KT-210-693

CONCEPTUAL FRAMEWORKS IN GEOGRAPHY

GENERAL EDITOR: W. E. MARSDEN

The Third World:
Diversity, Change and Interdependence

Michael Barke B.A. Ph.D.

School of Geography and Environmental Studies,
Newcastle-upon-Tyne Polytechnic

Greg O'Hare B.Sc. Ph.D.

Department of Geography, Derbyshire
College of Higher Education

*Maps and diagrams drawn by Ann Rooke and Andy Skinner,
cartographers at Derbyshire College of Higher Education*

N 0019220 1

NEWMAN COLLEGE
BARTLEY GREEN
BIRMINGHAM, 32.

CLASS	330.91724
ACCESSION	82601
AUTHOR	BAR

Oliver & Boyd

Acknowledgements

The authors and publishers wish to thank all those who gave their permission to reproduce copyright material in this book. Information regarding sources is given in the captions.

Oliver & Boyd
Robert Stevenson House
1–3 Baxter's Place
Leith Walk
Edinburgh EH1 3BB

A division of Longman Group Ltd

ISBN 0 05 003525 8
First published 1984
Second impression 1985

© Oliver & Boyd 1984. All rights reserved. No part of this publication may be reproduced, stored in a retrieval system, or transmitted in any form or by any means, electronic, mechanical, photocopying, recording or otherwise, without the prior written permission of the publishers.

Printed in Singapore by Kyodo Shing Loong Printing Industries Pte Ltd

Contents

Editor's Note   v
Preface   vi

1 Definitions and Profiles of the Third World   1
   A. The Third World   1
   B. Unity and Diversity   3
   C. Continuity and Change   14
   D. Dependence and Interdependence   17
   Conclusion   18
   Key Ideas   18

2 Physical Resources and Development   20
   A. Resources and Development   20
   B. Climatic Resources   24
   C. Plant and Animal Resources   31
   D. Soil Resources   37
   E. Environmental Hazards   39
   Conclusion   42
   Key Ideas   43

3 Human Resources and Development   45
   Introduction: Internal and External Factors   45
   A. Internal Economic Factors   45
   B. Internal Socio-economic Factors   48
   C. Internal Social Factors   58
   D. Internal Socio-political Factors   62
   E. External Factors   64
   Conclusion   70
   Key Ideas   71

4 Agricultural Systems   74
   A. Diversity and Change   74
   B. Farming and Land-use Intensity   76
   C. Subsistence and Commercial Farming   87
   D. The Role of Land Ownership   90
   Key Ideas   95

5 Agricultural Production and Reform   100
   Introduction   100
   A. The Importance of Agriculture   100
   B. Status and Performance of Agriculture   103
   C. Land Reform   108
   D. The Green Revolution   113
   Key Ideas   119

6 Mineral Resources and Manufacturing Industry:
   Geographical Perspectives   121
   A. Mineral Resource Exploitation   121
   B. Manufacturing Industry   136

	Conclusion	149
	Key Ideas	151
7	**Transport and Tourism**	154
	Introduction	154
	A. The Role of Transport in Economic Development	155
	B. Characteristics of Third World Transport Systems	162
	C. Tourism	173
	Key Ideas	178
8	**Population**	180
	Introduction	180
	A. Population Growth	180
	B. Population Distribution and Carrying Capacity	190
	C. Migration and Mobility	194
	Conclusion	202
	Key Ideas	203
9	**Urban Development**	206
	Introduction	206
	A. Urban Population Trends	206
	B. Urban Systems	214
	C. The System in Action	218
	D. Third World Cities: Generative or Parasitic?	227
	Key Ideas	232
10	**Forms of Settlement**	234
	Introduction	234
	A. Rural Settlement	234
	B. Urban Morphology	244
	C. Urban Social Geography and Housing Problems	253
	Conclusion: Convergence or Divergence?	264
	Key Ideas	265
11	**Interdependence: Trade, Aid and Technology**	268
	A. Demands of the Periphery	268
	B. International Aid	268
	C. International Trade	273
	D. Technological Transfer	280
	E. International Interdependence	283
	Key Ideas	284
	References and Further Reading	287
	Index	293

Editor's Note

An encouraging feature in geographical education in recent years has been the convergence taking place of curriculum thinking and thinking at the academic frontiers of the subject. In both, stress has been laid on the necessity for conceptual approaches and the use of information as a means to an end rather than as an end in itself.

The central purpose of this series is to bear witness to this convergence. In each text the *key ideas* are identified, chapter by chapter. These ideas are in the form of propositions which, with their component concepts and the inter-relations between them, make up the conceptual frameworks of the subject. The key ideas provide criteria for selecting content for the teacher, and in cognitive terms help the student to retain what is important in each unit. Most of the key ideas are linked with assignments, designed to elicit evidence of achievement of basic understanding and ability to apply this understanding in new circumstances through engaging in problem-solving exercises.

While the series is not specifically geared to any particular 'A' level examination syllabus, indeed it is intended for use in geography courses in polytechnics and in colleges of education as well as in the sixth form, it is intended to go some way towards meeting the needs of those students preparing for the more radical advanced geography syllabus.

It is hoped that the texts contain the academic rigour to stretch the most able of such candidates, but at the same time provide a clear enough exposition of the basic ideas to provide intellectual stimulus and social and/or cultural relevance for those who will not be going on to study geography in higher education. To this end, a larger selection of assignments and readings is provided than perhaps could be used profitably by all students. The teacher is the best person to choose those which most nearly meet his or her students' needs.

W. E. Marsden
University of Liverpool

Preface

This book was encouraged by the rapid increase of interest in Third World and 'development' geography during the past decade. It has three closely associated objectives. The first is to examine the tremendous diversity of the 'Third' or 'less developed' World, and to highlight the contrast between this area and the 'more developed' parts of the World. The second is to illustrate, against a general background of continuing poverty, many of the rapid socio-economic, environmental and political changes which have taken place in the Less Developed Countries in recent years. The third objective is to emphasize that the Less Developed Countries as well as the More Developed Countries not only influence, but strongly depend on one another in an increasingly interdependent world.

In pursuing this broad set of objectives for an area as large and as complex as the Third World, we were confronted with problems of data availability. For instance, up-to-date population census data for many parts of the Third World were not available at the time of writing (1981–2). This has meant that certain figures on population migration, urbanization, etc. are estimated rather than precise. Some data, such as quantitative information on religious practices, have not yet been collected by many Less Developed Countries. As data sources are not reliable, or as accurate as those for the More Developed Countries, many of the data presented in the text should be regarded as estimates.

Data source problems are compounded by, and relate to, those of material selection and generalization. It was not possible, for the 120 or so countries of the Third World, to cover topics as varied and diffuse as resources (Chapters 2 and 3), agriculture (Chapters 4 and 5), industry (Chapter 6), transport and tourism (Chapter 7), population and settlement (Chapters 8, 9 and 10) and international relations (Chapter 11) without a careful but severe selection of locations and themes. However, in order to give the student a feel for the Third World, we have felt it necessary to examine a relatively wide range of topics and locations. In so doing, a fair amount of generalization, unacceptable given a smaller region or narrower geographical focus, has been unavoidable. We would like to stress here that an essential accompaniment to the text is a good modern atlas.

As we have gleaned our material from a wide variety of sources, we hope that in reaching our conclusions we have not misrepresented or misinterpreted the work of others in the field. Nevertheless, the book reflects the collaborative effort of two workers from the northern 'developed' world writing about spatial patterns and processes in the southern 'underdeveloped' world. Accordingly, though we have attempted to remove from the text strong Eurocentric or ethnocentric bias towards the Third World, many of the views contained in the book relate to attitudes prevailing in a Western industrial society.

Finally we wish to thank all those who have assisted in the preparation and writing of the book, most especially our patient and helpful wives!

Michael Barke
Greg O'Hare
1983

1 Definitions and Profiles of the Third World

A. The Third World

Introduction

Three-quarters of the world's population, or around 3300 million people, live in a large group of independent nations in Africa, Asia and Latin America. The geographical location and extent of these countries, which are collectively known as the Third World, are shown in Figure 1.1. Despite its large area and population only about one-fifth of the world's wealth is produced in the Third World. It is this poverty, rather than population size or geographic extent and position in the lower and southern latitudes which gives the region its particular character.

Figure 1.1 Major world divisions. First, Second and Third Worlds and the 'North'–'South' division (indicated by the broken line).

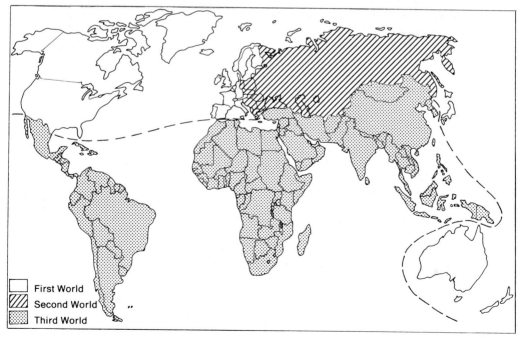

First World
Second World
Third World

The poor nations of the Third World or the 'South' are, however, politically distinctive. They form a third element in the world power structure and are differentiated from two other more wealthy power groups in the 'North'. They are distinct from those northern nations which have adopted a capitalist market economy. These developed market economies (DMEs) are sometimes referred to as the 'First World' and include all of Western Europe, the United States, Canada, Australasia and Japan. The poor countries of the South are also differentiated from the Second World of socialist states including the USSR and Eastern Europe, which have adopted a centrally planned economy (CPE). As socialist states, China, Cuba, Tanzania, North Korea, Vietnam and a number of others belong to the Second World; but in view of their universal poverty they are assigned to the Third World.

1. Terminology: a note

Different terms have been used at various times to indicate the development state or condition of the Third World. No single term, however, can define completely the development condition of a country or region, since development is a complex economic, social and political phenomenon.

Many of the earlier terms such as 'colonies' and 'territories' used in the nineteenth and early twentieth centuries, and 'primitive', 'backward' and 'undeveloped' used in the 1930s and 1940s are no longer in general use. Conversely, some more recent descriptions which are less harsh, less Western and less superior in tone, for example the 'underdeveloped', and the 'less developed' countries, together with the 'South' and the 'Third World' itself, have become increasingly popular. The titles the 'Less Developed Countries', abbreviated to LDCs, and the counterpart 'More Developed Countries' (MDCs) are useful because they emphasize more than the others that poverty is a relative and not an absolute notion. Some countries are poorer or less poor than others in terms of various criteria. The terms LDC and MDC possibly give undue emphasis to economic growth, and underplay many substantial changes in economic, social and political affairs that have taken place in Third World countries. Nevertheless, these terms (together with the Third World) will be generally used throughout the text.

2. The principal themes

This book provides a spatial perspective on the Third World in relation to three closely related themes. The first theme concerns the concepts of *unity* and *diversity*. Unity or uniformity in the Third World is examined through a survey of the area's general patterns of poverty and underdevelopment. Not every region or country experiences similar levels of development, however. A very poor LDC such as Bangladesh, with an annual gross national product (GNP) of $90 per head of population (capita) is clearly at a very different stage of development from a better-off country such as Kuwait, with a GNP of $17 000 per capita per annum. Thus, it is necessary to recognize the diversity of the Third World or its local, regional and national inequalities in development.

The second principal theme is that of '*continuity and change*'. Poverty and underdevelopment have persisted in certain parts of the Third World for decades and even centuries. Such unchanging patterns are an illustration of the 'continuity' in development which can be found in the Third World. At the same time, many rapid changes have taken place in certain areas of the Third World, especially since the 1950s. These changes, whether social, economic, environmental or political, are referred to as developmental changes and are the result of what is called the 'development process'. Such changes, beneficial or adverse, induced by local or foreign influences, provide an important dynamic and geographical focus for this book.

While the Third or Less Developed World is highly dependent on the More Developed World for trade, aid and technology, the latter is becoming in turn increasingly dependent on the former for markets and raw material resources (e.g. oil). These concepts of '*dependence and interdependence*', where regions and countries from all over the world not only influence but strongly depend on one another, form the third main theme of the book.

ASSIGNMENT

1. Examine the following terms used to describe the Third World: colonies, territories, undeveloped, underdeveloped, emerging or developing, poor, less developed, never to be developed, the Third World, the South, the Majority World. To what extent do they reflect a Western or Eurocentric viewpoint?

B. Unity and Diversity

Introduction

The LDCs share various basic features of underdevelopment, and are quite distinct from the MDCs. Ways of earning a living, for instance, in poor agricultural LDCs such as Bangladesh (Plate 1.1) and Mongolia (Plate 1.2) show a number of common features of

Plate 1.1 Bangladesh, a poor agricultural LDC. The most important activity in this country is tropical wet rice cultivation. Such 'permanent' systems of agriculture involve the use of much human and draught animal power. As shown, the fields are cultivated using a double oxen plough, before the onset of the Monsoon and planting with wet rice. Great care is taken in levelling, flood control and seed bed preparation, and animal manure as well as human 'night-soil' are used as fertilizer. (*Photograph: R. P. Wainwright*)

Plate 1.2 Mongolia. Although much of the Third World is tropical and sub-tropical, Mongolia has a continental climate with a wide range of temperature between summer and winter. Rainfall is low and the predominant vegetation forms are grassland and semi-desert. Here a nomadic pastoralist tends his livestock (mostly sheep) well wrapped against the severe winter. (*Photograph: E. Hallam*)

Plate 1.3 Hong Kong: a relatively rich industrializing LDC. In the foreground is the modern metropolis of Victoria which is situated in the north of Hong Kong Island. To the left across the harbour on the mainland is the built up area of Kowloon. (*Photograph: R. Beck*)

poverty and hardship. However, despite uniformity, tremendous diversity exists within the Third World. This diversity exists, firstly, between whole countries. Poor agricultural countries such as Bangladesh, with its permanent intensive rice cultivation and Mongolia with its extensive pastoral nomadism are not only different from each other but are clearly at a very different level of development from say a more wealthy industrializing LDC such as Hong Kong (Plate 1.3). Secondly, equally large and stark contrasts are found within individual LDCs as exist between different regions and across various socio-economic groups. There is, for example, in Zambia, a considerable socio-economic and cultural gulf between the obvious destitution of many tribal groups living in rural districts, and the relative opulence of a small imported (European) elite who work and live in mining and urban/industrial areas. Finally, because of diversity within both the LDCs and the MDCs the transition from the category of LDC to MDC is very gradual. There is not a great deal of difference between the more developed LDCs such as Argentina, and the least developed MDCs, such as Portugal.

1. Unity in the Third World

(a) *Shared characteristics and the development gap*

Geographers and economists have identified a range of common economic, social, cultural and political attributes of the LDCs. Table 1.1 shows, in general terms only, the position of the LDCs and the MDCs with respect to 28 of such characteristics. The table serves to highlight what has generally become known as the 'development gap' between the rich and poor countries. This development gap is demonstrated by the large number of 'low', 'poor' and 'non-advanced' conditions recorded by the LDCs and the 'high' and 'favourable' conditions reported by the MDCs. Where the LDCs do provide local 'highs' this often involves some negative aspect, such as high population increase, and high infant mortality.

The development gap between the LDCs and the MDCs can be quantified as shown in Figure 1.2. The Third World has three-quarters of the world's inhabitants and independent states, and occupies about 60% of its land area. However, only about three-sevenths of global (marketed) food production, one-quarter of international trade, one-fifth of world income and energy consumption, one-seventh of world manufacturing, one-ninth of all money spent on education and one-twenty-fifth of global expenditure on health, takes place within the Third World.

(b) *Economic criteria*

Income level. The most common standard used to describe the poverty of the Third World is that of income level expressed in terms of aggregate output such as the gross national product (GNP). The latter can be defined as the total value of all goods and services produced by the economy over a period of time (usually one year). GNP per capita, i.e. GNP divided by population, is commonly used to rank countries on a scale of development (see Table 1.2). This statistic is more easily measured and quantified than other types of development indicator, such as social well-being, or health. This does not mean, however, that income data are precise, scientific or objective measures of development. They are simply more easily available.

There are at least four limitations to using income level as an indicator of a country's development. Firstly, placing a value on all goods and services is difficult since a sizeable proportion of production within a LDC does not enter the market economy. Because a lot of goods and services are not marketed there is a strong tendency to undervalue economic

Table 1.1 General characteristics of the LDCs and MDCs.

Criteria	Development gap	
	LDCs	MDCs
Economic condition		
1. Productivity	Low	High
2. Income (GNP)	Low	High
3. Income inequality between regions and social classes	High	Moderate
4. Capital formation and savings	Low	High
5. Economic growth (absolute rate)	Low	Moderate
6. Energy consumption	Low	High
7. Levels of technology	Low	High
8. Type of Production (a)	Subsistence	Commercial
(b)	Primary (e.g. minerals, food)	Industrial
9. Agricultural population	Large	Small
10. Infrastructure: transport, housing, hospitals	Poor	Good
11. Market size	Small	Large
12. Trading relations	Unfavourable (depending on primary products)	Favourable
13. Balance of payments problems	Severe	Moderate
14. Technological dependence	High	Low
Social condition		
15. Human nutrition	Poor	Good
16. Health levels	Low	High
17. Infant mortality	High	Low
18. Life expectancy	Poor	Good
19. Literacy	Low	High
20. Technological skills	Low	High
21. Size of populations	High	Moderate
22. Rate of population growth	High	Low
Cultural and political condition		
23. Society	Peasant	Industrial
24. Status of women	Low	Moderate
25. Behaviour	Traditional	Modern
26. Ethnic/cultural variety	High	Low
27. Political stability	Low	High
28. Government	Authoritarian/ military	Democratic/ socialist

output. Much production in the Third World is for personal subsistence (see item 8, Table 1.1). This means that many articles are home-made, labour is often exchanged between families and villages and many goods and services are bartered. Secondly, it is difficult to give a proper international value to the income of a country since comparisons between currencies, exchange rates and conversion to US dollars are not easily computed. Thirdly, it is often very difficult to obtain accurate and reliable population data for every country. Indeed, data collection of all types presents massive problems in the LDCs. Finally, per capita GNP is only a crude average. It does not reveal the distribution of the national income between regions and various socio-economic groups.

Despite these limitations GNP per capita is useful as a broad expression of the material well-being of nations. No matter how much adjustment is made for the aforementioned limitations, enormous differences are still apparent in per capita income and levels of well-

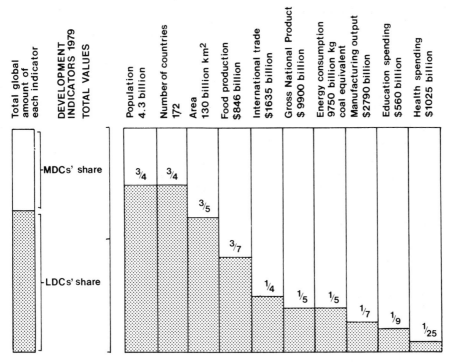

Figure 1.2 The distribution of global 'wealth' (development indicators) between the LDCs and the MDCs.

being between the LDCs and the MDCs. It is staggering that just over one-quarter of the countries shown in Table 1.2, which contain about one-half of the world's population, had an income in 1981 of less than about $370 per person per annum.

(c) Social and welfare criteria

(i) *Hunger and malnutrition.* Low income levels are usually associated with poor and abject living conditions. Low levels of health in the Third World are closely associated with hunger and malnutrition. While in the industrialized countries of the West food (calorific) intake may exceed requirements by about 20%, in the Third World many millions of people exist on diets whose calorific content is below the accepted minimum of 2200, which is the lowest amount required for the average adult *at rest*. It is often the protein supply and, most significantly, the animal protein provision which are extremely low in the LDCs. While on average the inhabitants of the Third World receive about one-half to two-thirds of the total protein necessary for healthy development, (35–55 grams/day instead of about 70 g/day) their consumption of animal proteins is generally less than one-third of the accepted minimum levels (5–15 g/day instead of 40 g/day).

The global distributions of the average daily per capita calorie and protein intake for different countries are shown in Figures 1.3 and 1.4. These patterns clearly differenti-ate the rich from the poor countries. While most of the North enjoys daily calorie consumption levels of over 3000 calories per capita, many LDCs have low borderline

Table 1.2 Classification of countries according to GNP per capita. (Source: *World Bank Development Report, 1981*)

	GNP per capita 1979 ($)		GNP per capita 1979 ($)
LDCs		**LDCs**	
Low-income countries		Middle-income countries	
Kampuchea, Dem.	—	Thailand	590
Lao PDR	—	Philippines	600
Bhutan	80	Congo, People's Rep.	630
Bangladesh	90	Nicaragua	660
Chad	110	Papua New Guinea	660
Ethiopia	130	El Salvador	670
Nepal	130	Nigeria	670
Somalia	—	Peru	730
Mali	140	Morocco	740
Burma	160	Mongolia	780
Afghanistan	170	Albania	840
Vietnam	—	Dominican Rep.	890
Burundi	180	Colombia	1010
Upper Volta	180	Guatemala	1020
India	190	Syrian Arab Rep.	1030
Malawi	200	Ivory Coast	1040
Rwanda	200	Ecuador	1050
Sri Lanka	230	Paraguay	1070
Benin	250	Tunisia	1120
Mozambique	250	Korea, Dem. Rep.	1130
Sierra Leone	250	Jordan	1180
China	260	Lebanon	—
Haiti	260	Jamaica	1260
Pakistan	260	Turkey	1330
Tanzania	260	Malaysia	1370
Zaire	260	Panama	1400
Niger	270	Cuba	1410
Guinea	280	Korea Rep. of	1480
Central African Rep.	290	Algeria	1590
Madagascar	290	Mexico	1640
Uganda	290	Chile	1690
Mauritania	320	South Africa	1720
Lesotho	340	Brazil	1780
Togo	350	Costa Rica	1820
Indonesia	370	Romania	1900
Sudan	370	Uruguay	2100
Middle-income countries		Iran	—
Kenya	380	Portugal	2180
Ghana	400	Argentina	2230
Yemen Arab Rep.	420	Yugoslavia	2430
Senegal	430	Venezuela	3120
Angola	440	Trinidad and Tobago	3390
Zimbabwe	470	Hong Kong	3760
Egypt	480	Singapore	3830
Yemen PDR	480	Greece	3960
Liberia	500	Israel	4150
Zambia	500	Capital-surplus oil exporters	
Honduras	530	Saudi Arabia	7280
Bolivia	550	Libya	8170
Cameroun	560	Kuwait	17100

Greece, Yugoslavia and Portugal are normally regarded as forming part of the more developed world, though in this classification their low GNP per capita places them in the less developed realm.

Table 1.2 (*cont.*)

	GNP per capita 1979 ($)		GNP per capita 1979 ($)
MDCs		**MDCs**	
Developed market economies (DMEs)		Developed market economies (DMEs)	
Ireland	4210	Belgium	10920
Spain	4380	Germany Fed. Rep.	11730
Italy	5250	Denmark	11900
New Zealand	5930	Sweden	11930
United Kingdom	6320	Switzerland	13920
Finland	8160		
Austria	8630	Centrally planned economies (CPEs)	
Japan	8810		
Australia	9120	Bulgaria	3690
Canada	9640	Poland	3830
France	9950	Hungary	3850
Netherlands	10230	USSR	4110
United States	10630	Czechoslovakia	5290
Norway	10700	German Dem. Rep.	6430

consumption levels in the region of 2000–2500 calories per person. The extent of low calorific intake shown in Figure 1.3 reinforces suggestions that as many as 800 million people in the Third World suffer from severe hunger or undernutrition. If the distribution of low calorie intake sketches the outlines of the Third World, low protein intake (or malnutrition) brings that shape into sharper focus. Almost all of the Third World has gross protein intake levels less than the 70 grams per capita recommended for healthy development. Only Argentina and Uruguay in Latin America and a number of countries in southern Africa enjoy consumption levels in excess of this figure.

(ii) *Life expectancy, infant mortality and literacy.* In recent years a number of institutions, both public and private, have tried to devise indicators that measure progress in physical well-being more effectively than does GNP. A new social indicator of progress called the 'physical quality of life index' (PQLI) was devised by the Overseas Development Council (ODC) in 1977. This index is a composite expression of three characteristics namely, life expectancy, infant mortality and the literacy rate.

The PQLI is calculated as follows. For each of the three criteria the performance of individual countries is placed on an index scale of 0–100 where 0 is an explicitly defined 'worst' performance and 100 represents an explicit 'best' condition. A 0% literacy rate for a country would register 0 on the index scale. Similarly the lowest life expectancy of 38 years at the age of one year (Vietnam) and the highest infant mortality rate of 229/1000 (Gabon) would be given 0 in the index scale. As performance improves for each characteristic to full literacy (100%), maximum life expectancy of 77 years (Sweden) and to minimum infant mortality of 7/1000 (theoretical minimum) index values systematically increase to 100. Thus for each increase of one point on the index scale (0–100) literacy rates increase by one point, infant mortality decrease by 2.2/1000 and those of life expectancy increase by 0.39 years.

By averaging the separate index values for the three criteria giving equal weight to each, a composite index value is obtained. This is the PQLI and it is scaled automatically to an index of 1–100.

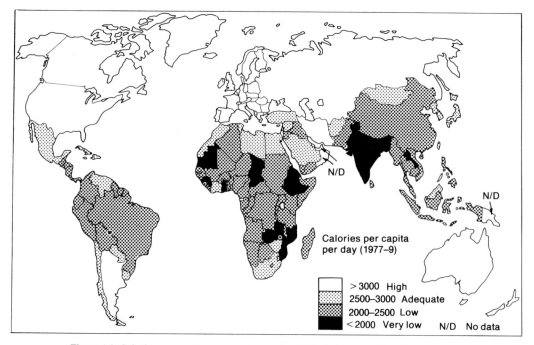

Figure 1.3 Calorie consumption per capita per day 1977–9. (Sources: *World Bank Development Report, 1981; FAO Production Yearbook, 1981*)

Figure 1.4 Daily per capita protein intake (grams) 1977. (Copyright *Third World Quarterly*, 1980)

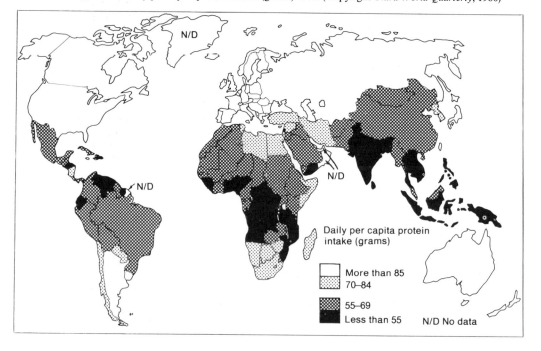

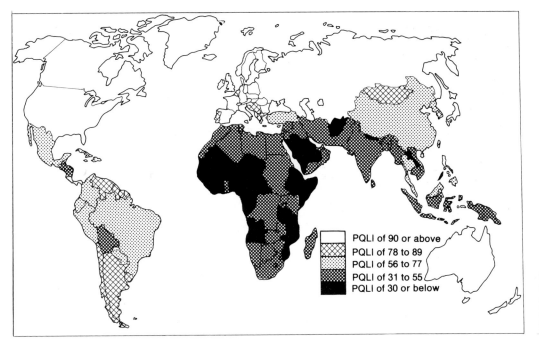

Figure 1.5 PQLI map of the world. (Source: Morris, 1979)

Figure 1.5 offers a broad expression of the PQLI relationships between countries. This demonstrates that high PQLI values of 90 or more, arbitrarily chosen to represent a high level of physical well-being, graphically distinguish the MDCs from the LDCs. Indeed 'basic minimum levels of human need' equivalent to achieving a PQLI value of about 77 are attained by few LDCs and many fall well short of this target.

2. Diversity in the Third World

(a) Diversity criteria and the internal development gap

Criteria used to draw out the common character of the Third World can be employed also to emphasize its tremendous variety. For instance, the LDCs may all share a PQLI value of less than 90, but LDCs with scores of less than 30, mostly in Africa and Asia, experience very different circumstances from those LDCs, mostly in Latin America, with scores between 78 and 90 (see Figure 1.5).

The wide development gap *between* Third World countries is universally recognized. Some popular international classifications of different groups of LDCs at varying levels of development will now be examined.

(b) Economic criteria

Income level. Examination of Table 1.2 reveals the tremendous variation in per capita income levels throughout the Third World. The World Bank has designated three categories of LDCs on the basis of income level. These include: firstly, the low-income countries with per capita GNP levels of less than $370 (in 1981); secondly, the middle-income countries with income levels between $370 and $4150, and thirdly the capital

11

surplus oil-exporting LDCs with income levels over about $4500. Indeed, some of the richest members of the latter group are better off in money terms than the MDCs themselves. The capital surplus oil exporters are generally classified as LDCs because of a very unequal *distribution* of income within their countries, as well as low levels of development in other fields, such as agriculture, industry, education, health services.

(c) General development criteria

A number of general development classifications, using a range of criteria, have been used to define the most impoverished as well as the most developed states. The former include (i) the Least Developed and (ii) the Most Seriously Affected Countries and the latter (iii) the Newly Industrializing Countries.

(i) *The Least Developed Countries (LLDCs).* The Least Developed Countries were initially defined in 1971 by the UN General Assembly using three main criteria: a per capita GNP of $100 or less (in 1981 about $350); a 10% or less share of manufacturing in the GNP; and a literacy rate of 20% or less. In addition to countries meeting all of these criteria borderline cases in which one criterion may be met and others nearly met are included in the Least Developed Country grouping. All have an extremely low level of exploitation of their natural resources. Agricultural output is very low or is stagnating relative to population increase, and starvation and disease are very real issues for many of the inhabitants. In addition, manufacturing industry is minimal, there are extreme scarcities of skilled labour and a very low volume of exports. Many of the Least Developed Countries are also constrained by one or more geographical or climatological handicaps. It will be noted from Figure 1.6 that many of them are located in the sub-Saharan belt of Africa (the Sahel) and are ravaged by drought. Moreover 15 of the 30 or so Least Developed Countries are landlocked (see Figure 1.6) while others suffer from tiny geographical extent or difficult and mountainous terrain.

(ii) *The Most Seriously Affected Countries (MSACs).* The Third World depends heavily on the import of energy (oil), food and capital equipment for the maintenance and expansion of its economies. The rapid increase in the price of these essential imports during the 1970s brought a range of different problems for the LDCs. Groups of countries reacted differently to the price rises. The major oil-exporting countries of the Middle East and elsewere benefited enormously from the oil price increases and were thus able to increase their imports of manufactured goods from the MDCs. Some middle-income countries (such as Brazil, Mexico) borrowed heavily in the international markets; while some increased their exports to cope with the rising import bill. Although a very few low-income countries were helped by good crop harvests and more aid, the majority of them, together with a number of middle-income countries, were very seriously affected by the price rises. They were beset by many problems and could neither increase their exports nor borrow much; they had to cut imports and endure stagnation. The distribution of these Most Seriously Affected Countries, first defined by the United Nations in 1974, is shown in Figure 1.6. It will be noted that they are a somewhat larger group than the Least Developed Countries (45 countries as opposed to 30) but perhaps not surprisingly incorporate many of them.

(iii) *The Newly Industrializing Countries (NICs).* Figure 1.6 shows also the distribution of a very different group of LDCs, namely the most developed LDCs. These 'Newly Industrializing Countries' (NICs) including Brazil, Mexico, Taiwan, Singapore, Hong Kong, Argentina and South Korea are defined as having the ability to export successfully manufactured goods (as opposed to just primary products) into the world market. No

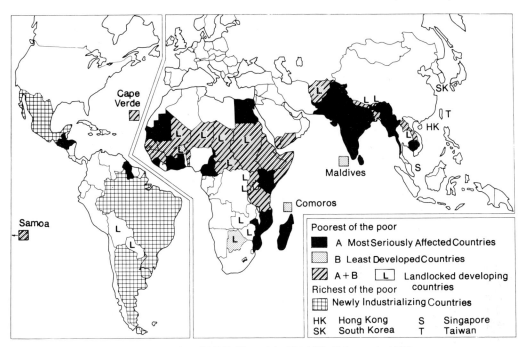

Figure 1.6 The least and most developed LDCs (Copyright *Third World Quarterly*, 1982)

doubt as other countries modernize and diversify their economies, for example Colombia, Turkey, Egypt, Malaysia and South Africa, they too will eventually be included in this select category.

1. *Use the data in Table 1.3, with reference to the text.*
   (a) *Convert literacy rates, life expectancy and infant mortality rates for each country into their index values.*
   (b) *Average the three index values to produce the PQLI score for each country. Check your results against the PQLI data of Figure 1.5.*
   (c) *Rank the given countries according to their PQLI scores, i.e. from 'worst' (lowest) to 'best' (highest).*
   (d) *How does the PQLI ranking compare with the given order of countries in Table 1.3 which is based on per capita GNP?*
   (e) *Give possible reasons for any discrepancies in the two rankings.*
2. (a) *Refer to Figure 1.6 and an atlas. Make separate lists of the countries belonging to (i) the Least Developed, (ii) the Most Seriously Affected and (iii) the Newly Industrializing Countries.*
   (b) *Mark those Least Developed Countries which are (i) arid and drought-ridden; (ii) landlocked; (iii) suffer from difficult terrain; (iv) possess tiny geographic extent. Summarize your findings.*
   (c) *What relationship exists between Newly Industrializing Countries and their position and size? Explain your conclusions.*

Table 1.3 Literacy, life expectancy and infant mortality rates for selected countries. All data refer to the early 1970s. (Source: Morris, 1979)

Country (ranked in order of increasing GNP per capita)	Literacy rate age 15 and over (%)	Life expectancy at age one (years)	Infant mortality rate (per 1000 live births)
Bangladesh	22	53	132
Burma	60	56	126
Afghanistan	8	48	182
India	34	56	122
Sri Lanka	81	70	45
Niger	5	46	200
Indonesia	60	55	137
Nicaragua	58	60	123
Colombia	81	67	97
Brazil	66	65	82
Hong Kong	77	71	17
United Kingdom	99	72	16
Saudi Arabia	15	52	152
Sweden	99	75	8

C. Continuity and Change

1. Continuity: unchanging patterns in basic poverty

(a) *The widening income gap within countries*

There is within countries of the Third World a backcloth of persistent poverty and inequality for substantial numbers of people. The basic characteristics of Third World poverty (outlined in Section B) are relevant as much today as they were in the 1950s when the plight of the people in the LDCs was being drawn into increasingly sharp focus. As Dwyer (1977) has pointed out, 'There is little reason to think that the basic contours of deprivation in the Third World delineated by Buchanan in 1964 have changed in any significant degree.' Despite the efforts of thirty years of what has been called 'development' and more specifically of the United Nations' two Development Decades (1960–70 and 1970–80) very little impact has been made to alleviate the poverty of the very poorest groups in the Third World.

Dwyer (1977) has demonstrated how fairly recent and rapid economic growth in Kenya and Mexico has increased and not narrowed the income gap between rich and poor within these countries. Taking the LDCs as a whole it has been estimated that economic growth in the last 20 years or so has effectively bypassed perhaps as much as one-third of the entire population. It has been the already better-off groups, such as the landed classes, professional and technical personnel, highly skilled (and a small fraction of the unskilled) industrial workers, which have benefited from economic growth. For the substantial and increasing portion of the population in the very poorest groups, improvements in income and welfare have been negligible. In many cases their situation has even, in absolute terms, been worsening.

14

(b) *The widening income gap between countries*

The income gap between the MDCs and the LDCs and between states in the Third World itself is also increasing. Table 1.4 shows that on the whole the income of the MDCs has grown at a slightly greater relative rate per capita than the LDCs between 1950 and 1980. Since the MDCs were already the recipients of much higher absolute incomes in 1950 these growth rates are suggestive also of a widening absolute gulf in income level between the two groups of countries. The absolute rise in income per capita of the MDCs during this period was $6530 whereas that in the LDCs was a mere $346. Moreover, the benefits of growth which have taken place in the LDCs have been very unequally distributed between states.

As indicated in Table 1.4, the middle-income LDCs have grown much faster in both relative and absolute terms than the low-income LDCs, increasing their absolute per capita GNP by $940 as opposed to merely $80 between 1950 and 1980. This widening gap between groups of countries within the Third World is more graphically demonstrated in Figure 1.7. Clearly it is the already better-off regions and countries (e.g. Latin America, North Africa and the Middle East) rather than the poorer areas (e.g. South Asia, sub-Saharan Africa) which are developing faster.

Table 1.4 The widening development gap as measured by GNP. (Source: *World Bank Development Report, 1981*)

	Per capita GNP constant (US $)			Absolute growth in per capita GNP	Average annual percentage growth in per capita GNP	
	1950	1960	1980	1950–80	1950–60	1960–80
MDCs	4130	5580	10660	6530	3.1	3.2
LDCs	315	371	661	346	2.1	3.1
(a) Middle-income	640	820	1580	940	2.5	3.3
(b) Low-income	170	180	250	80	0.6	1.7

Note that many LDCs have achieved higher growth rates of their GNPs *per se* than a number of MDCs but their higher population growth rates reduce the benefit *per capita*.

Figure 1.7 The widening internal development (income) gap. This is expressed as GNP per capita in 1960, 1970 and 1980 for major regions of the Third World. (Source: *World Bank Development Report, 1980*)

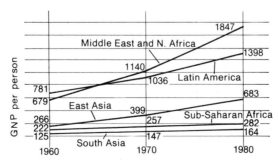

15

2. Change

Despite the continuation of poverty for substantial numbers of people in the Third World some very important changes have nevertheless taken place in the LDCs in recent years.

(a) Rapid and accelerated change

Many aspects of change in the LDCs are developing at a rapid and, in some cases, at an accelerating rate. One only has to refer to the remarkable contrast between the political maps of Asia and especially Africa in 1939 with those of the early 1980s to gain an impression of the staggeringly rapid political changes which have occurred in these continents. Figure 1.8 shows huge areas in Africa that ranked as British, French, Belgian and other European territories in 1939, and have been transformed, especially since the 1960s, into independent states.

The pace of political transformation is matched, if not exceeded, by the astonishing speed with which certain economic, social, cultural and environmental changes are taking place. In the last 20 to 30 years some countries, such as Taiwan and South Korea, have made remarkable economic advance. They are now important semi-industrial nations and in several years' time may deserve to join the ranks of the MDCs. While Tanzania has stagnated in some economic respects, it has made considerable social and political progress. Its community (socialist) health and education schemes have resulted in major improvements in life expectancy levels and in literacy rates (see Chapter 3). One of the most significant changes of all to have taken place relates to population. Population growth and especially urban expansion has been particularly rapid in many Third World countries during the post-war period (see Chapters 8 and 9).

Figure 1.8 Political transformation in Africa 1939–82. (Source: Steel, 1974)

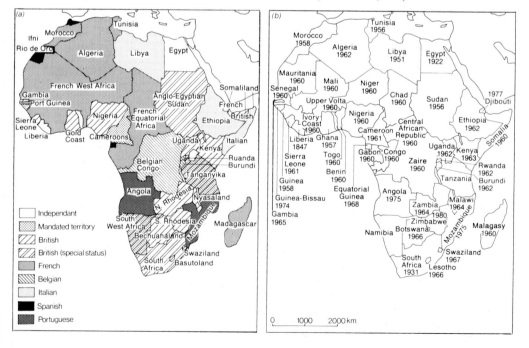

16

(b) Spatial aspects of change

In several respects the spatial distribution of human activity in the Third World has been increasing. Forests are continually being cleared, especially from equatorial areas; new lands, in particular in Latin America, are being opened up for settlement and agriculture; and new mineral deposits have been developed throughout the LDCs. In both market economy LDCs (e.g. Brazil) and socialist LDCs (e.g. Tanzania, China) specific programmes have been implemented to develop more fully their rural and less progressive regions at a distance from the metropolitan centres.

Despite the increasing dispersal of human activity the dominant spatial pattern of change in the Third World has been a massive *concentration* of social and economic activity. We have seen that it has been the already better-off groups, the more developed regions, the more developed LDCs which have benefited most from recent economic growth.

In particular, present patterns of economic and social activity have encouraged rapid urban development especially in the largest cities. During the post-war period most of these centres have more than trebled their populations. Industrial and commercial activities have rapidly expanded in the major cities and, to a lesser extent, in favoured but concentrated industrial complexes outside the major metropolitan districts. The spatial impact of these changes has been to concentrate both population and economic activity more than ever before. In many cases rural–urban contrasts in income and welfare have been magnified because many rural areas have been side-stepped by economic growth and development.

ASSIGNMENTS

1. *Using Figure 1.7 and Table 1.4, describe the growing income gap*
   (a) between the MDCs and the LDCs, (b) within the LDCs themselves.
2. *(a) Describe the pattern of the former European colonies in Africa shown in Figure 1.8.*
   (b) Compare the speed of the decolonization process under the British and the French.

D. Dependence and Interdependence

Introduction

It is well known that the LDCs are highly *dependent* on the MDCs for trade, aid and various forms of technology (see Chapter 11). For instance, 85% of the light manufactured goods and over 90% of the heavy industrial and transport equipment imported by the LDCs come from the industrialized countries of Europe, North America and Japan. It is less realized that, in their turn, the MDCs are becoming increasingly reliant on the LDCs for resources and as a major market for their export products. As an example, the countries of the Third World provide 50% of the domestic requirements of non-energy-producing materials (e.g. zinc, copper, silver, mercury) for the industrialized countries (see Chapter 6). Because of improvements in communication and increasing fears of resource scarcity, the functional interdependence between different parts of the world is probably more deep seated today than at any previous time. This theme of interdependence where countries, regions and even groups of people are becoming increasingly dependent on each other will now be examined a little further.

1. Interdependence

(a) Oil price increases (political decision making)

The four-fold increase in the price of oil in 1973 by the Organisation of Petroleum Exporting Countries (OPEC) along with other increases since then, not only interrupted economic growth in the North, but also debilitated further the already weak economies of the oil-importing LDCs. Rapidly enlarging oil import bills have reduced the capacity of the LDCs to import goods and services such as capital equipment and technical advice necessary for the build up of local industry. Moreover, as oil is a vital ingredient in programmes of agricultural development and extension (for mechanization and local fertilizer manufacture), domestic food production has been curtailed at a time when population and thus demand for food has been increasing. Energy and food crises, population growth and economic development are becoming globally intertwined both in space and time.

(b) Natural disasters (unforeseen events)

Global change can be affected by unforeseen events as well as by political decision making. For instance, the especially cold winter of 1971–2 throughout Eastern Europe effectively destroyed one-third of the Russian winter wheat crop. This deficit was alleviated not by expanding the spring wheat crop of the USSR, but by purchasing grain from the very large surplus stocks of the USA over a three-year period (1972–4). The consequence of this transaction, which all but emptied the granaries of the USA, was that food prices soared all over the world. In the same year (1972) a late monsoon heavily damaged the crops of the Indian sub-continent resulting in a disastrous loss of food supply. Then drought hit parts of Africa (where it still continues today) and China and, while the latter was acquiring whatever foodstuffs were left in the market, millions of people in Africa and India faced starvation. Most of the world's supplies of wheat had been sold and nowhere was grain to be found. In a similar situation a few years earlier, millions of tonnes of wheat had been rushed from North America to avert disaster in the Third World, but on this occasion only 200 000 tonnes could be made available.

Conclusion

Thus, our spatial perspective on the Third World comprises three principal themes. (1) Against a general backcloth of continuing poverty and underdevelopment there exists considerable *diversity* in human and physical circumstances. Superimposed on these conditions (2) *change* is taking place, sometimes at staggering rates, altering past, creating present, and encouraging future, geographical patterns. Finally, (3) countries, regions and peoples within the LDCs and the MDCs are becoming increasingly locked together in global partnership, and *interdependence*.

Key Ideas

A. The Third World
1. A large number of poor independent countries, concentrated in the lower and southern latitudes, constitutes the region known as the Third World.
2. This poor, heavily populated and extensive region is distinct from two more wealthy 'northern' regions namely the First World of market economies and the Second World of socialist states.

3. A variety of terms has been employed at different times, and with different degrees of suitability, to describe the countries of the Third World.
4. This book is concerned with the themes of unity and diversity, continuity and change, and dependence and interdependence within the Third World.

B. Unity and Diversity
1. The countries of the Third World share a number of common economic, social, environmental and political characteristics.
2. The poor or adverse nature of many of these characteristics in the Third World may be used to highlight the 'development gap' between the LDCs and the MDCs.
3. Per capita income is the most commonly used standard to denote the poverty or low level of development of the LDCs.
4. Low levels of living in the Third World are also illustrated by widespread hunger and, in particular, malnutrition.
5. The Physical Quality of Life Index (PQLI), a composite indicator of literacy, infant mortality and life expectancy levels, is an alternative indicator to per capita income, demonstrating the gulf in social conditions between the LDCs and the MDCs.
6. Tremendous diversity exists within the Third World.
7. On the basis of income level, three main groups of LDCs are commonly designated, namely the low-income, the middle-income, and the capital surplus (oil-exporting) countries.
8. On the basis of a range of social and economic indicators, other hierarchical groups within the Third World including the Least Developed, the Most Seriously Affected, and the Newly Industrializing Countries, have been officially designated.

C. Continuity and Change
1. There exists an unyielding backcloth of persistent poverty for large numbers of people in the Third World.
2. The development gap between the MDCs and the LDCs and inside the Third World is increasing with time.
3. Despite continuing poverty many socio-economic, environmental and political aspects of change are developing at a rapid and even accelerating rate in certain parts of the Third World.
4. The dominant spatial pattern of change in the Third World has been a massive concentration of social and economic activity, especially in urban areas.

D. Dependence and Interdependence
1. The LDCs are highly dependent on the MDCs for trade, aid and technology.
2. The MDCs are dependent in turn on the LDCs for resources and as a major market for their exports.
3. The world is an interdependent system where countries and regions from all over the globe not merely influence but strongly depend on one another.

Additional Activity

1. (a) Describe the Third World in terms of its uniformity, unchanging character and dependence on the MDCs.
   (b) Describe the main patterns of diversity, change and interdependence in the Third World.
   (c) Why is it important for geographers to study the themes mentioned in (a) and (b)?

2 Physical Resources and Development

This chapter and the next examine the constraints and opportunities offered by resources in Third World development. Resources can be classified into natural resources on the one hand, i.e., unchanged materials of the 'land', and into labour and capital resources on the other. The latter are used in the exploitation of the former to create wealth. In this chapter, particular attention is given to the natural resources (including natural hazards) and Third World development.

A. Resources and Development

1. Nature and distribution of resources

The role of natural and human resources in Third World development is difficult to evaluate precisely. Firstly, resource value is inherently difficult to measure and assess. For example, how does one assess in simple economic or quantitative terms the exact value of a diverse flora, a good soil or even a skilled workforce? Secondly, the resource base of the Third World is by no means fully known or understood. Very few LDCs have been geologically surveyed in any detail and little is known of the precise distribution of other natural resources including vegetation (see Plates 2.1, 2.2), soils, water supplies, minerals and power. In view of this, it seems difficult to justify either the traditional view that the natural resources of the Third World are exceptionally rich, or the modern view of the Third World as poor or inferior in natural resources. Thirdly, although it is convenient to separate out resources into physical and human, and more specifically into single resources such as mineral supplies and labour skills, the interaction and interdependence of resources may be so close that it is impossible to identify any particular resource as the crucial one influencing development. Clearly, development takes place within the total environment or ecosystem with its complex of interacting physical and human resources.

Despite such deficiencies in information about the known value and complexity of resources, the uneven distribution of resources in the LDCs is generally acknowledged, both between and within countries. Table 2.1 shows a seven-fold classification of LDCs based on territorial extent, population size, and extent and nature of physical resources. Included in the classification are 'overpopulated' countries such as those in South Asia (India and Pakistan) and China with a diverse resource base (category 7) and small 'relatively overpopulated' countries with a narrow resource endowment such as Jamaica and Sri Lanka (category 2). The relatively large number of countries with little or moderate population pressure are differentiated (categories 2–6 inclusive) on the basis of both geographic size and primary export potential.

Plate 2.1 A ferry crossing in Sierra Leone. Transport in the LDCs is beset by many problems. Not only are transport systems frequently rudimentary; note the simple 'dug outs' in the foreground, and the unpaved lateritic road on the far bank, but the natural environment also presents difficulties. Apart from mountains and desert, wide or fast-flowing rivers often have to be crossed. The vegetation here is also particularly difficult to penetrate as it is derived secondary tropical rain forest. Several emergent trees (e.g. palms) give the impression of an open forest, but there is a dense plant undergrowth or jungle which can hamper the unwary traveller. (*Photograph: M. Barke*)

Plate 2.2 Traditional cattle herding in the savannas, northern Nigeria. The vegetation here is described as 'parkland' savanna, i.e. there is a dominant grassland layer together with a significant cover of woodland and trees. Within traditional pastoral systems the social and religious value of cattle (often of Zebu type) is far more important than their economic value. As there is a tendency to keep large numbers, overstocking and overgrazing can be a problem. To the south of the area shown, in the more humid (i.e. more than 1000 mm of rainfall) savanna lands, cattle rearing is restricted because of the tsetse fly and sleeping sickness. (*Photograph: I. Brightmer*)

Table 2.1 A classification of Third World countries. (Source: Auty, 1979)

Size	Rural population pressure	Primary export range and prospects	Examples
1. Small	Overpopulated	Narrow: unfavourable	Haiti
2. Small	Some pressure	Narrow: favourable	Kuwait
3. Small	Some pressure	Narrow: unfavourable	Mali
4. Small	Underpopulated	Diverse: moderate	Central African Republic
5. Medium	Some pressure	Narrow: favourable	Malaysia
6. Medium	Underpopulated	Diverse: favourable	Nigeria
7. Large	Overpopulated	Diverse: varying	India

2. Natural resources and development

(a) Passive or active role?

Many analyses grossly exaggerate the importance of natural resources in development. A number of geographers, for instance, have tended to discuss physical factors at length, to give little weight to human factors and to suggest that levels of development are somehow causally linked or actively determined by the quality and quantity of natural resources. In no sense, however, are natural resources responsible for development and economic growth; they possess no deterministic power. Evidence for this statement arises from the poor correlation between the occurrence of resources and levels of development. For instance, Africa, India, China and Brazil have large quantities of untapped resources but are not highly developed. Similarly, Switzerland and Japan have shown that high levels of development are possible on the basis of apparently meagre natural resources.

An interesting quantitative relationship between natural resources per inhabitant of various regions of the world and their level of development as measured by the per capita production of goods and services was observed by Cole (1981), as shown in Figure 2.1. Natural resources index values (a compound measure based on the size of region, its cultivated land, its minerals and fuel) are plotted on the horizontal axis. Production index scores, (calculated using the sum of data on energy, mineral and steel production, energy and food consumption and the availability of hospital beds) are plotted on the vertical axis. The world average index value in each case equals 100. Areas falling on the line XY imply a direct correlation or close balance between levels of natural resources and production. Although Cole's data must be considered notional and relative they make it clear that very few areas coincide with the line XY. Indeed calculations highlight the occurrence of regions at a distance from the line and thus a very poor correlation between resources and production. Venezuela, the Persian Gulf area and Amazonia all have relatively favourable levels of natural resources per capita but are little developed. In contrast, Western Europe, Japan and north-east USA are highly developed but have a relatively poor resource base. Cole places most of China, India and the rest of South Asia

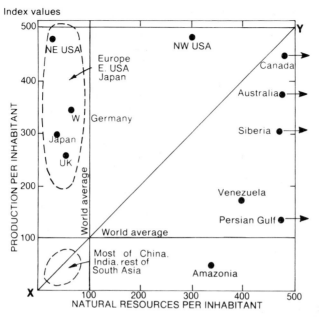

Figure 2.1 Relation between natural resources and production for selected world regions and countries. See text for explanation. (Copyright Cole, 1981. Reprinted by permission of John Wiley & Sons Ltd.)

slightly below line XY in the lower left hand corner of the graph: thus both production and resources per inhabitant in these regions are less than the world average with natural resources slightly greater than their production suggests.

The view that the economic development of the LDCs has little if anything to do with the 'internal' possession of natural resources is particularly favoured by economists. It has been argued that economic growth is principally determined by capital or human skills which are seen as the 'engines of growth'. Resources need not be situated within a country, and necessary raw materials can be imported. To a large extent resources deficiency can be compensated for by capital, or labour and entrepreneurial (risk-taking) skills, and technology.

There can be little justification for ignoring natural resources altogether, however, in any development analysis. Resources often play more than merely a passive role. It is worth noting that many LDCs do not have the external trading potential, capital accumulation, technology or labour and entrepreneurial skills to enable them to make up for limited natural resources.

(b) Compromise view

There is some evidence to show that the possession of natural resources is important especially in the early stages of economic development. Thus, natural resources are more important for the LDCs with their shortage of human and technological skills than the MDCs with their massive trading potential and their larger supplies of capital, labour skills and technology. For many LDCs, rich resources may have great significance as sources of exports, capital accumulation and foreign exchange. In this context,

23

diversification of resources may be less important than the size of one or two resources, if the resources are large enough and long-term demand is steady and strong.

Notable examples of countries which have been able to accumulate large amounts of capital (which may be exported or appropriated by a few: see Chapter 3) in recent years from mineral exploitation include South Africa (gold and diamonds), Zambia (copper), Brazil (iron and manganese) and of course the oil-exporting countries of the Middle East, North Africa, Nigeria, Mexico and Venezuela. Formerly, agricultural resources such as coffee in Brazil and beef in Argentina were likewise significant in raising large reserves of capital for these countries.

Physical resources, however, operate within the limits and possibilities set by their nature and location. Mineral exploitation may be limited by difficulties of access (see Chapter 6). Many of the best potential hydro-electric sites in the Third World (from the physical point of view of rainfall) are associated in the tropics with difficult forest vegetation, the lowest population densities and low economic activity generally. A poor distribution or lack of resources may place serious limits on growth and development. This may be the case for the thirty or so most destitute or Least Developed Countries (see Figure 1.6) of the Third World which have severe geographical, climatological and terrain difficulties.

In view of the evidence which is now accumulating concerning the possible destruction of renewable resources such as forests and soils, and the perhaps imminent exhaustion of many non-renewable resources (e.g. oil, metals), the relative importance of natural resources in the economic development of the Third World may increase in the future.

A more detailed analysis of the role of natural resources in Third World development, including climate, biological conditions and soils will now be given. The importance of minerals and power supplies will be dealt with in Chapter 6.

ASSIGNMENTS

1. *Note the major features of Table 2.1.*
   (a) *Outline the relationship between the size of a country and (i) its population; (ii) its resource base as measured by its primary export prospects.*
   (b) *Assign each of the following seven countries to their most suitable category in Table 2.1, one for each category: South Africa, China, Jamaica, Niger, Algeria, Cameroun, Qatar.*
   (c) *Can you find a place for (i) the Newly Industrializing Countries (NICs); (ii) a country such as Saudi Arabia which is both large and underpopulated in the classification. Comment on the reasons for any difficulties encountered in finding such places.*

B. Climatic Resources

Introduction

By controlling supplies of energy and moisture, climate has a major effect on the development and distribution of ecological systems (or ecosystems) and the vegetation, animals and soils they comprise. Accordingly, it is a major determinant of farming and general land use. Also, by influencing the distribution of ecological conditions associated with the growth of pests and disease it exercises an influence on the health and condition of plants, animals and humans.

1. Climatic Patterns

Owing to the sheer size of the Third World, the uneven distribution of land and sea and regional variation in relief and altitude, climatic diversity in the LDCs is considerable. A great number of climate types can be distinguished. In broad terms, however, and excepting the montane climates of mountainous areas (e.g. Tibet, Andes), the presence of warm and cool temperate climates in southern Latin America and Africa and continental type climates in northern China and Mongolia (see Plate 1.2), most of the Third World is embraced by one of four main climatic regions. These are the moist tropical (equatorial), the tropical monsoon, the tropical wet and dry (savanna) and the arid climates. Figure 2.2 shows the spatial distribution of these major climatic regions and Figure 2.3 provides a profile of their chief attributes. It should be noted that the major climatic zones shown merge gradually into one another over large distances, and that much internal climatic variety exists within each gross climatic backcloth.

2. Temperature

(a) Insolation and thermal distribution

Most countries of the Third World enjoy high levels of incoming solar radiation throughout the year, the resource on which all plant (and animal) productivity ultimately depends. As a result, over much of the Third World temperature conditions are generally quite high and striking in their relative uniformity. In the moist tropics, in particular, temperatures are constantly high with a diurnal range greater than the annual range which

Figure 2.2 Distribution of climate in the Third World and adjoining areas. (Sources: Trewartha, 1954; Meigs, 1953)

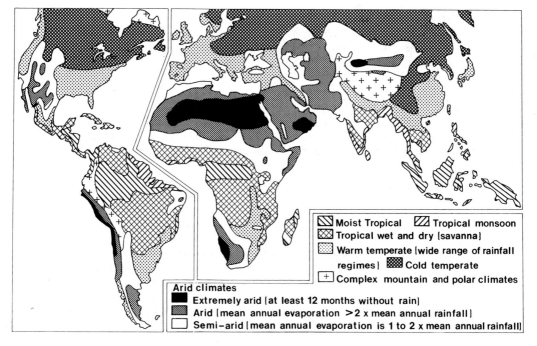

25

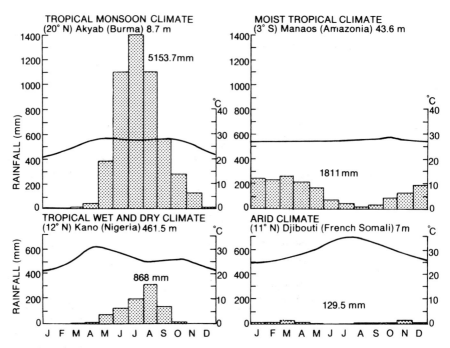

Figure 2.3 Rainfall and temperature profiles of four stations in the tropics. (Data compiled from average monthly figures from Gates, 1965)

seldom exceeds 3 Celsius degrees (see Figure 2.3). Summer (maximum) temperatures are higher in the tropical wet and dry and tropical monsoon climates and their annual ranges are correspondingly greater: about 11 °C and 8 °C respectively. The arid climates of the tropical Third World are noted for showing the largest range of both diurnal and seasonal temperatures.

(b) Effects on the ecosystem and the human response

In only a few areas of the Third World (mountainous zones, north China, southern Argentina) do low temperatures radically limit biological productivity; over most of the region plant growth is possible throughout the year. Indeed in tropical areas where high amounts of insolation are received, such as south China, India, the Philippines and Taiwan, multiple cropping is a feature with two and sometimes four crops per year being common; a fact which is of vital significance in raising crop yields and production. Variations in day length across the Third World, however, affect the performance of some traditional tropical plant varieties. Traditional varieties of rice appear to be sensitive to small variations in day length (the photo-period) and yields for this crop are highest not in the moist tropics where day length seldom exceeds 12–14 hours, but in such mid-latitude countries as south China, the Philippines and Taiwan. Here longer day lengths of 14–16 hours greatly benefit photosynthetic processes within the plant.

Long periods of high temperatures, however, are thought to limit soil fertility by speeding up the loss of organic matter from soils through enhanced 'burning' or oxidation. Also, by increasing the rate at which moisture leaves the soil by (*a*) direct

26

evaporation and (b) transpiration (water flow) through plants (a + b = evapo-transpiration), high temperatures exacerbate problems of moisture deficiency and drought, especially in areas of low rainfall.

3. Rainfall

(a) Seasonality, reliability, intensity

Compared with temperature, variations in rainfall and water supply are enormous in the Third World. In the tropics and sub-tropics rainfall rather than temperature determines the seasons, and the amount and timing of precipitation are the chief criteria for distinguishing the various tropical climates shown in Figure 2.2.

Though rainfall appears well distributed throughout the year in the moist tropics (see Figure 2.3) total amounts tend to be excessive, with values in the region of 1500–2500 mm being not uncommon. Abundant rainfall is also a feature of the tropical monsoon climate; and many areas with this climate have annual rainfall totals in excess of the moist tropics. Rainfall annual totals in the tropical wet and dry climates tend to be much less, averaging about 500–1500 mm. Unlike the moist tropics, the seasonal distribution of rainfall throughout the year in the tropical monsoon and tropical wet and dry climates (as the latter's name implies) tends to be very uneven. The presence of a wet and dry season (rainfall deficiency in the winter period) is a paramount feature of both these climates, the length and occurrence of which varies with location, the proximity to rain-bearing air masses, the regional pattern of relief, and the distribution of land and sea. For instance, in the seasonal wet and dry climates of Africa, the dry season might last for as little as 2–3 months close to the moist tropics but may extend to 8–9 months near the wet and dry/arid zone climatic boundary (see Figure 2.4). In the arid climates themselves annual rainfall amounts are extremely low (usually less than 250 mm) with little seasonal variation.

Figure 2.4 Climate, vegetation and crop variation between the equator and the tropics taking West Africa as an example. (Source: Manshard, 1979)

Number of humid (or dry) months	10–12 (0–2)	9–10 (2–3)	7–9 (3–5)	$3\frac{1}{2}$–6 (6–$8\frac{1}{2}$)	2–$3\frac{1}{2}$ ($8\frac{1}{2}$–10)	1 (11)	0 (12)
Mean annual precipitation	Mainly > 2000 mm	Mainly > 1500 mm	Mainly > 1000 mm	750–1000 mm	> 400 mm	Under 400 mm	
Simplified transect sketch							
Typical economically useful plants	Rubber, tropical timbers	Oil palm, cocoa, coffee	Yams	Cotton, millet, groundnuts	Ground nuts		
MAIN VEGETATION	MOIST TROPICAL FOREST	MONSOON FOREST	WET SAVANNA	DRY SAVANNA	THORN BUSH SAVANNA	SEMI-DESERT	DESERT

27

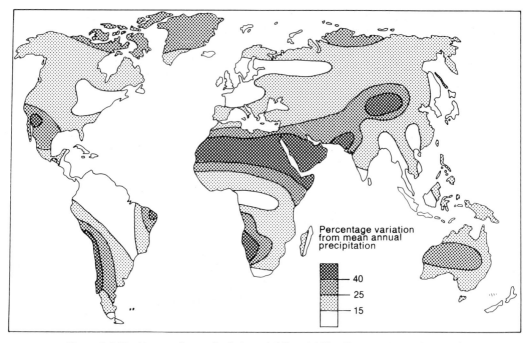

Figure 2.5 World map of annual relative rainfall variability (Source: Trewartha, 1954)

One of the most significant attributes of rainfall in many LDCs is its high variability whether on an annual, seasonal or daily basis. In general terms the lower the rainfall the more unreliable or periodic it is in its occurrence. Considering the large extent of arid and sub-humid climates in the Third World (Figure 2.2) it is not surprising that rainfall variability in Third World countries tends to be high and on the whole greater than in temperate latitudes. As shown in Figure 2.5, in areas such as East Pakistan and the sub-Saharan Sahel zone of Africa total rainfall in any one year can be expected to exceed or fall short of the mean annual amount by an average of 40% or more. This contrasts with typical annual variability values of 10–20% or less in many of the MDCs.

While seasonality in rainfall in the Third World exerts an overall control on water availability, and high variability imposes a degree of uncertainty, the characteristics of individual rainstorms are also important, particularly their intensity, duration and frequency. A large proportion of rainfall in the Third World, in humid and arid climates alike, occurs in storms of high intensity. It has been claimed that as much as 40% of the rainfall in the tropics, as opposed to about 5% in temperate areas, falls at intensities of at least 25 mm per hour, a figure at which rainfall becomes erosive. In temperate latitudes intensities rarely exceed 75 mm/hour, and then only in summer thunderstorms, but in the tropics intensities of 150 mm/hour occur regularly and rates of 340 mm/hour for a few minutes have been recorded.

(b) Effects on the ecosystem and the human response

The considerable variation in rainfall across the Third World in space and time is crucial firstly in determining patterns of vegetation and soils and, secondly, in influencing people's use of agricultural land resources. Poor water availability provides the major agricultural constraint in the Third World.

(i) *Annual and seasonal distribution of rainfall.* In parts of the moist tropics (particularly when tropical rain forest is cleared), abundant rainfall throughout the year, together with constantly high temperatures and humidities, reduce the fertility of soils. Such climatic conditions encourage excessive weathering, the rapid decay and loss of organic matter by bacterial action, and the removal of soil mineral nutrients by intense leaching (see Figure 2.6). Further, these climatic conditions do not favour the optimal growth of many cereal crops including wheat, rice, maize and sorghum, which tend to be replaced by tree and root crops such as palm oil, cocoa and yams (see Figure 2.4).

The marked seasonal variation in rainfall distribution in certain parts of the Third World has a number of consequences which vary with total rainfall amounts. In parts of

Figure 2.6 Nutrient circulation in selected semi-natural and agricultural ecosystems in the Third World. (Source: Gersmehl, 1976)

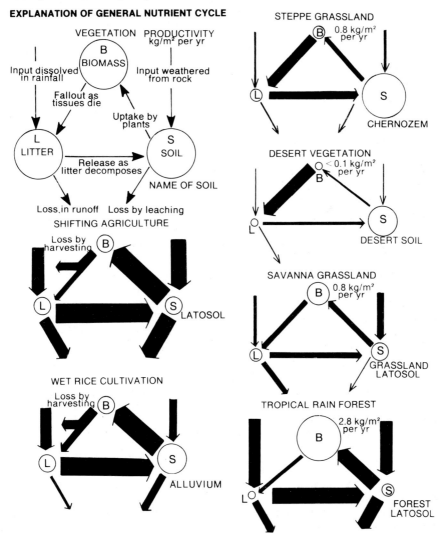

the monsoon lands, such as Bangladesh, where excessive seasonal flooding causes destruction to crops, property and lives, too much rather than too little precipitation in the rainy season is the problem. By contrast, in both the tropical monsoon and the seasonal wet and dry lands a lack of rainfall in the dry (winter) season induces problems of soil moisture deficiency. Seasonal soil moisture deficiencies give way to permanent year-long deficiencies and drought in the semi-arid and arid zones where extremely low rainfall totals are greatly exceeded by constantly high rates of evapo-transpiration.

In the wet and dry tropics (savanna lands) and in the arid zones moisture deficiency severely limits crop and livestock production over wide areas. Apart from the barren deserts of the extremely (hyper-) arid regions, most arid and semi-arid lands include thinly vegetated desert fringes that sustain only nomadic pastoral populations (Plates 1.2 and 2.2) and their grazing animals, together with smaller areas, in Central Asia, Latin America and Africa, which support pockets of settled population, crops and livestock (see Figure 4.1). In these arid areas, and in most of the savanna lands, periodic dry farming is practised which is restricted to drought tolerant crops such as maize, millet, sorghum and groundnuts. In the better endowed savanna and arid zones, especially on alluvial lowlands adjoining large rivers, rainfall deficiencies can be overcome by irrigation. In hot climates irrigation makes cultivation possible throughout the year and greatly enlarges not only crop diversity (e.g. rice, wheat, maize, sugar and vegetables) but also the yields which can be expected. Perennial irrigation systems, for instance in Eygpt (Nile) and in the Punjab (Indus), can run into difficulties, however, and excessive soil moisture evaporation can lead to problems of soil salinization (see Section E).

(ii) *Intensity of rainfall.* A range of ecological and agricultural problems is associated with the high intensity of tropical rainfall. At rates in excess of 25 mm/hour, it leads to soil surface compaction, reduced infiltration, excessive run-off and soil erosion. Soil erosion is especially severe where there is little vegetation cover to afford protection of the land. This situation is characteristic not only in the moist tropics and monsoon lands where land has been cleared for agriculture; but also in the more arid wet and dry climates where, at the end of the dry season, the vegetation is already at an absolute minimum and the soil has been hardened and dried by the sun. The erosion hazard can be lessened by cropping systems which minimize, in both space and time, the extent to which the soil is bared or, on sloping ground, by the construction of terraces.

Many areas of badly eroded land in the Third World, from the high Andes of Colombia and Peru to the Deccan of India, bear testimony to the erosive power of tropical rainfall in association with population pressure, unwise cropping practices and a lack of effective soil conservation. Plate 2.3 illustrates the kind of damage which can occur when soils are laid bare to the full intensity of tropical rainfall.

(iii) *Variability and uncertainty.* Probably the most serious single climatic hazard in the LDCs arises from the high variability and uncertainty of rainfall. This is problematic from an agricultural point of view since rainfall tends to be either too much or too little for crop production. In the Philippines nearly 4450 mm of rain fell in Luzon in one month alone (July 1972). It affected 0.3 million hectares of rice plantations, and reduced yields from 1720 kilograms per hectare (kg/ha) in 1970 to 1490 kg/ha. Such abundant and intense rainfall also destroyed nearly one-third of the sugar crop which is the country's main export earner. In the Sahel of Africa, persistent drought has helped to reduce steadily the total area of millet cultivation in Chad from 1.3 million hectares in 1961 to 0.8 million hectares in 1973. The yield during the same period decreased from 840 to 540 kg/ha. Moreover, the distribution of rainfall during the growing season, that is, the precise timing of rainfall is an equally critical factor. In the monsoon lands the time of the

Plate 2.3 Severe gully erosion in the central Andes of Peru, caused by heavy tropical rainfall acting on land cleared of its (forest) vegetation cover for cultivation. Cultivation has taken place for many centuries in this area. The soil between the gullies is still cultivated and a cereal crop has just been harvested. (*Photograph: J. P. Cole*)

onset of the monsoon rains can easily determine the difference between a good or bad crop year. If the Monsoon arrives earlier than usual, land and crops may not be prepared. If the rains are late in arriving the growing period may be critically foreshortened. Some of the worst famines of Southern Asia in recent years have resulted not from the outright failure of the Monsoon itself, but from its not arriving as early as expected.

ASSIGNMENTS

1. *'In general the lower the rainfall the more irregular it is likely to be in its occurrence.'*
   Assess the validity of this statement with reference to Figures 2.2, 2.3 and 2.5.
2. *Analyse and assess the agricultural significance of (a) rainfall distribution, (b) rainfall intensity, (c) the uncertainty and unreliability of rainfall in the Third World.*

C. Plant and Animal Resources

1. The main vegetation types

(a) Origin and distribution

In theory, the distribution of vegetation within Third World ecosystems reflects chiefly the distribution of the main climatic types outlined in the previous section. Thus tropical rain forest (Plate 2.1) is associated with the moist tropics, savanna vegetation (Plates 2.2 and 2.4) with the tropical wet and dry climate, tropical monsoon forest with tropical monsoon climate and desert vegetation (Plates 1.2 and 2.5) with arid and semi-arid climates. Figure 2.4 illustrates for West Africa an idealized case of gradual change from tropical rain forest to monsoon forest, to tree, bush and grass savanna, to desert vegetation as the dry season increases in duration and intensity away from the equator. It may be noted also that a number of vegetational forms associated with warm and cool temperate climates are found in the Third World. These include the temperate grasslands (steppe) of the Argentinian Pampas and the South African Veldt; grassland and mixed woodland formations in northern China, and grassland and montane vegetation patterns in areas of high altitude.

In reality, vegetation patterns are much more complicated owing to influences of soil, relief and biotic factors including humans. Thus, as shown in Figure 2.4, while the distinction between tropical rain forest and monsoon forest may be determined by a true climatic limit based on the nature of seasonal drought (i.e. 2–3 months), the same cannot be said for the various types of savanna vegetation. Despite the gradual change from wooded to grass savanna in response to increasing aridity, in many tropical areas there is little correlation between the amount and duration of precipitation and the occurrence of savanna forms. For instance, savanna occurs in areas with 500–3750 mm of rain per annum and from eight months of consecutive drought to none. Most savannas are probably human-induced and are due to cutting and burning and animal grazing over long periods of time. Though the presence of drier conditions between the moist tropics and the semi-arid lands possibly favours grassland development, grassland is very rarely a climatic climax vegetation in the tropics except where altitude or waterlogging limit tree growth. In the same way, desert vegetation on the fringe of desert areas may not be a reflection of climatic aridity only. For instance, the increase in drought tolerance and/or the absence of vegetation in the savanna/arid boundary of the Sahel in Africa and elsewhere is as much to do with actual land use (e.g. overcropping and overgrazing) as with climatic aridity (see Section E).

(b) Size and growth rate

Figure 2.6 shows the movement of minerals (nutrients) within a number of Third World ecosystems as a simplified series of stores and transfers. Such a model of nutrient circulation consists of a biomass store (the volume of the plants and associated animals) which as tissues die contribute material to the litter store. As litter is decomposed, nutrients are released to the soil store where they are available for plant uptake. Losses of minerals from the cycle, from leaching and run-off, are compensated for by inputs from rainfall and rock decay. Because the biomass circles are proportional to the vegetation formations themselves the tropical rain forest (TRF) is clearly outstanding in the large amount of living plant material it contains. With no drought or frost in the moist tropics to limit either growth or decay, mineral transfer between the stores is rapid and continuous. The rate of growth of the TRF is thus exceptional and averages about 2.8 kg of dry matter (carbon) production per square metre per year. With seasonal drought occurring in the savanna and both drought and frost in the steppe grasslands nutrient circulation is reduced. The growth rate of the two grassland formations is less than one-third (0.8 kg/m^2 per year) that of the TRF and their respective biomasses are also considerably decreased. Desert vegetation is notable for its negligible biomass and productivity, a consequence of prolonged year-long drought.

Plate 2.4 Drought resistant baobab trees in the dry 'Sudan' savanna of western Senegal. The dry season here lasts for 8–9 months and has helped reduce the ground vegetation to a bare brown plain. This land is occasionally grazed and burnt over and may be used, during the wet season, to grow groundnuts and millet under rotational fallow cultivation (*Photograph: G. P. O'Hare*)

Plate 2.5 Desertification and Warfare: the human consequences. Even as drought ravages large areas of Somalia, a human flood of hungry and war-weary refugees continues to pour in from neighbouring Ethiopia. It has been estimated that about 1.3 million refugees are already in the food camps in Somalia. More than 90% of the refugees are women and children. Here hungry refugees arrive at the Harar camp in Somalia (Beletweine). (*Photograph: Popperfoto, Arild Vollan*)

2. Resource value of vegetation and wildlife

(a) Forest and woodland

In many LDCs forests, after the soil itself, must be looked upon as potentially the chief natural resource. Firstly, forests have a many-sided ecological role to play which affects human life in many ways. Given the hazards of the climatic environment, forests help to restrict floods, soil erosion and soil water evaporation. They also provide habitats for a wide variety of plants and animals. The tropical rain forest with an estimated one-half of the world's species must be considered (at least for the inhabitants of the MDCs!) as the globe's primary ecological and scientific resource. Secondly, as a source of timber for construction, fuel, cellulose, resin, gums and camphor, forests represent a major biological and economic resource for the peoples of the Third World.

(i) *Exploitation of timber.* In recent years there has been a very large increase in the production and export of roundwood timber by the LDCs (see Table 2.2). Tropical

Table 2.2 Aspects of world timber (roundwood) production. (Sources: *United Nations Statistical Yearbooks, 1965, 1978*; FAO, 1981)

(a) *Total timber (roundwood) production (1964 and 1977) by the LDCs and MDCs*

	1964		1977	
Region	Volume (million m³)	Percentage share	Volume (million m³)	Percentage share
LDCs	943	47	1667	57
MDCs	1054	53	1242	43

(b) *Timber production by type of wood and by region (1977)*

Region	Coniferous percentage share	Broadleaf percentage share	Total share	Percentage of world production
World	44.3	55.7	100	100
Africa	3.5	96.5	100	15.1
S. America	13.5	86.5	100	9.8
Asia	19.7	80.3	100	32.1
N. America	77.5	22.5	100	18.2
Europe	65.8	34.2	100	10.3
Oceania	38.7	61.3	100	1.0
USSR	82.0	18.0	100	13.5

(c) *Output and export of main forest products by the LDCs and MDCs (1977).*
     (Units in million cubic metres)

Region	Fuel wood	Industrial timber	Total timber	Processed industrial timber		Export of timber	
	(I)	(II)	(I) + (II)	Sawnwood, panels	Pulp & paper	Un- processed timber	All processed products
LDC	1386	281	1667	84	23	47	15
MDC	148	1094	1242	458	244	68	119

hardwoods such as teak and mahogany are highly valued. Moreover, some of the reasons which have previously kept the export of tropical hardwoods to relatively low levels, including difficulties of cutting and transporting heavy hardwood timber, of selecting species of value from mixed species composition rather than pure stands, and inaccessibility have now been overcome by modern technology. Tropical forest clearance by transnational companies using advanced high-powered technology has reached alarming proportions.

One calculation has suggested that mechanized and organized deforestation in parts of South East Asia, Africa and increasingly in Latin America is clearing in total an area equivalent to the size of Wales each month! It can, however, be difficult for tropical forests to regenerate when large areas are felled. This fact together with the present weak policies of afforestation by Third World governments may mean that such rates of extraction, if they continue, will effectively exterminate the tropical rain forest, and with it its rich assemblage of fauna and flora, by the early twenty-first century.

(ii) *Fuel and the original energy crisis.* While tropical timber represents an important resource for certain LDCs and foreign-based trans-nationals, tropical woodlands are absolutely vital as a source of domestic firewood (fuel for cooking) for the vast majority of poor people in the LDCs (see Table 2.2(*c*)). Because the principal population loci are situated not in the timber-rich moist tropical rain forests but in monsoon forest areas which have already been largely cleared and disturbed, and in the grass-dominated savannas, there is a severe firewood shortage. In the savanna lands of north and central Nigeria 50 million people lack enough firewood while 15 million people in the moist southern forests can be said to have too much. Of the 2000 million or so people in the Third World who rely on firewood to cook their daily meals at least one-half have difficulty finding sufficient firewood, and about 150 million people simply cannot lay their hands on enough firewood to meet even minimal needs. The search for firewood, and the forest cutting it entails, is creating larger areas of denuded forest land at a distance from settlement zones. The time spent by the average family in searching for and collecting fuel wood, which sometimes takes as much as 3–4 hours per day, is increasing. For many families it now costs as much to heat their supper bowl as to fill it.

(b) Domesticated species and wildlife

The resource value of other biological components of Third World ecosystems may now be mentioned. Many traditional crop varieties and livestock breeds in use today, although commonly tolerant of marginal environments or indifferent management, are not particularly productive. Native Indian or Venezuelan cattle, hardy animals adapted to survive adverse and highly competitive environments, are not as effective meat producers as their European counterparts. By the same token many traditional food crops and fodder grasses (e.g. of the savanna), which are adapted to soils of low fertility and uncertain moisture regimes, do not give high yields per hectare even when introduced to better environments or conditions. Though there have been many attempts (e.g. the green revolution) to improve this situation with the substitution wherever possible of native plants and animals by new high-yielding varieties, results have not been as successful as originally hoped (see Chapter 5).

This condition does not apply to the wildlife resources of the LDCs. In contrast to introduced cattle, the wild herbivorous game of the tropical savannas, such as zebra, antelope and wildebeest, make extensive use of the often scarce forage of these areas and are very efficient converters of it into meat products. They are also less susceptible than livestock to tropical pests and diseases such as trypanosomiasis (sleeping sickness).

Despite efforts to establish various game farming programmes, the potential value of game resources has not been effectively realized, for reasons of taste, problems of domestication, transport and marketing facilities. Nevertheless herbivorous and carnivorous game animals (lions, cheetahs) are a considerable tourist attraction in many countries such as Kenya and Tanzania and along with other aesthetic and scenic resources may support an important and lucrative industry (see Chapter 7).

3. Pests and disease

Species diversity and unchecked growth

Human poverty is the principal cause of pest and disease in the LDCs. Nevertheless, natural environmental conditions, especially in the tropics, promote the incidence of pestilence and poor health. It may be recalled that tropical regions are extremely rich in species of plant and animal, and environmental conditions often increase the rate at which these species grow and develop. Such high species diversity and growth rate carries with it attendant problems. Tropical frost-free environments which encourage the fast and unchecked growth of vegetation and crops also favour the development of (1) weeds which compete with crops for moisture, light and nutrients, and (2) the parasitic fungi, insects, spider mites, eel worms and virus diseases which reduce crop yields and cause crop failure.

(i) *Biological losses.* The Third World compares unfavourably with the MDCs in terms of estimated annual biological losses of crops to pests, diseases and weeds. Average harvest losses for all crops by these agents alone in Africa and Asia have been estimated to range between 40% and 45% whereas the corresponding figure for Europe is less than 25%. Examples of pest attack on crops in the Third World are endless. They include coffee rust which eliminated the Arabic coffee industry in Sri Lanka and blister blight in tea which was a very serious menace in India, Indonesia and Sri Lanka until control measures were found. Other examples are the effects of stem borers and 'blast' on rice in Asia; cotton pests in Egypt, Peru and Nicaragua; 'sudden death' of the Zanzibar cloves; 'wither tip' of the Dominican limes; and the Panama disease of the Caribbean and Latin American bananas. Every crop or cereal has at least one serious pest that affects its yield.

Conditions in the tropics are also conducive to the transmission of gastro-intestinal and other parasitic diseases in humans and animals. Parasitic diseases are almost universally distributed in domestic animals throughout the tropical world. These disease organisms not only increase mortality; they are also responsible for retarded development of young animals, reduced yields of milk and meat, lowered wool production and impaired working capacity of draught animals.

(ii) *Management difficulties.* It is obvious therefore that, compared with temperate environments, many more (fast-growing) varieties of weeds and pests have to be suppressed if agriculture is to be efficient. This in turn demands more human labour and draught animal power for weeding and pest control. Farmers in the Third World find the management of weeds and pests particularly difficult because they are not educated in effective control measures, and they have little access to pesticides, insecticides and fertilizers.

ASSIGNMENTS

1. Examine Figure 2.4 and Plates 2.1, 2.2, 2.4 and 2.5.
   (a) Compare the height, spacing and composition of the main vegetation types.

(b) To what extent are these vegetation types influenced by (i) climatic variation, (ii) human and grazing activity?

2. *Examine the possibilities for, and the constraints against, Third World development offered by*

    (a) traditional domesticated plants and animals,

    (b) game animals,

    (c) the variety and rapid growth of many living organisms in the Third World.

D. Soil Resources

1. Opportunity or constraint?

Because soils are the result of the interaction of a large number of variable factors, it is not surprising that a diverse range of soil conditions is found throughout the Third World. For example, as shown from Figure 2.6, soils of the savanna grasslands, and especially those of the tropical rain forest contain relatively small amounts of nutrient reserves. Soils of desert regions are much richer in nutrients while those found in association with temperate grasslands (steppe) hold exceptional quantities.

Despite such diversity, the soils of the Third World, and especially in the tropics, are often regarded as of inferior quality and as posing fundamental problems for economic development. It has been suggested that soils represent, after water availability, the second major agricultural constraint of the Third World. Nevertheless, such impressions are to an extent Western in concept and arise as much as anything from a failure to understand tropical soils. As we shall see (Section 1 (b)), tropical soils are often better than they are made out to be and not everywhere do they impose restrictions on agriculture.

(a) Soil constraints

The most characteristic soil of the tropical Third World is the latosol; it occupies extensive areas not only under the various types of tropical forest but also in association with the tropical savanna grasslands. Forest latosols are often intensely leached and highly acidic, lacking both mineral nutrients and organic matter. Such soils contain large amounts of iron and aluminium clays, the former giving them their renowned reddish colour. They also have a poor structure and accordingly have a low capacity for holding water and nutrients. The latosols of the savanna grasslands share certain features of the forest latosols. They are less intensely leached, however, and may contain higher amounts of nutrient bases as well as organic matter in the surface layers (see Figure 2.6). The grassland latosols are also ravaged by seasonal drought and are especially difficult to work at the end of the dry season when they are baked and hardened by the sun. For these reasons it has been estimated that less than one-half of the latosol area of the Third World could be used for growing crops.

In the arid and semi-arid zones of the Third World large areas of desert and semi-desert soils exist. In the absence of downward leaching and intense weathering, these soils have usually a high nutrient level (Figure 2.6) and some are potentially fertile. But without irrigation they are rendered virtually unusable by permanent water deficiency.

Finally, all tropical soils are very prone to the dangers of erosion from heavy downpours especially when vegetation is cleared for agriculture.

(b) Soil potential

While it is true that land of generally low fertility is a feature of the Third World, opportunities for development are not everywhere restricted by poor soils. Not all tropical latosols are infertile. The surface texture of many tropical latosols is often very good and may remain friable, loose and workable. Within the tropics there are many notable areas of exceptional fertility including rich alluvial soils supporting intensive farming and high population densities. In this respect, South and South East Asia appear to be more richly endowed than either Africa or Latin America. In the former area civilizations have brought into effective use areas of fertile alluvial soils along rivers, flood plains, deltas and coastal areas. In the Ganges Valley, in the Mekong and Yellow River deltas and elsewhere annual silt renewal serves to maintain fertility at a high level and gives opportunity for intensive agricultural development based on paddy rice cultivation (see Figure 4.1).

While other areas of the Third World are less richly endowed with alluvial soils, significant areas do exist in Latin America including the Amazon, in the Congo Basin and in the Southern Sudan in Africa. In many of these areas, however, intensive agricultural development has not taken place. This may be because the population is not large enough or does not have the technical skills necessary for such development. Another reason may be critical differences in the physical and ecological conditions of the river basins themselves. The great rivers of Asia bring down soluble plant food that has been removed from the soils upstream in the catchment area. Unlike the soils in Latin America and Africa, much of this soil derives from outside the tropics proper, where different processes operate and higher soil fertility exists. Elsewhere in the tropics, fertile volcanic soils, more localized than alluvial areas, are also found. Intensely farmed mineral-rich volcanic zones in Asia (Indonesia, Java, Deccan), Africa (parts of East Africa, Rwanda, Cameroun) and Latin America (Caribbean Islands, parts of Mexico, Costa Rica and Colombia) testify to the relatively good prospects which such soils offer development.

Areas of the Third World experiencing more temperate climates often possess areas of high fertility. These include the mineral-rich chernozem soils of the steppe grasslands of the Argentinian Pampas and to a lesser extent the South African Veldt with their commercial grain and livestock farming. Less important but worthy of mention are the forest soils of tropical mountains that are high enough to escape the sterilizing effects of the high temperatures of the lowlands. The fertile humus-rich soils of the White Highlands in Kenya which support crops of coffee, maize, tea and vegetables (Plate 5.1), and similar areas in other parts of East Africa, provide cases in point.

2. Eurocentric view of tropical soils

Although soil is a fundamental agricultural resource, its precise role in development is difficult to assess. This is because the productive capacity of the land is dependent not only on the 'inherent fertility' of the soil itself and its internal physical, chemical and biological conditions; but also on external climate, the type of crop grown, the incidence of pests and disease, and management practices. What is meant by inherent fertility in temperate lands is often of a different nature and may have less agricultural relevance in the Third World. For instance, one of the most important tropical crops, wet rice, does not require fertile soil in the conventional sense but a soil capable of holding standing water. Moreover, many tropical soils are deficient in calcium, but most traditional tropical crops are adapted to such soils and do not require much calcium. Indeed Western impressions of low soil fertility in the tropics have arisen as a consequence of the failure of European farming techniques in tropical areas. Many attempts to establish intensive Western-based continuous agricultural production in the moist tropics, to replace indigenous forms of extensive sporadic cultivation (e.g. shifting cultivation), have ended in calamitous failure. Such techniques have involved, for instance, deep ploughing which has damaged soil structure, and clean weeding together with planting in rows which has been responsible for accelerating soil erosion and the leaching of nutrients. European methods of cultivation have also tended to leave the soil exposed to the sun which in turn has 'burned away' (oxidized) its essential organic compounds. Thus indigenous local farming practices which might appear inefficient to people living in the temperate latitudes are often ecologically suited to their environments and help to maintain the condition of tropical soils at a reasonable level.

ASSIGNMENT

1. (a) Assess the fertility of tropical latosols and hot desert soils.
   (b) Examine the role of Western bias in affecting European impressions and use of tropical soils.
   (c) Critically examine the links between areas of fertile alluvial and volcanic soils and that of dense agricultural populations in the LDCs.

E. Environmental Hazards

1. Natural hazards

A natural hazard can be defined as an extreme environmental disturbance triggered by the forces of nature. Catastrophic natural events (e.g. flood, drought and storm) can cause considerable destruction to land, life and property and are frequently responsible for restricting, if not reversing, economic and social development. Figure 2.7 shows the areas in the Third World where, over the past 50 years, particular hazards or combinations of hazards have involved the loss of more than 100 lives in a single incident (except for active

Figure 2.7 Natural hazards in the Third World which over the past 50 years have involved the loss of more than 100 lives in a single incident (volcanoes excluded). (Source: Doornkamp, 1982)

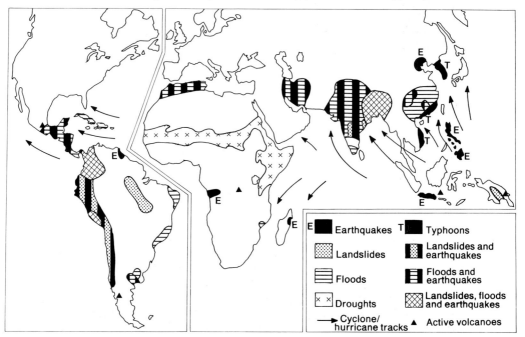

39

volcanoes). It is clear that catastrophic natural hazards are widespread in the Third World. Moreover they are particularly concentrated in areas of heavy population (see Figure 8.7), a fact which magnifies their human significance. In 1973 alone, 100 000 people died in the Sahel (sub-Saharan) drought (1968–74) and 6 to 7 million became dependent on food handouts from national and international agencies. Particularly vulnerable to earthquakes are countries in South East Asia, Mexico and those on the west side of South America. On 31 May 1970, an earthquake at Ancash–Chimbote in Peru led to 52 000 casualties, and over $500 million worth of damage was done to property.

The adverse effects of natural hazards in the Third World are compounded by poverty. For instance, storm damage in Florida can be more easily overcome than similar destruction in Jamaica because of the much greater wealth (to buy construction materials, medical facilities) of the former area.

2. Human-induced hazards

Natural hazards are not restricted to national boundaries (Figure 2.7) and many are greatly exacerbated by human action. For instance, in 1978, India suffered some of the worst flooding in its history with tens of thousands killed and at a cost of $1000 million. This was due not only to heavy rain in neighbouring mountainous Nepal, but also to massive forest clearance in that country.

Many Third World ecosystems are being seriously degraded by human activity (see Tivy and O'Hare, 1981). Three notable examples of soils and vegetation being impoverished are the processes of laterization, desertification and salinization.

(a) Laterization

Widespread woodland clearance by peasant cultivators and foreign trans-nationals in parts of the humid tropics is leading to severe environmental deterioration. A reduction in the quality of the environment is due to the accelerated loss of soil nutrients by (a) tree removal, and (b) leaching and erosion, and may ultimately lead to the development of laterization. This is the process whereby nutrients and silica compounds in the soil are removed downwards leaving a deeply weathered parent material rich in compounds of iron and aluminium.

(i) *Removal of the tree biomass*. It is clear from the nutrient circulation model in Figure 2.6 that removal of the tropical rain forest effectively breaks the rapid but 'self-contained' nutrient circulation from soil to plant biomass to litter and back again to soil. Since the majority of the nutrient reserve of the TRF, unlike the forest ecosystems of temperate latitudes, is contained in the forest biomass rather than in the soil or litter, the removal of the felled wood represents a considerable and instant loss from the system's nutrient reserves.

(ii) *Increased leaching and erosion*. Secondly, forest removal and its replacement by grassland, crops and other herbaceous vegetation exposes the soil to the effects of sunlight, heat and rain, which all increase further the loss of much of the remaining nutrient stock in both litter and soil. For instance, under conditions of constantly high temperatures and humidity, the bacterial decomposition of residual litter in the soil is rapid. If soils are cultivated after deforestation, larger surfaces of soil may be exposed to greater amounts of oxygen, a process which rapidly 'burns up' or depletes the soil organic matter. Without the protection afforded by the multi-layered forest canopy, deforested land is susceptible to greater impact from tropical rainfall. This creates larger amounts of surface run-off and accelerated soil erosion, flooding and the sedimentation and silting of rivers and reservoirs. In addition, high rainfall inputs to the soil, together with low rates of evapo-transpiration in the absence of forest, favour intense leaching. This leaching leads to laterization by removing nutrients and silica while leaving iron and aluminium compounds to accumulate in the soil. If such degraded parent material is dried out by the sun, or if the looser soil surface layers are severely eroded by rainfall, hardened brick-like 'lateritic crusts' may appear at the soil surface. Laterization is becoming a serious problem in the moist tropics and in the savannas since it causes long-term and often irreversible changes in the ecosystem. Lateritic crusts are not easily re-afforested and their cultivation becomes difficult if not impossible.

(b) Desertification

(i) *Process.* Away from the more humid tropical areas, other forms of ecosystem destruction are being enacted on a growing scale. In areas of low and fluctuating rainfall (see Figures 2.2 and 2.5) and where human populations exist there is a tendency to increase livestock numbers and/or the extent of the cultivated area in good rainfall years. Conversely, during periods of alternating drought such extensions quickly exceed the carrying capacity of the land to support them: the net result is overstocking and excessive cultivation. Overgrazing and overcultivation together with widespread woodcutting in the dry lands of the Third World have been responsible in recent years for a marked deterioration in the quality of vegetation and soils. The result has been an increase in the area of desert-like surfaces, or desertification (see Plate 2.5).

Such land-use practices destroy the vegetation and remove precious organic matter from the soil. Organic matter loss and direct soil compaction by large numbers of livestock can lead to a breakdown in soil structure. A compacted structurally poor soil has little ability to absorb moisture so that, when the rains do come, large amounts of surface water tend to collect. As this water is rapidly lost through high rates of evaporation, the soil becomes arid and harsh, and desertification results.

(ii) *Pattern.* The desertification hazard is greatest in the fragile arid, and especially in the semi-arid, ecosystems where population pressure and land-use is relatively severe. Little risk from desertification is encountered in the extremely (hyper-) arid belts where deserts already exist and where there is little human activity. There is also only modest risk in the sub-humid savanna zones where, though population and land-use pressure may be higher in absolute terms, there is much less climatic stress and more vegetation cover.

The areas of the Third World most at risk from the desertification process are illustrated in Figure 2.8. One area which has been very seriously affected by desertification is that of the Sahel. Since the late 1960s the Sahelian belt of sub-Saharan Africa from Senegal to Somalia (see Plates 2.4 and 2.5) has suffered from a prolonged period of climatic drought. Climatic aridity in this area, coupled with widespread pastoral nomadism and more localized subsistence cultivation, have seriously devastated large areas of arid and semi-arid grass, scrub and tree ecosystems, converting them into desert-like vegetation-free surfaces. The human consequences of desertification in the Sahel (as elsewhere) have been considerable. Vegetation destruction and drought have resulted in the widespread decimation of livestock; soil desiccation and structural deterioration have been responsible for marked falls in crop yield and outright crop failure. Tens of thousands of people have died because of famine and an estimated 6 million persons have been displaced from their homes. Most of this large refugee population, forced to migrate south into the more humid and already highly populated regions of the savanna, has exacerbated problems of population and land-use pressure in these areas.

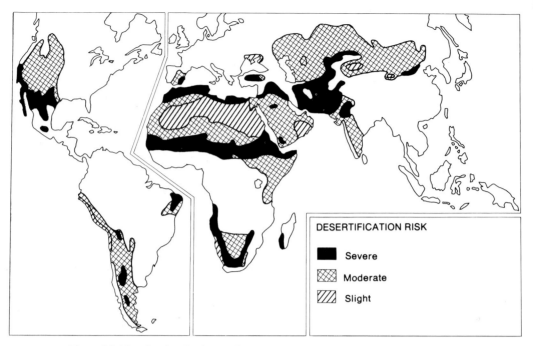

Figure 2.8 Map showing the degree of desertification hazard in the Third World and selected
neighbouring areas (Source: FAO, UNESCO and WMO, 1977)

(c) Salinization

In the better-endowed areas of the savanna and arid zones, especially on alluvial lowlands
adjacent to large rivers, problems of drought or desertification have been overcome by
irrigation. In regions where irrigation has been practised for some time, for example the
Lower Indus, the Nile, the Peruvian coast or more recently in north west Mexico, Jordan,
north east Brazil and Patagonia, the excessive application of irrigation water has led to
problems of increasing salt content in the surface layers of the soil. Where underground
drainage is poor, unused or unevaporated irrigation water builds up towards the surface
causing waterlogging and, as water near the ground surface evaporates, the deposition of
salt. This process of salinization and the creation of 'saline deserts' is to varying degrees
undermining the already critically low levels of land productivity in many parts of the
Third World. In common with laterization and desertification, salinization is reducing
yields, causing crop failure and eventually land abandonment in virtually every one of the
LDCs with land under irrigation. In India, for instance, despite strenuous corrective
measures such as improving drainage and flushing out salts with fresh water, over 6
million hectares (compared with a total national irrigation area of 40 million hectares)
have been severely damaged by salinity and many areas rendered unusable. In China, on
at least one-fifth of the irrigated area of some major regions, yields have been reduced by
salinization and tens of millions of hectares throughout the country are more or less sterile
because of salt.

Conclusion

This chapter has attempted to show that physical conditions (natural resources and
hazards) provide both opportunities and constraints for development in the LDCs. Most

workers would probably agree, however, that it is the human resources of a country–its population, skills, technology and capital–and not its physical or material resources, which determine the character and pace of its development and change. These issues are explored in the next chapter.

ASSIGNMENT

1. (a) *Examine the factors which lead to the development of laterization, desertification and salinization.*
   (b) *Summarize the implications of these three processes for human populations.*

Key Ideas

A. Resources and Development
1. The quality and quantity of resources in the Third World is by no means fully known or understood.
2. Resources, both natural and human, are generally very unevenly distributed throughout the LDCs.
3. Resource values are difficult to measure and the role of resources in development is not easy to assess.
4. The importance of natural resources in development has often been either exaggerated or underestimated.
5. Natural resources may influence development, especially in its early stages, but they do not determine its direction and rate.

B. Climatic Resources
1. Excluding temperate and montane climates, four main climatic types are found in the Third World, namely moist tropical (equatorial), tropical monsoon, tropical wet and dry and arid/semi-arid climates.
2. Variations in climate have a marked effect on the development and distribution of ecosystems and on the human use of agricultural resources.
3. Temperature conditions are relatively evenly distributed throughout the LDCs and do not directly or seriously limit plant production and agricultural potential.
4. Compared with temperatures, variations in rainfall and water supply in the Third World are enormous.
5. In many areas the amount, intensity and above all the unreliability of rainfall strongly affect the use of agricultural land resources.

C. Plant and Animal Resources
1. Four main tropical vegetation types are found in the Third World, namely tropical rain forest, monsoon forest, savanna grasslands and desert and scrub.
2. Outside the tropics, various temperate grasslands and woodlands exist, and complex montane vegetation is found in large highland areas throughout the Third World.
3. Vegetation formations vary in species composition and structure, and reflect not only climate but also the influence of soils, relief and biotic factors, especially humans.
4. The ecological and economic value of forest resources are enormous, but they are being reduced by over-exploitation.
5. Other biological resources such as game animals could be increased in value by better management and use.
6. The pest and disease problem of the Third World is in part a function of climate.

D. Soil Resources

1. The most extensive soils of the Third World, the latosols and desert soils, tend to offer limited scope for agricultural development.
2. The latosol is an intensely leached, highly acidic soil found in association with tropical forest and grassland areas.
3. Desert soils often contain reasonable reserves of mineral salts (nutrients) but unless they are supplied by irrigation, water deficiency renders them virtually unusable.
4. Localized areas of fertile alluvial and volcanic soil support dense populations in the tropics.
5. Western impressions of low soil fertility in the tropics are due in part to the failure of Western-based agricultural methods in these areas.

E. Environmental Hazards

1. Catastrophic natural hazards, which can limit and even reverse economic development, are widespread in the Third World.
2. Human action often exacerbates the adverse effects of extreme natural events.
3. Many Third World ecosystems are being degraded by human-induced hazards.
4. Deforestation has resulted in severe soil leaching, erosion and flooding.
5. Laterization represents a severe form of soil sterilization, and results from the excessive leaching of mineral salts and silica compounds, leaving a parent material rich in compounds of iron and aluminium.
6. In arid and especially semi-arid zones, population and land-use pressure is causing a deterioration in the quality of vegetation and soils and an increase in the area of desert-like surfaces (desertification).
7. In many regions where irrigation is practised problems of increasing salt concentration in the upper layers of the soil, or salinization, are being created.
8. Laterization, desertification and salinization have been responsible for a decline in agricultural productivity and in some cases land abandonment.

Additional Activities

1. Refer to Table 2.2, a good atlas and the text.
   (a) Examine the reasons for, and the implications of, increased timber production by the Third World.
   (b) Describe and explain the variations in the nature and extent of timber production by region in Table 2.2(b).
   (c) What is the main use of timber in the LDCs and MDCs? Give reasons for your answers.
   (d) In what other ways can forests be regarded as an important resource?
2. (a) Examine Figure 2.8 and briefly describe the distribution and extent of the desertification hazard.
   (b) Compare the pattern of desertification risk with:
       (i) the distribution of rainfall reliability shown in Figure 2.5,
       (ii) the location of the main climatic types, illustrated in Figure 2.2,
       (iii) the spatial pattern of the main agricultural types indicated in Figure 4.1.
       (iv) Explain your findings.
   (c) Outline general ways in which the spread of desertification might be arrested in terms of (i) climate change, and (ii) alterations in land-use practice and management.
3. Discuss the relationship between (a) minerals, (b) climate, (c) ecological resources and Third World development.

Human Resources and Development

Introduction: Internal and External Factors

A number of observers have suggested that the obvious poverty of the Third World is a result of some internal deficiency or inferiority in its human resources. Others have contended that the underdeveloped nature of the LDCs is due to an external deficiency or constraint created by their dealings with other regions, especially the MDCs. The subject of 'internal' human resource deficiency is dealt with in Sections A to D; that of external constraints on development in Section E of this chapter.

A. Internal Economic Factors

The lack of Western-style development in the Third World may be a consequence of a deficiency in one or other of the factors necessary for production, such as land resources (Chapter 2), labour and capital. In particular, several economic theories or models have emphasized a link between capital shortage in the Third World and the state of underdevelopment.

1. Capital

(a) Vicious circles of poverty

One model which emphasizes the possible connection between capital shortage and poverty in the LDCs, is the concept of 'the vicious circle of poverty'. As shown from Figure 3.1 this model states that at the individual level a poor person (A) cannot pay for an adequate supply of food (B), thus is physically weak (C) and is unable to work efficiently (D). As a consequence the person is unable to earn much money (E), is poor (A) and cannot afford sufficient nourishment (B) and so on. At the level of an entire economy, low productivity (A) leads to low real incomes (B) and eventually to low savings (C), to low investment (D) and hence capital shortage (E). A shortage of capital prevents the effective utilization of resources (F) and thus acts as a brake or blockage to productivity (A) and so forth.

Although these models are useful, they are inadequate as a total explanation of poverty and underdevelopment. Firstly, the assumption that an initial state of poverty is the sole cause of continuing poverty is simplistic since it does not explain the root cause of the initial poverty. Secondly, as there is no consideration of social conditions, these models imply, quite incorrectly, that societies in the LDCs are static and unchanging entities. Thirdly, they do not distinguish between LDCs, which they assume are all at the same stage of development. No account is taken of the fact that wide variations exist both

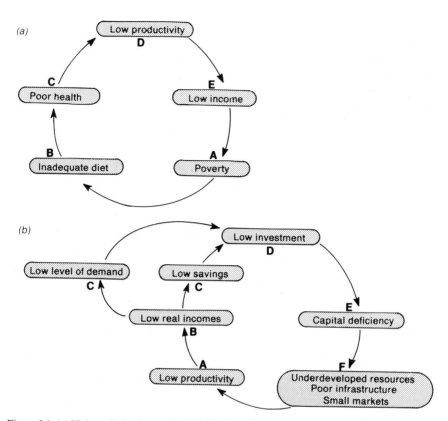

Figure 3.1 (*a*) Vicious circle of poverty: individual level; (*b*) Vicious circle of underdevelopment: economic system. (Source: Nurkse, 1953)

within and between LDCs (see Chapter 1). Finally, they do not give any clues as to how an individual or country can 'break out' of the cycle. This is an important issue because not all countries are poor: some must have broken the cycle in some way.

(*b*) *Capital as the engine of growth*

Some economic observers have argued that countries can break out of the cycle of poverty through the mobilization of resources, especially capital. They argue that large capital accumulations are necessary for economic growth and that the LDCs can acquire this capital in three main ways:

(i) through foreign financial flows in the form of both government (official aid) and private investment, from the MDCs;

(ii) by internal accumulation through higher taxes and forced savings;

(iii) by exporting natural resources such as minerals, or producing cash crops.

The relative and absolute importance of each of these three sources of capital will vary from one country to another. For instance, India and Brazil have benefited from foreign government and private investment from the MDCs. China has managed to develop internal sources of capital through domestic savings while the OPEC countries (oil-exporting) have amassed vast amounts of foreign currency through the export of crude oil. Though clearly not all LDCs can accumulate sizeable capital reserves in these ways it may be useful to pursue the idea of capital-led economic growth if only to see how it may be attained – by some.

2. A general theory of economic growth

(a) Rostow's stage model

A very popular theory of economic growth is the stage model of economic development introduced by W. W. Rostow in 1960 (see Figure 3.2). This model gives us some insight into how the cycle of poverty may be broken and economic growth achieved. Through primarily external influences, a poor country is able to move from stage 1, *the traditional society*, where a subsistence economy predominates, to stage 2, where the installation of roads and railways, and the formation of a new social and political elite, encourage *the preconditions for take-off*, with cash cropping and extractive industry playing a key role. As productive investment increases to above 10% of national income, *the take-off*, the third and critical stage, is reached. At this stage there develop one or two significant manufacturing sectors with high rates of growth, and a political, social and institutional structure which favours growth. After take-off, self-sustaining growth may be achieved. Thereafter there follows stage 4, or *the drive to maturity*, during which the impact of growth is transmitted to all parts (i.e. not just 'enclaves' and specific industries) of the economy. Finally, with stage 5, a shift in sectoral dominance to industries such as durable consumer goods (automobiles, washing machines) ushers in *the age of high mass consumption*.

Figure 3.2 Rostow's stage model of economic growth (1960). (Source: Rostow, 1971)

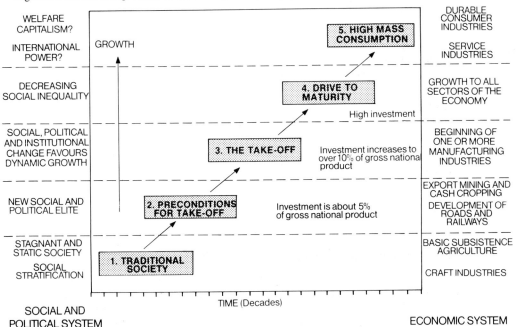

(b) Some criticisms of the model

Although the Western industrial countries may all have moved through these developmental stages over different time scales (indeed, the model is Eurocentric and based on the historical experience of the MDCs), it is unlikely that the same path can be easily or faithfully undertaken by the vast majority of the LDCs. Evidence has shown that capital investment alone is not sufficient to promote 'take-off' as described by Rostow. Despite large injections of capital into the economies of certain LDCs over the last two to three decades, most LDCs, especially in Africa and Asia, are still at the traditional stage. Very few have reached the preconditions for take off, (perhaps Mexico, Brazil, India, Colombia), and fewer still have achieved take-off itself (perhaps some NICs, e.g. Hong Kong, Taiwan, Singapore, S. Korea). There are two main reasons for this. Firstly, it seems likely that there need to be fundamental structural changes in society before increasing productive investment can take place. This would include for example, conditions which encourage people to save and invest and lead to the development of an entrepreneurial or business class. A second fundamental point is that the whole international economic situation confronting the LDCs today is very different from that which faced the MDCs when they were undergoing economic 'take-off'. The passage from a traditional agricultural to an advanced industrial economy may be, in global terms, a once and for all process. Those countries which industrialized and developed first (the MDCs) did so because they could make use of virtually the whole world as a source of raw materials and a market for their processed goods. Under existing international conditions, the MDCs may have effectively 'closed the door' on the LDCs.

Thus social and political as well as economic conditions appear to be pertinent to the process of economic growth and development. Let us look now at such conditions in the Third World.

ASSIGNMENTS

1. *Assess the strengths and weaknesses of the 'vicious circle' concept.*
2. *Read again Rostow's stage theory of economic development outlined in Section 2(a) and shown in Figure 3.2.*
   (a) Consider the selected characteristics of development for the five groups of countries shown in Table 3.1.
   (b) Estimate the general level of development (stages 1–5) of these countries using Rostow's ideas.
   (c) Give reasons for your estimations and discuss the merits and disadvantages of Rostow's model in the light of these.

B. Internal Socio-economic Factors

Introduction: the labour force

In view of the size and rate of growth of Third World populations (see Chapter 8) there is little doubt that the labour force of the LDCs is adequate in quantity. What is more uncertain is the quality of this labour supply in terms of the physical health, skills and knowledge of individuals. As we shall see, health and education levels are deficient in the Third World. Such deficiencies may well contribute, together with high rates of population increase and low investment rates, to the low rates of labour productivity in the Third World, and in turn to the state of underdevelopment.

Table 3.1 Some indicators of development for selected countries. (Sources: *World Bank Development Report, 1981*; United Nations, 1981)

	1979 Per capita GNP (US$)	1977 Share of agriculture in total GDP	1977 Share of mining in total GDP	1977 Share of manufacturing in total GDP	1970–80 Gross domestic investment: average annual growth rate (%)	1977 Literacy rate	1977 Circulation of daily newspapers per 1000 population	1977 Population per passenger vehicle
Group 1								
Bolivia	1099	17.1	10.8	13.3	6.3	62.7	26	153
Liberia	500	16.1	22.8	8.8	5.2	9.1	8	141
Group 2								
France	9950	4.7	0.8	27.5	2.0	97	205	3
USA	10630	2.7	2.6	24.3	1.9	99	287	2
Group 3								
Hong Kong	3760	1.4	0.0	23.6	12.5	77.3	368	35
Turkey	1330	26.0	1.2	17.9	10.1	60.3	41	88
Group 4								
Chad	110	40.4	1.0	10.8	(−0.5)	5.6	—	724
Mozambique	250	56.3	0.6	6.1	(−8.4)	11.4	4	109
Group 5								
Spain	4380	9.4	1.3	26.7	2.5	91.2	128	6
USSR	4110	17.7	51		—	99	396	—

1. Health and disease

(a) General measures of health

One of the simplest ways of revealing the gross inequalities in health levels between the LDCs and the MDCs is by the use of life expectancy and/or infant mortality data. (See Table 1.3 and the PQLI map of Figure 1.5.) Life expectancy in the LDCs increased by a dramatic 50% between the early 1940s and the early 1970s but this rapid improvement began to falter in the 1960s and has continued to slow down. Today, in the LDCs as a whole, life expectancy at birth is about 53 years while in the MDCs it is around 70 years. As shown from Table 3.2 (and Table 1.3), there are significant differences between Third World regions and countries. Poor African countries south of the Sahara, together with those in South Asia, generally report the lowest levels of health, while the Latin American countries, which are among the wealthiest of the LDCs, report health levels approaching (at least in statistical terms) those of the MDCs. Health and GNP levels are not everywhere correlated, however, and countries such as Sri Lanka (health levels higher than incomes suggest) and regions such as the Middle East (lower than incomes suggest) provide notable exceptions. Such anomalies are the result, in part, of differences in the degree of health care provision. Sri Lanka has a fairly active health care programme while the Middle East, in general, has done relatively little to improve health levels among the majority of its people.

(b) Provision of health care

(i) *Present status and concentration.* In measures for health improvement as well as in levels of health the LDCs lag far behind the rest of the world. Unlike the inhabitants of the MDCs most people in the Third World are not being reached by the benefits of modern health care. As shown from Table 3.2, in the LDCs there is a serious shortage of hospitals, doctors, nurses and medicines. One reason for the narrow coverage provided by public health facilities can be found in the low government expenditure on health expressed either as a percentage of GNP or on a per capita basis. Government health outlays in about one-quarter of the LDCs is less than 1% of GNP and $1 per capita, and in about one-half it is less than $5 per capita. At higher levels of GNP per capita, health expenditures and thus services increase; but still remain much lower than the MDCs where expenditures are often above 5% of GNP and in excess of $400 per capita.

Another explanation for restricted health care coverage is that, of the money spent on health care, a relatively large proportion goes to maintain a small number of expensive modern hospitals and highly (often Western-) trained, medical personnel. Moreover, the large majority of medical facilities are concentrated in the capital city or major urban areas and are thus most accessible to a small number of privileged and wealthy urban citizens. In this way many LDCs spend 80% or more of health resources on 20% of their population. Further, because of a lack of roads and reliable affordable transport or simply of ignorance or reluctance to use available medical services, most patients visiting health facilities come from the immediate vicinity. In India one study has shown that the population of a community attending a dispensary decreased by 50% for every additional half mile (0.8 km) between the community and the facility. Thus the overwhelming majority of people in the LDCs especially the poor in rural areas, do not have access to any permanent form of health care.

(ii) *Primary health care.* The realization of the possible inappropriateness of such narrow Western-based oversophisticated medical care has caused some recent shift in emphasis in

Table 3.2 Health levels, medical services and some other factors affecting health in selected regions and countries. (Sources: *World Bank Development Report, 1980*; United Nations, 1981)

Region & country	Per capita GNP (1977)	Per capita food supply		With access to safe water (%)	Population			Adult literacy rate	Life expectancy	Infant mortality rate per 1000 (under age 1 year)
		Daily protein intake (g)	Daily calorie intake		Per hospital bed	Per doctor	Per passenger vehicle			
	(i)	(ii)	(iii)	(iv)	(v)	(vi)	(vii)	(viii)	(ix)	(x)
Sub-Saharan Africa										
Ethiopia	110	59.8	1822	7	171	84850	—	10	39	165
Kenya	270	61.3	2176	17	773	8840	128	40	53	51
Ghana	380	40.1	2125	35	648	10200	146	30	48	63
South Asia										
Bangladesh	90	37.2	1816	53	4868	11350	2562	22	47	140
India	150	46.2	1904	31	1620	4100	784	36	51	122
Sri Lanka	200	39.3	2061	20	330	4010	339	78	69	45
East Asia										
Indonesia	300	39.3	2041	11	1625	16430	279	62	48	—
Philippines	450	38.4	2025	50	639	3150	115	87	60	72
Malaysia	930	45.0	2495	62	—	4350	23	60	67	35
N. Africa & the Middle East										
Morocco	550	68.2	2617	55	739	11100	53	28	55	117
Turkey	1100	81.1	2893	75	476	1720	88	60	61	—
S. Arabia	6040	53.2	2017	64	840	2220	9.2	—	48	—
L. America										
Guatemala	790	53.8	2024	40	457	2500	77	46	57	75
Brazil	1360	57.8	2468	77	264	1650	20	76	62	—
Argentina	1730	106.7	3367	66	176	530	13	93	71	59
MDCs										
UK	4420	86.6	3223	100	117	670	3.8	99	73	16
Sweden	9250	82.1	3059	100	66	580	3.2	99	75	8

medical provision. The idea that a simple low-cost but widespread system of primary health care (PHC) should be made available to populations in the LDCs has gained some acceptance. Consequently, within many LDCs an increasing use is being made of a relatively large number of semi-trained peripatetic health workers to improve general health levels. Also, rather than treating illness after the symptoms have arisen (curative medicine) emphasis is being given to environmental and preventive measures, that is, establishing patterns of behaviour to restrict the spread of disease. In Tanzania (see Section (f)) preventive work is now based on a widespread immunization programme for tuberculosis, measles and other diseases. Moreover as shown in Plate 3.1, many children there suffer from malnutrition, even though protein may be available. Because of various taboos and traditions children are given mainly maize, which is relatively protein deficient, while adults commonly consume protein-rich groundnuts as part of their diet. Accordingly, education schemes are attempting to emphasize the importance of giving the young a diet of groundnuts mixed with milk and maize.

Such primary or community-orientated health care is the key to the ambitious but necessary goal of the World Health Organization (WHO) and its member countries that 'health for all' should be achieved by the year 2000.

Plate 3.1 Lower slopes of Mt Kilimanjaro, Northern Tanzania. Small leaved coffee bushes and broad bladed banana trees can be seen in the cultivated plot in the background. Though one of the most fertile areas in the country, the thin condition of the children shows that there is hunger here. Factors contributing to this include poor agricultural methods and the custom of giving children maize rather than protein-rich groundnuts in their diet. Continuing drought since 1975, when this picture was taken, will have exacerbated the situation further. Simple or intermediate toy technology is represented by the home-constructed wooden bicycle! (*Photograph: J. P. Cole*)

(*c*) *Patterns of disease*

The most widespread diseases occurring in the tropics and sub-tropics alike are (1) those transmitted by human faeces, i.e. the intestinal parasitic and infectious diarrheal diseases, (2) various airborne diseases including tuberculosis, meningitis and measles, and (3) various nutritionally related diseases, such as kwashiorkor (protein deficiency) and pellagra. These disease groups are also the major causes of death in the LDCs. A study of deaths among children of 5 years and less in selected areas of Latin America revealed that over 70% of all deaths were directly due to these three groups of disease.

Other debilitating and fatal diseases are more limited to particular geographical areas or particular ways of life. (4) The various vectorborne diseases (e.g. malaria, trypanosomiasis, bilharzia) are those where the disease agent or organism (pathogen) is transmitted to humans by a vector or carrier (e.g. mosquito, snail). They are less widespread than the ubiquitous groups (1–3) and figure less prominently in gross mortality and morbidity (disease) statistics. Nevertheless, there has been a startling increase in their incidence since the 1970s, despite major efforts to control them.

By far the most important tropical vectorborne disease is malaria. This disease is widely distributed throughout tropical areas of Africa, Asia and Latin America. Because of the susceptibility of mosquitoes (the insect vector which transmits the disease) to low humidity (below 60%) and to low temperature (the insect's activity is curtailed below 16°C) there is a general absence of malaria from hot desert and upland areas in the tropics and temperate zones. Malarial eradication programmes launched in the 1950s and backed by international agencies such as WHO have been successful in many countries where they have been implemented. However, because of a decline in preventative action, such programmes have suffered recent setbacks and there has been a resurgence of the disease in Turkey, Indonesia, Sri Lanka and in the Indian sub-continent. The number of new malarial cases increased by over 235% between 1972 and 1976: in 1982 over 150 million suffered from the disease.

A second important vectorborne disease which affects humans and livestock is trypanosomiasis or 'sleeping sickness'. As shown in Figure 3.3, it is transmitted by the tsetse fly (Glossina species) which prefers wooded and bush savanna country in hot relatively humid lowland areas. Despite control measures, including the destruction and sterilization of breeding sites of the tsetse (e.g. bush clearance and spraying with insecticides), the separation of game (which act as 'carriers' of the disease) from livestock, and the treatment of infected stock and humans by drugs, the disease is still a major problem. Trypanosomiasis causes high mortality in much of tropical Africa and widely prevents stock-keeping (see Plate 2.2). At present about 45 million people are affected by

Figure 3.3 The Tsetse fly–game–human–livestock cycle in the disease trypanosomiasis.

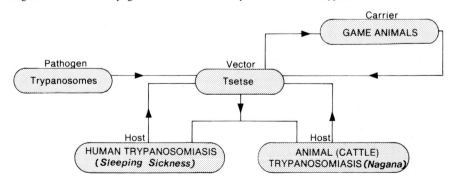

the disease. Finally, (5) the various contact diseases such as leprosy and tetanus, which are spread by direct contact between individuals, are generally of relatively minor significance except in limited areas.

(d) Causes of disease

Though the tropical environment is well suited to the growth and spread of disease (Chapter 2, Section C), low health levels in the Third World are largely a function of poverty. Inadequate nutrition, crowded and insanitary conditions, together with a lack of medical services, lie at the root of health problems.

(i) *Malnutrition.* Widespread undernutrition and malnutrition (Plate 3.1) are a characteristic of many LDCs (see pages 7–9 and Table 3.2), which contribute substantially to the incidence and severity of health problems. Although malnutrition may not be a major *primary* cause of death, it is of immense importance as a secondary and contributing factor. Nutritional diseases such as rickets (vitamin D deficiency), kwashiorkor (protein deficiency), beri-beri (vitamin B_1 deficiency) and marasmus (shortage of both calories and protein) reduce resistance to other (endemic) diseases, such as intestinal parasitic diseases, malaria, typhoid. Disease itself can contribute to malnutrition. Epidemics of diarrheal diseases, for instance, are often followed by outbreaks of nutritional disease.

(ii) *Insanitary conditions.* Probably the most important reason for the unhealthiness of the Third World is the lack of decent sanitary facilities and supplies of clean drinking water. The great majority of people, especially in rural areas, do not have proper access to modern community water supplies and waste disposal systems. Approximate data shown in Figure 3.4 and Table 3.2 on the proportion of population served by clean drinking water and adequate sewerage facilities indicate that in general this proportion is very low and that it tends to increase with the level of socio-economic development. Figure 3.4 shows that about 60% of the population of the more wealthy regions namely Latin America, North Africa and the Middle East, are well served by adequate water and sanitary facilities but this proportion falls to between 20% and 30% for poorer areas, such as South and East Asia and to under 20% in Africa south of the Sahara. Further, although urban areas are by no means adequately served, it is particularly in the rural areas where facilities are most restricted. In Pakistan only 5% of the rural population of 60 million but 75% of the 30 million urban population are well served with water supply. Of Iraq's urban inhabitants, 100% and 75% respectively are supplied with water and

Figure 3.4 Access to safe water and sewage services in major regions of the Third World (Source: World Bank, 1980)

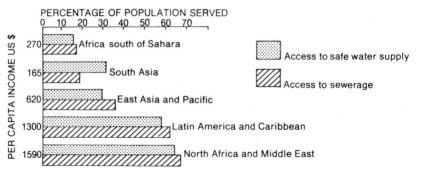

sewerage services, while the corresponding figures from rural areas are only 11% and 10%.

In the presence of insanitary and overcrowded conditions, faecally related diseases, other intestinal infections, as well as typhoid, dysentery and cholera spread easily. It has been estimated that about 80% of the disease problems of the LDCs can be related to poor water supply and sanitation.

(e) Health and economic development

There is no doubt that ill health is one of the greatest obstacles to economic and social development in the Third World. Ill health imposes economic costs in at least three ways:

(i) Illness impairs people's ability to concentrate, students' ability to learn, and the availability and productivity of labour. As much as one-tenth of people's normal activities may be disrupted by illness in the Third World. The removal of even a few days' labour because of ill health can be devastating. If, for instance, a farmer suffers a severe attack of malaria (shivering and fever lasting several days) at a crucial period during the farming calendar, for example at sowing or harvest time, the consequent loss of labour may result in damage to crops and food shortage. This may spell starvation for the family.

(ii) Illness consumes scarce financial resources. Health services may be limited but the costs of treating illness are still a burden on the community.

(iii) Enormous waste occurs when poor health conditions restrict settlement in areas with fertile land or other natural resources. The occurrence of 'river blindness', a disease transmitted by the bite of blackflies that breed near running water, has restricted access to land and resources in West Africa (see Figure 10.1) and has also resulted in the abandonment of villages. In some West African river-valley communities a fifth of the adults may be blind because of the disease. Sleeping sickness, in both animals and humans, strongly restricts livestock rearing in many lowland hot wet tropical lands in Africa. The tourism potential or the export of cash crops of areas may also be undermined if disease conditions are prevalent.

Paradoxically, the attainment of better health may pose, in certain areas, a threat to well-being. In Kenya, increased medical facilities have helped to reduce infant mortality and improve life expectancy. The result has been a rapid increase in population (almost 4% per annum) which is now placing considerable pressure on existing resources. Against these trends, in many countries (e.g. China, India) family planning/child spacing programmes form an important part of campaigns to raise the level of health while at the same time reducing population expansion.

(f) Tanzania: primary health care

Socialist Tanzania, in a vigorous programme of primary health care, has transformed its medical services into a positive health care system. From preoccupation with curing the ills of the few who could pay for its services in the cities it has turned to the provision of preventive services for the entire population.

The relatively inexpensive training of paramedical personnel and the establishment of a new national network of health establishments have taken up the major share of medical expenditure in recent years. While the city hospitals took over 80% of the health budget in the 1960s, 60% now goes to support rural service. Three levels of health care have been created in the rural areas.

(i) *Rural dispensaries*. About 3000 of these have been set up every 2–4 km. The rural medical assistant who heads the dispensary is usually a local farmer. Though he has little training he is able to diagnose several basic diseases, such as malaria and anaemia, which he can treat using the simplest methods, for example by pills.

(ii) *Rural health centres*. Medical staff at the 300 or so health centres (average distance apart 15 km) have slightly more training and treat diseases such as bilharzia and hookworm with a careful course of treatment involving injections.

(iii) *District hospitals*. The most difficult diseases are passed on to the district hospitals of which there are about 65. Even here the health assistants are trained in two to three years at a cost of about $1200 as opposed to $12 000 over many years for a doctor.

Mass campaigns of instruction in hygiene and nutrition have been launched and wells are being drilled to provide safe drinking water within a kilometre of every dwelling place in the country. As the first hopeful return from these efforts, infant mortality has been reduced from 190 per 1000 live births in 1960 to 152 in 1977, and life expectancy has been increased from 37 years to 48.

2. Education

(a) Basic patterns and improvements

As with health, levels of education are generally much lower in the LDCs than in the MDCs. While most people in the MDCs are literate, almost three-quarters of the inhabitants of Africa, almost one-half of those in Asia and one-quarter of those in Latin America are illiterate. An impression of the generally low but nationally varied levels of literacy in the Third World is given in Tables 1.3, 3.1 and 3.2.

Nevertheless, during the last 20–30 years some substantial advances have been made in the field of education in the Third World. For the period 1960–75, enrolment in primary schools more than doubled from 163 million to 370 million. For the first time more children in the 6–11 age group were in rather than out of school in the Third World. By 1975 only 121 million (38%) of the 6–11 primary age group were not enrolled in schools.

Such basic improvements have resulted in reductions in Third World illiteracy. Between 1960 and 1975 the average level of illiteracy dropped from 59% to 50%. At the national level, too, advances in the ability of people to read and write have been spectacular.

(b) Re-appraisal

At the same time, after almost three decades of rapidly increasing enrolments and hundreds of billions of dollars of educational expenditure, the plight of the average citizen of Asia, Africa and Latin America seems little improved. The benefits which are supposed to accrue in countries which adopt expanded educational systems – a rise in the levels of living especially for the poor, the provision of equal opportunities for all, the reduction of cultural divisions between diverse and often fractious ethnic groups, the encouragement and spread of modern Western attitudes – have been shown to be greatly exaggerated.

(c) Nature of education programmes

(i) *Present status and concentration*. Most schooling, particularly in the primary sector, is characterized by a shortage of even the most rudimentary equipment (Plate 3.2), poor

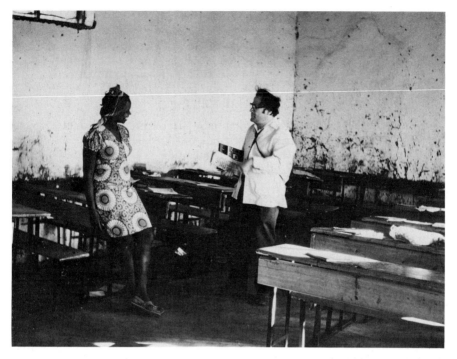

Plate 3.2 An English and Tanzanian teacher converse in a secondary school at Iringa, south central Tanzania. Note the rudimentary schooling facilities: simple wooden desks and benches and the absence of books and audio-visual aids; the school itself is a converted tobacco storage and processing factory. Many schools in the Third World have no buildings at all and use the shade of trees as roofs. (*Photograph: J. P. Cole*)

teacher training facilities and high rates of absenteeism. High 'drop out' rates occur, especially among the poorer children whose labour (particularly girls') is needed on the family plot or the domestic front (care of younger children). These facts partly explain the poorer levels of education among women in the LDCs. Parents' inability to pay for uniforms or transport to school also restricts the access of the poorer children to education.

Moreover, the formal education system in most LDCs is with minor exception a direct transplant of the system in the MDCs. Just as the international transfer of sophisticated physical technology (e.g. iron and steel, rubber factories) may be ill suited to societies in the LDCs (Chapter 11, Section D), the transfer of intellectual technology from highly urbanized and industrialized countries may be similarly ill suited. The adverse effects of Eurocentric educational systems transferred to the LDCs tend to reveal themselves in a number of ways. Firstly, because transplanted Western systems are geared to the availability of jobs in the modern urbanized sector they have encouraged the drift of qualified individuals from rural to urban areas. Secondly, the need for suitable qualifications to secure attractive high urban incomes has increased the demand for and the provision of secondary and tertiary education at the expense of the primary sector. Increases in the former benefit the already better-off urban groups who can afford such advanced education; decreases in the latter put at a disadvantage the already disadvantaged, the rural poor. Thirdly, Eurocentric educational systems transferred to the LDCs have encouraged the international migration of high-level educated workforce, the so-called 'brain drain' from poor to rich countries. Fourthly, the pursuit of Western-based ideas and philosophies has directed much attention away from local issues such as appropriate technology, labour-intensive techniques, and preventive low-cost medicine.

Thus, instead of being a force for equality, education in most LDCs acts to increase rather than to decrease social and income inequalities. It maintains and increases the development gap not only within the LDCs–between rich and poor, and rural and urban areas–but also between the LDCs and the MDCs.

(ii) *Informal and basic education.* The World Bank has recently suggested that the only way to make primary education in the LDCs universally available by the year 2000 is to provide a new low-cost education called 'basic education' as a supplement to standard primary schooling. Unlike the formal system with its emphasis on examinations and paper qualifications, designed for urban areas, it is envisaged that 'basic education' will provide pupils with some functional and practical skills which will fit the specific needs (e.g. health, food supply) of local rural communities. Included within this new education programme, for instance, is a plea for the greater education of women and girls. Measures such as these will help to improve family planning and health as well as increasing the generally low social status of women in the Third World (see Section C).

In conclusion, suitable programmes of education are essential at all levels in the development process. The greater education of females, for example, will improve local domestic and agricultural activities and will give women the opportunity to participate more widely in economic development. Also, increasing various types of technical skill and training among the inhabitants of the Third World should lessen the present 'intellectual' dependency of the LDCs on expatriates, and allow the LDCs to build up an indigenous technical capacity for economic development.

ASSIGNMENTS

1. *Study Table 3.2 and Figure 3.4.*
   (a) Describe the variations in health levels shown.
   (b) To what extent can the data be used to explain (i) poor health levels in the Third World, and (ii) improved health conditions among the more socio-economically advanced countries.
2. *(a) Analyse the main types of disease found in the Third World.*
   (b) Discuss the factors which influence their distributions.
   (c) Assess their impact on (i) general physical well-being, and (ii) economic development.

C. Internal Social Factors

1. Social dualism

The concept of social dualism within the Third World is generally accredited to the Dutch economist J. H. Boeke (1953). While working in Indonesia he discerned two distinctly different societies within one area. One society, the indigenous society, was seen as traditional, often static, feudal and fatalistic, and was regarded as representing society before (and after) the advent of colonialism (see Section E). The other society, the modern one, was regarded as rational, Western, dynamic, profit oriented and a product of colonial import. This work led some other authorities to suggest that many traditional modes of behaviour and outdated social attitudes of the indigenous society prevent the adoption of new ideas and techniques necessary for economic growth. At the same time, little credit was given to the traditional society, and few explanations of the way in which it functions. Thus social factors alone, rather than capital, or the supply of technology or skilled labour were seen as responsible for limiting the transfer of economic development from the MDCs to the LDCs and, more specifically, from the modern sector (where it has been introduced) to the larger traditional sector. Underlying all these explanations of course is the rather ethnocentric assumption that the traditional society should change to the modern one, that everyone should adopt the Western capitalist viewpoint, and that all people are acquisitive rational economic human beings.

2. The indigenous society: the Western viewpoint

(a) Social constraints

(i) *Class structure.* Many LDCs, especially in Latin America and parts of South East Asia, have a class structure which prevents individual advancement because it is composed of a small elite of landowners, priests, elders and autocratic rulers, and a very large undifferentiated lower class of peasants. These elites have either monopolized commerce or seized its proceeds. Many of the land owners have not been innovators and have resisted economic change for fear of losing their social and political power. In Africa, on the other hand, one of the main obstacles to development is often seen to be a lack of a well-developed indigenous capitalist class. Thus, in many parts of the Third World there is no sizeable rural or urban middle and 'capitalist' class to provide leadership and into which the enterprising individual can climb.

(ii) *The division of labour: custom, caste and sex.* Many customs and behavioural attitudes within peasant societies decide who shall do a particular job. In India, for instance, where such an occupational caste system is at its most extreme, artisans and merchants can only follow their father's occupations.

The division of labour within traditional societies is also determined by the relative status of men and women. Normally, operations involving strenuous physical labour (e.g. forest clearance, ploughing) are left to men. Because of their relatively higher levels of formal education, technical training and geographic mobility, men have better access than women to jobs in the commercial, managerial and industrial field. By contrast, various socio-cultural and political obstacles restrict the economic participation of women in many Third World societies. Much of their work tends to be tedious and time-consuming and confers low social and political status. In general, women are confined to domestic activities (looking after children, fetching water and firewood), agricultural work (tending the farm plot, especially sowing and weeding) and local processing and manufacturing work (food processing, textiles, pottery). (See Plate 5.2.)

The dichotomy between male and female employment in the Third World is not everywhere so clear cut, however. For instance, merchant occupations are normally the sole preserve of males in large parts of Africa and Asia, yet in South Ghana many important merchants, for example fruit and vegetable sellers in the local markets, are women. In central India, farming operations involving men *and* women are the predominant overall pattern. Women are also extensively employed in factory and industrial work, especially in South and South East Asia, as cheap labour.

Analysis of women's occupations in Sri Lanka exemplifies their inferior position and reflects their poor educational opportunities. In 1973, 90% of the plantation labourers were female, 75% of all textile workers, 60% of packaging workers, 54% of teachers and 30% of the typists, doctors and medical technicians.

Women's role in economic development in the Third World is undergoing change. Their socio-economic status has increased where traditional values are breaking down. In central India, for instance, males are sharing more of the agricultural and food processing work. In Sri Lanka, women increased their labour force participation from 13% to 25% between 1959 and 1970. Conversely, economic growth with increasing mechanization has reduced women's already low socio-economic position. In many paddy rice-growing areas of India, hulling machines have encroached upon traditional female-operated pounding systems. Flour mills have increasingly taken over home grinding operations in the wheat areas.

Present Third World development policies are biased towards male employment and thus effectively bypass one-half of the population. Though women probably grow more than one-half of the food in the Third World, they are rarely consulted in land reform and other agrarian programmes (Chapter 5, Section C). The recent claim (1982) by the Communist Party in China, one of the most egalitarian countries in the world, that women are inferior to men, contributing only about 2% to national and cultural progress, does little to improve the development participation of women in the Third World.

(iii) *Religious and cultural attitudes.* Religious and cultural traditions in the Third World are immensely varied and complex. In Nigeria, for instance, the predominant religions are Islam with its chief adherents in the north and south west of the country, and Christianity (mostly Roman Catholicism) in the southern and central regions. Traditional faiths which include ancestor-worship and animism (belief in the spiritual qualities of inanimate objects) are widespread throughout Nigeria. Communities which are nominally Christian or Islamic may also adhere to strong traditional religious beliefs. Reliable data on the various religions of the Third World are very difficult to obtain, a fact which makes generalizations about them even more hazardous.

Nevertheless, many traditional religious and other cultural attitudes in the Third World with their unbridled concern with superstition and their disregard of rationality and science are thought to limit economic opportunity in many ways, including the use of resources. In Africa and Asia, there are some classes or communities which take a religious and in this specific case a non-commercial attitude to livestock, fail to exploit their cattle to best advantage in terms of work, meat or milk and carry excessive numbers. Under Hindu laws, breeds of poor quality cattle cannot be killed or restrained from breeding even though their numbers may be so excessive as to cause a deterioration of land and a drain on the farmers' resources. In some tribal groups in Africa, such as the Masai of East Africa, the Fulani of West Africa, there may be a similarly excessive accumulation of livestock in order to achieve social prestige or to enable men to pay for new brides!

(iv) *Communal organization: the extended family and the tribe.* The extended family which consists of grandparents, parents, sons and daughters, their wives and husbands and children living together is a common feature, especially in Africa and Asia. So too is the tribe in Africa, particularly south of the Sahara (see Figure 3.5). This is a group to which the individuals feel a strong sense of belonging and which is united by a common language and culture. Both forms of social organization (though now on the decline in many areas) are thought to limit economic progress. It is argued that in such communal modes of organization, where property and possessions are owned and pooled by the unit and where production is part of social relationships rather than an economic process, there is little scope for personal advancement and the adoption of new ideas and techniques. The enterprising individual who 'gets on' is expected to share his or her good fortune with all the members of the family or tribal group.

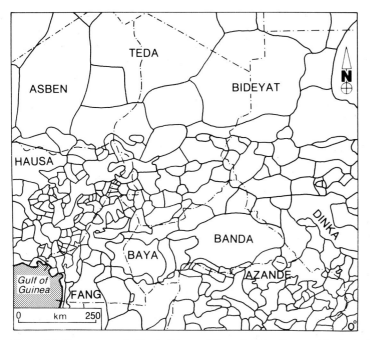

Figure 3.5 The pattern of tribes in West and Central Africa (Source: Murdock, 1959)

Conversely, there is little incentive to work hard, given the knowledge that the family will support the individual in times of hardship. Further, in many communal groups, decisions, for instance to change farming, cannot be made by the individual. They have to be made by the group, more commonly by the head of the group who is likely to be old, authoritarian and traditional, and opposed to change and development.

(b) Social advantages

Social and cultural attitudes do not always limit economic advance. Unswerving family/company loyalty in South Korea, Taiwan and elsewhere in South East Asia are reckoned to form the basis for the present high economic growth rate of these areas. However, even where social values do limit economic progress, they form part of a stable and protective social system. Many attitudes and customs in the Third World, which seem strange to a person from the MDCs, are nevertheless well adapted to the society in which they function and are successful since they have existed in modified form for centuries.

Further, many Eurocentric analyses of social and cultural attitudes in the LDCs are riddled with misunderstanding, if not outright prejudice. Claims that farmers in peasant societies are lazy and work few hours, are unambitious and poor adopters of new ideas, must be examined in the context of Third World environments not Western ones. Firstly, if peasant farmers *do* work less than their counterparts in the MDCs, it is probably due to the relative simplicity of agricultural systems, and the marked irregularity of labour inputs, rather than to laziness, poor diet or even the enervating tropical climate. Secondly, peasant farmers are unlikely to adopt innovative cropping techniques not because they are unambitious and inherently conservative, but because subsistence farming is associated with a high degree of risk and uncertainty. In areas where farms are small and cultivation is dependent on a highly variable rainfall, peasant farmers and their families will be exposed in poor years to the very real dangers of starvation. Thus a small farmer may be very reluctant to shift from a traditional technology and crop pattern which has proved adequate over the years to a new one which promises higher yield but which many entail higher risks of crop failure.

ASSIGNMENT

1. Examine the concept of 'social dualism' as applied to Third World societies.
   (a) With reference to the indigenous society make a list of the cultural values and modes of behaviour which are thought to limit socio-economic progress.
   (b) What are the inherent 'strengths' of the indigenous society?
   (c) What possible social and cultural links are there between the indigenous and modern societies?
   (d) Can it really be claimed that the traditional society has been untouched by the wider processes of social change?

D. Internal Socio-political Factors

Political and social unrest are diagnostic features in the Third World. They are a function of a number of issues. These include the abject poverty of much of the peasantry, the great cultural cleavages between different national groups, the glaring socio-economic inequalities, and the land system (see Chapter 4) which has concentrated political as well as social power in the hands of small elites. They are also a result of 'nations' being formed by 'lines drawn on a map' by former colonial rulers which have cut across traditional boundaries and communities (see Section E). There is also political interference by external states, in particular the USA and the USSR.

1. National integration and plural societies

One of the most pervading aspects of the Third World is the wide variety of its peoples, their cultures, values and behavioural attitudes. Societies within and between the LDCs are strongly divided by deep-seated differences of kinship, race, religion and custom. These diverse or 'plural' societies have prevented Third World governments from bringing their populations together, culturally and socially, into a single territorial unit and establishing a common national identity.

Figure 3.6 shows, in the broadest sense only, the extent to which the LDCs have been able to integrate effectively their communities. In comparison with the nation states (nationally integrated unit) in Europe and America the Third World shows a wide spectrum of national and social structures. The traditional societies of West and Central Africa (Black Africa) consist of a loose aggregate of many tribal groups, but where one may dominate the other, set within often arbitrary colonial inherited boundaries (Figure 3.5). In contrast are those states of North Africa and the Middle East where by virtue of relatively greater cultural homogeneity (e.g. Islam) societies have become partially integrated. Many countries in Southern and East Africa, though dominated numerically by traditional societies, have considerable and often politically and economically dominant settler groups (e.g. Europeans in South Africa and Kenya). Also distinguished are the countries of South and South East Asia with their substantial minorities, including sizeable immigrant groups such as the Chinese, whose role in the area's economic life may be disproportionate to their numbers. The colonial derived states of Latin America are controlled by a small introduced white (European) elite with a dominant mestizo population (white and Indian mixture) and an occasionally large and compact Indian community existing outside the social and political framework of

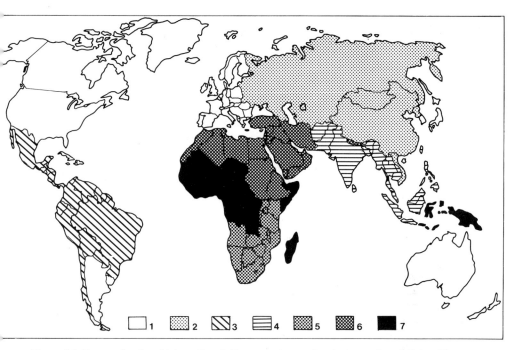

Figure 3.6 Degree of national integration. 1. European-type national states;   2. socialist multi-national states;   3. colony-derived societies with marginal indigenous populations;   4. Asian societies with large indigenous minorities;   5. traditional societies with considerable settler groups;   6. partially integrated traditional societies;   7. traditional societies lacking political integration. (Source: Buchanan, 1971)

the state e.g. Indians in the highlands of Peru and Ecuador. A number of countries including China, North Korea, Vietnam, Cuba and Tanzania have used socialism to achieve some degree of cohesion and integration of their national groups. The failure of Third World countries to integrate effectively their diverse national communities has been suggested as a reason for their underdeveloped condition. A sufficient mass of population has not been brought together to achieve the wholesale social and political change needed for economic development.

2. Problems of independence

The attainment of independence by most of the countries of Latin America in the nineteenth century and of Africa and Asia in the twentieth century has meant that there has been relatively little time for these countries to adjust to their various political, social and economic problems. Political change and instability are commonplace in the Third World and may be a reflection of new-found independence. Governments which are run or established by undemocratic military groups change hands with considerable frequency. Political revolutions in the Third World, whether inspired by parties from the right or left, or from internal or external forces, are commonly accompanied by social unrest, civil war and much human misery.

A powerful manifestation of political dissent is the wide variety of movements which seek to revise either political boundaries or political allegiances which have mostly been erected by the colonial powers in the past. Separatist movements aim to create a new state out of one or more already established and are often inspired by politically active groups such as the Kurds in the Middle East, the Tamils in Sri Lanka and the Yoruba and Ibo of Nigeria. Other movements seek a re-adjustment of state frontiers as, for example, West Pakistan sought along the northern border with India in Kashmir; while regionalist movements attempt to achieve some or more autonomy for peoples within their established state as, for example, the poor negro and mestizo population did in north east Brazil.

Finally, political upheaval can lead to outright open warfare between states, and may lead to changes in government or boundaries or both. Since 1945, the majority of the 150 or so wars which have been fought and the 50 million people killed have been overwhelmingly located in the LDCs. We only have to examine the major conflicts between states in the last ten years in the Far East (Vietnam/USA), in Central Asia (Afghanistan/USSR), the Near East (Israel/Jordan, Lebanon), the Middle East (Iran/Iraq and Yemen), East Africa (Ethiopia/Somalia; Uganda/Tanzania), Southern Africa (South Africa/Angola; Rhodesia (Zimbabwe)/Botswana, Zambia, Mozambique), North Africa (Libya/Sudan), Central and South America (El Salvador/Honduras; Argentina/UK) to realize that most modern warfare is acted out in the Third World.

It is worth emphasizing that the LDCs are politically, as well as economically, manipulated by the MDCs. Whether it is direct interference in the affairs of nations such as the USA in Vietnam or the USSR in Afghanistan; or indirect involvement such as the supply of weaponry, military personnel or ideology (capitalism versus communism) to the Third World, the rest of the world lends its support to conflict and war in the LDCs. The whole question of external interference in the economies and societies of Third World countries relates directly to their prospects for development and will be considered in the next section.

ASSIGNMENT

1. *Study Table 3.3.*
   (a) *Briefly describe the relative proportions of GNP spent on health, education and armaments for the countries shown.*
   (b) *What do these data suggest about government priorities in the Third World?*
   (c) *To what extent do the public expenditure patterns explain poor health and education levels in the LDCs?*
   (d) *Suggest how variations in armament spending may be used to highlight zones of conflict and warfare (see page 64) in the Third World.*
   (e) *'One way of improving health and education in the LDCs is to radically reduce arms spending.' Discuss.*

E. External Factors

1. Underdevelopment as process

Until recently, the main suggestion has been that underdevelopment is an initial condition or state maintained from within the LDCs as a result of some deficiency or blockage in their physical or human resources (the neo-classical approach). However, underdevelopment may be a process resulting from the interaction between the MDCs and the LDCs (the radical approach). In other words, as shown from Figure 3.7, development and underdevelopment can be seen as part of the same overall process of developmental change. As development has proceeded in the MDCs, its corollary underdevelopment, has occurred in the LDCs. This more radical interpretation suggests that development can

Table 3.3 Expenditure on health, education and arms as a percentage of GNP in selected LDCs.

	GNP per capita ($ US) 1977	Public expenditure		
		Health (% GNP) 1976	Education (% GNP) 1977	Armaments (% GNP) 1977
LDCs				
Ethiopia	110	0.9	2.3[1]	4.5[1]
India	150	1.2	2.9	3.2
Tanzania	190	1.9[1]	4.7	4.6
Kenya	270	1.8	5.0	4.1
Mauritania	270	1.1	5.8	11.6
Philippines	450	0.7	1.7	3.3
Zambia	450	2.6	6.1	9.2
Jordan	710	1.2	3.5	16.7
South Africa	1340	0.4	1.3	4.5
Brazil	1360	1.2	3.2	1.1
Iran	2160	1.5	5.1	10.8
Israel	2850	2.4	6.8[1]	26.5[1]
UK	4420	5.2	4.5	4.7
Global LDC share	20%	4.5%	11%	25%

[1] 1975

Note that in contrast to health and education, arms spending in the Third World has rapidly increased in the last 20 years.

Figure 3.7 The process of development and underdevelopment and the core–periphery hypothesis.

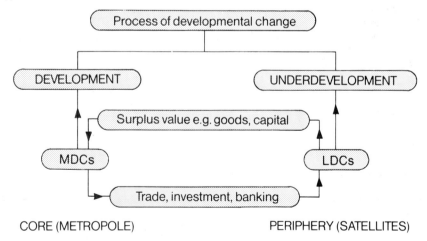

CORE (METROPOLE)   PERIPHERY (SATELLITES)

proceed only if there are available regions (productive land) and peoples (labour) capable of producing what's called a 'surplus value', expressed as a surplus of goods and capital. This surplus generates development in the receiving areas (MDCs) which lie at the centre or metropole of the World space economy. At the same time the regions or satellites

(LDCs) of the periphery from which economic surplus is extracted become steadily more depleted of resources and so become underdeveloped.

2. Importance of historical perspective

The radical approach to underdevelopment suggests that the key to understanding the development gap between rich and poor countries lies in the past. It states that the origins of international inequality can be traced firstly to the spread of mercantilism and trade from the sixteenth and seventeenth centuries, and secondly to the spread of political colonialism starting in the sixteenth but increasing especially in the nineteenth century. The metropolitan countries of Europe including Spain and Portugal in the sixteenth and seventeenth centuries and more pertinently Britain, Germany, France, Netherlands and later Belgium and Italy in the nineteenth century are seen to have become highly industrialized and developed nations through the international exploitation of the colonies over which they held political sovereignty. An impression of the way in which, for instance, Africa was 'carved up' into colonies by the European states is given in Figure 1.8. Most of the countries we now call the Third World fell under the political domination of Europe. It could be argued that although not all LDCs became colonies (e.g. Ethiopia, Thailand) they were (as many still are) dominated economically from abroad with effects in the economic field similar to those under colonialism.

3. Some benefits of colonialism

Some would argue that colonialism has had beneficial effects on the economic, social and political structures of the LDCs. Colonial governments established law and order, suppressed tribal conflict and civil war, safeguarded private property, established and organized basic transport and health services. Contacts with the metropole acquainted the colonial population with new wants, crops, commodities and methods of cultivation and served to establish new markets for local produce.

In South Asia the British were responsible, at great expense, for the development of a frontier defence system of elaborate proportions, for the establishment and maintenance of a transport (railway) network of continental proportions and for the creation of public projects unmatched in any other world colonial area. The latter included, for instance, the irrigation system and settlement of the Punjab, and the reclamation of the Bengal and Irrawaddy lower deltas. Not all surplus value was extracted by the British: many products were processed for local and South East Asian markets, for example Indian textiles, cotton, jute, sugar and coal. Moreover, a century of colonial rule did not greatly disrupt or challenge the traditional social pattern. In some instances British rule protected the traditional pattern against the penetration of militant Muslim populations, and from the penetration of commercial agents into peripheral regions, such as Nepal, Bhutan.

4. Disfunctional effects of colonialism

Despite such advantages, the overall impact of colonialism has been deeply disfunctional. Colonial exploitation has seriously undermined and distorted pre-colonial economic, social and political structures. These points will now be briefly examined.

(a) *Economic legacy*

(i) *Expansion of agriculture and mining.* The principal economic motive of colonial exploitation was to secure, as efficiently as possible, agricultural raw materials and minerals from the colonial territories and to despatch these commodities, as quickly as possible, to the homeland.

In agriculture the internal colonial administration established new patterns of cropping. It identified those crops which grew locally or which could be introduced to the colony with export value. Everything was done to increase the productivity and quality of these export crops including research into new varieties, pest and disease control, improved credit, transport and marketing facilities. By contrast little attention was paid to food production which employed a far greater number of people and represented a larger amount of agricultural produce. As land was converted from food to export crops, subsistence food production stagnated and there was a need to import food from neighbouring regions or other countries.

In this way many countries of the tropical zone in Africa, Asia and Latin America were given the role of supplying the MDCs with a range of agricultural exports needed as industrial raw material. These included commodities such as sugar, tobacco, tea and coffee, cocoa, groundnuts, palm oil, cotton, rubber and sisal. In the more temperate countries of South America and Southern Africa, European techniques were transplanted at an early stage and countries such as Argentina and Uruguay became noted for the supply of agricultural commodities, particularly beef, which requires an extensive use of land.

Since mineral commodities were also highly sought after by the European industrial nations, a third group of countries came to be dominated by the export of primary mineral products to the MDCs. In Central and South America such countries included Mexico, Chile, Peru, Bolivia, and later Venezuela. In Asia most of the Middle Eastern countries, notably Iran, Iraq, Saudi Arabia, Kuwait, as well as Malaya in the Far East came to be included. In Africa, Zambia, Zaire, Liberia, Mauritania, and more recently Libya, Algeria and Nigeria, are of this type.

The export of primary mineral and agricultural products from the periphery to the centre had little capacity to transform the overall economies of the LDCs. A change from subsistence food to export crop production did not bring any new major technologies. Mining was largely foreign owned and controlled, and provided little employment. Both activities depended on a specialized infrastructure. Road and railway systems (Chapter 7) were designed (and distorted) to meet the goal of export only and this did not really benefit the rest of the economy. As a whole, export activities did little to improve the standard of living of many workers or to increase the size of domestic markets through increased demand for products.

(ii) *Economic dualism and the enclave economy.* The foundations of what is called the dual economy were firmly laid during the era of colonialism. Commercial agriculture and export mineral production functioned fairly (but not entirely) independently of the rest of the economy. This highly specialized sector was seen as modern, dynamic and capitalist. The other sector was traditional, inward looking and pre-capitalist, and based on subsistence agriculture. As the modern sector was limited both in areal extent and in the numbers of workers it employed compared with the traditional sector, it was regarded as an 'enclave' economy within the much more extensive subsistence agricultural economy.

Thus, just as it is possible to conceive of cores (MDCs) and peripheries (LDCs) on a global scale, it can be acknowledged that colonialism inspired cores (enclave economies) and peripheries (rural subsistence sector) within Third World countries themselves. Figure 3.8 identifies a number of core areas in South Asia established in the colonial period. Virtually all originated before 1947 and were dependent on the primary cores in North West Europe, especially the London core of lowland England. There is a distinction, however, between the seaboard cores (1–6) and other cores (7–13) and their

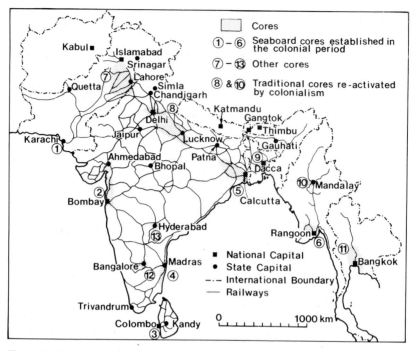

Figure 3.8 Cores in South Asia. (Source: Kirk, 1981)

location related to the railway network and the post-colonial political territories of the area. While the seaboard cores of Bombay (1665), Calcutta (1697) and Madras (1639) can be associated with the early mercantilist period, trade, and the East India Company in particular, a number of the other cores in the area were established or re-activated by the rise of industrialization in the British core. Thus, new peripheral nuclei developed in Ceylon (1815), lower Burma (1824) and Karachi (1824) in the nineteenth century, and those around Delhi, Lahore and Mandalay in the twentieth century. It is interesting that cores around Islamabad in West Pakistan and Dacca in East Pakistan (Bangladesh) are largely a product of new political conditions created in these post-colonial territories.

(iii) *Disturbed and vulnerable economies.* Colonialism disturbed and mis-shaped the economies of the LDCs. In the absence of industry, the agricultural sector became grossly inflated, polarized between inefficient food production for local consumption and the production of export crops for the world market. Commercial agriculture and export mining became very vulnerable in character since they depended a great deal on circumstances (e.g. demand and thus prices) in the MDCs. Trade in the LDCs came to depend on the export of inexpensive primary raw materials to the industrialized countries in exchange for highly priced manufactured goods. Moreover, trade became highly dependent on a narrow range of export commodities, and on a small number of trading partners in the LDCs (see Chapter 11, Section C and Table 11.3).

(b) *Social legacy*

The political and economic domination of the periphery by the metropole also activated, and indeed depended on, social adjustment in the LDCs. Of these adjustments the most important include critical shifts in settlement form and function (Chapter 10), in population (Chapter 8) and in the relation of people to the land (Chapter 4).

(i) *Population change*. International colonialism left an indelible mark on populations in certain parts of the Third World. In Central and South America, in particular, immigrant groups of Spanish and Portuguese came to dominate the indigenous Indian populations so thoroughly that the latter became a minority struggling to preserve its cultural identity. Domination was achieved through changes in racial structure and the size of native populations. For instance, sexual relations between Spanish and Indian people were common during the early colonial period, the progeny of which helped form the basis of what is today Spanish America's most common racial type: the mestizo. In Latin America, the combined forces of warfare, forced labour, psychological and socio-economic disruption and, above all, susceptibility to Old World and European diseases (measles, smallpox, influenza and typhoid) substantially reduced indigenous populations. Such agents are reported to have reduced the population by 1650 to one-twentieth of its pre-conquest size of about 25 million. The dramatic decline of native population in many areas, the general scarcity of population in the lowlands, and the labour demand of the mines and plantations which became established as the colonies developed, encouraged the importation of negro slaves. During the colonial era, it is estimated between 5 and 8 million Africans were brought to Latin America, the largest numbers settling in intensive lowland agricultural areas including north east Brazil and the Caribbean.

Colonialism also caused the re-distribution of population at local and regional scales. In Latin America the concentration of native populations into towns (the *reducciones*) which the Spanish ordered for the more effective control of labour for mines and field, was particularly significant in this respect. Likewise the later creation of large estates (*haciendas*) owned and administered by Spaniards but worked by slaves and then by hired labour had the effect of drawing and concentrating displaced Indians on estate lands. In Kenya (and elsewhere in Africa) populations were forced to migrate to, or permitted to settle in, only the 'native land units'. By contrast, an immense amount of land was reserved at the pleasure of the Crown (Crown Land) or administered for European settlement (the White Highlands) or set aside for Asians, Europeans and Coastal Arabs (alienated land outside the Highlands).

(ii) *Changes in land-holding*. Colonial exploitation undermined rural structures and disturbed social patterns in other ways. Private land ownership was encouraged wherever possible at the expense of native communal forms of ownership, such as with cocoa and oil palm smallholdings in West Africa. At times, especially in Africa and Latin America (e.g. banana plantations in the Caribbean), land came under direct foreign ownership. In addition, the establishment of law and order, greater social stability and rudimentary health and social services under colonialism acted to increase substantially the rate of population growth. Population increase and the consequent pressure on land resources (exacerbated by foreign land ownership) led to increased land fragmentation and to a decrease in the size of both farms and individual plots of land. In turn, population pressure and land fragmentation led to overcultivation, to land exhaustion and finally to declines in crop yield. All led to the increasing poverty and debt which Third World farmers now find themselves in.

(c) *Political legacy*

There can be little doubt that the political systems of the Third World are distinctive and that they owe many of their features to the historical experience. Political colonialism, for instance, can be seen in the number, size and geographical demarcation of political units.

Many LDCs have varied considerably in size and shape owing to the intense struggle for colonies among the industrialized countries during the nineteenth century. As a result the Third World has 134 (73%) out of 185 national units making up the world. Moreover, 76 out of 102 countries with less than 5 million people are to be found in the LDCs. At the same time there are a number of countries, such as China, with 1000 million, India (650 mill.), Indonesia (135 mill.), Brazil (110 mill.) and Nigeria (75 mill.).

A large number of the European colonies which later became independent states were established in a relatively short period of time. The 'mad scramble' for Africa by European countries took place in less than 50 years (1870–1920). Boundaries were imposed with such haste that scant regard was paid to the existing distribution of ethnic and cultural groups, to former indigenous empires and to ancient ethnic cores (see Figure 3.5). Like cultures were split asunder and diverse and often conflicting ethnic groupings were amalgamated by colonial boundary demarcation–boundaries which in many instances remain unchanged today. One not surprising legacy of such boundary imposition is the propensity for ethnic and cultural conflict within and between countries.

5. Post-colonial experience: perpetuation of dependency

(a) Neo-colonialism

Despite achieving political independence in the nineteenth and twentieth centuries (see Figure 1.8) the LDCs are still economically dependent on the MDCs. This situation of continuing dependency, or neo-colonialism, is maintained by trade flows, international banking organizations, and private investment, particularly in the form of the vast transnational corporations and foreign aid programmes (see Chapter 11). These mechanisms enable the MDCs to continue their exploitation of the LDCs in the post-independence era.

Neo-colonialism has social, cultural and political connotations as well as an economic dimension. There is a continuing intellectual and cultural dependency of the LDCs on the MDCs. To some Latin Americans, Asians and Africans, Paris, London, Rome, Madrid and Amsterdam still represent the only sources of real culture. This external orientation for all things Western means that many forms of economic dependence (trade, technology) are accentuated: imported products are valued more highly than local goods, foreign university degrees more highly than local degrees, foreign consultants more than local experts. Moreover, by military intervention, for example by the USA in Vietnam and the USSR in Afghanistan, and in the establishment of pro-USA (e.g. El Salvador) and pro-Soviet (e.g. Cuba) governments, the MDCs continue physically to dominate the LDCs.

ASSIGNMENT

1. (a) *Define and explain the process of colonialism.*
   (b) *Examine with reference to specific examples the ways in which colonialism has (i) benefited; and (ii) constrained economic, social and political development in the LDCs.*
   (c) *Define and explain the process of neo-colonialism.*

Conclusion

It is not possible to be dogmatic about the reasons for the underdeveloped condition of the Third World. Though it is reasonable to argue that human rather than physical factors are responsible, it is difficult to assess the precise role of the individual human factors involved. Arguments which signal internal social, economic and political resource deficiences as the prime cause of underdevelopment are counterbalanced by viewpoints emphasizing external deficiencies in the relationship between the LDCs and the MDCs. Moreover, human factors do not always constrain progress. For instance, better levels of education and health among the inhabitants of the Third World suggest, at least in theory, an improved human resource base from which development can proceed.

Key Ideas

A. Internal Economic Factors
1. Underdevelopment in the Third World may reflect some internal deficiency or constraint in its human resources.
2. The concept of the 'vicious circle of poverty' has often been used to express a link between capital shortage and underdevelopment.
3. Such 'vicious circle' models tend to be inadequate explanations of poverty.
4. A very popular theory of (capital-led) economic growth is the stage model of economic development by Rostow.
5. This model suggests that a poor country may become highly developed by moving through given developmental stages, namely (1) the traditional society; (2) the preconditions for take-off; (3) the take-off; (4) the drive to maturity; and (5) the age of high mass consumption.
6. This Western or Eurocentric model may be inappropriate as an explanation of economic development in the Third World countries.

B. Internal Socio-economic Factors
1. There is a wide gap in health and education levels and services between the MDCs and the LDCs.
2. There are five major disease groups which affect the inhabitants of the Third World, namely (1) faecally related; (2) airborne; (3) nutritionally related; (4) vectorborne and (5) contact.
3. Diseases belonging to the first three groups are the most widespread and serious.
4. Vectorborne diseases such as malaria and sleeping sickness are relatively less widely distributed, being located in specific geographical areas.
5. Widespread poverty rather than climatic conditions lies at the root of the health problems of the LDCs.
6. Lack of clean drinking water and sanitation are responsible for about four-fifths of the disease in the Third World.
7. Poor health seriously limits economic development because it lowers labour productivity, uses scarce financial resources in its improvement, and restricts settlement, tourism and even trade.
8. Low educational and organizational skills also inhibit labour productivity and economic development.
9. Education and health programmes in the LDCs are often direct transplants of Western systems.
10. Eurocentric education and health systems are often ill suited to the needs of the LDCs.
11. Widespread, low cost, 'basic education' and 'primary health care' programmes may be more appropriate to the practical needs of the LDCs.

C. Internal Social Factors
1. Third World societies are often spoken of as 'dual' societies because a relatively small modern society exists side by side with a large indigenous one.

2. Traditional attitudes and modes of behaviour within the indigenous society are thought to prevent the adoption of new ideas and techniques necessary for progress.
3. Various class structures in the Third World including the presence of a small privileged elite and a very large lower class of peasants, and the absence of a 'capitalist' class, tend to obstruct social and economic development.
4. Various socio-cultural and political obstacles restrict the economic participation of women in many Third World societies.
5. Other forms of social organization such as the extended family and the tribal group, together with religious attitudes, may also restrict progress.
6. Many values, attitudes and behavioural patterns which pervade Third World society nevertheless confer a measure of stability and protection.

D. Internal Socio-political Factors
1. The indigenous society is separated from the modern society and is itself internally divided by deep-seated differences of kinship, race, religion and custom.
2. Such diverse or 'plural' societies make it difficult for Third World countries to integrate effectively their national communities and to participate in economic development.
3. Political instability is reflected in both internal and external conflict, i.e. in civil strife, in movements which seek to revise political boundaries and allegiances, and in open warfare.

E. External Factors
1. Underdevelopment may not be an initial state or condition, maintained by internal resource deficiency, but a process generated by the interaction between the LDCs and the MDCs.
2. As the MDCs have developed, the LDCs have underdeveloped.
3. The key to Third World underdevelopment would seem to lie in the past, in colonialism.
4. Colonialism may have benefited the LDCs by establishing law and order, providing basic transport and health services, and by introducing new ideas and technologies.
5. The overall impact of colonialism has been deeply disfunctional with adverse economic, social and political effects.
6. Localized or 'enclave' economies specializing in export cash cropping and mining were established in the colonial era and have become vulnerable to fluctuations in market demand.
7. Colonialism warped existing social structures by causing changes in population and in the relationship of people to the land.
8. The number, size and shape of political units in the Third World can be traced to the domination of the MDCs over the LDCs during the colonial period.
9. Despite political independence, the LDCs remain economically, socially, technologically and culturally dependent on the MDCs.
10. These continuing national forms of dependency are referred to as neo-colonialism.

Additional Activities

1. Trace the changes which have occurred in the economic development of Taiwan and organize these changes according to the stage model of economic growth by Rostow. See Mountjoy (1979), Weston (1980) and Freeberne (1972).
2. Carefully examine the data shown in Table 3.2.
   (a) Find from Chapter 1, Section B the minimum or recommended per capita daily protein and calorie requirement.

(b) Calculate using columns (ii) and (iii) the daily protein and calorie supply as a percentage of this requirement.

(c) Rank from lowest to highest the different regions according to their average (i) protein, and (ii) calorie supply. Comment on any differences between the two sets of rankings.

(d) Are the distinctive dietary characteristics of the regions shown in Table 3.2 also highlighted in the world maps of food intake (Figures 1.3, 1.4)

(e) Discuss the links between food consumption and the degree of access to safe water (column iv) with life expectancy and infant mortality data (cols. ix, x)

(f) Examine the variations in the levels of medical provision (cols. v, vi) between the different regions and countries and comment on your analysis.

(g) Explain how variations in levels of transport availability and education (cols. vii, viii) can influence the effectiveness of health provision.

(h) Assess the relationship between per capita income and the information shown in columns (ii) to (x) for the selected countries.

3. List the factors thought to be responsible for the underdeveloped condition of the Third World. Which, in your opinion, are the most important?

4 Agricultural Systems

A. Diversity and Change

A diverse range of agricultural systems is found in the Third World. This diversity is an outcome firstly of variations in the physical environment. At the continental scale the major farming systems of the Third World (Figure 4.1) can be seen to relate to the main patterns of climate, vegetation and soils (Chapter 2). For instance, livestock farming is not usually practised in lowland equatorial areas. Here a hot, wet and enervating climate, together with the associated prevalence of pests and disease, makes the breeding and rearing of cattle especially difficult. Figure 4.2 shows that at the local scale the influence of soils becomes more discernible. The main commercial crops of cocoa and oil palm in the Krobo district of south east Ghana are grown on the better soils, on flat reasonably fertile deep red loams.

The role of physical environmental conditions in influencing agricultural patterns in the Third World should not be overstated, however. Agricultural contrasts are also a product of human and cultural factors. For instance, the limits of cultivation in the Third World depend not only on natural conditions (e.g. altitude, aridity) but also on the economic, social and technical attributes of different farming groups. In some areas of the Third World it is possible to find examples of a whole range of agricultural systems, from hunting and shifting agriculture to vast commercial plantations, within a few kilometres of each other. Among the Fulani of West Africa there are both sedentary cultivators and nomadic herdsmen.

Agricultural diversity cannot be separated from agricultural change. In recent years there have been three major aspects of change within Third World farming systems. Firstly, there has been in general an increase in the intensity with which land is used. Secondly, a drive towards commercialization and the use of modern scientific methods (see Chapter 5) has become apparent in certain areas. Thirdly, there have been both subtle and dramatic alterations in land tenure or the way land is held and owned (see Chapter 5).

Figure 4.2 A cross section profile of a typical sequence of land-use in the Krobo district, south east Ghana. (Source: Manshard, 1979, copyright Bibliographisches Institut, Mannheim)

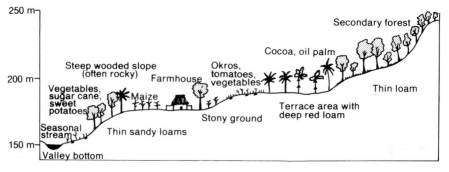

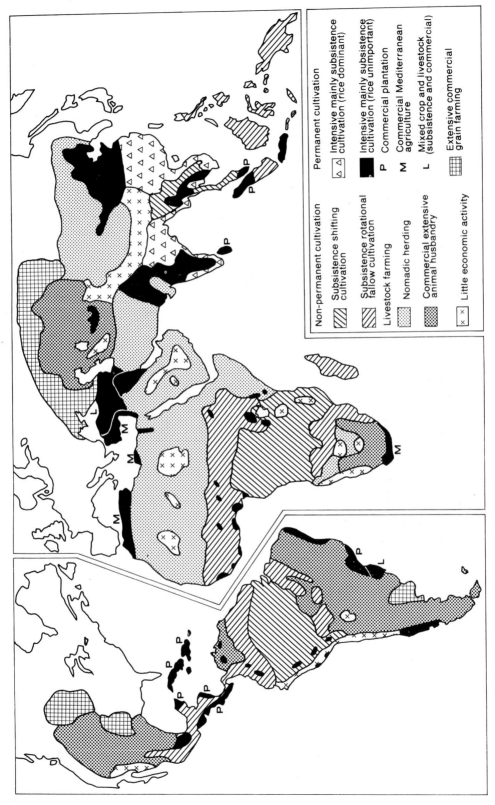

Non-permanent cultivation

Subsistence shifting cultivation

Subsistence rotational fallow cultivation

Livestock farming

Nomadic herding

Commercial extensive animal husbandry

Little economic activity

Permanent cultivation

△ Intensive mainly subsistence cultivation (rice dominant)

Intensive mainly subsistence cultivation (rice unimportant)

P   Commercial plantation

M   Commercial Mediterranean agriculture

L   Mixed crop and livestock (subsistence and commercial)

Extensive commercial grain farming

Figure 4.1 Map of agricultural types in the Third World and adjoining areas.

B. Farming and Land-use Intensity

Farming in the Third World varies considerably according to the intensity with which land is used. There are extensive systems, such as shifting agriculture and nomadic pastoralism, and intensive systems such as wet rice cultivation. Between these two extremes there is a wide range of transitional forms, such as the various kinds of rotational (bush and grass) fallow cultivation.

1. Extensive systems: shifting agriculture

(a) Nature and distribution

Where population densities are low there is little need to farm intensively to produce sufficient food to support the population. As a consequence, over much of equatorial and tropical Africa and Latin America and in parts of South East Asia, where population densities rarely exceed 10–12 persons/km², an extensive form of agriculture known as shifting cultivation has traditionally been relied on (see Figure 4.1).

The main features of shifting cultivation (called 'ladang' and 'milpa' in parts of Asia and Latin America respectively) are well known. The cultivator clears, with the help of an axe or machete a chosen area of vegetation which is usually forest or bush (Plate 4.1). The biggest trees as well as those which provide some economic return (e.g. oil palm, kola) are often left standing. The cut wood, which may be supplemented by brushwood collected from neighbouring areas, is assembled into large heaps, allowed to dry, and burned at the end of the dry season. Immediately after the first rains of the wet season, the sowing and planting of crops takes place on the cleared soil which has been 'fertilized' by mineral ash from the burned vegetation. The major crops grown under this system vary from region to region. In West Africa, upland rice, together with root crops including yams, cassava and sweet potato, tend to predominate in the wetter forested zones, while grain crops such as maize, millet and sorghum are characteristic of the drier forested zones. A wide range of primary and subsidiary crops are often grown in the cleared plots. The Iban of Sarawak, for example, grow cucumbers, pumpkins, cassava, maize and pineapples on land which is sown with upland rice.

As shown in Figure 2.6, when shifting or 'slash and burn' agriculture takes place within tropical rain forest ecosystems, important modifications occur to the nutrient cycle. Biomass is removed by felling and burning, although some nutrients are transferred to the litter and soil. Nutrients (and energy) are diverted from the immediate cycle not only by crop harvest but also by increased rates of leaching (page 40). As a result of these processes and the large net loss of nutrients from the site, cleared plots can only be used for a short time. Progressive weed infestation and rapidly falling crop yields (Figure 4.3) will often cause plots to be abandoned after two or three years of cultivation. The natural plant cover is left to re-establish itself over a long period (about 20–25 years) to allow the slow build-up of nutrient reserves (humus) in the soil. The time during which the vegetation re-establishes itself is called a fallow period. With short cultivation and long fallows a lot of land must be available for the farming to be effective. For a 2-year cultivation, 20-year fallow cycle only about 9% of the suitable land in one holding is cultivated at any one time. Systems of shifting cultivation are usually classified as such where the amount of land so cultivated does not exceed 33%.

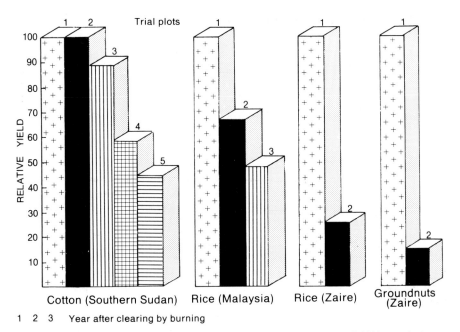

Figure 4.3 Reduction in yields with continuous cropping under the system of shifting agriculture in the humid tropics. (Source: Ruthenberg, 1980)

(b) *Status of the system*

(i) *Advantages*. Some authorities suggest that shifting cultivation is an efficient and ecologically sound system. It may be one of the few proven systems which makes possible the cultivation of soils of generally low fertility without large technical inputs. Provided that burning is not too severe and frequent, and the vegetation is allowed to recover fully, fertility can be maintained (see Figure 4.4a, b). By clearing small patches within the forest, leaving the larger trees and planting crops to give reasonable cover, soil erosion is reduced and not too much ecological disturbance results to the ecosystem. The characteristic crop diversity of the system has many advantages. Each crop takes its own particular requirements from the soil; the cultivator, by mimicking the diversity of the natural vegetation, causes a more balanced depletion of the soil nutrients. Furthermore the intermixture of crops discourages the rapid spread of diseases which can ravage single stands. By growing a wide range of crops the cultivator is able to produce different types of food ready to eat during the year. If conditions are unfavourable for one crop it is unlikely that they will be unfavourable for all. In addition, relatively little effort is needed to produce the desired harvest: the system is thus fairly productive in terms of yield per worker-hour.

(ii) *Disadvantages*. Other people condemn shifting cultivation as wasteful and harmful, and criticize it on a number of specific grounds. The system encourages tribal or communal ownership of land, rather than private ownership which may be more likely to improve farming efficiency and incentive. The frequent movement of not only the cultivated plots, but also people and settlement makes the provision of public services such as schools, hospitals and roads difficult. It appears that overuse of the system in an area does result in vegetation and soil degeneration (Figure 4.4c). Moreover a great deal of organic matter in and above the soil is destroyed by burning (Plate 4.1). Such material may

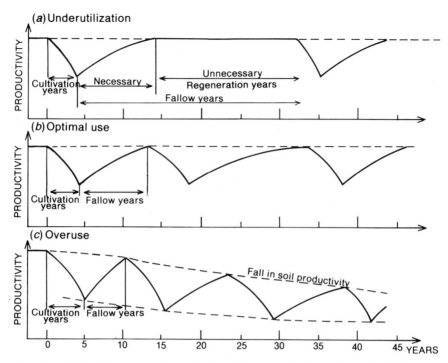

Figure 4.4 Relationship between soil productivity in shifting agriculture and length of fallow. (Source: Ruthenberg, 1980)

Plate 4.1 Shifting cultivation, Yucatan, Mexico. A relatively large plot (the milpa) has been cleared with cutlass and fire from the tropical low jungle. Maize, along with beans and pulses can be seen growing between the charred tree stumps. Some weeding is carried out, but apart from mineral ash no inputs of fertilizer or manure are made. Cultivations lasting about two years are followed by fallows of seven to eight years. Relatively short fallows are possible because the low rainfall (about 750 mm) and shallow limestone soils of the area avoid the worst effects of leaching. (*Photograph: G. P. O'Hare*)

be better used for timber, firewood, leaf manure, and various wood distillation products. Burning creates mineral ash but the fertility value of this ash lasts for a short period only owing to excessive leaching. Another problem is that the system of cultivation does not prevent weed infestation. Finally, and most importantly, it is capable only of producing low yields per hectare from a relatively large area of potentially usable land. Thus, the system cannot support a large population. Beyond a certain limit of about 10–12 persons/km^2, variants of the technique, or completely different systems, have to be introduced.

(c) *Shifting cultivation: The Bemba of Zambia*

On the upland savanna plains of Zambia, the Bemba practise an interesting form of shifting cultivation called the 'chitimene' system. Wide areas of the upland plains have poor latosolic soils (see Figure 4.8a and b) low in plant nutrients. The biomass or volume of vegetation of the open savanna woodland and its store of nutrients is also relatively small. Accordingly, the Bemba are obliged to concentrate the accumulated nutrients of a wide area, i.e. about 2.4 hectares of woodland, into a smaller plot of about 0.4 hectares. The branches of trees and other vegetation from the large plot are cut down during the dry season and dragged to the main central area, where they are stacked and then burned. Burning clears the ground of low vegetation, makes the surface soil more friable and adds fertile ash. When the rains come, finger millet, (which is the staple crop), sorghum and maize are sown broadcast, and gourds and marrows are planted as an edge crop. After this initial grain crop, groundnuts and beans can be grown successfully on the plot in the following year. After two to three years soil fertility declines, weeds begin to proliferate and the plots are eventually abandoned, sometimes for several decades to allow the restoration of fertility. As plots are cleared further and further from the village (up to 12–16 km at times) the Bemba build temporary huts on the plots to live in while they are working there. When distances become too great the people may decide to move the village to a new site where fields can be cleared close to the settlement.

The Bemba system of shifting cultivation is on the decline now. Many of the men have left their villages to find work in the mines of the copper belt (see pages 132–5). The women, who have always carried out much of the agricultural work (sowing, planting, weeding), find it difficult to clear the main farm plots as well, without the assistance of the men. Many Bemba have moved their upland villages to more lowland sites near the main roads and railway lines. The availability of commerical opportunities here, such as selling produce to travellers, as well as the general occurrence of more fertile soils (Figure 4.8b, c) has encouraged semi-permanent rotational (bush) fallow and permanent cultivation systems (Figure 4.8e).

2. Transitional systems: rotational (bush and grass) fallow cultivation

(a) *Nature and distribution*

As population density increases and land becomes scarce it may no longer be possible for farmers to move to fresh uncultivated areas. Ways of dealing with the twin problems of increasing the food supply and maintaining soil fertility have been devised. The principal technique is to increase the period under crops and shorten the length of the fallow. The first stage in this process of agricultural intensification is represented by rotational fallow cultivation. This system is found in parts of Latin America and Asia, and is now the most widespread type of agriculture in tropical Africa (see Figure 4.1). In the latter it occurs especially in the savanna zones, from Senegal (Plate 2.4) and Sierra Leone to northern Nigeria in West Africa to southern Chad and Sudan, as well as in parts of East and Southern Africa, for example, Kenya, Tanzania, Zambia (see Figure 4.8e), Angola, Botswana and Mozambique. Rotational fallow cultivation can support population densities of up to 250 persons/km², especially in some of the more fertile and less leached savanna areas.

With rotational fallow cultivation, the fallow period, ranging between about 15 years (bush fallowing) and 5 years (grass or planted fallow) is not as long as that left by the shifting cultivators, and the semi-natural ecosystems are not allowed to re-establish themselves completely. The shorter fallow maintains them as essentially bush (hence the name) or grasslands rather than as secondary forest. With this system the percentage of land cultivated at any one time ranges between 33% and 66% so that in general terms as much land remains in fallow as under cultivation.

The shorter fallow period itself is not sufficient to restore fertility. In face of longer periods of cultivation, the fallow cultivator, using a hoe (or in more intensive systems a plough), attempts to maintain soil fertility by more careful preparation of the seedbed, more frequent weeding, and the application of greater amounts of manure.

(b) Land-use zonation

One notable geographical consequence of the more stationary nature of rotational fallow cultivation is that zones of different cropping sequence develop around more fixed settlements. Cropping patterns may be determined by variations in soils and relief (Figure 4.2), or by distance from the hut or village (Figure 4.5). In the latter case the intensity of cropping decreases in proportion to the distance from the farmstead. Land close to the houses (dungland and gardens; see Plates 4.2 and 4.3) is often permanently cultivated since it is frequently enriched with household waste, crop residues and manure from free-ranging cattle, sheep, goats and poultry found in the village. This land is cultivated continuously without fallow, and special crops are grown either because they make heavy demands on the soil (tobacco, cotton) or require constant attention during growth (vegetables and maize) or are used frequently in cooking (indigo, fruit). Adjoining this inner zone of permanent 'garden' cultivation in concentric circles of varying size is an intensive fallow system which is the most important zone in terms of total production. The fields here are often used for growing the staple food (and cash) crops, and the fallow period is used mostly as pasture (see Plate 4.2). Long fallows between the cropping years in the outermost zones mean that shifting cultivation is practised. The land-use zonation patterns are not static, however. New circles of land-use overlap the old ones with the long-term movement of homesteads; and the sons of fallow cultivators may move into the bordering bush or forest to develop 'extension' areas.

(c) A rotational (bush) fallow system: eastern Nigeria

In south east Nigeria increasing population pressure has caused a shift from shifting cultivation to bush fallowing. Extensive areas have also been planted with perennial tree crops such as the oil palm, which has become an important cash as well as a local subsistence crop (see Figure 4.6). Under the oil-palm cover, cropping with manioc, yams and maize alternates with several years of bush fallowing. Fallow periods of more than six years with a predominance of maize or yams indicate an ample availability of land. Less than six fallow years and an increasing reliance on manioc (a more starchy and less-soil-demanding crop) indicate land shortage.

The intensity with which the land is used decreases with distance from the village or compound.

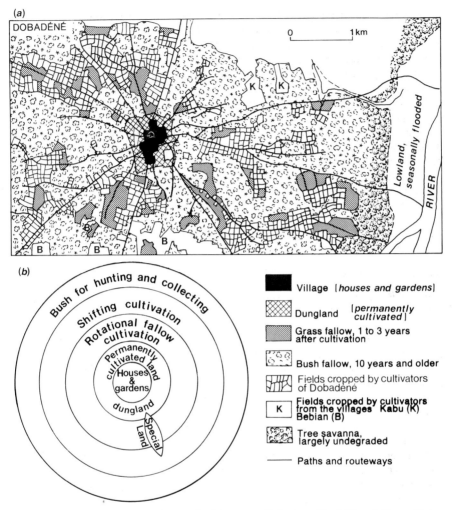

Figure 4.5 (*a*) Land-use zonation in a semi-arid savanna, Dobadene, Chad, West Africa. (*b*) An idealized model of the spatial organization of land-use common in the savannas of tropical Africa. (Source: Ruthenberg, 1980)

(i) Small *compound plots* (i.e. gardens adjacent to the settlement) are farmed with great intensity. The greatest variety of plants are found here and there is a close integration of tree crops, (e.g. oil palm, coconut palm, bananas) and arable farming (yams, manioc, maize and vegetables). Labour and material inputs (e.g. household refuse, goat manure, and organic matter imported from the surrounding fields) are high, as are crop yields (28 tonnes per hectare). Though the compound plot occupies in general less than 10% of the crop area, it can produce one-third to one-half of the farm output.

(ii) The slightly larger *homestead fields* close to the compound are usually covered by oil palms and produce arable crops within an intensive fallow system. Where population density is high, rotations of $1\frac{1}{2}$ crop years and $3\frac{1}{2}$ fallow years may occur. Yams which grow well under the shade of the oil palms are interplanted with manioc and then with

Plate 4.2 Permanently cultivated land within an African compound, Bwiam Village, the Gambia. Manure for this 'dungland' is provided by free-ranging pigs and poultry and by cattle which are tethered to the posts in the foreground. Nutrient-enriched land like this is cultivated with maize year after year in the wet season since this crop is ravaged by weaver birds if it is grown outside the compound. Beyond the line of baobab trees and the compound fence in the distance are large fields which are used on a rotational fallow basis. These fields are cultivated every 2–3 years with the main cash crop (groundnuts) and some food crops (millet, sorghum, sesame). In the fallow period the land is used as forage for free-ranging cattle. (*Photograph: G. P. O'Hare*)

Plate 4.3 Garden cultivation, Bwiam Village, the Gambia. On this intensively cultivated garden plot close to the village a wide range of vegetables is grown, including tomatoes, onions, lettuce, ochra and peppers. These crops are cultivated by the women of the village who add dung and household waste to the soil as fertilizer, and ash to the crops as an insecticide. In this garden, which is about 1 hectare in extent, eight wells have been dug to provide a permanent supply of irrigation water. Beyond the garden, near the river, rice is grown every year on seasonally flooded land. (*Photograph: G. P. O'Hare*)

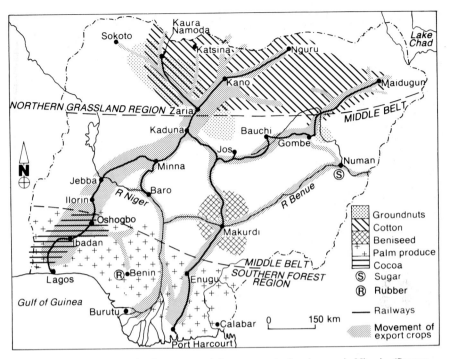

Figure 4.6 Export crop production zones and the movement of cash crops in Nigeria. (Source: Grove, 1967)

maize. In the second year manioc becomes the predominant crop to be superseded later in the year by fallow.

(iii) The *distant fields*, which are much larger and have usually a low-density oil-palm cover, produce food in an extensive bush-fallow system. After fire clearance manioc is grown and interplanted with groundnuts and maize. Fallows traditionally last 6–8 years, but even here they have already been reduced because of land pressure.

Little or no mulching or manuring is practised on the homestead and distant fields and crop yields are correspondingly low (about 3 tonnes/ha). The fields, especially those of the homestead, provide most of the starch (root crops) and fat (oil palms) for the household members, and supply organic matter for mulching for the compound plots.

3. Intensive systems: permanent cultivation

(a) Nature and distribution

Under permanent farming, fallows virtually disappear and are replaced by large areas of continuous cropping. More than 66% of the available land is cultivated at any one time. Farmers make use of numerous labour-demanding techniques, such as manuring, weeding, terracing and water control, to maintain yields. Because yields per hectare are greater under permanent cultivation than other systems, it can support high densities of population, usually over 250 persons/km². A comparison of Figure 4.1 with Figure 8.7 shows that the great majority of the people of the Third World are supported by intensive permanent systems of agriculture.

83

(*b*) *Types of permanent cultivation: variety and status*

(i) *The humid tropical lowlands.* Many attempts to introduce permanent systems of farming into the humid and sub-tropical lowlands have been unsuccessful. It may be recalled from Chapter 2, Section D that the introduction of European-based systems of permanent cultivation have been particularly disastrous. During the famous British-sponsored groundnut scheme in Tanganyika (Tanzania) (1947–9) about 90 000 hectares were cleared and abandoned with the loss of some £70 million. A group of 40–50 French farmers settled in 1949 at Auberville (Congo-Brazzaville) and started farming according to European patterns but abandoned the site after a few years. Of Ghana's 30 large-scale mechanized state farms established in the early 1960s only a few survived and losses were heavy. It appears clear that unless high and costly inputs are made such systems cannot be maintained because of rapidly declining soil fertility and environmental deterioration.

Some success has been achieved, however, with the use of perennial and tree crops as opposed to annual crops. The former mimic the forest vegetation, offer soil protection, are less choked by weeds and demand less of the soil and nutrient store than the latter. As well as providing high yields of calories per hectare (e.g. bananas) such crops offer, where markets are available, high remunerative returns (e.g. rubber, coconuts, cocoa, coffee). Evolution of this kind of cropping has taken place on a large scale. Nowadays, in tropical Africa (Nigeria, Ghana) and Asia (Malaysia, Indonesia, Sri Lanka) hundreds of thousands of hectares that were previously utilized by shifting and fallow systems now support cocoa, oil palms, tea, bananas and coffee.

(ii) *Fertile areas: wet land cultivation.* Systems involving permanent cultivation have been successfully introduced, in some cases for several millennia, in areas of exceptionally fertile soils. Such soils include tropical soils weathered from basic volcanic rocks (e.g. in Java) or tropical soils liable to seasonal flooding. Volcanic soils are very fertile because they have considerable reserves of nutrients; land which is continually being flooded has silt deposited on it which renews the reserves of nutrients in the soil. Very high densities of population can be supported by the permanent use of these fertile areas. Locally population densities in Java and Bangladesh reach over 2000 persons/km²: the highest agricultural population density in the world.

Wet land cultivation in fertile deltaic areas is the most successful form of permanent cultivation in the tropics. The crop produced under these conditions is swamp or paddy rice. South East Asia has led the way in this type of farming. The ancient wet rice cultivation systems on the banks of the great rivers of Asia (Red, Mekong and Ganges: see Plate 1.1) and Africa (Nile) have been possible because of the annual replacement of top soil by flood waters (Figure 4.1). Details of the nutrient-conserving attributes of paddy rice cultivation are shown in Figure 2.6. Not only is there fertile silt renewal but the flooded fields of the rice paddy system help to retard litter decomposition and to reduce run-off loss. Nutrients are thus retained in the litter and soil stores. In view of the considerable success of paddy rice cultivation many authorities urge its expansion throughout the tropical world where conditions permit. Although fertile flood plains of similar extent to those in South East Asia may not exist in the rest of the Third World (see page 38), irrigable plains are by no means uncommon.

There are, however, a number of difficulties involved in their utilization. Environmental requirements for successful wet land cultivation are fairly exacting. Firstly, there must be flood plains of reasonable extent with constant annual renewal of silt. Secondly, very large quantities of water are essential to provide the necessary flooding. This normally means that rainfall must be heavy and correctly distributed throughout the year, but it is possible for riverine lands in comparatively dry areas to be inundated with flood waters received from distant areas of heavy rainfall upstream, as happens in the inland delta of the Niger in Mali. Thirdly, quite lengthy dry periods are needed for the ripening and harvesting of the crop. It is largely for this reason that truly equatorial climates with their constant cloud cover and lack of a dry season are not well suited to rice cultivation.

Where suitable land does occur, human circumstances should also be favourable. Firstly, high densities of population are usually needed to provide the motivation and the large workforce necessary for such cultivation. The clearance of swamp vegetation, the establishment and maintenance of separate and bunded fields, the construction of terraces on sloping ground and the constant care of the growing rice crop (e.g. moving it from nursery beds to the main fields) are all tremendously arduous and unpleasant tasks. Secondly, such work also needs to be highly organized and demands a relatively high level of operational efficiency. It is no coincidence that the ancient civilizations of South East Asia with their large, well organized and technically skilful populations have mastered the art of paddy rice cultivation. Thirdly, many areas are not yet suited to wet land agriculture because of cultural constraints. In parts of the American and African tropics the production of swamp rice is not an indigenous activity. In these areas the staple foods include root crops (yams, cassava, groundnuts and sweet potatoes) and upland cereals especially upland rice, maize and various kinds of millet and sorghum. Thus the establishment of wet rice cultivation in some of these areas would require a major cultural shift in long-established eating habits as well as in long-practised cultivation techniques.

And yet rice farming is increasing in importance in tropical Africa and America. In parts of the Amazon lowlands, in valleys of Central Mexico (Plate 4.4), on the fadamas (seasonally flooded riverine lands) of northern Nigeria, and along the coastal swamps of

Plate 4.4 Rice is a traditional crop in a number of Mexican states such as Veracruz and as here in Morelos, south central Mexico. There has been a recent expansion in the area of wet rice cultivation and yields have been improved using new better-adapted high-yielding varieties. In the background, wooded savanna land is used for extensive cattle rearing. (*Photograph: G. P. O'Hare*)

85

Sierra Leone and Liberia a start has been made, and further development may continue to take place.

(iii) *Other areas of permanent cultivation.* In terms of area, most permanent cultivation in the tropics is found in semi-arid and savanna areas where leaching problems are less pronounced. A large part of India (the Deccan) and a rapidly growing part of the semi-arid and savanna lands of Africa (see Figure 4.1) are cropped annually by rain-fed agriculture. Although yields here do not continue to fall drastically under continuous cropping (as in the humid tropics) they stabilize, unlike the fertile areas, at a low level. In view of this low level 'steady state' trap, almost all production here, unless enhanced by fertilizer and especially irrigation inputs (Punjab, Sudan), is at a low level of output with high drought risks and a great deal of erosion hazard.

The development of intensive permanent arable land-use in densely populated tropical highlands (e.g. South and Central America, the mountains of South India, the highland areas of East Africa), and in the more temperate areas of the Third World, has been pursued with a good deal of success. For instance, permanent cultivation is widely practised in the Mexican Highlands, where the intensive production of maize and beans has led to the development of a large and stable Indian population. It would seem that the decline in soil fertility which accompanies more intensive land-use without fertilization is less pronounced in such tropical highlands than in hot humid lowland areas. Yields usually stabilize as in the temperate zones (e.g. Argentina, Central Chile, Southern Africa) at a level sufficiently high to make permanent cultivation advantageous, even without heavy inputs of fertilizer.

(c) *Permanent cultivation in the savannas: the Hausa*

One of the largest areas of permanently cultivated land in tropical Africa is in Hausaland in northern Nigeria (see Figures 4.1, 4.6). The most densely populated zone is around the city of Kano (see Plate 4.5) where most of the land is cropped every year. Population density and the proportion of permanently cultivated land declines with distance from the city. The main crops here include sorghum (guinea corn), millet and cow peas while groundnuts are both the main cash crop and local food crop. In the fields, which are usually small and rectangular, the crops are grown in various combinations on ridges, and weeding is done with care. Fertility tends to be low and is maintained by a variety of means. Within a few kilometres of Kano, waste from the slaughter houses, refuse dumps and latrines is applied to the fields. The group of children in Plate 4.5 are carrying refuse from the city's rubbish tip to their family's fields. At greater distances from Kano, manure for the fields comes from cattle, sheep and goats which graze the impoverished grasslands and stubble fields in the dry season. During the wet season, when the crops are growing, the animals are kept in stalls.

Seasonally flooded areas or land close to water courses which can be irrigated (the fadamas) are normally cultivated in the dry season when the other fields lie fallow. Some valuable crops are grown under irrigation, particularly onions and peppers, sugar cane, maize and, increasingly, rice.

ASSIGNMENTS

1. (a) *Give a reasoned account of the nature and distribution of shifting cultivation using the information contained in Figures 4.1, 4.3, 4.4 and 2.6.*
   (b) *What are the main advantages and drawbacks of the system?*

Plate 4.5 Children collecting domestic refuse to fertilize permanently cultivated land near Kano, northern Nigeria. Sorghum (guinea corn), the staple crop, has been harvested and stacked. In the background small permanent rectangular fields hedged with grass, shrubs and cacti to protect crops against livestock may just be made out. (*Photograph: I. Brightmer*)

2. (a) *Refer to the idealized land-use zonation model shown in Figure 4.5b and note its salient features.*
   (b) *Draw out the similarities and differences between this model and (i) the land-use patterns illustrated in Figure 4.5a, (ii) the case study material in Section 2 (c) and (iii) the information in Plates 4.2 and 4.3.*
3. (a) *List the environmental and human conditions which favour the development of wet rice cultivation.*
   (b) *What factors have encouraged/constrained the expansion of paddy rice cultivation outside South East Asia?*
4. *Analyse and explain the argument which maintains that as population density increases so too does the intensity of agricultural land-use.*

C. Subsistence and Commercial Farming

Introduction

So far we have been considering essentially subsistence farming where agricultural production is geared mainly to domestic consumption. The selling of produce in the market place, on the other hand, is one of the chief attributes of commercial farming. It is often difficult in practice to distinguish between subsistence and commercial farming in the Third World since there is a gradual continuum of change between the two types and many transitional stages occur. On the island of Luzon in the Philippines, for example, a typical farmer may plant maize, sorghum and upland rice using methods akin to rotational fallow cultivation. Such crops are used primarily for family consumption but small amounts may be sold locally from time to time to pay taxes. In addition, copra extracted from coconut trees grown on the farm is carried to nearby villages where it is bought by agents of copra-exporting companies.

1. Subsistence farming

Motivation and risks

On the subsistence farm there is a tendency for a wide range of crops to be grown but output and local consumption will be more or less equivalent. Unlike commercial farming, only the simplest of tools and methods are used on the subsistence farm and capital investment is correspondingly small. Crop output per hectare is highly variable, however. In South Asia, where there is population pressure, the subsistence cultivator attempts to secure as large an output as possible from each unit of land. In those parts of Africa where there is low population density the farmer aims to maximize production in relation to the work involved rather than to produce as large a yield as possible from each hectare. Most production in excess of family requirements may be difficult to keep owing to lack of storage facilities, or impossible to sell because of lack of buyers or transport or even of knowledge of places requiring extra food.

For the subsistence farmer the most important thing is to grow sufficient food for the whole family every year, to avoid the possibility of starvation. The main motivating force in the peasant's life is thus the maximization of the family's chances of survival and not the pursuit of income or profit. The peasant is 'risk avoiding' and may be very reluctant during periods of high risk and uncertainty to shift from a traditional technology and crop pattern, which over the years have become familiar, to a new system which promises higher yields per hectare but which may entail greater risks of crop failure. When sheer survival is at stake it is more important (and rational) to avoid a bad year when there is general crop failure than to maximize the output of the better years. New methods (e.g. new seeds, different cash crops, fertilizers) which appear to the outsider to be improvements on the old may give larger yields in some years but certainly not in all, and when they do not it could mean starvation for those concerned. Thus it should not be concluded that peasant cultivators are backward, irrational, slow at adopting new ideas out of ignorance, or even just plain lazy. They often operate in a wholly rational, if conservative, manner.

2. Commercial farming

(a) Motivation and risks

The main goal of the commercial farmer is to maximize yield per hectare, usually of one of two specialized cash crops, to sell in the market place. To maximize personal income, farmers need to acquire, usually from local agricultural research institutions, specialized knowledge of the small number of commercial crops which they use. In addition, the commercial farmer may rely on imported capital inputs including machinery, fossil fuels, fertilizers and pesticides, as well as an efficient and reliable water supply to maintain and increase yields. There are large variations among commercial agricultural operators with regard to the use of such technology. Examples range from the simple knapsack pesticide spray used by the Nigerian and Sudanese peasant cultivator to the large combine harvester used by the Rhodesian (Zimbabwe) and Argentinian farmer.

The commercial farmer may have to deal with risks and uncertainties quite different from those which face the subsistence cultivator. In brief these include, firstly, increased demands on, and competition for, land in areas undergoing successful commercialization. Secondly, commercial operators are highly dependent on an external supply system, over which they have little control, not only for their input supply but also for product disposal in the market place. Thirdly, by selling their produce in the market place small-scale commercial farmers become exposed to low and widely fluctuating prices for their cash crops (see Chapter 11, Section C3).

(b) Development of cash cropping

Commercial agriculture has been adopted in different ways over different time periods, and has met with varying degrees of success in different areas of the Third World (see Chapter 3, Section E).

Commercial farming may completely replace, especially where population densities are fairly low, indigenous systems, as in the establishment of the commercial plantation. More commonly, however, commercial systems have been grafted onto indigenous economies. This has involved (1) the substitution of native by improved local varieties of crop (e.g. oil palm, groundnuts in West Africa), (2) the introduction of exotic annual crops (e.g. American cotton and tobacco in West Africa) and (3) the introduction of perennial and tree crops in the case of cocoa, coffee, bananas, tea and rubber in various parts of the Third World (Ghana, Malaysia, Sri Lanka).

On many occasions cash cropping has been a virtual failure because of an inability of the innovators to comprehend local physical and cultural conditions. Unsuccessful attempts by the Ford Motor Company to introduce rubber plantations in Brazil and by the British Government to develop commercial groundnut production in Tanganyika (now Tanzania) are notable examples (see page 84). In other areas, by contrast, the swing from subsistence to cash cropping has made great progress. The introduction and development (often with national government assistance) of cocoa production in Ghana and Nigeria, of rubber and oil palm in Malaysia, of tea in Assam and Sri Lanka and of sugar in the West Indies are examples.

Although the greater part of agricultural production remains in the hands of the subsistence cultivator, and the total agricultural area occupied by largely commercial systems remains relatively limited, commercial agriculture has been showing considerable increase both in area and total production in recent years. It may be appropriate to mention that there can be losers in this process. As shown in the criticisms of the green revolution (Chapter 5) many small farmers can be impoverished by new technologies and commercial developments.

(c) Spatial distribution of commercial agriculture

As cash crop farming was initially stimulated and has been maintained by international trade, it is not surprising that areas in the Third World which are accessible by road or rail to port and other export-handling facilities have developed intensive cash crop production. Figure 4.6 serves to illustrate this point. In Nigeria, as indeed in West Africa as a whole, there is a good relationship between the distribution of the principal areas of commercial agriculture and the movement of cash crops to the main ports via the

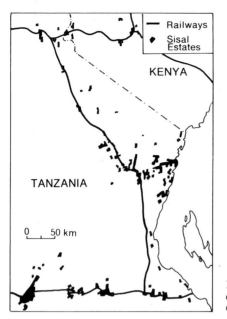

Figure 4.7 Railways and sisal estates in north east Tanzania and southern Kenya. (Source: O'Connor, 1971, p. 270)

transport system. In East Africa the sisal plantations of Tanzania are also clearly associated with the transport (railway) system (see Figure 4.7).

Increasing commercialization has also been in response to local domestic opportunities and markets which have been improved by the export economy itself. Many cultivators have taken advantage of the growing demand for cash crops by an expanding urban/industrial market. Most large urban centres in the Third World are becoming increasingly associated with zones of commercial farming in their vicinity.

ASSIGNMENTS

1. *(a) What are the major features of subsistence and commercial farming?*
   (b) Carefully examine the claim that peasant cultivators are poor adopters of new ideas and techniques.
2. *Refer to Figure 4.6.*
   (a) Examine the distribution of the main areas of cash crop farming in Nigeria.
   (b) Explain this variation in terms of prevailing climatic conditions (see Figure 2.4).
   (c) What effect does the type of transport (road, rail, river) have on the movement and destination of the main cash crops?

D. The Role of Land Ownership

Introduction

Land tenure, or the way in which land is held and owned, is also crucial to the identification and description of separate agricultural systems. Discussions of land tenure usually involve: (1) an analysis of the spatial distribution of individual land holdings, including their size and shape, and whether the individual plots which make up the farm are together (contiguous or consolidated) or separated by distance (scattered or fragmented); and (2) reference to the form of ownership of land, whether it is under communal (collective), feudal, private or state control. In the Third World, land tenure exists in considerable variety, some forms of which (e.g. communal, feudal) have been considered obstacles to agricultural change and economic development (Chapters 3 and 5). In many LDCs, various historical circumstances (Chapter 3) have led to a very uneven distribution of land ownership where peasants are subjugated by landlords. This is especially true in Latin America, parts of Asia (excluding China, North Korea and North Vietnam) and in the Middle East and North Africa. Comparable systems do not exist for sub-Saharan Africa where both historical and cultural influences and the availability of relatively more land per capita have resulted in a different pattern of land tenure. In the latter area, although there is increasing private and state ownership of land, the usual system is one of tribal ownership. Here all land is owned by the community as a whole, though each farmer or family has some security of tenure on the land which he or she is cultivating.

1. Land tenure patterns

(a) Latin America: latifundia/minifundia system

The latifundia system, with large centrally managed estates worked by semi-serf peasants, has been a feature common to many LDCs especially in Latin America and the Middle East. The most obvious manifestations of this system are (1) a high degree of land ownership in the hands of a few wealthy landlords; (2) a large proportion of landless labourers among the peasantry who sell their labour, when conditions allow, for sub-standard wages on neighbouring large estates or commercial plantations; and (3) insecure land-holding arrangements for the remaining rural peasantry.

A peasant belonging to the latter group may be able to till an inadequate piece of land either within or outside the latifundia. This plot of land may be owned by the peasant but more often it will be rented from or pawned to a local landlord or moneylender. Peasants who rent land may have to give up to the landlord as much as 80% of their produce either in cash (cash tenancy) or in kind with part of the crop itself (share-cropping). Others work the landlord's land for nothing at different times of the year. In other cases tenant farmers must provide both output and free labour to the 'patron'. Under such a system, land ownership provides not only economic benefits for the landlord but also, and often more importantly, social status and political power.

In Latin American countries that have not experienced major land reforms in the last 60 years (see Chapter 5 on land reform), such as Brazil, Argentina and Guatemala, generally 3–4% of the landowners own between 60–80% of the agricultural land. Indeed 50% of the land (in estates of over 1500 hectares) is held by a mere 1–2% of the population, a degree of land concentration far greater than any other comparable world region. Table 4.1 provides a dramatic picture of such pronounced inequalities of land ownership in five Latin American countries. In those countries with dense indigenous populations, such as Guatemala, sub-family farms or minifundias, defined as being too small to provide employment for a single family (two workers), are very numerous accounting for 85–90% of all farms. But in no case do they occupy more than 15% of the total agricultural land. In the less densely populated countries of Argentina, Brazil and Colombia, the minifundias constitute between 22% and 44% of all farms; but occupy

Table 4.1 Number, area, productivity and employment of farms of various size classes in selected Latin American countries (percentage country total in each case). (Sources: Barraclough & Domike, 1966; Todaro, 1977)

| Size class of farm: | Small farms (minifundia) | Moderate-sized farms | | Large estates (latifundia) |
| | | Family farms | Medium-sized farms | |
Number of farm workers:	0–2	2–4	4–12	12 and over
Argentina				
Number of Farms	43	49	7	1.0
Total farmland	3	45	15	37
Value of agricultural product	12	47	26	15
Labour employed	30	49	15	6
Brazil				
Number of farms	23	39	33	5
Total farmland	0.5	6	34	59.5
Value of agricultural product	3	18	43	36
Labour employed	11	26	42	21
Chile				
Number of farms	37	40	16	7
Total farmland	0.2	8	13	78.8
Value of agricultural product	4	16	23	57
Labour employed	13	28	21	38
Colombia				
Number of farms	64	30	5	1
Total farmland	5	25	25	45
Value of agricultural product	21	45	19	15
Labour employed	58	31	7	4
Guatemala				
Number of farms	88	10	1.9	0.1
Total farmland	14	13	32	41
Value of agricultural product	30	13	36	21
Labour employed	68	13	12	7

less than 5% of the total farmland. The latifundias on the other hand, defined as those farms large enough to provide work for more than 12 people, occupy as much as 60% of the agricultural land (in Brazil) yet comprise less than 5% of the total farms of the countries shown.

(b) Asia: Small farms and high tenancy

In many countries of South and South East Asia the degree of land-holding concentration is only slightly less. Although accurate data on land ownership are scarce partly because of the complexity of tenures, it seems that in most Asian countries (except China, North Korea and North Vietnam) a small elite group of large landowners control some 20–40% of the farm area and have better access to resources such as credit, capital and fertilizers. However, ownership in Asia is highly decentralized through tenancy and share-cropping. Large land-holdings have not for the most part been operated as centrally managed latifundia, by squatters, landless workers and tenant share-croppers. By contrast they have been rented out to cultivators in numerous smallholdings. Indeed in many Asian countries 50% of all farmland may be tenanted.

(c) Sub-division and fragmentation

The economic and social implications of heavy land ownership concentration, parti-cularly in Latin America, and of tenancy, especially in Asia, are exacerbated by the crucial factor of population pressure. Population pressure causes sub-division and fragmentation of already inadequate-sized farms so that agricultural production may decline to bare subsistence levels or below. The existence of large and growing numbers of people crowded onto too little land is a serious problem in most of Asia and is becoming one in parts of Latin America. Asia has over 30% of the world's crop land area but over one-half of its population (see Table 5.1). Already in many parts of India, Indonesia and the Philippines peasant holdings are less than 1 hectare. In Taiwan, South Korea and Nepal the proportion is nearer to 0.5 hectare. In Central America, rapidly growing indigenous populations have resulted in the sub-division of the minifundias into much smaller plots of land: the microfundias. There are already about 75 000 microfundias in Guatemala yielding an average income that is less than one-third that provided by its minifundias. Fragmentation is also acute in the populous Andean region where holdings are often split into 15 or 20 separate plots.

As holdings shrink and fragment, farm output, particularly in bad years, falls below subsistence levels and chronic poverty becomes a way of life. Asian and Latin American peasants are forced to borrow even more money from the moneylenders at exorbitant interest rates (50–200%). As most cannot repay these loans they are compelled to sell their land and become tenants with large debts. Since land is scarce, they are forced to pay high rents to the landlord or moneylender in cash or kind. Since labour is abundant, wages are extremely low. They are thus caught in a vice of chronic poverty, if not in a downward spiral of underdevelopment. Peasants in Asia and Latin America are sharing a common experience in that they are being transformed from small proprietors to tenant farmers and share-croppers, then to landless rural labourers, to jobless vagrants and finally to migrant slum dwellers on the fringes of the modern urban areas (see Chapter 10).

2. Land tenure and crop production

Introduction

Smallholdings have always been responsible for the bulk of agricultural production, if not of large-scale export production in the Third World. In terms of general food production, the smallholding has as its counterpart the large low-cost low-input estate (latifundia). In relation to the production of cash export crops, the smallholding contrasts with the high-cost capital-intensive plantation.

(a) Smallholdings and large estates

Evidence from a wide range of Third World countries indicates that small farms are generally more efficient, i.e. lower-cost producers of most agricultural commodities. Small farms generally have higher inputs and outputs per unit area than the larger estates. Indian government studies in several states recorded output per hectare figures 10–30% greater on smallholdings. Table 4.1 demonstrates quite clearly that though the latifundias may be relatively efficient producers of food in terms of the low amounts of labour they employ these farm units are inefficient in relation to food output per hectare. The latifundias produce only about one-half of the food output by value that their relative areas would suggest. In contrast, the minifundias can supply in relative percentage terms a value of produce up to about four times (and the family and medium-sized farms a value up to about twice) that of the area of the land they occupy. The minifundias of Colombia and Guatemala are responsible for a greater value of agricultural output than the latifundias despite occupying respectively only one-ninth and one-third of the latifundias' land area.

A major reason for the relative economic inefficiency of large estates is the poor utilization of productive farm resources. In Brazil, the latifundias, with an average area 32 times larger than that of the family farms, invest only 11 times as much. A considerable portion of the arable latifundia land is left idle. In the five countries shown in Table 4.1 only about one-sixth of the latifundia land is cropped regularly and only 4% is cropped every year, the rest being pasture and semi-natural vegetation. Thus the most unfortunate characteristic of the large estates for agricultural development is their extensive use of land, often the best land in the country for soil quality and accessibility. Moreover, as relatively large numbers of landless labourers and tenant farmers are employed on these farms, there is considerable under-utilization of labour. It follows that a redistribution of these large unused lands to family farms would probably raise national agricultural output and productivity (see Chapter 5, Section C).

(b) Smallholdings and plantations

The other variant of the large estate, the commercial plantation, is very different from the extensively worked, centrally managed, latifundia whose produce tends to be used locally or nationally. The plantation is usually conceived as a large-scale agricultural/industrial enterprise that is both capital and labour intensive. It raises and usually processes, mostly with the assistance of organized labour, agricultural tropical commodities designed for the world market.

(i) *Variety of plantations.* It is difficult to define precisely a plantation or plantation crop. A plantation in Malaya is defined simply in terms of size, as an enterprise 40 hectares or more in extent. On oil palm plantations in Malaysia a wage-earning labour force with no ties to the land produces the crop, whereas on sugar plantations (called centrals) in Fiji the labour force is given a degree of proprietorship over a smallholding in addition to payment for working in the plantation. Sometimes zones of smallholders or 'outgrowers' will cultivate a range of crops in addition to the commercial plantation product and will supplement the central plantation output. This latter type of production system, called the 'nucleus estate', may be set up as a new development as in many African schemes (e.g. the Gezira scheme in Sudan) or it may evolve from an existing plantation which agrees to accept outgrower produce.

Further, while the old traditional plantation was always foreign owned, today's modern, more industrial, variant is increasingly being operated with indigenous private and government ownership. Finally, there is no crop exclusively grown on plantations, though perennial crops, especially trees (oil palm, rubber, coffee), or shorter-term crops (sugar cane, bananas) are characteristic of the plantation. Oil palm and cocoa are peasant smallholding products in West Africa but are plantation products in Brazil, Indonesia and

Malaya. Rubber and oil palm are grown under both plantations and smallholdings in Malaysia.

(ii) *Plantation versus smallholdings.* Opinions about the relative merits of plantations compared with smallholdings in the production of 'plantation' crops have often been divided. However, it is generally acknowledged that the plantation system can produce, process, market and distribute a superior-quality product more efficiently than the smallholding. On the other hand, the low capital investment of the smallholding and the fact that the commercial crop is often a sideline to subsistence farming gives the smallholder greater flexibility in times of economic and political change. When prices are low the smallholder can fall back on subsistence production.

Although it is difficult to generalize, agricultural and especially cash crop production is being increasingly characterized by the smallholding rather than the large estate or plantation. For instance, most banana plantation cultivation in Central America is monocultural and rests in the hands of foreign trans-national companies (e.g. the US United Fruit Company). However, critics of such production claim that it has exploited local resources through 'soil mining', and local labour through low wages. As a result there has been a movement in the area to increase production from native smallholdings. In Ecuador, which is now the leading single exporter of bananas (28% of world total), most of the crop is produced by comparatively small-scale indigenous growers.

ASSIGNMENTS

1. Refer to Table 4.1.
  (a) Compare and contrast the five Latin American countries shown on the basis of their minifundia, moderate-sized farms (family and medium-sized farms) and latifundia.
  (b) Examine and explain the economic efficiency of the three classes of farm shown with reference to (i) yield per unit of land, and (ii) yield per unit of labour.

Key Ideas

A. Diversity and Change
1. Diverse agricultural systems in the Third World are the result of a complicated interaction between varied physical and human factors.
2. The effects of the natural environment on farming can be examined at different scales: from global to local.
3. Agricultural diversity is ultimately a reflection of variations in human and cultural factors.
4. Agricultural change involves an increase in intensification and commercialization and a shift in emphasis towards private and small-scale farming.

B. Farming and Land-use Intensity
1. Shifting cultivation, where plots of land are cleared and cropped at infrequent intervals, is a very extensive form of agriculture.
2. While shifting agriculture may be sound ecologically, it supports only a low density of population and is thought to limit economic and social development.
3. Where population densities increase shifting agriculture gives way to systems with much shorter fallows, as in rotational fallow cultivation.
4. In areas of rotational fallow cultivation concentric zones of decreasing land-use intensity may develop with distance from settlements.
5. Most people in the Third World are supported by permanent field cultivation.

6. Permanent cultivation has been introduced with different degrees of success in different parts of the Third World.
7. Wet rice cultivation represents the most successful form of permanent cultivation in the tropics.
8. The human and physical requirements of wet rice cultivation are exacting, and its large-scale expansion outside South East Asia remains in some doubt.

C. Subsistence and Commercial Farming
1. The main concern of the subsistence cultivator is to avoid risk and uncertainty, and to produce enough food annually for survival.
2. Where peasant farmers have not responded to obvious economic opportunities it is usually for sound rational reasons and not because they are irrational, backward or lazy.
3. The commercial cultivator is chiefly motivated to maximize yields per hectare and cash incomes.
4. Increasing land pressure, a high dependency on an external supply system, and low and fluctuating prices for cash crops, present problems for commercial operators.
5. Many factors have influenced the development of cash cropping including international trade, the availability of transport, expanding domestic markets and the policies of national governments.
6. Transport facilities have played a crucial role in the global, regional and local distribution of cash cropping.

D. The Role of Land Ownership
1. A high concentration of land ownership, insecure tenancy arrangements for peasant cultivators, and large numbers of landless labourers are the chief features of land tenure in certain parts of Latin America, North Africa and Asia.
2. A variety of conditions are responsible for transforming small proprietors to tenant farmers and share-croppers and eventually to landless rural workers.
3. The smallholding is in general more intensively worked and a more efficient producer of most agricultural produce than the extensively operated, centrally managed estate.
4. A plantation is a large-scale agricultural/industrial enterprise that is both labour and capital intensive which raises and usually processes agricultural commodities designed for the world market.
5. In general terms agricultural and, in particular, cash crop production are being increasingly characterized by the smallholding rather than the large estate or plantation.

Additional Activities

1. (a) Examine the relationship between the main patterns of climate, vegetation and soils outlined in Chapter 2 and the distribution of the main agricultural types shown in Figure 4.1.
   (b) What other factors influence the distribution of the principal farming systems?
   (c) Examine the effects of these factors.
2. Refer to Table 4.2 and the text.
   (a) Describe the types of change which take place under increasing land-use intensification.
   (b) Account for such changes with reference to (i) variations in population density, (ii) variations in land (soil) quality, (iii) degree of commercialization, (iv) size and type of farm holding.

Table 4.2 Types of land-use intensity. (Source: Boserup, 1965)

Type of culti-vation	Cropping length	Fallow length	Type of fallow	Tools in use	Fertilizer	Labour inputs	Productivity per hectare	Productivity per worker-hour	Population density
Extensive Shifting	1 to 2 years	20 to 25 years	Tree	Axe and digging stick	Ash	Land clearance, fire/axe	Low	High	up to about 10–12/km^2
Extensive/ intensive Rotational fallow	About 5 years	5 to 15 years	Bush and grass	Hoe and plough	Ash and manure	Weeding, seed bed preparation	Medium	Medium	10–250/km^2
Intensive Permanent	Annual and multi-cropping	Few months, negligible	Alter-native crops	Plough	Manure and compost	Weeding, irrigation, terracing	Relatively high	Low	over 250/km^2

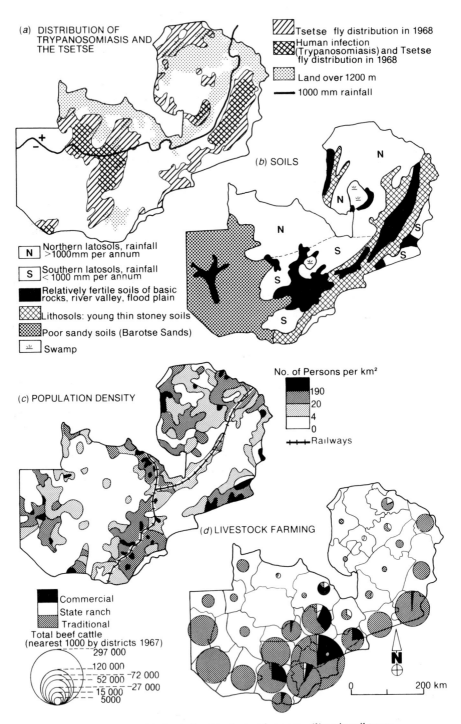

(a) DISTRIBUTION OF TRYPANOSOMIASIS AND THE TSETSE

Tsetse fly distribution in 1968

Human infection (Trypanosomiasis) and Tsetse fly distribution in 1968

Land over 1200 m

1000 mm rainfall

N Northern latosols, rainfall >1000mm per annum

S Southern latosols, rainfall <1000 mm per annum

Relatively fertile soils of basic rocks, river valley, flood plain

Lithosols: young thin stoney soils

Poor sandy soils (Barotse Sands)

Swamp

(b) SOILS

(c) POPULATION DENSITY

No. of Persons per km²

190
20
4
0

Railways

(d) LIVESTOCK FARMING

Commercial

State ranch

Traditional

Total beef cattle (nearest 1000 by districts 1967)

297 000
120 000
72 000
52 000
27 000
15 000
5000

N

0   200 km

Figure 4.8 Zambia in maps: (a) physical and ecological features; (b) main soil types; (c) population density and railway lines; (d) livestock rearing; (e) farming types. (Source: Davies, 1971)

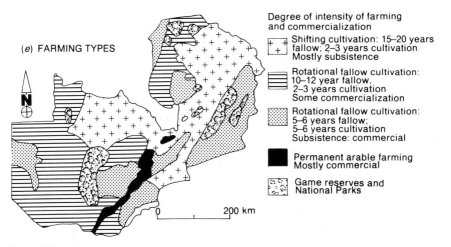

(e) FARMING TYPES

Degree of intensity of farming
and commercialization

Shifting cultivation: 15–20 years
fallow; 2–3 years cultivation
Mostly subsistence

Rotational fallow cultivation:
10–12 year fallow,
2–3 years cultivation
Some commercialization

Rotational fallow cultivation:
5–6 years fallow;
5–6 years cultivation
Subsistence: commercial

Permanent arable farming
Mostly commercial

Game reserves and
National Parks

0   200 km

Figure 4.8 (*cont.*)

3. Re-read the section on soils in Chapter 2 and the section on the tsetse fly and trypanosomiasis disease in Chapter 3 (page 53). Refer to the series of maps on Zambia in Figure 4.8(*a–e*).

(a) Account for the distribution of tsetse fly in relation to (i) altitude, (ii) the location of game reserves.

(b) What are the possible implications for humans and livestock in areas of tsetse fly distribution?

(c) Suggest why tsetse fly populations may be kept at bay in areas of human occupation and settlement.

(d) Critically examine the relationship between the intensity of cultivation and (i) the distribution and quality of soils, (ii) the distribution of population density. Give reasons for your answers.

(e) Examine the factors responsible for the distribution and extent of (i) commercial and subsistence cultivation, (ii) commercial and subsistence livestock rearing.

5

Agricultural Production and Reform

Introduction

Agriculture is of outstanding importance in the Third World. It is a major source of employment, an important earner and a valuable support for the economies of the LDCs. Yet agricultural investment and productivity have remained low, and food production has barely kept pace with population expansion. Many attempts have been made by the LDCs to increase agricultural output. These have included (wherever possible) programmes of increasing the cultivated area, as well as enhancing crop yield through the application of modern scientific methods. Some countries have also attempted to improve agricultural performances and the conditions for farmers by re-organizing the way land is held and owned in land reform.

A. The Importance of Agriculture

1. Land, work and people

(a) Rural population and cropland

As shown from Table 5.1, over 92% of the world's rural population and over one-half of the world's cultivated land are in the Third World. Asia itself has more than 70% of the world's rural population and approximately 32% of the world's cropland. Africa has 14% and 12%, respectively, while Latin America, with 6.2% and 10% respectively, has as many rural dwellers as North America, Europe and the USSR put together.

The pressure of rural population on the amount of arable land is, as shown from Table 5.2, far greater in the Third World than in other regions. Asia has the lowest ratio of cropland to rural population of all the major regions, averaging 0.30 hectares per person. Of the Asian countries Burma has one of the most favourable ratios (1.08); but many Asian countries have extremely poor ones: for example, Bangladesh (0.16), China (0.19) and Nepal (0.21). Africa and Latin America as a whole have much better ratios (0.58 and 1.13 hectares per person, respectively); but they still do not approach those of Europe (1.95) and the USSR (5.04) and fall far short of North America (39.33). Of Third World countries the most and least favourable rural inhabitant per cropland ratios are found in Latin America. The former is represented by Argentina (7.03), the latter by Haiti (0.10).

(b) Employment provision

A very large percentage (60%) of the total active population of the Third World depends directly or indirectly on agriculture for a living (see Table 5.1). Percentages range from 35% in Latin America, to 59% in Asia, to 66% in Africa: a higher proportion than any

100

Table 5.1 Distribution of cropland, rural population, active agricultural workforce and cropland per rural person in the major regions of the LDCs and MDCs. (Source: *FAO Production Year Book, 1979*)

Region	(1) 1978 Land area (Mha)	(2) 1978 Cropland (Mha)	(3) World distribution (%)	(4) 1979 Rural population Millions	(5) World distribution (%)	(6) 1979 Agricultural population as percentage of total active population	(7) 1978–9 Cropland area per rural person (ha)
Africa	2965	169	11.9	292	14.4	66	0.58
Asia	2677	449	31.75	1477	72.9	59	0.30
L. America	2020	142	10.04	126	6.2	35	1.13
All LDCs	7589	741	52.4	1876	92.7	60	0.39
Europe	472	142	10.04	73	3.6	16	1.95
N. America	1835	236	16.7	6	0.3	2.5	39.33
USSR	2227	232	16.4	46	2.3	17	5.04
All MDCs	5485	673	47.6	148	7.3	13	4.55
World	13074	1414	100	2024	100	46	0.69

Table 5.2 Distribution of cropland per rural person, and contribution of agriculture to employment, GDP and export earnings in selected LDCs and MDCs. (Sources: *World Bank Development Report, 1980*; World Bank, 1975)

	1975 Cropland (kha)	1975 Cropland per rural inhabitant (ha)	1978 Numbers employed in agriculture as percentage of active population	1978 Contribution of agriculture to GDP (%)	1977 Agricultural share of exports (%)
Africa					
Ivory Coast	8860	2.22	81	21	89
Nigeria	21795	0.48	56	34	6
Rwanda	704	0.21	91	46	90
Uganda	4880	0.67	83	57	99
Zaire	7200	0.53	76	27	21
Asia					
Bangladesh	9500	0.16	75	57	42
Burma	18940	1.08	53	46	88
China	110300	0.19	62	—	37
India	164610	0.44	74	40	35
Nepal	2090	0.21	93	62	82
Philippines	8977	0.34	48	27	58
Latin America					
Argentina	26030	7.03	14	13	75
Bolivia	3090	1.08	51	17	17
Guatemala	1498	0.46	57	—	82
Haiti	370	0.10	70	—	53
Mexico	23817	1.01	39	11	39
Venezuela	5214	1.81	20	6	1
UK	7261	4.71	2	2	9
USA	176440	21.5	2	3	24
Japan	5510	0.26	13	5	2

other region. Table 5.2 provides data for individual countries. Many countries in Asia and especially in Africa have more than 70% of their population involved in agriculture. The three most populous countries in the Third World, namely, China (950 million), India (644 million) and Indonesia (136 million), have more than 50% of their population engaged in farming, and the fifth most populous, Bangladesh, with 85 million, has nearly three-quarters of its workforce similarly occupied. Even in the arid oil-rich countries of the Middle East and North Africa, where agriculture may be expected to be relatively unimportant, quite significant agricultural populations exist. This is in very sharp contrast to conditions in the MDCs where less than 10%, and in several cases less than 5%, of the working population obtains its living from farming.

2. Income and revenue

(a) Contribution to GDP

Not surprisingly, this large agricultural workforce generates a reasonably high proportion (about 35%) of the total gross domestic product of the LDCs, ranging from about 20% for Latin America to around 45% in Africa. Table 5.2 shows that in several LDCs, especially in Asia and Africa, agricultural activity is a major source of income and contributes as much if not more to total GDP than that of any other recognized leading sector, such as industry, manufacturing and services. Also, much agricultural output is never marketed so that if anything GDP contributions are undervalued.

(b) Export earnings

With the exception of certain minerals, including oil which dominates the trade patterns of a small number of oil-rich LDCs, the agricultural sector is a predominant source of foreign exchange earnings in many LDCs. Excluding oil, agricultural products and byproducts on average account for about 65% of the foreign trade of the LDCs. Table 5.2 shows the contribution which agriculture makes to the value of merchandise exports in a selected number of countries. Apart from those countries dominated by primary fuels and minerals, for instance, Nigeria, Venezuela, Saudi Arabia (oil), Chile (copper), Bolivia (tin and oil), or less commonly by manufacturing, for example, South Korea and Hong Kong, many LDCs depend heavily on the export of primary agricultural produce for foreign exchange earnings. This dependence is highest among the poorer lower-income group of LDCs such as Burma (88%), Rwanda (90%) and Uganda (99%); but is still surprisingly large in more developed and even 'industrializing' countries such as Mexico (39%), Brazil (64%) and Argentina (75%).

ASSIGNMENTS

1. (a) Refer to columns 1 and 2 in Table 5.1. Calculate the percentage of land within each major region which is cultivated and give reasons for your findings. Consult an atlas, if necessary.
   (b) Examine and explain the variations between the LDCs and the MDCs in their rural and agricultural populations.
2. Refer to Table 5.2.
   (a) Discuss the variations in total cropland and cropland per rural inhabitant for the selected countries shown.
   (b) Examine the extent of dependency on agriculture within and between the various regions shown.

B. Status and Performance of Agriculture

Despite the importance of farming in terms of land-use, employment provision and income creation, the agricultural sector has consistently failed to fulfil its basic function: that of adequately feeding the inhabitants of the Third World. This unfortunate situation, emphasized by the dietary patterns of the Third World shown in Figures 1.3 and 1.4, can be traced to the nature and productivity of agricultural systems.

1. Agricultural productivity

Agricultural productivity both in relation to output per person and per hectare is generally low. Table 5.3 compares agricultural productivity between major world regions. As shown, crop yields of wheat and rice per hectare in the Third World are much smaller than those found in the MDCs. Even greater disparities are revealed when output per worker is considered. On this basis American farmers are on average about 120 times more productive than the farmers of the Third World.

(a) Explanation of low productivity

Explanation for this low agricultural productivity is a source of some controversy. Most authorities agree, however, that poor agricultural performance is determined by a complex combination of constraints: environmental (poor climate and soil resources), economic (lack of financial credit, capital equipment), socio-cultural (resistance to adoption of new ideas; population growth) and institutional (unfavourable land tenure).

(i) *Low levels of technology.* As indicated in Table 5.3, agricultural technologies in the poor countries are basically traditional rather than modern. They use relatively high amounts of human and draught animal power (Plate 1.1) and few advanced technical

Table 5.3 Agricultural productivity (outputs) and technological inputs by major world region. (Sources: FAO, 1980; *FAO Production Year Book, 1979*)

Region	Outputs					Inputs		
	(1) Crop yield (100 kg/ha) 1979		(2) Output of cereals per capita per annum 1979	(4) Consumption of commercial fertilizers per annum 1978/79		(5) Number of tractors 1978	(6) Area of arable land per tractor 1978
	Wheat	Rice	(metric tonnes)	(million metric tonnes)	(metric tonnes per hectare)	(thousands)	(hectares)
Africa	8.5	14.3	0.4	1.1	0.006	203	697.8
Latin America	14.4	18.9	2.1	6.2	0.044	899	157.6
Near East	14.4	42.4	1.5	2.7	0.033	539	150.4
Far East	15.5	20.7	0.9	8.6	0.032	436	605.5
All LDCs (including China)	14.6	25.1	1.0	29.1	0.039	2701	274.5
North West Europe	35.4	54.1	9.5	21.0	0.15	6804	14.09
North America	21.2	51.4	120.4	22.1	0.10	5026	46.9
USSR	15.6	39.3	7.5	29.4[1]	0.12[1]	2515	92.2
Japan	30.6	62.4	2.4	5.0	0.90	1050	4.7
ALL MDCs	20.4	55.7	11.4	77.5	0.11	17090	39.4

[1] USSR and Eastern Europe

inputs. By contrast, agricultural operations in the MDCs use low levels of human and animal power, and very high technical inputs such as fossil fuels, modern machinery, fertilizers, pesticides, hybrid seeds and water. Traditional methods of farming in the Third World have remained relatively unchanged over time. Some of the reason for this can be traced to the special conditions of subsistence farming with its high risks and un-certain rewards (page 88).

(ii) *Population growth.* Rapid population growth (see Chapter 8) has exacerbated problems of technological backwardness by putting pressure on existing resources. Population in the rural areas of the LDCs has continued to increase in absolute numbers during the last three decades. This is despite a marked reduction in relative growth rates, during the most recent decade, because of rapid migration out of the rural areas to the cities. Where fertile land is limited, especially throughout Asia, but also in many parts of Latin America and Africa (Table 5.2), rapid rural population growth has led to an increase in the number of people living on each unit of land. Given unchanging traditional farming methods with simple technologies and traditional seeds, as more and more people are forced to work on a given piece of land, their marginal productivity will decline. The result of this 'law of diminishing returns' is a continuing decline in real living standards for the rural peasantry.

(iii) *Low investment in agriculture.* One of the main reasons for agriculture's low productivity is that agriculture has for long been regarded as a low-status low-priority sector in development planning. During the 1950s and throughout most of the 1960s the share of total national investment allocated towards agriculture in a sample of 18 LDCs was approximately 12% even though agricultural output in these countries constituted almost 35% of their GNPs and more than 60% of their total employment. This neglect of agriculture and the accompanying bias towards investment in other sectors of the economy–in the urban and industrial sector in particular–can be traced to a long misplaced emphasis on rapid industrialization as a means of achieving successful economic development and progress.

There is evidence that since the mid 1960s some greater priority has been given to agriculture in Third World national development plans. In Nigeria, for instance, where Federal investment in agriculture during 1949–62 ranged between only 3.5% and 5.6% annually, public funding is now running at 15%. In India, the allocation of public funds to the agricultural sector has recently risen to about 25%. Despite these increases, agriculture still tends to be viewed as a passive supporting sector in the overall economy rather than as playing a dynamic and leading role. Agriculture has been starved of investment in order to supply low-priced food and labour (a consequence of low prices given to farmers for their crops and a general lack of work on the land) to an expanding industrial economy.

2. Methods of increasing food production

(a) *Expansion of the cultivated area*

Low levels of food production and population pressure on land resources can be relieved either by expanding the cultivated area and/or by increasing yields. The amount of new land, which can be brought into cultivation is reckoned now to be very limited in the Third World however. The annual rate of expansion of new land brought under cereal cultivation in the market economy LDCs, for instance, fell throughout the 1950s, 1960s and 1970s from 1.8% to 1.5% to 0.9%. The expansion of new acreage slowed down in all major regions, with the exception perhaps of Africa, and particularly in Latin America and the Near East where growth rates have declined by about two-thirds over the same period.

(b) Increasing yields

In contrast to the low-cost expansion of the cultivated area increasing the yield per hectare is much more expensive and usually requires a higher level of technology and management. Only in recent years in the Third World has a concerted effort (known as the green revolution) been made to develop technology to raise yields of staple food, as opposed to export cash crops. As a result, since the 1960s most increases in cereal production can be attributed to a rise in yield rather than an expansion of the cultivated area. The contribution of yield to production increases for the LDCs as a whole (excluding the Centrally Planned Economies) rose from 45% in the 1950s to 56% in the 1960s and to as much as 67% in the 1970s.

3. Food production and population

(a) General stagnation of output

Yield increases have not, however, counterbalanced the reductions in the rate of acreage expansion. There has been a general slowing down in the rate of cereal production between the 1950s and 1970s in all major regions of the Third World. Production declines in Africa, the Far East and Latin America have been particularly dramatic in the 1970s. This decline has meant that food production has barely kept pace with the rapid rise in populations in the Third World. Figure 5.1 shows the annual relative changes in the

Figure 5.1 Total and per capita food production in the LDCs and MDCs, 1961–5 to 1979. (Source: *FAO Production Yearbook, 1980*)

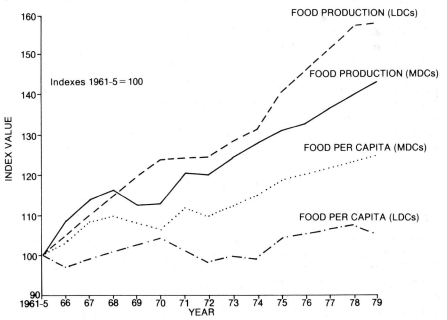

output of food both in total and per capita within the LDCs and the MDCs from 1961–5 to 1979. Although food production in the LDCs has increased at a higher relative rate than in the MDCs, absolute gains in food production have been less in the former than in the latter area. This is because the absolute level of food production in the MDCs was already higher than in the LDCs in 1961–5. More importantly, food production per capita in the LDCs, in contrast to the MDCs, has shown very little improvement since 1961–5.

(b) Regional and national diversity

Grouping all nations of the LDCs together masks the increasing disparities in rates of food production among separate regions and individual countries. For instance, the data shown in Figure 5.2 clearly indicates the worsening position of Africa relative to Asia and Latin America. Although food production per capita in Asia and Africa was actually less in the early 1970s than in 1961–5 because of bad weather conditions, Asian food output per capita made a slight recovery, while African production continued to decline for the rest of the decade. In 1979 people living in Africa had on average only about nine-tenths of the food supply available to them in the early 1960s.

Figure 5.3 shows that considerable variation also exists between countries. The increasing food crisis of Africa is starkly revealed by countries such as Chad and Kenya which are considerably worse off in terms of per capita food production (up to 25%) than they were in the 1961–5 period. While actual food production has been seriously reduced

Figure 5.2 Total and per capita food production by major Third World region 1961–5 to 1979. (Source: *FAO Production Yearbook, 1980*)

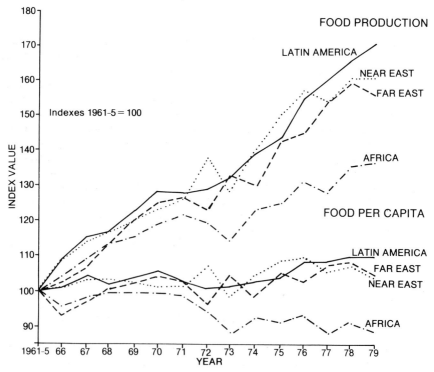

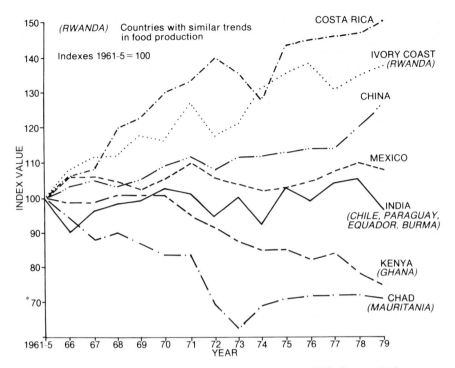

Figure 5.3 Food production per capita in selected LDCs 1961–5 to 1979. (Source: *FAO Production Yearbook, 1980*)

in countries of the African Sahel including Chad, Mauritania and Upper Volta, as a result of prolonged drought, those such as Kenya and Ghana have failed to improve their human/food balance essentially because of very rapid population expansion. Not all parts of Africa, however, have shown declining rates. The Ivory Coast and Rwanda have markedly improved food output in relation to population increase. While Costa Rica and China represent countries in Latin America and Asia respectively which have increased food production per capita, many others are showing signs of relative stagnation. For instance, India, Mexico and the Philippines have all significantly expanded food production in the past two decades but most gains, especially in India, have been offset by population increase.

The general conclusion inferred from these trends in food production per capita is that hunger and malnutrition within the Third World are likely to persist if not increase in many areas. Many of the poorest countries of the Third World are entering a worsening situation. Food production per capita declined as a result of high population growth rates in the 1960s in 56 out of 128 LDCs. In the 1970s the number of countries in this danger increased to 69.

ASSIGNMENTS

1. (a) *Examine the links between agricultural outputs and inputs shown in Table 5.3 for the selected regions.*
   (b) *What other factors not covered in Table 5.3 need to be taken into account when explaining low agricultural productivity in the Third World?*

2. *Study Figure 5.1.*
   (a) Calculate the average annual percentage increase in food production (total and per capita) for the LDCs and MDCs.
   (b) What do your results tell you about (i) absolute gains in food production, (ii) rates of population increase in the two areas?
3. *Study Figures 5.2 and 5.3.*
   (a) How far do food production trends for individual countries confirm those of the regions to which they belong?
   (b) Comment on the role of (i) adverse weather and climate, (ii) population increase, in food production trends for individual countries.

C. Land Reform

Introduction

It may be recalled from Chapter 4, Section D, that much of the inefficiency in the use of both land and labour in Third World farming is related to (1) a highly unequal distribution of land ownership (2) a high degree of tenancy and share-cropping which creates insecurity and lack of incentive, (3) a tendency for farms to be fragmented and for plots of land to be scattered and (4) an increasing number of people with no direct title to land at all. Accordingly, many authorities believe that such unsuitable land tenure systems constitute a major obstacle to agricultural development. They contend that agricultural progress will only be achieved through major structural and institutional changes in land-holding or in what is called land reform.

Land reform can be defined as intervention in the prevailing pattern of land ownership, control and usage in order to change the structure of holdings, improve productivity and broaden the distribution of social and economic benefits. There is a difference between land reform and the wider concept of *agrarian reform*. The latter involves the modification of a wide range of conditions that affect the agricultural sector and may include not only changing land ownership patterns (land reform) but also altering price policies in favour of farmers, increasing the availability of credit, supplying inputs in the form of machinery and fertilizers and providing infrastructural support such as improved marketing, transport, housing and education. Land reform may be a necessary condition for agrarian reform but is seldom sufficient for increasing agricultural output. Many a land reform has failed because of the failure to back up the reform with necessary complementary agrarian measures.

1. Types of land reform

Land reform may involve one or more of the following:

(*a*) the *redistribution* of public and private land in order to change the patterns of land distribution and size of holdings. Usually this involves expropriation, sometimes with compensation, of some or all of the land of the big landowners. Such land may be assigned to a relatively large number of landless or semi-landless peasants usually in individually owned farms (e.g. Bolivia, Morocco, Tunisia) but sometimes into communal units, as in the Mexican *ejidos* and the Peruvian worker co-operatives. Thus an increase in the number of small and medium-sized farms and a reduction in the number of large holdings results. Alternatively, all land can be nationalized and regrouped into state-owned holdings all of which might be large, as in China and Cuba.

(*b*) Another form of land distribution is the *consolidation* of individual holdings. This method attempts to improve the poor spatial organization and layout of individual farms when fields are inconveniently located with respect to one another or where fields are an awkward shape for current farming techniques, say in narrow strips and wedge-shaped plots. As shown from Figure 5.4, fragmented traditional Kikuyu farms in Kenya have been regrouped into contiguous blocks of land. The Kikuyu farmers were given, in addition to technical assistance, individual legal titles to the new enclosed farms (see Plate 5.1) which were comparable in area to all their previous holdings. Yet consolidation schemes are not highly developed. They have taken place only in a few countries in Africa (e.g. Kenya) and Asia (e.g. Pakistan and several Indian States).

(*c*) A third type of reform is *tenancy reform*. This usually involves improvements in tenancy contracts such as providing more security of tenure, introducing more equitable crop sharing and rent arrangements. In Taiwan, during the early stages of their reform, rent was reduced from over 70% to a maximum of 37.5% of the crop value and security of tenure was fixed at six years. Workers and tenants were eventually made owners of the land they worked. However, a large number of ineffective tenancy reforms testifies to the difficulty of administering such types of reform. In South Asia, evasion and subversion by landlords, political bribery and indifference has stultified the progress of tenancy improvements.

(*d*) Fourthly there is *land tax reform*. In theory an increasing land tax would gradually force the owners of large estates to intensify production to pay for the higher taxes or to dispose of or sell a large part of their holdings. To date, land tax reform remains a theoretical notion in the Third World where many countries do not have the political will to exploit the advantages of this system.

Figure 5.4 Patterns of Kikuyu land holdings (*a*) before and (*b*) after land consolidation. Shading shows holdings of one landowner. (Source: Grove & Klein, 1979)

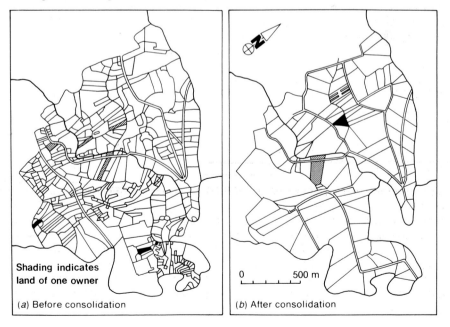

Shading indicates land of one owner

0   500 m

(*a*) Before consolidation

(*b*) After consolidation

Plate 5.1 Consolidated privately owned smallholdings in Kikuyu country, Central Highlands, Kenya. The lower temperature, adequate rainfall (750–1000 mm) and fertile volcanic soils of this highland area support permanent mixed farming. Relict forest and rough grazing land are found on the higher and steeper slopes, while mixed arable farms predominate in the lower areas. Subsistence crops (e.g. maize, bananas and sweet potatoes) are grown together with those which bring a cash income (e.g. coffee, vegetables and milk). The landscape is dotted with roundhouses and (smaller) grain stores behind the trade centre (foreground) and local school (left in foreground). (*Photograph: Kenya Information Services issued by FAO*)

(*e*) As an alternative to proper land reform, settlement schemes and *new land colonization* projects have been an interesting agrarian reform measure in certain parts of the Third World, in particular in Latin America. Land settlement has proved beneficial, especially where underutilized land offers potentially high returns on investment. In the Gezira scheme in the southern Sudan, fertile new irrigated land has been opened up under co-operative farming for the production of cash crops of cotton and sugar. Likewise, some measure of success has been achieved settling excess population from Java to Sumatra and from Luzon to Mindanao in the Philippines.

In general, however, as a means of reaching large numbers of landless people, or of relieving land pressure, colonization schemes are severely limited. They have proved very costly. Ten recent projects (supported by the World Bank) located in Brazil, Colombia, Ethiopia, Kenya, Malawi and Malaysia settled no more than 35 000 families at a cost of $190 million. Clearly the average capital requirement of more than $5000 per family severely restricts the prospects of such an agrarian measure.

Though extensive land resources exist in Latin America, (e.g. along the eastern foothills of the Andes and in Amazonia), as well as in certain other parts of the Third World (e.g. Indonesia and Zambia), many schemes have taken place in extremely remote areas of questionable fertility. Moreover, many of the settled families have lacked an understanding of how to work effectively the land they were given and have been short of credit, transport and general infrastructural support in the way of houses, hospitals and schools.

2. Factors in land reform

(a) Social and economic aspects

Many of the earlier land reforms (e.g. Mexico 1917 and Bolivia 1952) were largely motivated by social pressure, and were based on the egalitarian desire for the more even distribution of land and wealth. The realization that land reform could actually increase agricultural productivity, and in particular the formulation by the United Nations in 1951 of land tenure as an obstacle to economic development, meant that a strong economic objective was added to the original social and egalitarian motives behind land reform.

The break-up of large estates and the reduction in the size of holdings by land reform need not be associated with a reduction in food output. We have already shown that small farms are more efficient food producers than large ones and they are efficient in their use of labour (see Table 4.1). Where output has dropped initially after the rapid break-up of large estates, as in Bolivia and Iraq, evidence suggests that such shortfalls in production are temporary and productivity is later restored. However, when there is a danger of decreases in production from the dislocation of efficient estates, many reforms have exempted such 'model' farms from expropriation. Despite active land reform in Cuba and Algeria many large efficiently run estates have avoided dismemberment, though ownership has passed to the Government in question.

(b) Political aspects

The political factor in land reform is sometimes played down, yet in the last analysis it is often the most decisive. Many land reforms have proved unsuccessful because of a lack of political will. Indeed much of the political power necessary to implement reforms is in the hands of the group at which the land reform is most often directed: the landed aristocracy itself. Where sustained political commitment is lacking, as in the Philippines, Pakistan, India, Colombia and Brazil, reforms have been unsuccessful and only partially carried through. In contrast, Mexico, China, Taiwan, Kenya, Egypt, Iran, Bolivia and Cuba offer instances of countries where political effort in land reform has been fairly strong and where reform programmes have been relatively successful.

3. The Mexican land reform

(a) Development of the reform

Mexico's land reform, the first in Latin America, has its origins in the Mexican Revolution of 1910–17. During the period preceding the Revolution, land and wealth had become so concentrated that Mexico had the most inequitable system of land ownership in all Latin America. By 1910 some 1% of the population owned 97% of the land and 96% of the population 1% of the land.

Central to Mexico's agrarian reform has been a policy of land redistribution from large estates to peasant communities or village units (the ejidos). Very few modern estate lands

Table 5.4 Progress of the Mexican land reform, 1930–70.

Year	Redistributed land as percentage of farm land	Redistributed land as percentage of cropland	No. of beneficiaries as percentage of rural population
1930	6	15	25
1940	22	47	51
1960	26	43	42
1970	43	51	66

were actually expropriated before the 1930s, however. As shown from Table 5.4, only 6% of the country's land, amounting to 8.4 million hectares, had been redistributed among 25% of the rural families. Land redistribution was accelerated during the administration of President Cardénas (1934–40). By 1940, 22% of all farmland (29 million hectares) had been distributed to over one-half of the country's agricultural population.

Between 1940 and 1960 the pace of land redistribution slackened and more attention was paid to the private sector. Land concentration increased again, and the number of land reform beneficiaries, as a percentage of the (growing) rural population, actually decreased to 42% by 1960. In the 1960s under peasant pressure for renewed land reform, the pace of redistribution increased once again. Nearly all lands affected in this period, however, were pasture or arid lands and of low productive capacity. By 1970, as a result of the new effort, 43% of all land in farms (61 million hectares) was redistributed land. This land was held by almost two-thirds of the rural population.

(b) Benefits of the reform

There is little doubt that the Mexican land reform improved the social, economic and political status of the rural peasantry. It markedly reduced the degree of land hunger and concentration in the country. In the pre-reform year of 1923 the area in large estates (i.e. over 1000 ha) was estimated at 130 million hectares and included 82% of the farm area; but by 1970 their extent had been reduced to 42 million hectares or 32% of the agricultural land.

As well as fulfilling important social and political roles, the land reform programme also served an important economic purpose. The post-reform economic performance of Mexican agriculture has been better than that in most other Latin American agricultural sectors and output has managed to keep abreast of population increase (Figure 5.3). Agricultural production trebled between 1945 and 1975. Though such a situation has been assisted by many factors including the use of modern agricultural inputs such as new seeds and especially by irrigation, there is no doubt that land reform has also played a crucial role. It may be noted that the initiation of a marked increase in Mexico's agricultural output is associated with the period of the Cardénas administration (1934–40) when active land redistribution was taking place.

(c) Problems of the reform

The first and perhaps the main criticism of the reform is that considerable land concentration continues to exist. Ten thousand large estates (average size 4184 ha) remain and occupy about one-third of the total agricultural land. In 1970, the top 20% of private farmers received 60% of all private income and even in the ejido sector the top 20% of the ejidatarios accounted for 45% of all ejido income.

Land reform has reduced but has not completely solved the problem of the landless labour force which has increased in recent years. It needs to be recognized, that even if the aims of land reform had been completely fulfilled, and even if all the remaining estate land were to be handed over to the peasantry, high population growth has ensured that many landless workers and families would remain.

Owing to the pressure of people on the land through population growth the tiny minifundia unit has not been abolished. In 1970 there were over 0.5 million private farms with less than 5 hectares of land. Since these units covered about 880 000 hectares, the average size was 1.7 hectares. This contrasts with the pre-reform situation when less than 400 000 of these private farms occupied 1.2 million hectares and had a mean area of about 3.0 hectares. Further, though the average size of the ejido plot is about 30 hectares, in some areas where land pressure is high, such as in the Central Plateau near Mexico City, individual ejido plots are well below the official minimum of 10 hectares. Land shortage in Tlaxcala in Central Mexico, for instance, has resulted in ejidatarios receiving no more than 1 hectare apiece.

Finally, complementary agrarian measures such as the provision of credit, technical assistance and other public services have not kept pace with the efforts of land redistribution. It is unfortunate that government financial and technical support has been unevenly distributed. Such assistance has been concentrated in the more commercialized ejido and private sectors, to the exclusion of smaller and poorer ejidatarios and private smallholders.

ASSIGNMENT

1. *(a) Describe the main types of land reform.*
   (b) Which are the most effective, and why?

D. The Green Revolution

Introduction

In recent years attention has been diverted from land reform and the need for equity in land ownership patterns to a more direct concern for increasing food production in the LDCs. Central to this shift of emphasis has been the 'green revolution'. The green revolution can be defined as the application of modern Western-based agricultural techniques to traditional farming systems in the Third World using new high-yielding varieties (HYVs) of certain crops. While the new methods and HYVs have the potential to increase food production substantially, there is concern about the long-term appropriateness of the green revolution technology. Some success for the green revolution can be claimed on productivity and economic grounds; but the new agricultural methods have also been responsible for a number of disruptive environmental, social and political effects.

1. Progress and production

From the mid 1940s until the mid 1960s a team of agricultural scientists, supported by the Rockefeller Foundation, and working in Mexico at the Centre for Improvement of Maize and Wheat (CIMMYT), succeeded in developing new varieties (hybrids) of wheat and maize that yielded over three and two times respectively as much grain as traditional

113

Plate 5.2 Indonesia: rice growing using new high yielding varieties (HYVs) near Jakarta. Women in the Third World tend to carry out a lot of the domestic and agricultural work as well as all kinds of fetching and carrying (e.g. water, firewood). Here a group of women are taking home the harvest. (*Photograph: International Labour Office*)

varieties (TVs). Encouraged by CIMMYT success the International Rice Institute (IRRI) was set up in 1962 in the Philippines. From here new high-yielding varieties of rice were developed and spread quickly from the mid 1960s to the early 1970s to various parts of Latin America, Africa and Asia.

The new seeds, especially wheat and rice, have had their greatest impact in certain Asian countries, notably Taiwan (100% adoption), South Korea, India, Pakistan, the Philippines, Burma, Malaysia and parts of Indonesia (Plate 5.2). In Asia alone in the late 1970s more than 70% of the wheat and 30% of the rice planted was HYV. In the rest of the Third World HYV diffusion outside Mexico (Plate 4.4), Costa Rica and Columbia has been relatively limited.

(a) Production successes

There is little doubt that the new hybrids possess some notable advantages (Table 5.5) and that the new agricultural methods have been responsible for some dramatic economic and production successes. The role played by the green revolution in raising Mexican food output between 1945 and 1975 with its new HYVs of wheat and maize has already been mentioned (page 112). In South Asia, HYV wheat has been the main benefit of the green revolution and has shown its most spectacular increases in production in India and Pakistan. Indian wheat production more than doubled from about 10 million tonnes in 1963–4 to over 26 million tonnes in 1971–2 (see Figure 5.5). After some fluctuation in the mid 1970s, production rose to 35 million tonnes in 1978–9. Pakistan's wheat production doubled between 1963 and 1976. Those countries shown in Figure 5.3 which have managed to maintain if not increase food production per capita over time, (e.g. Ivory Coast, Rwanda, Burma, Philippines, Colombia) have benefited in varying ways from the availability of the new seeds and methods.

Table 5.5 Selected attributes of HYVs.

Advantages	Drawbacks
1 The new hybrid varieties are more responsive to fertilizer (especially nitrogen) than traditional strains.	1 They require heavy doses of chemical fertilizer (70 kg/ha average).
2 The yields per unit of fertilizer are higher.	2 They need careful weed control and a controlled supply of water.
3 The HYVs are short and stalky: the heads do not topple when heavy with grain (i.e. lodge).	3 They are more susceptible to pest and disease attack and require large applications of pesticides and fungicides.
4 With respect to rice they are non-sensitive to day length.	4 The new seeds must be produced each year by crossing carefully maintained purebred lines.
5 Their shorter growing period sometimes allows a second or third major crop.	5 They are less adapted to drought and with respect to rice to deep flooding or waterlogging.
6 They can give two to four times the yields of indigenous varieties.	6 They have low genetic variety.
	7 Some varieties have poor milling qualities and inferior taste.

Figure 5.5 The progress of the green revolution in India, 1959–79 (a) yields and production of wheat, rice and total grains and, (b) area of wheat, rice, irrigated land and high-yielding varieties (in hectares); and inorganic fertilizer consumption (in tonnes). (Source: *FAO Production Yearbooks*)

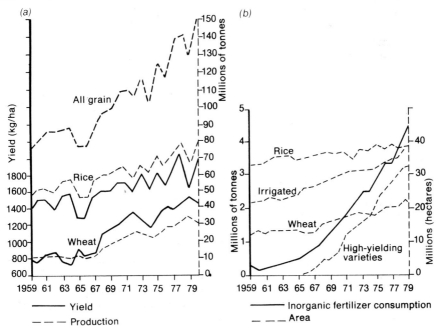

(b) Declining impact

Such was the early success of the new technology between the mid 1960s and early 1970s that enthusiasts went as far as to predict conditions of glut for the world's grain markets of the mid 1970s. Unfortunately such happy prospects of over-production never came to fruition. In 1972 the world's food situation took a turn for the worse and poor weather caused bad harvests in India, China, Australia, the USSR and in the Sahel (see page 18). Two years later as world prices for oil and fertilizer, vital ingredients of the new technology, shot to unprecedented levels, the green revolution slowed down. Since then the green revolution has failed to live up to its earlier promise. In certain areas it has unleashed a series of harmful environmental, social and political effects. These will now be considered.

2. Technical and environmental issues

(a) Technical considerations

As shown from Table 5.5, the new hybrids require, in order to give good yields, high doses (about 70 kg) of fertilizer per hectare. With double or triple cropping this requirement must be multiplied by a factor of 2 or 3. In 1970 the consumption of fertilizer in East Asia was only 14 kg/ha and in Africa it was a mere 0.5 kg/ha and much of the fertilizer had to be imported through foreign trans-national corporations. The potential fertilizer demand of the HYVs is way beyond the supply capacity of the world fertilizer industry and what the LDCs can afford. Because fossil fuels are needed in the manufacture of fertilizer, the oil price rises of the 1970s not only reduced fertilizer imports but also affected the domestic production of fertilizer in Third World countries themselves.

The new strains are also dependent for their success on a range of other technological inputs. Their short stature means that they are susceptible to weed infestation so that careful weed control, often using herbicides, is necessary. They are more susceptible than traditional varieties to disease and pest attack and require large regular amounts of pesticides and fungicides. The new HYVs depend ultimately for their success on large and controlled applications of water and thus demand good irrigation conditions. Many of the new strains are less adapted than indigenous varieties to drought and, in the case of rice, to deep flooding and waterlogging. As a result the HYVs are automatically excluded from large areas of the Third World with low, excessive or irregular rainfall. Because of the 'law of limiting factors' when any one of the aforementioned inputs of fertilizer, pesticides, herbicides, water are deficient as well as good seed, the new HYVs actually yield less than traditional varieties which are better adapted to marginal environments of drought, pest and low fertility.

(b) Ecological side effects

According to some geneticists, one of the most serious ecological side effects of the green revolution is the accelerating loss of genetic variety in plant crops. The large number of traditional strains is being replaced by relatively few HYVs, destroying the variability that is required for the continual development of new varieties. A second, more localized, ecological problem of the new technology is the creation of soil degradation and environmental pollution where heavy applications of fertilizers and pesticides have

116

occurred. Finally, the new HYVs have tended to displace protein-rich crops such as beans, pulses and oil seeds. It is interesting that the long delayed Indian sixth five-year plan will give high priority to an important programme for pulses and oil seeds.

3. Social and political issues

A question of some importance concerns the geographical and social distribution of benefits conferred by the green revolution. It has been argued that the spatial impact of the green revolution has been very uneven and as a result regional and personal income disparities have been exacerbated.

(a) Polarization of benefits: the rich get richer

The new technology has made most progress in the more environmentally favoured districts. Areas such as the fertile irrigated north west Indo Gangetic Plain have benefited from HYVs while areas such as the Deccan and Bengal, plagued by drought and flood respectively, have benefited little from the new seeds (see Figure 5.6). Aside from regional variations caused by the varying availability of controllable water supplies, the green revolution has also shown the greatest advances in the already more developed regions where the necessary infrastructure in transport, storage, mills and marketing channels have been established and where the farmers are more literate, progressive and able to respond to the new innovations. Moreover, the benefits from HYVs have been unevenly spread across social classes within regions.

Basically it is the richer, larger farmers who are benefiting most from the new seeds. This group can best afford to buy them and invest in other requisites of the green revolution package, such as fertilizer, pesticides and irrigation equipment. Small farmers, tenants, sharecroppers and landless labourers have gained little and have been prevented from adopting the new items because of a scarcity of financial resources. It has been estimated that the majority of the peasants (75–80%) in the rice belt of India and especially those operating under insecure oral tenancy leases have experienced relative *decline* in their economic position owing to the green revolution. Realizing the potential profitability of the HYVs, large landowners, in a bid to secure all benefits for themselves, have adopted capitalist methods of farming. These include increased use of material inputs and mechanization, direct employment of wage labour, withholding land from tenant cultivators, expansion of farming through the eviction of tenants and buying out smaller cultivators. The trend is thus for the concentration of good-quality, especially irrigated, land in the hands of larger modern farmers while subsistence farmers are left with poor-quality land.

(b) Effects on employment

Another disruptive effect of the new technology concerns its impact on employment. Initially the green revolution was seen as the answer to unemployment among the rural masses. Potentially the new varieties tend to be employment creating because increased yields and multiple cropping mean increased labour demands through irrigation, fertilizer application, weed control, bigger crops to be harvested, transported and marketed. However, in practice, labour-saving devices such as tractors, ploughs, tillers, sprayers, harvesters, threshers and power-driven wells are being increasingly introduced on larger farms. The trend towards mechanization has been facilitated by the fear of labour shortages, increased wages and labour disputes. In addition, all sorts of powerful

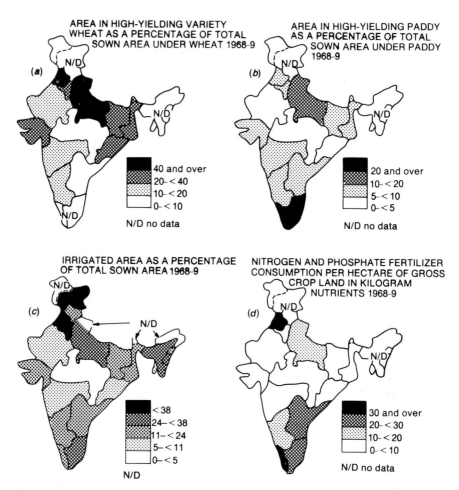

Figure 5.6 Spatial impact of the green revolution in India. Percentage area of (*a*) high-yielding variety wheat; (*b*) high-yielding variety rice; (*c*) irrigated land and (*d*) the per hectare consumption of fertilizers by state, 1968–9. (Sources: Chakravarti, 1973; Johnston, 1979)

individual and corporate bodies, including foreign and domestic industrialists, transnational corporations, politicians and even aid agencies have a strong vested interest in promoting the new mechanized technology.

Conclusion

The relative success of the green revolution has been the subject of some controversy. Advocates of the green revolution point to its marked production successes especially in Taiwan, South Korea, India, Pakistan, Mexico, Costa Rica and the Ivory Coast. They argue that food production in the Third World (Figures 5.1–5.3) has generally kept pace with population expansion because of the new programme. Critics of the scheme, on the other hand, claim that it has unleashed many adverse ecological, socio-economic and political effects. They maintain that by concentrating land ownership and creating unemployment and landlessness it is increasing the gap between rich and poor. Rather than relieving poverty the green revolution may actually be creating it.

ASSIGNMENT

1. (a) Carefully examine the development of the green revolution in terms of (i) economic and production issues, (ii) environmental and technical issues, (iii) social and political issues.
   (b) Assess the relative success or failure of the green revolution.

Key Ideas

A. The Importance of Agriculture
1. Agriculture is of outstanding importance in the economic and social life of the LDCs.
2. Agriculture is the major source of employment and contributes substantially to personal and national income as well as to foreign exchange earnings.

B. Status and Performance of Agriculture
1. The inability of agriculture to feed adequately the inhabitants of the Third World is largely a function of low agricultural productivity.
2. Low productivity in agriculture results from many factors including low levels of technology, increasing rural populations and low investment.
3. Since the mid 1960s most of the increase in the food supply has resulted from increasing yields rather than expanding the cultivated area.
4. Food production in the Third World has barely kept pace with rising populations though considerable disparity in rates of change in food production per capita exists between different regions and countries.

C. Land Reform
1. Land reform is intervention in the prevailing pattern of land ownership with a view to increasing productivity and broadening the distribution of social and economic benefits.
2. Population pressure on land resources together with a highly unequal distribution of land ownership has stimulated land reform legislation if not implementation.
3. Land reform may involve land redistribution, farm consolidation, changes in existing tenancy arrangements and land taxes, and as a possible alternative, new land settlement schemes.
4. Political factors ultimately determine the direction and extent of land reform.
5. The Mexican land reform has brought substantial improvements in the socio-economic condition of the rural peasantry, but land concentration and a growing mass of landless labourers still exist.

D. The Green Revolution
1. The green revolution is the application of modern Western-based agricultural techniques to traditional farming systems in the Third World using new high-yielding varieties (HYVs) of certain crops.
2. The new HYVs, especially wheat and rice, have been responsible for some notable food production increases.
3. They depend for their success, however, on a wide range of technological inputs including large doses of fertilizers, insecticides and herbicides, as well as a controlled and regular supply of water.

4. The green revolution technology has caused a number of harmful ecological side effects.
5. The benefits of the green revolution have become polarized with most progress being made in environmentally favourable regions and by the richer larger landowners.
6. Overall the green revolution may be an inappropriate technology and is no substitute for effective land reform.

Additional Activities

1. Read the article entitled 'The Green Revolution in South Asia' (Farmer, 1981), noting the conditions under which rice and wheat are grown and the difficulties experienced in introducing new high-yielding varieties of wheat and rice in India. Examine carefully Figures 5.5a, b and 5.6 which illustrate the development of the green revolution in India. Now answer the following questions.
   (a) How far has the increase in the production of the two grains been due to (i) expansion of the cultivated area, (ii) increase of yield?
   (b) Comment, with reference to both graphs and map, on the link between yield increases in wheat and rice and the adoption of the green revolution technology i.e. inputs of irrigation, fertilizer, pesticides and new hybrid seeds.
   (c) Compare the patterns of success and failure in the adoption of HYV rice and wheat shown in Figure 5.6a–d. Explain your answers.
   (d) Discuss the problems which India is likely to face in attempting to maintain the green revolution technology and of spreading its production benefits to less favoured areas.
2. 'The green revolution may be a short-term solution to agrarian problems in the LDCs but is no substitute for longer-term programmes such as land reform.' Discuss.

of world exports of bauxite and tin respectively. The bulk of such exports go to MDCs in an un-processed state and it is clear that there is considerable interdependence between some producing LDCs and some consuming MDCs. The spatial pattern of exports is of interest and demonstrates that some producing countries have considerable advantages because their location gives them access to certain markets. For example, Morocco exports phosphate rock to Western Europe, bauxite is exported from the Caribbean to North America, and a variety of minerals are exported from Mexico to the United States. Transport economies are a major factor in shaping this pattern and such countries are clearly in a more advantageous situation than a landlocked country such as Zambia or one more distant from major consumers, even as it... [illegible]... two-edged. Although proximity may imply a ready market for an exporter, it can also lead to the domination of the exporter by the importer. Japan's vast and expanding need for raw materials for its manufactured goods has opened up new sources of mineral supply in Asia and Oceania in the last three decades, especially in the Philippines, India and Indonesia. But these suppliers are dependent upon the state of world demand for Japan's exported manufactured goods, this in turn depending upon the general state of the world economy. A recession in demand is certain to have a severe effect upon such mineral producers. Furthermore, it is clear that for individual Third World countries a major source of revenue is derived from their export of just one raw material, or a limited range of them. For example, the mining sector accounts for 15% of total employment in Zaire, Zambia and Liberia, and in many other developing countries it accounts for more than 10% of GDP.

2. Problems in the economic development of mineral resources

It is obvious that not all LDCs can benefit from mineral resource exploitation as the distribution of resources is dependent upon geology. Thus, purely *physical* factors have a bearing on economic development. However, a number of economic, political and technical problems also affect the exploitation of known resources.

(*a*) *Accessibility*

The famous English geographer, L. Dudley Stamp had an instructive story to tell of the potential value (or otherwise) of mineral resources:

A good many years ago when I first went to Burma to prospect for oil in the Chindwin River basin, I was very much excited at finding a hill which seemed a solid mass of iron ore. It was obviously not high grade, but still, what a discovery! I rode back two days journey to the nearest telegraph, sent cables to secure a prospecting monopoly, and advised my head office at Rangoon of my action. The reply from headquarters came quickly. It read: 'What on earth do you think is the good of iron ore in the Chindwin stop get on with your work.' Thus I learned that accessibility is a factor of great importance in assessing the value of an iron ore deposit.

(From L. Dudley Stamp, *Our Developing World*, Faber 1960, p. 139)

Fifty years on, although technology has ensured vastly improved accessibility, similar limitations still apply. The value of mineral resources does, to some extent, still depend on their accessibility.

(*b*) *Price fluctuations*

Mineral prices are notoriously volatile. For example, a USA-based company began mining copper in Peru in 1969 when the price was £755 per tonne. Only one year later the price had fallen to £450 per tonne. A wide range of factors influence these price fluctuations and often prices are set in markets over which producing countries have no control. The geographical significance of this is that at one date the exploitation of a resource at point 'X' is economically viable but at a subsequent period its exploitation at the same location has become uneconomic, or its profitability reduced.

(c) External control

Because of the vast amounts of capital expenditure involved in the establishment of a modern mining industry and because of the limited amount of highly skilled labour, many LDCs have to seek capital and expertise elsewhere in order to exploit their own resources. This involves sacrificing control to powerful trans-national corporations. For example, before nationalization, two foreign companies controlled Zambia's copper production, and two US firms were responsible for 90% of Chile's copper output.

(d) Processing industries

One of the potential benefits of the exploitation of mineral resources in the LDCs is the opportunity this provides for industrialization: firstly through the processing of raw materials, and secondly through the development of industry utilizing such processed products. Such 'spin off' has not occurred to any great extent in the LDCs. In 1970 only 29% of the total mine production was actually processed within the LDCs.

(e) Knowledge

The effective development of a country's mineral resources requires a sound factual basis. Knowledge of the geology and some rudimentary data on mineral occurrences is an essential starting point, whether the development initiative comes from some trans-national enterprise or from the Government. Yet even this rudimentary knowledge may be lacking, and may impose severe obstacles to LDCs' efforts to mobilize fully their development potential.

(f) Divergent objectives

The interests of investors in mineral resource development in the LDCs and those of the host governments may not always be the same, and thus provide a source of conflict. A trans-national company will be primarily concerned with the maximization of profits and with spreading risks over the company as a whole, i.e. in several different countries. The Government of a LDC, however, will be concerned with maximizing the revenue it obtains from the trans-national within its territory. Furthermore, a national government is likely to take a different view of some of the environmental consequences of mineral exploitation, and to attempt to control or extract compensation for them. For example, subsidence produced by oil extraction is an increasing problem in the Lake Maracaibo field in Venezuela, and in Malaysia special legislation has had to be introduced in an attempt to prevent excessive silting of rivers due to tin mining activities. Such broader considerations are unlikely to be taken into consideration by trans-national firms, and may in fact be regarded as a nuisance.

3. Mineral exploitation and external geographical relationships

Earlier chapters have stressed that we live in an interdependent world. The exploitation of mineral resources obviously involves major *internal* geographical changes in a country, but equally important are the *external* geographical relationships involved. We shall now examine some of these through the examples of oil resource exploitation in the Middle East, and copper in Zambia.

(a) Oil prices and Third World countries

No topic demonstrates the degree of economic interdependence in the modern world more than oil. A large number of countries are major oil consumers who have to import oil. These include LDCs and MDCs. A much smaller number of countries produce oil primarily for export. Figure 6.2 illustrates both these groups. Without oil the countries of the second group would be of very limited significance on a world scale but in the last few decades they have risen to a position of great prominence; so much so that there is probably no other part of the world upon which so much economic, political, and diplomatic attention is concentrated as on that part of the world mainly responsible for oil export: the Middle East. This change of external relationships was quite sudden and produced a new economic situation with which much of the rest of the world is still attempting to grapple. In October 1973 OPEC quadrupled the price of oil from about $3 a barrel (a price that had barely changed for two decades) to about $12 a barrel and subsequent increases have taken the price to over $30 a barrel. These actions had immense implications for the rest of the world, as we shall now examine (see also Chapter 1).

(i) *Third World oil-consuming nations.* Figure 6.2 shows that many LDCs have a considerable dependence on oil for their energy needs. Out of more than 130 countries in the developing world, only five–Taiwan, India, South Korea, Zambia and Mozambique–now use more coal than oil.

Figure 6.2 Oil-importing and oil-exporting countries. (Source: Odell, 1981, p. 594)

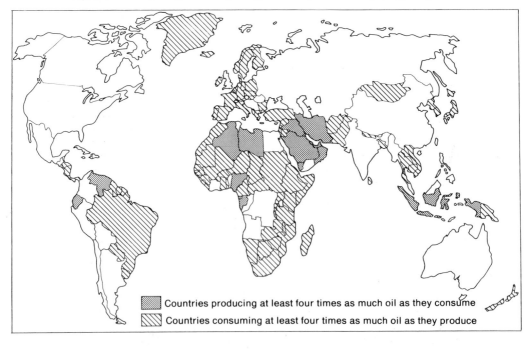

Countries producing at least four times as much oil as they consume

Countries consuming at least four times as much oil as they produce

The events of 1973 produced a decline in the already precarious economic position of the LDCs dependent upon oil. The poor oil-importing countries found that the oil producers in the Third World showed even less concern for their economic development problems than had the Western-owned oil companies that had previously supplied them. In order to buy the oil they needed so badly they had to go deeply into debt.

The disastrous impact of oil price increases was felt in other ways also. Because of the recession in the industrialized Western economies, itself largely induced by oil price rises, the demand for other primary raw materials decreased and Western economies became more protectionist. Many LDCs who depend on exporting these raw materials were faced with continued deterioration in their terms of trade, and their exports were unable to grow. At the same time, the LDCs have found it difficult to reduce their imports, many of which are necessary for development. Thus heavier and heavier loans have been necessary from the wealthy West, although the ability of the Western system to continue to supply loans at the rate required has increasingly become problematic. The ability of Third World countries to continue to repay their debts is doubtful. It has been calculated that about 40% of the earnings of the LDCs now goes to repay debts instead of being available for investment in fundamental development programmes.

(ii) *Labour migration in the Middle East.* The immense revenue made available to the Middle Eastern oil-exporting countries by their greatly enhanced profits has enabled them to develop other facets of their economies. To do this they have required additional labour, and a phenomenon common in other parts of the Third World, namely international labour migration, has grown to significant proportions in the Middle East in recent years. Table 6.3 shows the principal sources and destinations of such labour flows, and should be examined together with Figure 6.3. Countries such as Saudi Arabia, Kuwait, Bahrain, Iraq, the United Arab Emirates (UAE), Qatar, and Oman are the principal destinations for these labour movements and their oil wealth means that their per capita GNPs all exceed $4500. On the other hand, countries such as Egypt, Jordan,

Figure 6.3 The Middle East oil industry. (Sources: various, but mainly Odell, 1979, pp. 86–7). Inset shows major export routes for Middle East and African oil.

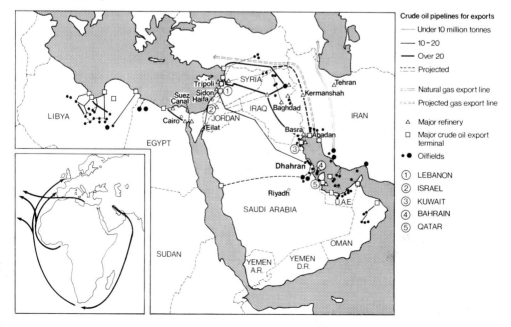

Table 6.3 Migrant workers in the Middle East. (Source: Birks & Sinclair, 1980)

Sources	Saudi Arabia	Libya	UAE	Kuwait	Oman	Iraq	Qatar	Jordan	Bahrain	Total
Egypt	95 000	229 500	12 500	37 558	4 600	7 000	2 850	5 300	1 237	395 545
Yemen A.R.	280 400	—	4 500	2 757	100	—	1 250	—	1 121	290 128
Jordan	175 000	14 150	14 500	47 653	1 600	5 000	6 000	—	614	264 517
Yemen D.R.	55 000	—	4 500	8 658	100	—	1 250	—	1 122	70 630
Syria	15 000	13 000	4 500	16 547	400	—	750	20 000	68	70 265
Lebanon	20 000	5 700	1 500	7 232	1 100	3 000	500	7 500	129	46 661
Sudan	35 000	7 000	—	873	500	200	400	—	400	44 373
Tunisia	—	38 500	14 000	49	100	—	—	—	—	52 649
Oman	17 500	—	—	3 660	—	—	1 870	—	1 383	24 413
Iraq	2 000	—	500	17 999	—	—	—	—	126	20 625
Somalia	5 000	—	1 000	247	300	—	—	—	—	6 547
Turkey	500	9 000	—	37	—	—	—	—	—	9 537
Iran	10 000	—	21 000	28 933	400	40 000[1]	4 000	—	1 982	106 315
Pakistan	15 000	4 500	100 000	11 038	32 500	5 000	16 000	—	6 680	190 718
India	15 000	500	61 500	21 475	26 000	5 000	16 000	—	8 943	154 418
Other Asian	8 000	500	2 000	1 103	200	—	2 000	—	981	14 784
Africa	10 000	500	—	107	400	—	—	—	57	11 064
Europe & America	15 000	7 000	5 000	2 028	2 800	500	846	100	4 442	37 716
Total	773 400	329 850	251 500	207 954	70 700	65 700	53 716	32 900	29 285	

Destinations

[1] Note These figures do not include migrant workers in Iran and pre-date the war between Iraq and Iran.

Syria, the Yemens, and Sudan all have per capita GNPs of less than $800. The latter group of countries also tend to have considerably larger populations than the former group.

The detailed patterns of labour flow (Table 6.3) reflect both political allegiances and spatial proximity. For example, in Saudi Arabia and Libya over 90% of the migrant workforce is Arab, but in the UAE only 24.5% is Arab and 65% is Asian. Although this pattern of labour flow appears to be mutually beneficial to both the richer sparsely populated countries and the poorer heavily populated countries, migrant labour in the Middle East, as elsewhere in the Third World, gives rise to a number of problems. In smaller countries such as Qatar and the UAE, immigrants outnumber the indigenous population and, as the number of non-Arabs grows, so too does the potential for cultural conflict. Furthermore, an excessive reliance on foreign labour prevents the development of a well-trained indigenous workforce. However, the problems for the countries exporting labour are probably more severe, as they lose their more skilled, better educated and younger males. This hampers their own prospects for economic growth. Finally, although remittances from workers overseas may be substantial (amounting to $600 million in Egypt in 1977), the available evidence suggests that little of this is invested in the productive economy. Thus the economies of the labour-exporting countries have benefited little, and inequalities within the Middle East have tended to grow.

(iii) *Geopolitical situation.* Figure 6.3 shows the main features of the Middle East oil industry in terms of producing fields, pipelines and major refineries. All students must be aware that the Middle East is one of the world's trouble spots. There are numerous ingredients in this situation, Arab–Israeli conflict being only one of them. One of the world's key areas in terms of global economic stability is located in the middle of a maelstrom of political instability, any facet of which is likely to erupt at any time.

In more local geographical terms, tensions arising from Arab–Israeli conflict have had a profound effect upon the oil industry and produced major spatial changes. For example, the initial establishment of Israel was immediately followed by the severance of pipelines that had taken oil from Iraq to Haifa. These were replaced by lines through Syria and the Lebanon where a new export terminal and a refinery were constructed at Tripoli (Figure 6.3). Examination of Figure 6.3 shows that the pipeline from Dhahran in the Persian Gulf to the Mediterranean deviated from the least-cost location, which would have taken it through Israel, via a more expensive route around the northern boundary of Israel to the port of Sidon. Possibly the most significant spatial change induced by political conflict, however, was the closure of the Suez Canal in 1967 as a result of which tanker traffic had to be completely re-routed via the Cape, although larger tankers were already using this route.

More recently, conflict in Iran, first with the Revolution and deposition of the Shah, and then with the war with Iraq, has emphasized the dangers of over reliance on the Middle East as a major source of energy, not just for the West but, as we have seen, for the developing world also. Unlike other raw material producers, the oil-producing countries have had a relatively un-interrupted demand for their product. Thus oil is a completely different primary product from copper, tin or cotton. It is only since the early 1980s that the demand for oil has ceased to rise year by year.

(b) Zambian copper

Zambia shares with a number of landlocked states in the Third World (see Figure 1.6) the problem of the transportation of a raw material upon which the national economy depends. Bolivia, Uganda, Zimbabwe and others face similar difficulties because of their geographical situation. To export their minerals or other products they must rely on the good will of other countries and attempt to secure international agreements. This is especially the case in Zambia where in 1978 copper accounted for 89% of the total foreign exchange earnings. The history of the industry and the efforts to capitalize on this resource in Zambia provide a good illustration of how external geographical factors can create problems.

(i) *Early problems*. The exploitation of Zambian copper could not occur until the railway reached the copper belt area in 1909 (Figure 6.4). This provided an outlet through Southern Rhodesia (Zimbabwe) to Beira in Mozambique. This route had many disadvantages, the most obvious being the high costs imposed by distance, not only the overland distance to Beira, but also the distance from Beira to the major markets in Europe. A second outlet was provided in 1931 with the completion of the Benguela railway from Lobito Bay in Angola, through the Katanga copper mines in the Congo (Zaire), to link with a line extending northwards through the Rhodesias. However, the full utilization of this shorter route to the west coast was prevented by the desire to secure more traffic for the Rhodesian railways. Obviously, this meant using the lines through what was then North and South Rhodesia and from there on to Beira.

(ii) *Events in the 1960s*. In 1961 the export of Zambian copper through Lobito Bay ceased entirely. One reason was that political troubles, especially in the Congo, created uncertain conditions. A further twist was added with the unilateral declaration of independence (UDI) in Southern Rhodesia in 1965, leading to an about turn. Newly independent Zambia was placed in a most difficult position: to continue to export copper through white-dominated Southern Rhodesia could be interpreted as economic support for

Figure 6.4 The Zambian copper belt and Central African railways.

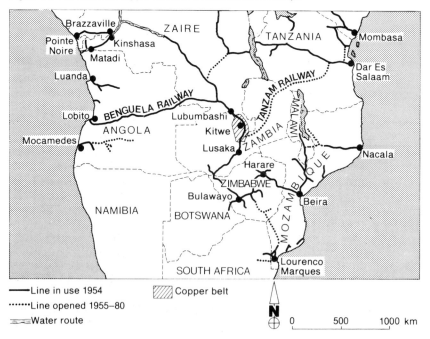

—— Line in use 1954

•••••• Line opened 1955–80

〰〰 Water route

▨ Copper belt

N

0   500   1000 km

130

that regime. Zambia was forced to seek alternative outlets, and the Benguela railway (Figure 6.4) again secured much of the Zambian copper traffic. However, civil war in the Congo (Zaire) and guerrilla activity made reliance upon this route highly risky and the Zambian Government even sought to export copper by air. Road exports via the Great North Road to Dar es Salaam gradually grew to greater significance and set the scene for a major new rail development linking Zambia and Tanzania.

(iii) *The Tanzam Railway.* This railway was to be financed largely from outside the two countries and thus brought in a further external factor: the finance and much of the labour and expertise coming from communist China. It is thus most ironic that the declaration of independence by socialist fearing whites in Southern Rhodesia should have provided the means for more direct communist involvement in Africa. In the early 1960s a railway line had been built from Dar es Salaam to the sugar-producing area of the Kilambero Valley in Tanzania and the declaration of independence by Southern Rhodesia made an extension through to Zambia seem desirable. Although part of it is in use, this rail link has not yet been completed. It is a final ironic twist for Zambia that the port facilities at Dar es Salaam have so far proved to be inadequate to cope fully with the extra traffic brought about by the line and that, with the independence of Zimbabwe, the line to Beira is open once more.

4. Internal spatial change: the geographical impact of resource exploitation

Mining activities produce distinctive geographical landscapes and create new nodes of economic activity. Thus, important spatial changes take place within countries as a result of mineral exploitation. We shall illustrate some of these changes in Chile and Zambia.

(a) *Nitrates and copper in northern Chile*

Northern Chile is characterized by an extremely inhospitable natural environment. There are places where no rain has ever been recorded and where pipelines have to be used to bring water from the wetter highlands to the east to the coast. The movement of people in this area, the establishment of towns and ports, and the laying down of transport routes are entirely due to mineral exploitation.

The main stimulus to the nitrate industry came with the discovery of its value as a fertilizer. The first nitrate field was at Tarapaca; it and other nineteenth-century fields are shown in Figure 6.5. The industry grew rapidly from the 1880s. Immigration took place from elsewhere in Chile and ports such as Iquique, Antofagasta, and Pisagua grew from literally nothing. Transport improvement was essential and several railways were built either by the nitrate companies themselves or by other investors. These routes were designed to provide the lowest-cost access from the 'oficinas' (the locations of the primary processing of the nitrates) to the ports located at the nearest points on the coast. Some parts of these routes were incorporated in a northward extension of the north–south railway, a line which almost certainly would never have extended so far north but for the presence of nitrates. In the 1920s the industry was severely affected by the rise in the manufacture of artificial fertilizers which used atmospheric nitrogen, and many of the former bustling 'oficinas' became virtually ghost towns. Chile still exports nitrates but holds only about 4% of the world market. As Figure 6.5 shows, the producing area has shrunk from about 150 sites in 1932 and is now concentrated on two sites: Maria Elena and Pedro de Valdivia.

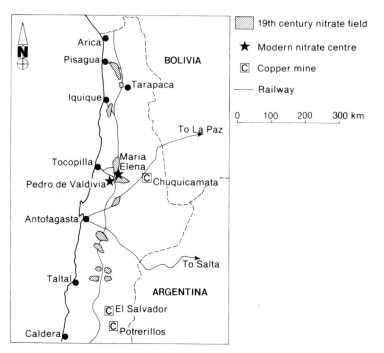

Figure 6.5   Mining in northern Chile. (Source: Odell & Preston, 1975, p. 148; Morris, 1981, p. 152)

To some extent the extraction of copper acted as a replacement industry for nitrates, although the precise location of the industry was different, the major sites being at Potrerillos and El Salvador in Atacama province, El Teniente and the huge mine at Chuquicamata in Antofagasta province. Although some population movements were set in motion by these developments, especially to Chuquicamata, now a town of 25 000 complete with smelting, refining and power production industries, their contribution to wider development was rather limited. Like the early nitrate industry, they have given rise to very few ancilliary industries either to supply the extractive processes or to assist in the marketing. Both nitrates and copper are export-orientated industries, the exploitation of which has largely been controlled from outside. Although important, they have failed to make any really fundamental contribution to development in northern Chile. Other industries, on the whole, remain absent from the region.

(b) The Zambian copper belt

The exploitation of Zambian copper has led to the development of an urbanized region in the north of the country (Figure 6.6). Except for Ndola the main towns are located near the seven copper mines. The total copper belt area contained some 750 000 inhabitants in 1970, 91 % of which lived in the eight towns (Plate 6.1). Thus, the existence of just one valuable resource has provided the basis for urban development in an otherwise thinly populated and backward region. With this have come services and infrastructure in the form of improved transport, educational facilities, hospitals and hotels, although it should be noted that the impetus for these came from the mining companies rather than from the old colonial administration in the 1930s.

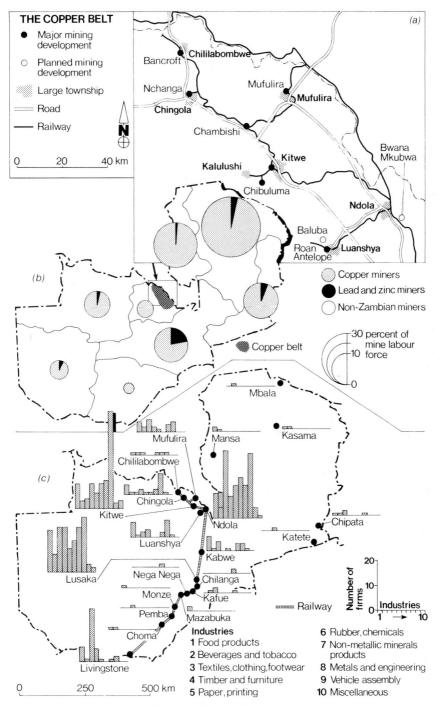

THE COPPER BELT

- ● Major mining development
- ○ Planned mining development
- ▨ Large township
- ═ Road
- ━ Railway

N

0   20   40 km

(a)

Chililabombwe
Bancroft
Nchanga
Mufulira
Mufulira
Chingola
Chambishi
Bwana Mkubwa
Kitwe
Kalulushi
Chibuluma
Ndola
Baluba
Roan Antelope   Luanshya

(b)

Copper miners
Lead and zinc miners
Non-Zambian miners

Copper belt

┌ 30 percent of mine labour
├ 10   force
└ 0

Mbala

(c)

Mufulira   Mansa   Kasama
Chililabombwe
Chingola
Kitwe
Ndola   Chipata
Luanshya   Katete
Kabwe
Lusaka
Nega Nega   Chilanga
Monze   Kafue
Pemba
Mazabuka
Choma
Livingstone

Railway

20
Number of firms   10
0   Industries
1 → 10

0   250   500 km

Industries
1 Food products
2 Beverages and tobacco
3 Textiles, clothing, footwear
4 Timber and furniture
5 Paper, printing

6 Rubber, chemicals
7 Non-metallic minerals products
8 Metals and engineering
9 Vehicle assembly
10 Miscellaneous

Figure 6.6 (*a*) Mines and towns in the Zambian copper belt. (*b*) Origins of mine workers employed in the copper belt region. (*c*) Distribution of firms in manufacturing industry. (Source: Davies, 1971, pp. 83, 93, 95)

Plate 6.1 Ndola township and industrial estate, Zambian copper belt. Zambia is not a very urbanized country but most of the modern economic development that does exist is concentrated in the towns, in a north–south belt coinciding with the copper belt in the north and extending southwards along the line of rail. Ndola is the oldest large centre and existed before the exploitation of copper when it functioned as an African trading centre and a centre of the Arab slave trade. Although not located on a copper mine, the infrastructure it already possessed made it an obvious choice for the headquarters of some of the mining companies when they began to exploit the copper belt region. The arrival of the railway in 1907 further added to Ndola's role and industry has developed quite successfully. There are copper and oil refineries and a large cement factory in the town as well as the trans-national firm shown in the photograph. (*Photograph: Compix*)

Ndola is the oldest town: it existed in the pre-mining period as an African trading centre (Plate 6.1). With the arrival of the railway in 1907 it became the commercial centre for the region and, although there is a mine in the vicinity, commerce and other manufacturing industries are significant. In the other copper belt towns, mining dominance decreases with increasing size, thus Chambishi, Kalulushi, and to some extent Chililabombwe, are exclusively mining centres. The larger towns (population about 100 000) of Mufulira, Chingola and Luanshya are primarily mining centres too but also possess manufacturing and service functions. Kitwe is the largest town on the copper belt and rivals Ndola as the regional 'capital'. Its relatively central location has attracted retail and service functions and additional manufacturing activity.

At the national level, Figure 6.6 gives a graphic impression of the remarkable concentration of modern manufacturing industry on the central axis formed by the north–south railway line, and especially the significance of the copper belt towns. Outside the copper belt, only Lusaka, and to a much lesser extent, Kabwe and Livingstone, have any significant industrial base. This contrasts fundamentally with northern Chile where the mineral extracting region is very much peripheral to the economic 'core' area of the country. However, this concentration of industry in Zambia does serve to illustrate the disparities existing between urban and rural areas, and Figure 6.6b, showing the origin of labour in the mines, indicates that labour is drawn especially from the northern rural provinces. Further south and east, much of the potential labour force has traditionally been employed in Zimbabwe and South Africa. As we have already noted in the context of international labour migration in the Middle East, this exodus of young workers is scarcely of benefit to rural areas and seems likely to hamper their development prospects (see Chapter 8). Thus, such regional concentration of modern economic activity is, in many ways, a mixed blessing for Zambia.

Conclusion: minerals and development

We have seen that many LDCs possess significant reserves of minerals yet experience problems in trying to maximize economic benefits from them. Although many LDCs have introduced special taxes to 'claw back' a fair share of returns from large mining enterprises, these sometimes introduce a climate of uncertainty and a withdrawal of investment. Perhaps more fundamental are the problems experienced in attempting to establish 'second-stage' industries associated with mineral resource exploitation, i.e. the processing of the raw material. Undoubtedly of great importance are the lack of energy resources and the capital to develop such resources in many LDCs (e.g. HEP). This greatly hinders the establishment of smelters and refineries and, together with the lack of demand from local indigenous industry, means that many LDCs export their products in a crude state and the revenue obtained per tonne is thus quite low. Value is added at each stage of the processing sequence. The value added by refining the metal ore first and subsequently exporting it is quite considerable, and the foreign exchange to be gained on export that much greater. However, the oil-producing countries are an exception. Oil-refining processes involve only a small reduction in bulk, so the crude material extracted from the earth already commands a very high price. Furthermore, demand from the MDCs is considerably higher and more constant for oil than for most of the metallic ores. There are few substitutes for oil, unlike metals. Thus countries such as Saudi Arabia and Kuwait are at a much greater comparative advantage in terms of the price they obtain for their resource than are countries such as Zambia and Jamaica which depend on metallic ores.

ASSIGNMENTS

1. (a) *Summarize the main features of Table 6.1 by describing the significance of mining and related industries and manufacturing industries in LDCs.*
   (b) *Using the data in Tables 6.1 and 1.2, examine the correlation (links) between:*
      (i) *per capita GNP and the contribution of manufacturing industry to GDP.*
      (ii) *per capita GNP and the growth rate in manufacturing industry,*
      (iii) *per capita GNP and the contribution of mining to GDP.*
      The best way to examine such links is to construct a graph, plotting the per capita GNP for each country against the other variables.
   (c) *Discuss and explain your results: do the countries with the highest per capita GNP figures have the largest manufacturing sectors and/or the most rapid rates of growth in manufacturing industry?*
   (d) *Suggest other ways in which the economic significance of mining and manufacturing to particular countries could be measured.*

2. *Carefully examine Table 6.3 and Figure 6.3.*
   (a) Construct a map to show (i) the main sources of migrant labour in the Middle East, and (ii) the main destinations.
   (b) Turn to Table 1.2 and for the countries named in Table 6.3 note their per capita GNP. Describe the relationships between national wealth and the tendency to import or export labour.

B. Manufacturing Industry

In this section we shall examine the levels and type of industrial development in the LDCs, then discuss trends in industrial location, and finally examine some problems of industrial development through case studies of Hong Kong and Nigeria.

1. Degrees and type of industrialization: diversity in the LDCs

(a) Levels of industrialization

Table 6.1 and Figure 6.7 indicate the significance of industrialization in a number of LDCs. Once again, it is apparent that there is considerable diversity. Heading the list are the so-called Newly Industrializing Countries, Brazil, Mexico, Argentina, Taiwan, Singapore and South Korea, countries where large numbers of industrial plants have been established in recent years. Many of these are large trans-national concerns, attracted by the availability of cheap, non-unionized labour. Other countries, especially in South East Asia, have shown quite high recent growth rates (Table 6.1): for example, Indonesia. A

Figure 6.7 Labour force in manufacturing industry: LDCs (Calculated from data in *World Bank Development Report, 1981*)

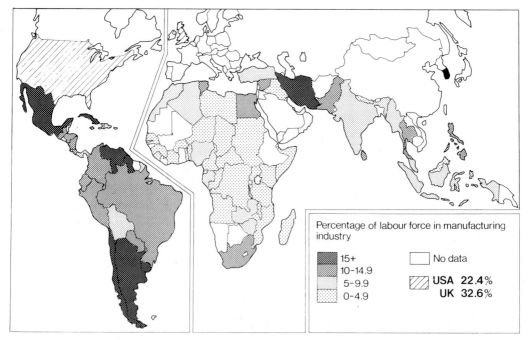

number of routine industrial functions of the assembly-line type are beginning to 'decentralize' from older industrial areas in the Pacific: the USA, Japan, and Hong Kong and other reasonably stable Asian countries have shown a marked increase in manufacturing industry as a result of such investment. Yet much of this is foreign owned. For example, it is estimated that while 90% of the electronics industry in Hong Kong is owned by local entrepreneurs, the corresponding figure for Singapore is only 20% and 50% for both Taiwan and South Korea.

However, many LDCs have less than 10% of their workforce in manufacturing industry. These include many of the smaller islands and a number of African countries. The latter, with just one or two exceptions, appear to be much less successful in attempts to industrialize than either South American or Asian countries. Nevertheless, it is clear from the data that levels of industrialization in LDCs are generally very low. As Figure 1.2 indicated, only about one-seventh of total world manufacturing takes place in the LDCs. Also, some of the large percentage growth rates shown in Table 6.1 should be treated with caution, as they represent growth from a very low starting figure.

(b) Stages of industrial growth

We may suggest a four-stage model of industrial growth in Third World countries:
Stage 1. traditional craft industries;
Stage 2. processing of primary products;
Stage 3. import substitution;
Stage 4. manufacture of capital goods and consumer durables.

(i) *Traditional craft industries.* There is a mistaken tendency to assume that industry in the LDCs is of recent origin, but many countries do have long-established craft industries, especially in textiles (Plate 6.2) and metal working. The Yoruba towns in Nigeria are a case

Plate 6.2 Mexico City: Indian woman and daughter engaged in traditional weaving. The survival of this traditional craft in a modern metropolis is largely due to the demand from tourists and wealthy residents of Mexico City, and suggests that the two sectors of the urban economy–the traditional and the modern–can co-exist quite happily. Some of the wealth created in the modern sector, and generated by tourism, is clearly spent in the 'lower circuit', enabling some employment to develop. Note, however, the employment of a young child, a characteristic feature of the 'lower circuit'. This family were migrants to Mexico City and lived in one of the many squatter areas. (*Photograph: M. Barke*)

in point. Cloth weaving, iron working, carving and leather working were all important manufacturing industries long before European contact. Here, as in other LDCs, colonial policies were disastrous for such industries. The import of cheap manufactured goods from European factories displaced many such crafts as the colonial territories came to be seen as providers of raw materials and importers of European manufactures. Some craft industries did survive, however, often in the remoter locations, and make an important contribution to the 'traditional' economy outlined in Chapter 3, Section A.

(ii) *Processing of primary products.* As many LDCs were seen as providers of raw materials for the West, it was inevitable that some processing of such raw materials should take place in the producer countries (Plate 6.3). This was especially the case when, in Latin America, a number of countries achieved independence in the nineteenth century. They naturally wished to enjoy a greater share of the benefits from their resources and the most typical development was the growth of port processing industries such as flour and sugar milling and meat packing. Inevitably, as such developments were on or near the coast, they frequently had limited relationships with the rest of the country and the economic structure, both in terms of markets and capital, was externally orientated.

(iii) *Import substitution.* The depression of the 1930s and the Second World War both had important consequences for industrialization in a number of LDCs. The reduction of imports from the MDCs helped the growth of indigenous industry especially that

Plate 6.3 Abandoned henequen factory near Mérida, Yucatan, Mexico. Henequen was a valuable crop in the eighteenth and nineteenth centuries, being used mainly for rope manufacture. The Yucatan peninsula became one of the world's leading suppliers and huge henequen plantations were set up. This gave rise to many decorticating factories where the fibre was extracted from the henequen leaves, cleaned in water and then hung out on racks to dry in the sun. These mills were located centrally in a group of fields or close to a village. In the twentieth century, demand has fallen, competitors have increased, and many of the plantations have become inefficient. The industry has declined in importance, resulting in the closure of many of the old factories. (*Photograph: G. P. O'Hare*)

requiring little capital and technology to initiate. Some new domestic industries were free from foreign competition and industries like textiles, furniture, printing and publishing, toy and hardware manufacture began to develop in a number of countries. After the Second World War, many LDCs achieved independence and, with this greater degree of control over their own destiny, many attempted more vigorous policies of industrial development. Import substitution was often a specific goal of such policies. Latin American countries were the first to adopt such measures, but Asian and African countries followed suit in the post-war years.

(iv) *Manufacture of capital goods and consumer durables.* The final stage is one of general industrialization where heavy industry has developed and provided the basis for the manufacture of items such as motor cars. However, such industries are frequently owned by foreign firms (Plate 6.1), and develop in LDCs because of cheap labour and tax concessions. For example, hourly wage rates for productive workers in the UK (1978) of 192p may be contrasted with those in South Korea, 32p; Taiwan, 30p; and Singapore, 20p. In other cases, where private capital is not forthcoming or where the dominance of trans-national corporations is felt to be undesirable, large-scale industrial development has been promoted through national planning. For example, China and India have each had a series of five-year national plans for economic development.

(c) Contrasts in types of industrial development

We have already seen that there are significant contrasts in the levels of industrial development in LDCs, and similar contrasts are apparent in industrial structure. A country such as Chad has barely any industry at all, other than a few craft manufactures, while countries such as India, Brazil and China have consciously developed basic industry: typical examples are iron and steel, heavy engineering and cement manufacture. Other countries have attempted to develop export-oriented industries, often with considerable success. The manufacture of toys, textiles and electrical goods in Hong Kong, South Korea and Taiwan are well-known examples. Elsewhere, domestic raw materials have provided the basis for industrialization. For example, Nigeria has promoted growth in cotton, vegetable oil, cocoa, food and fibre processing. Although such emphases may be recognized, it must be stressed that in countries such as India and China significant features from the earlier stages of industrial growth frequently co-exist with modern developments (see Section B3). It is unfortunate that, rather than the integration of these two aspects of manufacturing industry, a dual economy (Chapter 3, Section E) has developed, with 'traditional' activities on the one hand and more modern activities on the other. It may be said that the persistence of this dual economy, even in quite heavily industrialized countries such as Brazil and India, is one of the diagnostic features of the Third World.

2. Trends of industrial location

(a) Urban concentration

The major feature of the location of industry in the LDCs is its concentration into urban areas and, more than that, into the major cities. To quote one example, in Ghana there is a strong concentration on the three metropolitan areas of Accra-Tema, Sekondi-Takoradi and Kumasi, over 50% of Ghanaian industrial establishments being located in these three areas. What factors lie behind such concentration?

Table 6.4 Proportion of national manufacturing activity in African capitals. (Source: Mabogunje, 1980, p. 167)

City	Percentage	City	Percentage
Dakar	81	Brazzaville	33
Banjul	100	Kinshasha	30
Conakry	50	Addis Ababa	47
Freetown	75	Khartoum	60
Monrovia	100	Kampala	28
Abidjan	62	Nairobi	42
Accra	30	Dar es Salaam	62
Cotonou	67	Bukava	100
Lagos	35	Bujambura	80
Douala	50	Blantyre	73
Bangui	100	Lusaka	35
Libreville	100		

(i) *Port concentration.* Colonial influence ensured that if any industry developed it did so in locations where export was easy, i.e. in or near the major ports (Table 6.4). As the case of Ghana illustrates, even with independence, concentration on these ports has continued.

(ii) *Nature of industry.* Much industry in the LDCs is strongly linked to the market and to sources of labour because it is light industry: textiles, food and drink manufactures and light consumer goods. In comparison with capital goods industries such as chemicals and iron and steel, immediate access to the market and large centres of population tends to be much more important.

(iii) *Conservative decision making.* As so many firms in the Third World are foreign owned, decision making tends to be done from afar. To someone in New York or London, the obvious place to locate a firm in a Third World country is in the largest city; the place most likely to offer the necessary infrastructure and services. It is much more difficult to attract such firms to remoter rural areas or small towns.

These features inevitably strengthen the tendency towards urban primacy found in so many LDCs (Table 6.4; see also Chapter 9). As their populations are so poor, the market available for the goods produced by a modern factory is strictly limited and tends to be concentrated in the port and/or capital. Few LDCs can afford to build other plants elsewhere and foreign capital is even less likely to be forthcoming. Table 6.4 shows the degree of urban concentration of manufacturing industry in a number of African countries.

(b) Decentralization: problems and prospects

This concentration of economic activity into relatively few locations within a country has increasingly been recognized as undesirable. An obvious consequence is the growth of regional imbalance which in turn produces gross inequalities of services, infrastructure, and incomes. These factors encourage migration from backward areas to the centres of relatively greater economic prosperity, thus further hindering the efforts of remoter areas to begin development.

However, the realization of the long-term consequences of regional imbalance has promoted attempts to decentralize industry or to encourage its growth in locations away from the metropolitan core areas. The island of Puerto Rico provides a good example of this strategy (Figure 6.8). San Juan is the dominant centre with 20% of the island's population and 51% of the factories. For some time the Government has given attention

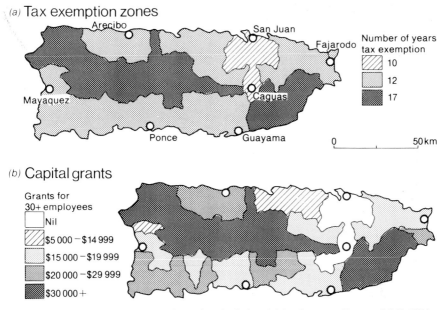

(a) Tax exemption zones

Arecibo   San Juan   Fajarodo

Number of years
tax exemption

10

12

17

Mayaquez   Caguas

Ponce   Guayama   0   50 km

(b) Capital grants

Grants for
30+ employees

Nil

$5 000 − $14 999

$15 000 − $19 999

$20 000 − $29 999

$30 000 +

Figure 6.8 Puerto Rico: Government incentives for industrial development (Source: Odell, 1974, p. 214)

to the spatial component of development and has devised a series of measures, including grants and tax exemption, to attract development to peripheral areas.

In India, industrial decentralization was strongly influenced by Gandhi, the great Indian independence leader, who had moral objections to large cities and large factories, feeling that the true Indian culture was found in the rural areas. Thus, he attempted to encourage the development of a decentralized village-based economy. This would be labour intensive rather than capital intensive and would employ the abundant labour force of rural India. In addition, the aim was to reduce transport costs by using raw materials and by selling in local markets. A campaign of support for small-scale industry thus began and has been encouraged ever since in India's five-year plans, mainly through the use of industrial estates. The number of estates designated increased from 12 in 1951 to over 700 in 1966.

Although the degree of success is limited, successive Indian governments have retained their faith in this policy of industrial decentralization. Table 6.5 shows the distribution of industrial estates in the state of Madhya Pradesh and we may use this example to test how effective the policy of industrial decentralization has been. Although estates were scheduled in 19 urban centres and 26 semi-urban throughout the state, it is only with the urban estates that work has progressed to any extent and only nine were functioning by 1967. Table 6.5 indicates that the larger places such as Indore and Gwalior were the best served, contrary to the intentions of the policy of decentralization.

Furthermore, since less than 20% of the units surveyed are based on local raw materials (indeed, many are based on imported products, especially in engineering) and selling in local markets is not characteristic (except in the case of food processing), little economy in transport costs seems likely. Finally, as the figures show, the employment generated in these industrial estates is not large and many of the production units, far from being labour intensive, use automated methods.

Table 6.5 Industrial estates in Madhya Pradesh. (Source: Brown, 1969)

Location	No. of units	No. of employees	Units engaged in				1961 population (thousands)
			General engineering	Chemicals	Electrical engineering	Other	
Indore Pologround	115	2218	68	22	10	15	395
Indore Fort	21	263	9	5	2	5	
Gwalior	45	501	27	7	4	7	301
Jabalpur	27	349	12	5	4	6	367
Bhopal	20	260	15	—	2	3	223
Ujjan	12	246	7	3	1	1	144
Raipur	14	266	5	4	1	4	140
Ratlam	3	26	2	1	—	—	87
Burhanpur	5	48	2	—	—	3	82
Total	262	4277	147	47	24	44	

Table 6.6 Industrial growth in Hong Kong. (Sources: Cheng, 1970; Chiu and So, 1983)

Year	No. of recorded factories[1]	No. of workers	Exports (mill. Hong Kong $)	Mean size of establishment (employment)
1948	1 160	61 714	No data	53.2
1953	2 131	100 902	No data	47.3
1958	3 765	168 138	1260.2	44.7
1963	7 467	302 234	3831.0	40.5
1968	11 257	458 940	8438.4	40.8
1973[2]	24 701	497 216	No data	20.1
1978	41 240	816 683	40 712	19.8

[1] Factories employing more than 15 workers only
[2] All factories in Victoria, Kowloon and Old Kowloon only

3. Problems of industrial development: case studies

In this section we shall examine two examples of industrial development in the Third World. These illustrate problems associated with different levels of industrialization, and locational trends and problems within each region.

(a) Hong Kong: problems of rapid industrialization

In many ways Hong Kong may be regarded as the 'success story' of the Third World. Yet the massive industrial and economic growth achieved in this tiny enclave in the last 30 years has not been achieved without cost, pollution, congestion, low incomes and appalling living standards for many (Plate 6.4). Nevertheless, the growth is spectacular, as Table 6.6 shows.

Plate 6.4 Chaotic land-use patterns in Hong Kong. As this photograph of Kowloon graphically illustrates, Hong Kong contains some of the most crowded communities in the world. These tenements are not just heavily sub-divided dwellings, they also contain shops and restaurants on the ground and first floors; and, more remarkably, small industrial units and workshops also proliferate, even in upper storeys, manufacturing an immense variety of commodities. The traffic generated by these business uses adds to the pedestrian and motor traffic congestion in the streets below. This is made worse by the encroachment of unofficial market stalls and street hawkers. An area such as this clearly represents a major planning problem. (*Photograph: United Nations*)

Table 6.7 Hong Kong's industrial structure, 1978 (Source: Chiu and So, 1983)

Size of firms (employment)	Manufacturing establishments (Number)	(Percentage)	Persons engaged (Number)	(Percentage)
1–9	27 205	66.0	108 066	13.2
10–49	10 751	26.0	227 239	27.8
50–99	1 918	4.7	131 733	16.1
100–499	1 225	3.0	222 827	27.3
500–1999	136	0.3	112 825	13.8
2000 and above	5	0.01	13 993	1.7
Total	41 240	100.00	816 683	100.0

(i) *Factors in industrialization.* Lacking in raw materials, fuel and power, the Hong Kong economy is based on entreprenuership and cheap labour and, although 'laissez faire' is the predominant philosophy of the Government and the people, the state has played an important part in the provision of infrastructure, especially the construction of docks, roads, reservoirs and housing. The colony was initially established as a port for the China trade, and for more than a century Hong Kong's income was derived from this *entrepôt* trade, with few manufacturing industries being present. The influx of refugees from communist China changed all this, together with the cessation of the colony's role as entrepôt for China, that country being closed for foreign trade. The refugees from the communist regime naturally included many business people as well as a labour force with a wide variety of skills. Gradually, industries began to develop in Hong Kong, initially aimed at home consumption, but many of which slowly began to look for foreign markets. Textiles formed the initial backbone of the industrial economy but other products rapidly developed.

(ii) *Nature of industry.* An important feature is the relatively small size of the industrial units (Table 6.7). Most start as family or individual enterprises and the capital normally comes from personal savings or family loans. Thus the small firm occupies a very important place in Hong Kong's industrial structure and growth. However, the environment within which many of these small firms have developed (Plate 6.4) now poses major planning problems and contrasts markedly with newer larger industrial developments (Plate 6.5) which tend to separate spatially. Many are found in Tsuen Wan and Kwun Tong new towns. Although these 'new' industrial areas have three-fifths of all industrial workers, the older areas of Victoria and Old Kowloon (Plate 1.3) still retain their vitality; the number of establishments doubled in both areas between 1968 and 1973.

(iii) *Land-use problems.* However, such growth poses considerable problems which find their principal expression in the chaotic land-use patterns within the older areas (Plate 6.4). In Victoria and Old Kowloon a complex mix of residential, industrial, commercial and institutional land-use is found. Figure 6.9 indicates something of this complexity. A major problem is the infiltration of residential land by industrial 'squatting', and the factories fail to conform to official safety regulations or ignore lease conditions (e.g. as to type of land-use). Extremely high densities result, both in factories and houses. An official survey showed that an average of only 7 m² was available for each person employed in one of these inner city areas compared with twice as much in the industrial zone of Kwun Tong new town. It is obviously highly undesirable for housing and industrial land-uses to be located in such close proximity. Many of the industries are small bakeries and noodle shops where flies and vermin abound, and in other industries there

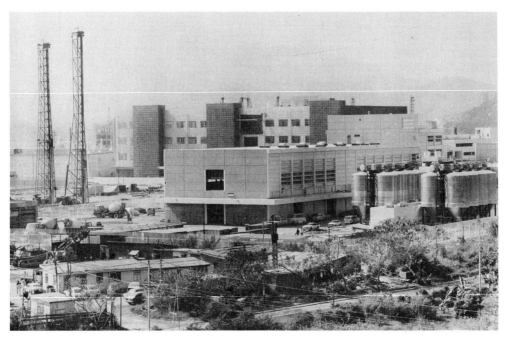

Plate 6.5 Tai Po industrial estate in Hong Kong's New Territories. This fast-developing estate covers 45 hectares and is being constructed and managed by the Hong Kong Industrial Estates Corporation, a non-profit-making body funded by government loans. Major Hong Kong and overseas companies have already taken up sites at Tai Po. Their products range from heavy machinery, automobile parts, hand tools, electronic and electrical equipment, ceramic and glaze materials, polyurethane products to food and beverages. (*Photograph: Hong Kong Government Office*)

are noise problems, fire hazards and fumes (especially from bleaching and dyeing activities).

Despite such problems it cannot be denied that these areas do make a major contribution to Hong Kong's economy. The Government is attempting to maintain the vitality of small-scale industry even in its clearance schemes. Owners of industries and workshops in squatter areas are paid compensation on clearance and some are offered premises in one of the 28 flatted factories opened by the Housing Authority. These consist of five-storey or seven-storey blocks divided into standard units of 18 or 23 m². About 10 000 such units are now in use, mostly employing about five or six workers each. The most typical industries are jewellery, glove and shoe manufacture, metalworking and plastics. Certain trades are excluded, especially those with noise, dust and fire risks.

Although many problems have obviously resulted from this very rapid expansion of industry in Hong Kong, it does indicate that rapid industrialization is possible, under the right circumstances. Yet, it must be conceded that Hong Kong's growth has owed much to chance and that the initial stimulus came from the communist revolution in China and the resultant influx of very able people who saw little place for themselves, their skills or their capital in a communist regime.

(b) Nigeria: industrial patterns at different scales

The theme of scale is a useful one for the description and analysis of industrial development. In this section we shall examine industry in Nigeria at three scales: national, regional, and local.

145

Legend:

- Residence
- Shop
- Restaurant
- Food factory
- Other factory
- Warehousing/storage
- Medical services

0   50   100 metres

N

Storage
of
refuse

Kowloon City
Alms House

Bottom map

Top map

A   B

Figure 6.9 Land-use mixing in old Kowloon. (Source: Leeming, 1977, p. 154)

(i) *The national level.* Before the Second World War, like most other colonial territories, Nigeria had scarcely any manufacturing industry. Yet the country possessed several advantages for industrial growth. There was a fairly large market and a range of mineral and power resources. Against this may be set the shortage of indigenous capital and the weak purchasing power of the majority of the population, together with a lack of experience of industrial labour and management.

Nigeria's industrial development since the 1950s has been based on two principles: the processing of goods for export, and substitution for the many imported manufactured goods. The former strategy involves the development of canning factories for fruit, mills for palm oil and groundnut oil extraction, and the establishment of cotton ginneries for producing cotton lint. Until 1958, 50% of industrial production was of this type. With independence, import substitution became a more desired aim, both to improve the balance-of-payments situation and to lead to a take-off into self-sustaining industrial growth. Nigeria has the advantage of being the largest producer and exporter of crude oil in tropical Africa. Oil exports accounted for 90% of all export earnings in 1974. Although such revenue is most welcome and helps to fund other projects, the oil industry has created very few employment opportunities in the Niger delta where the oil is extracted. The country's industrial structure is dominated by processing and consumer industries which account for about 80% of the factories, 90% of the industrial workforce and 90% of the value added. The two major consumer industries are: food, beverages and tobacco; and textiles and clothing (34% and 17% respectively of the total value added in industry). The production of capital goods such as cement, bricks, machinery and iron and steel is responsible for only about 10% of the value added. Limited capital and technology, and the small size of the national market, handicap further growth in this sector.

Figure 6.10 Distribution of industry in Nigeria. (Source: mainly White & Gleave, 1971, p. 180)

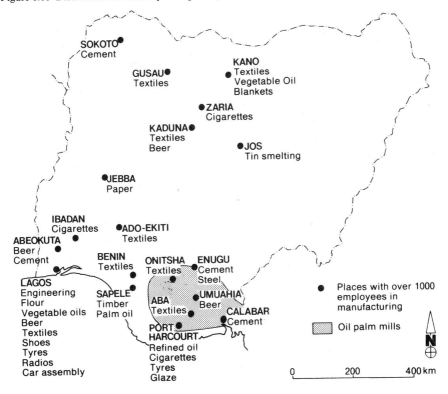

(ii) *Regional patterns*. Turning to regional patterns, as one would expect, the Lagos area contains the largest concentration of industries, although there has been significant growth in recent years in Kano, Kaduna and Zaria (Figure 6.10). Elsewhere, modern industry is limited, although craft industry thrives. As we have already noted, primary processing activities are among the first to emerge and therefore their distribution is quite widespread. In the north, groundnut oil mills are concentrated on Kano, the centre of this agricultural crop, while palm oil extraction predominates in the east. Large-scale plants have been constructed in association with palm oil plantations at Sapele and Calabar. Timber processing is an expanding activity and the African timber and plywood factory at Sapele is the largest in West Africa. Canning and bottling of local fruit and fruit juices have developed in the forest zone (Fig. 4.6) between Ibadon and Lagos while coca-processing plants are restricted to the western states. This wide range of processing industries, utilising local products, has produced a widespread distribution of processing (Fig. 6.11). However, in other industries, for example cement and brick manufacture, a widespread distribution occurs because transport costs are high for such bulky products.

A further category of industries consists of those which are essentially market orientated. Cotton textiles is the best developed such industry in Nigeria, giving rise to a variety of manufacturing processes (Figure 6.11). There are 13 ginneries scattered through the production area and these supply lint to the mills which show a more concentrated pattern. Kaduna is the main centre, with a secondary concentration at Lagos. There is a

Figure 6.11 Cotton industry in Nigeria (Source: White & Gleave, 1971, p. 184)

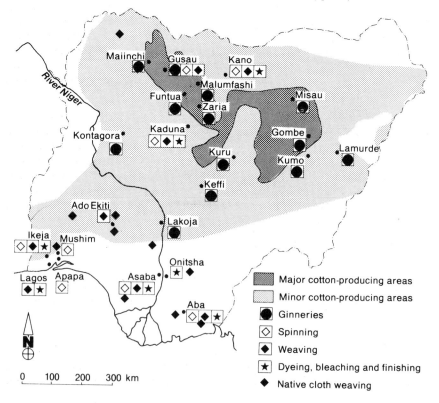

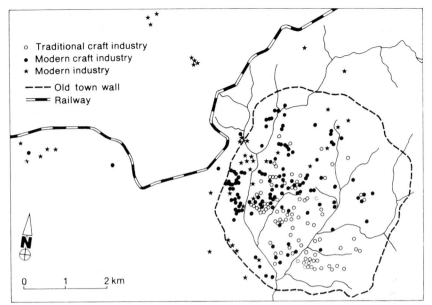

Figure 6.12 Distribution of industry in Ibadan. (Source: White & Gleave, 1971, p. 267)

small specialist weaving and finishing plant and two firms making blankets at Kano, while large integrated mills exist at Asaba, Ado Ekiti, and Aba. One factor encouraging industrial concentration is the development of linkages and this appears to be occurring in the case of the Nigerian cotton industry. Another rapidly expanding industry is tobacco manufacture; Oshogbo, Port Harcourt, Ibadan, Zaria and Ilorin all have plants and meet 80% of Nigeria's needs. To these industries we can add those that use imported raw materials: flour milling, breweries, bottle manufacture, assembly industries and chemicals all tend to be concentrated in the ports for obvious reasons.

(iii) *Industry at Ibadan.* At the local scale Figure 6.12 shows the distribution of industry in Ibadan. Traditional crafts such as spinning and weaving are carried out in compounds or on the verandahs of houses. Pottery, however, is carried on near raw material sources. Small mills, grinding maize and beans tend to be located near the food markets. In general, these traditional crafts are found within the old town walls and are more concentrated in the southern and western areas. Modern crafts are more widely scattered, and some are found outside the walls. Larger-scale industries are sited on or near the major routes in the newer parts of the city.

Conclusion

It is clear from these case studies and the earlier discussion that industrial development in the Third World faces many problems. In conclusion we can attempt to summarize some of these.

(*a*) *Problems associated with people*

(i) There is a major problem in training and equipping an adequate labour force. Considerable investment in training and education is necessary but, clearly, this is a slow

149

process and is likely to produce problems of social change and adjustment. It is extremely difficult for people from an agricultural background to adapt quickly to working in factories, as the rhythms and routine of work are entirely different.

(ii) There is a shortage of entrepreneurs, people who are prepared to take risks and initiate new developments. Despite the dramatic example of Hong Kong, over much of the Third World entrepreneurship in manufacturing industry is either lacking or is not regarded highly by the elite. Land ownership confers much more status, and money may be spent on luxury goods imported from abroad rather than on investment in indigenous industry.

(iii) The populations have limited purchasing power. Poverty is a recurrent feature of the Third World but, even more than this, inequality predominates. This concentration of wealth into relatively few hands means that the market for manufactured goods is bound to be limited, although the total populations are frequently large.

(b) Problems associated with money

(i) There is a lack of capital to invest in manufacturing industry yet modern industry requires a higher per capita investment of capital than ever before, and possibly more per worker in the Third World than in the Developed World. Capital is scarce and, as we have observed in several places, subject to competing demands.

(ii) Foreign investment has to be encouraged if there is little indigenous capital, yet, perversely, many Third World countries frighten away foreign investment. Political instability often persuades foreign investors that the risks are too great, but such investment is frequently important in the 'priming' actions, especially the all-important infrastructure–the railways, roads, port developments and airfields–which are necessary if the rest of the economy is to be developed.

(c) Problems associated with the international economy

(i) In the nineteenth century, the first industrial nations had no rivals for many of their products. Experimentation was possible, often in a rather leisured manner. The countries attempting to industrialize in the modern world face a host of competitors, both from within their own ranks and from the highly developed economies.

(ii) Because of this and because of the narrow market represented by the domestic demand, many attempts have been made to expand the potential market by creating wider economic groupings such as the Latin American Free Trade Association and the East African Common Market. Yet, frequently, the effectiveness of such groupings has been threatened or destroyed by national self-interest or political instability, as for example in East Africa.

(iii) Many of the industrial assets of Third World countries lie with their primary products but, compared with the past, and with the single exception of oil, primary products are now less significant in industrialization. The Western world now uses more synthetic products and has economized quite spectacularly on the use of basic raw materials.

(iv) Even within the Third World, automation and the global spread of advanced technology threatens even the limited proportion of the workforce who are employed in industry. For example, with the increased automation of the Venezuelan oil industry, employment is falling in the western region (Maracaibo) and consequently the Government has felt it necessary to plan the new town of El Tablazo in an attempt to diversify the industrial and employment base.

(d) *The circle of poverty*

As we have seen, it is possible to identify a wide range of problems in the industrialization of the Third World. It is clear that the vast majority of Third World countries are caught in a circle of poverty (Figure 3.1), out of which only a few such as Hong Kong and Taiwan appear capable of breaking. Low incomes mean that there is little surplus that can be saved or used for purchasing manufactured goods. This means that in the country as a whole the rate of accumulation of capital, upon which industrial investment depends, is very low. Thus, labour intensive occupations continue with low productivity and low incomes. It is only rarely that Third World countries have managed to escape from this circular process.

ASSIGNMENTS

1. *Examine Figure 6.7.*
   (a) Describe the pattern and diversity of manufacturing employment among the LDCs.
   (b) Explain the pattern and diversity in terms of: (i) general level of income (Table 1.2), (ii) the availability of energy and mineral resources, (iii) the existence of a skilled labour force and entrepreneurship, (iv) a 'good' geographical position in terms of trade with the MDCs.
2. *Study Table 6.4 and refer to a good atlas.*
   (a) Locate the cities listed.
   (b) Comment on their location within the countries concerned.
   (c) Examine the level of development of the countries using the indicator of per capita GNP (Table 1.2).
   (d) Discuss the relationship between the proportion of national manufacturing activity in the major city and the per capita GNP level of the country.
3. *Examine Figure 6.8 carefully. Imagine you are a Puerto Rican industrialist about to establish a new factory employing 50 people for the manufacture of footwear. 60% of your market is likely to be in the San Juan metropolitan area, the remaining 40% is elsewhere on the island. What factors would (a) lead you to locate in San Juan, and (b) locate elsewhere on the island?*
4. *Refer to Figure 6.9 and Plates 6.4 and 6.5.*
   (a) List the problems and advantages of industry locating in close proximity to other land-uses.
   (b) Explain why industry may need to 'decentralize' from areas like those shown in Figure 6.9 and Plate 6.4.
5. *Examine Figures 6.10, 6.11 and 4.6.*
   (a) Describe the distribution of the various industries in the different parts of Nigeria.
   (b) Account for the patterns of industrial location with respect to: (i) raw material supplies, (ii) the transport network, (iii) local, national and foreign markets, (iv) sources of power.

Key Ideas

A. Mineral Resource Exploitation

1. There is considerable diversity within the Third World in the production and export of minerals.
2. There is an important distinction between the possession of significant resources of minerals and the ability to exploit those reserves.
3. Many Third World countries are major producers of just one mineral commodity.
4. The developed nations tend to be the major consumers of minerals that are produced by the LDCs.
5. Patterns of export and import are often strongly influenced by proximity.
6. Accessibility is a major factor in the ability to exploit mineral resources.
7. Price fluctuations in the world market can render the exploitation of a mineral at a particular location uneconomic.
8. Many Third World countries have to employ 'Western' capital and expertise to exploit their resources.
9. Few Third World countries enjoy the additional economic benefits of processing and manufacturing industries related to their resource exploitation.
10. The exploitation of mineral resources has profound implications for the external geographical relationships of countries as well as producing internal spatial changes.
11. Many Third World countries depend on oil for their energy needs, and their economies have been badly damaged by the oil price increases in the 1970s.
12. Much of the world's oil supply comes from one of the most unstable regions in the Third World: the Middle East.
13. External relationships have a major influence on landlocked countries like Zambia in their attempts to exploit their resources.
14. The exploitation of valuable mineral resources can lead to settlement and transport provision in entirely inhospitable areas, although the regional economy remains entirely based on extractive industry.
15. By contrast, other industries may be attracted to mining areas if they provide the only modern infrastructure within a country.
16. Oil-exporting countries in the Third World obtain a much greater financial return from their resource than countries exporting metallic ores.

B. Manufacturing Industry

1. There are a number of rapidly industrializing countries in the Third World, but in many others manufacturing industry is insignificant.
2. It is possible to recognize a four-stage model of industrial development in Third World countries.
3. Elements from different stages often exist side by side producing a 'dual' economy.
4. Most industry in Third World countries is concentrated into urban areas and often into the largest one or two cities.
5. Many countries have attempted to decentralize industry, often with only limited success.
6. The rapid industrialization of Hong Kong owed much to the influx of entrepreneurial skills and cheap labour.
7. Major environmental problems have resulted from uncontrolled industrial development in Hong Kong.
8. Manufacturing industry in Nigeria is typical of many Third World countries, being based on the processing of primary goods for export, and the substitution of goods that were formerly imported.

9. Although craft industry is widespread, and the location of industries involved in processing raw materials is strongly influenced by the type of agriculture, modern industry is highly localized in the major urban centres.
10. Within a large city such as Ibadan, different types of industry seek different locations, influenced by factors such as labour, transport, size of enterprise.
11. In their efforts to industrialize, many LDCs face major problems owing to labour supply problems, capital shortage, and the nature of international trade.

Additional Activities

1. Using the data in Table 6.5, calculate the location quotients for the number of units in each category of industry. Use the formula below:

$$\frac{\text{Number of units in industry } I \text{ in area } X \text{ as a percentage of the regional total of units in that industry}}{\text{Number of units in area } X \text{ as a percentage of all units in that region}}$$

(For more details on the calculation of location quotients, see Bale (1981, pages 126–8, 162–3).)
For example, the location quotient for the chemical industry in Jabalpur is:

$$\frac{\dfrac{5}{47} \times 100}{\dfrac{27}{262} \times 100} = 1.03$$

A location quotient of more than 1.0 indicates that a specific type of industry is more concentrated in the city concerned than is industry generally.
Comment on your findings on the localization of industry on industrial estates in Madhya Pradesh, especially in relation to the size of towns.
2. Tabulate the land-uses in Figure 6.9 (including residential) and, for a similar 400-metre stretch of an older commercial core in a British city, plot and tabulate the ground-floor property uses. Compare and contrast (a) the number of establishments, and (b) the type of establishments.
Discuss the reasons for and against the mixing of industrial and workshop land-uses with commercial and residential uses.
3. Using Figure 6.12 calculate the mean centre of gravity of each type of industry of Ibadan. For the method of calculation see Daniel and Hopkinson (1979, pages 178–80).
Plot the centres of gravity. Compare the distributions with Figure 10.12. Comment on and account for the distribution of different types of industries in Ibadan.
4. Refer to Chapters 2, 3 and 6. Discuss the problems facing the LDCs in their attempts to industrialize, under the following headings:
(a) raw materials and power supplies,
(b) availability of capital,
(c) skills and levels of technology,
(d) dominance of the 'traditional' sector,
(e) markets at home and abroad,
(f) international control of trade.
5. From the figures in the text and from other relevant reading, give evidence for the concentration of industry into a limited number of cities in the LDCs. Make a list of the problems and dangers involved in such concentration.

7 Transport and Tourism

Introduction

The existence of an effective transport system may be viewed both as an indicator and an initiator of development. Figure 7.1 shows how the MDCs have a greater provision of roads and railways than do the LDCs. The MDCs possess just over 25% of the world's population but account for 88% of the rail traffic and 72% of the lorries and buses. Many economists believe that transport is the single most important factor in development. Without an effective transport system, exchange cannot take place, and it is exchange–of commodities, people and ideas–that allows an economy to grow. However, economic growth depends on many other factors and to isolate transport as the prime determinant may be a little simplistic. In the first part of this chapter we shall attempt to put transport in its proper perspective as a factor in economic growth.

It is clear that transport is a major agent of spatial change. Transport improvements may lead to new opportunities being created in new locations, as they improve

Figure 7.1 Density of roads and railways: world wide. (Own calculations from data in Kurian, 1979)

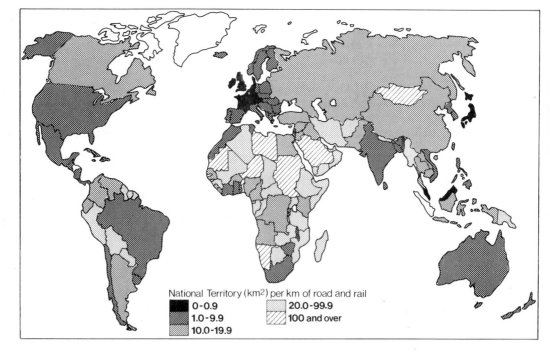

National Territory (km²) per km of road and rail

- 0-0.9
- 1.0-9.9
- 10.0-19.9
- 20.0-99.9
- 100 and over

accessibility and change the relative location of places and phenomena. Such spatial changes are not always beneficial, however, and improved transport may impose additional burdens, whether it be in the Amazon basin or in the centres of the large cities of the Third World. Although the precise role of transport in economic development and its positive or negative aspects as an agent of spatial change are the subject of debate, there can be little doubt about the role that ports play in Third World economies. As so many countries depend upon the export of a limited range of goods, the efficiency of handling such products, and the economies that can be made in dealing with them at the points of entry and exit, are vital for many LDCs.

In the third section of this chapter, we shall turn attention to the growth of tourism in some Third World countries, a feature that owes much to improved transport and accessibility at the global scale. Tourism now makes a significant contribution to the economies of a number of developing countries, and is dominant in some of the smaller ones. Many others are anxious to develop tourism as a source of additional income yet, as we shall see, the real benefits that tourism brings to Third World countries may be questioned.

A. The Role of Transport in Economic Development

1. Transport and development: an initiator, permissive or negative factor?

Table 7.1 indicates major contrasts between the LDCs and the MDCs in the possession of motor vehicles. The USA has 70 times the number of private cars and 24 times the number of commercial vehicles per 1000 population as Kenya has. Such contrasts do not mean that massive investment in transport will automatically induce economic growth. Rather they imply that transport improvements are one important feature of the overall process of development. Indeed, we can identify three possible viewpoints on the relationship between transport and development: that transport is an initiator of economic development; that it is a permissive agent which, along with several other changes, may induce economic growth; and finally that, in certain circumstances, transport may have a negative effect on development.

Table 7.1 Motor vehicles per thousand inhabitants, 1976. (Source: Kurian, 1980)

Country	Cars	Commercial Vehicles	Country	Cars	Commercial Vehicles
Nepal	0.3	0.2	Ivory Coast	19.9	12.6
Bangladesh	0.4	0.3	Angola	21.9	6.1
Chad	1.4	1.6	Mexico	41.3	15.8
Bolivia	1.6	3.2	Malaysia	42.1	14.5
Pakistan	2.7	1.3	Jamaica	55.6	14.5
Ecuador	6.3	10.0	Argentina	80.9	35.1
Egypt	6.4	1.5	Spain	148.7	30.3
Kenya	7.0	5.1	Kuwait	230.1	81.2
Philippines	8.8	6.4	United Kingdom	260.0	33.9
Mozambique	10.4	2.5	West Germany	307.5	22.0
Peru	17.6	9.2	Sweden	350.4	19.7
Iran	17.8	3.3	Australia	375.6	88.3
Zambia	18.0	13.0	USA	506.7	121.5

(a) Transport as initiator

Perhaps the clearest example of transport being used as an initiator of economic growth is to be found in communist China. On coming to power in 1949, the communists had very clear ideas about their transport policy, and especially that for the railways. The pre-war pattern of railways (Figure 7.2) was a reflection of the colonial era. The system had developed with foreign capital and initiative and largely served foreign needs, concentrating on the main points of contact with the outside world–Canton, Tsingtao, and especially Shanghai–and being limited to the eastern part of the country, especially the economic core of the centre north. Not surprisingly, in the period up to the Second World War approximately three-quarters of Chinese industry was located in the coastal regions. The new Government determined that the railways were to assist the deliberate dispersal of industry away from the 'imperialist-dominated' large cities and ports. Such dispersal was also necessary from a strategic point of view, making the country less vulnerable in wartime. Also, some means of better integrating the country was desirable and improved communications to the interior were vital. Figure 7.2 shows how these policies produced a new railway system opening up western and central areas. So important was transport considered to be that, under the first five-year plan in 1953, 13% of total investment was in railways and a further 3.8% went to the other forms of transport.

Figure 7.2 Railway network of China, 1949 and 1979.

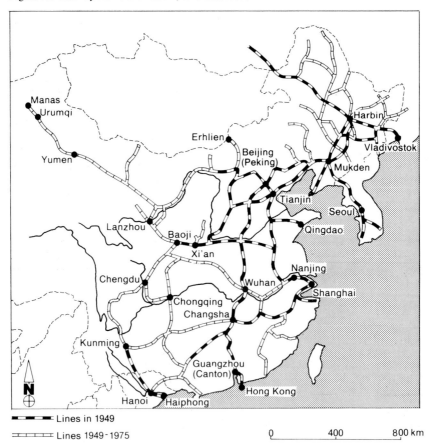

Lines in 1949

Lines 1949-1975

0   400   800 km

In the north west, the Xinjiang (Sinkiang) Friendship Line terminated at Baoji in 1949 (Figure 7.2) but has since been extended through Lanzhou to Urumqi (the capital of Zinjiang) and Manas. Both Lanzhou and Urumqi have developed as manufacturing cities, the latter having grown in population from about 60 000 in 1949 to about 300 000. It is a centre of iron and steel, cement, agricultural machinery and textile production. The railway has allowed the exploitation of the Karamay oil field, discovered in 1955, and located 300 km north west of Urumqi. Crude oil is carried by pipeline to Manas, then by rail to Yumen for refining. Thus, what was formerly one of the most isolated and backward regions of the world, with little or no economic development, has been transformed by the growth of communication linkages.

The role of transport may be equally significant in agricultural development (Figure 4.7). In an isolated community with no adequate road or rail links to the outside world there is little incentive to produce more than is required for local consumption, even if the area is ideally suited for a range of crops whose produce is in demand elsewhere. Furthermore, the production and marketing of perishable commodities such as meat, milk, fruit and vegetables depends not just on transport, but on fast transport.

(b) Transport as a permissive factor

Despite the obvious importance of transport in economic development, other authors argue that it should be regarded more as a permissive factor than an initiator. Transport by itself does not necessarily produce economic growth and other factors are of considerable importance. There has to be productive capacity or some resource base that can be exploited, and there has to be a demand or market for the products. In other words, for economic growth to take place and for transport links to be viable there must be complementarity between the area of production and the area of consumption. Regardless of the amount and quality of transport links between the two, without this complementarity there is unlikely to be much economic growth generated.

We may cite the case of Nepal to illustrate this point. Since the 1950s, transport development has had a prominent place in Nepal's development priorities (Plate 7.1), and the length of all-weather roads has increased from 88 km to 2035 km and of 'fair'-weather roads from 288 km to 1553 km. Despite this investment, the actual utilization of the road system remains very low. Many of the highways link locations that either have no commercial surplus for sale or have very limited purchasing power; others link areas with the same surplus commodity. Thus the overall benefit from this transport investment is very limited. Agricultural production showed no appreciable increase over the period 1961–74 and, although factors other than transport obviously were responsible, it is clear that the development of transport alone is not sufficient to promote economic growth. It is vital that, when new areas are opened up by improved transport, complementary investments must also be made.

(c) Transport as a negative factor

Under certain circumstances transport development may be positively harmful to an area, as again illustrated in Nepal. During the construction of the apparently impressive highway system, considerable labour which would otherwise have been employed on farms was attracted to the construction sites. In the mountainous areas where the size of farms was very small and productivity extremely low, whole families abandoned the land in favour of this new and apparently more lucrative way of earning a living. Thus population decline and land abandonment, both negative features, were an unforeseen consequence of transport improvement. Similarly, in many LDCs it has been noted that

Plate 7.1 A young Nepalese porter gazes towards the beginning of a road being built with British Government finance. The road may speed up communications in eastern Nepal but it will deprive this boy and thousands of others of a livelihood. They earn their living carrying loads on their backs between the plains in the south and the hill town of Dhankuta, making the 22-km journey by foot up a steep rocky trail. (*Photograph: Christian Aid*)

improved transport into predominantly rural areas often provides a stimulus to rural-to-urban migration (see Chapter 8). For example, in the densely populated but poor north east of Brazil, new roads built to help the movement of agricultural produce and industrial development have led instead to migration from the region to the south.

Transport development can also prove to be negative in a different way. As part of Nepal's transport programme, a new road (the Siddartha Rajmarga) was opened in 1968 leading from India northwards through Butwal and on to the town of Pokhara. Indian manufactured goods could then be transported into Nepal at less cost and their price in the local markets of Pokhara and Butwal fell below that of locally produced goods. The result has been the decline of several traditional handicraft and 'cottage' industries. Furthermore, Nepalese labour is now 'exported' to India over this improved transport route. Clearly, as far as the Nepalese economy is concerned, such transport investment has in some ways produced negative results.

2. A model of transport and economic development

In this section we shall describe a model of the historical sequence of transport and economic development and then compare it with an actual example.

(a) The model

Figure 7.3 illustrates the essential features of this idealized model. The first phase (*a*) begins with a scattering of small ports or trading posts along the coast. Each has an

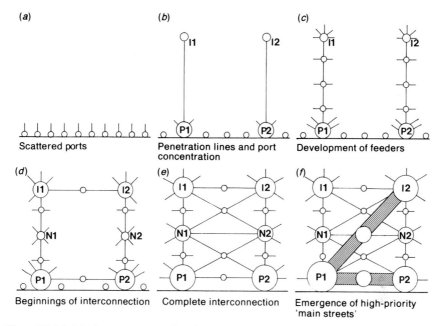

(a) Scattered ports

(b) Penetration lines and port concentration

(c) Development of feeders

(d) Beginnings of interconnection

(e) Complete interconnection

(f) Emergence of high-priority 'main streets'

Figure 7.3 Model of transport network development in the LDCs. (Source: Taaffe, Morrill & Gould, 1963.)

extremely localized hinterland from which commodities are gathered for export, and there is scarcely any interconnection between the ports. In the next phase (b), however, the interior begins to be penetrated, but only from certain points, P1 and P2 in this case. As these lines of penetration become more permanent, transport costs to P1 and P2 are reduced, and the areas served by P1 and P2 thus enlarged. Also at this stage, inland trading posts are established, I1 and I2, where commodities are gathered together and sent to their respective ports, P1 and P2. Thus, a concentration on these ports begins. Once this domination is established, 'feeder' routes begin to focus on these major ports and their interior centres (stage c). These feeder routes enable the larger ports to further enlarge their hinterlands at the expense of the smaller places and small localized 'nodes' begin to develop as trading villages along the major lines of penetration. As feeder development continues (stage d) certain of these nodes (N1 and N2) become focal points for networks of their own. In the next phase (e), the larger feeder routes begin to link up, eventually forming a completely interconnected network. Once this level is reached, the final phase (f) will soon follow and is characterized by the emergence of truly national 'main streets' or major trunk routes. Since larger places grow at the expense of smaller, the result is a set of high-priority linkages between these largest places and this, of course, adds further to their accessibility and 'centrality' and enables them to grow still further.

(b) The reality

Figure 7.4a, b illustrates some of the basic features of the development of Ghana's transport network. In 1900 numerous small scattered ports can be easily identified (Figure 7.4b), these normally being located at a European trading station or at the mouths of rivers. Penetration into the interior consisted mainly of tracks through the bush

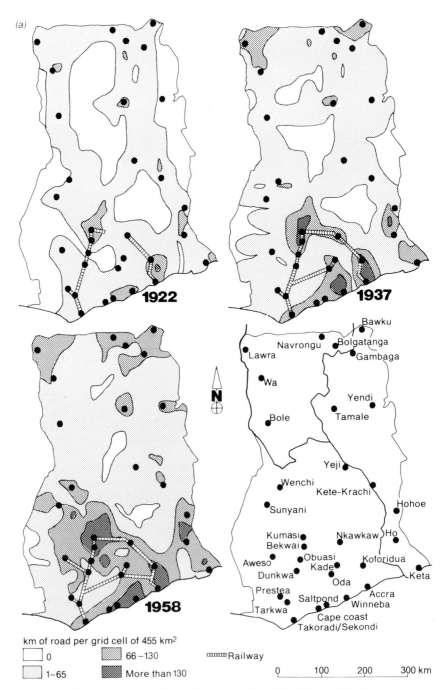

(a)

1922

1937

Bawku
Navrongu Bolgatanga
Lawra Gambaga
Wa
Yendi
Bole Tamale

Yeji
Wenchi Kete-Krachi
Sunyani Hohoe

Kumasi Nkawkaw Ho
Bekwai
Aweso Obuasi Koforidua
Kade
Dunkwa Keta
Oda
Prestea Accra
Saltpond Winneba
Tarkwa Cape coast
Takoradi/Sekondi

1958

km of road per grid cell of 455 km²

□ 0   ▨ 66–130   ⊓⊓⊓⊓ Railway
□ 1–65   ▨ More than 130

0   100   200   300 km

Figure 7.4 (*a*) Railway growth and increasing density of roads in Ghana, 1922–58. (*b*) Port concentration in Ghana, 1900–25. (Source: Taaffe, Morrill & Gould, 1963)

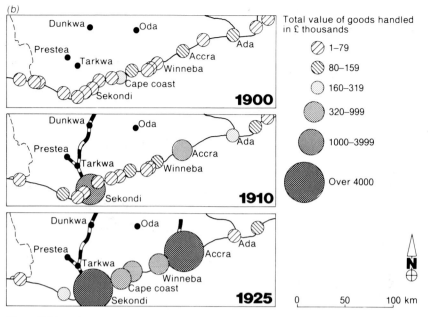

Figure 7.4 (*cont.*)

connecting the ports to very small hinterlands. The second phase of development is probably the most important and is characterized by the emergence of the first major penetration lines from the sea coast to the interior. The later phases of development typically evolve around these lines of penetration and ultimately there is a strong tendency for them to develop into the major trunk routes.

In Ghana the desire to reach Kumasi, the tribal centre of the aggressive Ashanti, was the primary motive for the development of the first penetration lines. Although the motives were not primarily economic in the first place, the port of Sekondi, from which the penetration took place, benefited immensely. This was especially so by 1910 with the building of the railway to Kumasi. Adjacent ports suffered a rapid decline in traffic. The eastern railway penetration, from Accra to Kumasi, was much slower; the gradual expansion of the cocoa-producing area to the north of Accra was the main reason for this line. Penetration north of Kumasi was entirely by road, largely because there were no minerals to provide the necessary economic incentive for further railway building.

We noted that such penetration was followed by lateral interconnection as feeder lines began to move out both from the ports and from the nodes along the penetration lines. Figure 7.4a shows the sequence of road development in Ghana from 1922 to 1958. In 1922 Ghana had just reached the stage of lateral interconnection. Linkages along the coast are apparent and interconnections are obviously more marked, the links east and west of Tamale providing a good example of links between intermediate nodes. In 1958 the network was reasonably well developed with only a few places without road links but these links were centred on relatively few locations, enabling them to emerge as significant urban centres. The concentration of trading activities on certain favoured ports as a result of these processes is clearly shown in Figure 7.4b. In summary, the model of transport development shows a reasonable fit with reality in Ghana.

1. *Use the data in Tables 7.1 and 1.2.*
    (a) *draw a graph to relate per capita GNP to (i) the number of cars per 1000 inhabitants and (ii) the number of commercial vehicles per 1000 inhabitants for the countries shown.*
    (b) *Account for the close relationship between the number of private cars and GNP, and the much poorer relationship between the number of commercial vehicles and GNP.*
    (c) *What factors apart from GNP influence the numbers of commercial vehicles?*
2. *Use a good atlas and tracing paper.*
    (a) *Trace the railway patterns in the following countries and regions: (i) Brazil, (ii) India, (iii) Africa south of the Sahara but excluding South Africa.*
    (b) *To what extent do the railway 'systems' fit the pattern shown in Figure 7.3?*
    (c) *Attempt to explain the contrasts between the three areas.*
    (d) *Comment on the usefulness of the model shown in Figure 7.3 in explaining these railway systems.*

B. Characteristics of Third World Transport Systems

Numerous obstacles prevent the development of efficient transport systems in many LDCs. This section examines transport systems under the headings of river, rail, road, air and sea, and the problems and potentialities associated with each will be discussed. It is clear that the problems are many, ranging from physical obstacles such as deserts, forests, mountains and rivers (Plates 2.1, 7.1, 7.2 and 7.3) to political ones such as the special problems of landlocked states and the existence of superimposed national boundaries that make little economic sense, and then to the purely human problems of lack of trained labour, expertise and efficiency. We must also consider the extent to which the transport

Plate 7.2 The Bosporus Bridge, Turkey. This huge bridge, built by a British firm, has considerable symbolic significance in Turkish life. It joins Europe and Asia and is regarded as a symbol of progress. It has partly replaced the many ferries which daily crossed the Bosporus with 'intercontinental' commuters, buses and lorries. The bridge and its peripheral highway system bypass the bottleneck of the old core of Istanbul and the ferry crossing of the Bosporus; the bridge itself is 6 km north of the city centre. The photograph is taken looking towards the Asian shore of the Bosporus, and passing beneath is a typical coastal trading vessel, of great importance in Turkey. The completion of the bridge has not been without controversy, and great fears have been expressed that uncontrolled urbanization could result on the Asian shore, where quite large areas of natural forest remain. (*Photograph: M. Barke*)

Plate 7.3 The Pan-American Highway in southern Colombia. Although a major achievement, the Pan-American Highway in the high Andes is scarcely comparable to major highways in Europe and North America. The difficult terrain and the inherent dangers for motor traffic are clear from the photograph. Heavy rain caused a landslide which, in turn, caused the vehicle shown to leave the road. Such difficulties are relatively commonplace. As can be seen, the highway at this point does not have a permanent tarmacadamed surface. (*Photograph: T. D. Douglas*)

systems are complementary or competitive. Unnecessary duplication of transport infrastructure is expensive and a waste of scarce resources in the LDCs. Yet, as much internal development has to be financed by external trade and as many of the major exports of the LDCs are bulky and at a low price per unit of weight (agricultural products and some minerals), it follows that transport costs are likely to make up a large proportion of the total price. Thus it is very important that transport costs be reduced to a minimum.

1. River transport

An examination of the maps of numerous LDCs may lead one to conclude that river transport offers considerable potential, being especially suitable for the transport of bulky commodities in large quantities. Many of the great rivers of the world, the Amazon, Nile, Ganges, Niger, Mekong, etc. run through Third World countries. Although some are used extensively, the obstacles posed by many others are formidable. In West Africa, for example, only in Nigeria and the Gambia are the rivers of significance for transport and in the latter country the commercial significance is reduced by the peculiar political boundaries. Many of the rivers have indirect courses, thus prolonging journey times. Many are seasonal and have a vast range of rise and fall which makes continuous navigation difficult. Finally, many have irregular courses with stretches of low gradient interrupted by rapids or waterfalls. Few are navigable for any distance from their mouths, one of the factors that delayed the exploration of the continent. Nevertheless, at a more local scale, some rivers or stretches of rivers are significant.

In South East Asia similar problems and a similar pattern of localized and seasonal use exist. The Mekong River, for example, has a course interrupted by deep gorges and rapids where the speed of the current makes navigation hazardous. Elsewhere in South East Asia, waterways are locally significant. In Thailand, timber and rice reach Bangkok primarily by water and in the wet season the only transport available over much of the Chao Phraya delta is waterborne.

In Latin America, although the continent is apparently entered quite easily along the major rivers, their role as lines of transportation is similarly localized. On the Paraná–Paraguay river system the heavy silt load makes the river suitable only for shallow draught vessels and barges. Although the main channel of the Amazon is navigable over large distances, its upper reaches and most of its tributaries have many rapids. In Colombia the river Magdalena has been used as a major transport artery, but this is in spite of its many difficulties and due also to the lack of alternatives rather than because of the suitability of the river. Its middle section is heavily braided, shallow and meanders a great deal. River ports, once relatively thriving, have been left stranded by frequent changes of course. Until 1914 the river carried virtually all Colombia's foreign trade but since then road and rail alternatives have been provided and diverted the majority of traffic away from the river.

Finally, it must be noted that many LDCs are simply devoid of rivers suitable for navigation, for example East Africa and most of the Andean countries of Latin America. Although in a localized sense water transport may be significant and even vital in a number of countries, its overall role is rather limited.

2. Rail transport

(a) General issues

Until the 1920s and 1930s, railways were virtually unchallenged as the principal transport medium involved in economic development. However, Table 7.2 indicates the advantages of modern freight transport by road. Delays are likely to inhibit the use of railways and are a major factor in the advance of road transport in many LDCs.

Although the rail delays indicated in Table 7.2 are a negative feature, railways do have a comparative advantage over road transport in moving large volumes of heavy traffic at low cost (Table 7.3), while road transport competes more effectively in higher value commodities and perishables.

Table 7.2 Average time by rail and road between Bombay and other destinations (freight traffic). (Source: Owen, 1968)

Centre	Average no. of hours by		Centre	Average no. of hours by	
	rail	road		rail	road
Poona	48	8	Calcutta	216	180
Baroda	72	45	Satara[1]	144	15
Ahmedabad	72	65	Sangli[1]	168	24
Nagpur	96	55	Indore[1]	192	50
Hyderabad	120	65	Bangalore[1]	192	50
Madras	192	80	Mysore[1]	240	60
Delhi	192	150			

[1] Including transhipment at change of rail gauge

Table 7.3 Comparative costs of road and rail haulage in India (rupees per tonne). (Source: Owen, 1968)

Distance (km)	Railways		Road	
	Bulk commodities	Light merchandise	13-tonne tractor and trailer	8-tonne truck
50	6.5	14.9	5.7	9.8
100	7.3	16.0	9.7	17.1
150	8.2	17.2	13.3	23.2
200	9.0	18.3	16.6	29.6
250	9.8	19.5	19.9	35.3
300	10.6	20.7	22.6	42.2
400	12.4	23.0	29.8	55.8
500	13.9	25.3	37.1	69.4

Not all railway systems are inefficient but most are elderly and reveal many of the drawbacks of their initial construction. In West Africa, railways were often constructed hurriedly through little-known territory, with military and political considerations paramount. The land was often difficult to survey and consequently many lines have severe gradients and excessive curvature, and many routes were badly located for economic development. To add to these difficulties, operating costs are frequently very high. The maintenance of track, embankments and cuttings is very expensive but vital where, for example, rainfall causes frequent landslips and washouts. Many of the railways penetrating inland from the West African coast have unproductive 'middle belts' where population density is low and very little traffic is generated, as on the Lagos–Nguru railway (Figure 4.6) between Oshogbo (291 km from Lagos) and Zaria (987 km from Lagos). Furthermore, most of the routes in West Africa were independent lines of penetration from the coast to the interior, so nothing like an integrated rail network has emerged.

Many railways in the LDCs were initiated with quite specific objectives in mind. For example, the early railway system in Malaya was created to serve the needs of the tin mining industry. Similarly, in Latin America most of the railways feed specific ports. In the nineteenth century the lack of an integrated system did not appear too severe a handicap since most of the lines were oriented towards export but, more recently, the inadequacy of these earlier transport routes has frustrated attempts at national integration.

New rail investment has taken place, however, and the stimulus is often the exploitation of specific and frequently isolated resources. For example, in Brazil a 970-km line is to lead from the Sierra dos Carajas iron ore deposits to Itaqui near São Luis in the north east. A line built for similar purposes but which also demonstrates the role of 'superimposed' political boundaries is the railway linking Nouadhibou to Zouerate in Mauritania. The line takes a large loop to the south to remain in Mauritanian territory. In many places major construction problems were met, particularly in stabilizing the sand dunes and building embankments and cuttings. Near Nouadhibou a 1900-metre tunnel had to be built through a granite escarpment at a cost of £3 million. Because of the length of the desert crossing (16 hours), the number of trains is kept to a minimum, another factor detracting from the profitability of the line. Sand abrasion and the weight of the trains put considerable wear and tear on the track so that maintenance costs are high. Because of the absence of any economic activity in the area crossed by the line, the only freight is the iron ore and mining company supplies.

It is only in the special circumstances of a highly valued mineral deposit that such developments are likely to proceed. It is virtually certain that most Third World countries will never develop a fully integrated rail network, but will remain characterized by relatively few isolated lines, used mainly for mineral traffic or agricultural export. East Africa illustrates this.

(b) Railways in East Africa

Figure 7.5 shows the principal railway lines of East Africa. The first line dates from 1893, leading inland from Tanga. Other important lines at this early stage were the Uganda railway from Mombasa to Kisumu, opened in 1902, and the Tanzanian Central line (built between 1905 and 1914). The former saw a branch built to Kampala in 1931. The period after the Second World War marked a second stage. The Southern Province line and the Mpanda branch in Tanzania, and the Western Uganda extension are the main developments (Figure 7.5). In addition a new link between the Tanga and Central lines was opened in 1963.

The earliest lines had a considerable effect on the areas they served. The Mombasa–Kisumu line was vital in the development of a commercial economy in Uganda and stimulated settlement and economic growth in the White Highlands of Kenya. The distribution of commercial agriculture in Kenya is still closely related to the railway and Nairobi itself had its origin as a rail camp. The Central line in Tanzania was less

Figure 7.5 East Africa: main railways, ports and hinterlands. (Source: Hoyle & Hilling, 1970, p. 241)

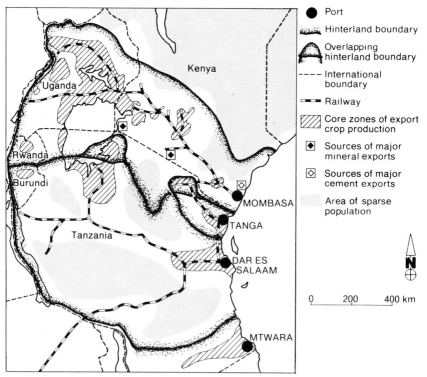

successful, as much of the trade was in seasonal products, and an irregular pattern developed. The line was built by German colonists, primarily for political reasons, and operated at a loss for many years. Similarly the Southern Province line in Tanzania was built partly because of political factors. It was part of the ill-fated East African Groundnut Scheme and extended from the newly developed deep-water port at Mtwara to Nachingwea. The line was an almost complete failure, especially after the collapse of the groundnut scheme, and between 1954 and 1961 lost £1.7 million. The Mpanda line was a similar failure, built for a specific purpose (to exploit a lead deposit) which turned out to be less productive than originally thought. For most of its length the line passes through uninhabited country infested with tsetse fly and has had little impact on this area. The Western Uganda extension to the coppermine at Kilembe was rather more successful in the short term but as copper reserves have dwindled it must draw traffic from other sources to remain viable. Yet its impact so far in this respect is disappointing. For 96 km west of Kampala it passes through quite densely populated fertile country and carries some agricultural products, but further west is an area of low and unreliable rainfall where even grazing is hampered by tsetse fly. Once again the railway's impact has been very limited.

In East Africa there is a clear contrast between the economic success of the early railways and the very limited achievements of the lines built more recently. The railways built before 1930 opened up the country in a way that is now impossible as competitive forms of transport are widespread and more flexible.

3. Road transport

(a) General issues

As we have seen, railways are geared primarily to export and only stimulate development at limited locations along their lengths. Road transport is much more flexible and capable of serving local needs. The road transport industry also has scope for considerable small-scale entrepreneurship, unlike other forms of transport. Road traffic has seen a major growth in the last few decades (Plate 7.3), in many countries resulting from the colonization of new agricultural areas.

Many roads in the LDCs are not useable in all weathers. This is especially so in tropical Africa where most of the roads are seasonal and even the main trunk roads are subject to frequent floods and landslips (Plate 2.1). Thus, roads can be costly to build and even more costly to maintain. Time-consuming ferries can also interrupt road transport. To achieve a fully efficient transport system it is important that road and rail should be integrated to ensure complementarity between the two systems, with railways taking longer-distance bulk loads, and road transport catering for local traffic and smaller, fragile or perishable commodities.

(b) Roads in Latin America

In recent years Latin America has witnessed some quite spectacular highway proposals. Figure 7.6 shows the routes of three such proposals, the Pan-American Highway, the Trans-Amazonica, and the Carretera Marginal de las Selva. The idea of a Pan-American Highway was first proposed in 1923, the idea being to try and promote closer economic ties between Latin American countries. The road extends 45 648 km from Cuidad Juarez

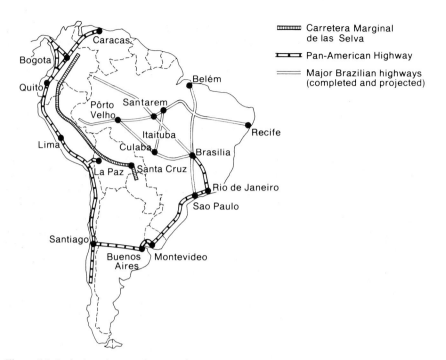

Figure 7.6 Latin American road proposals.

in north Mexico to Chile and Brazil and, apart from a section between Panama and Colombia, is now complete (Plate 7.3). Most of the route forms part of each country's main road network. However, the best-maintained sections tend to link the productive areas within individual countries. For example, in Colombia the link between the three largest cities has been paved while the section south of Popayan, running through much poorer areas, remains unsurfaced. Political factors delayed progress on some sections of the route: for example, between Arequipa and La Paz the route partly duplicates the Southern Railway of Peru and the La Paz–Guaqui railway in Bolivia. The Peruvian rail company fought against improvement of the road and the granting of lorry permits as this would obviously affect their competitive position, especially as the rail traffic had to be shipped across Lake Titicaca in Bolivia. Despite these, and other, difficulties, the road is a relative success and together with the growth of intercontinental trade groupings has stimulated more international commerce in Latin America.

The Carretera Marginal de las Selva provides a considerable contrast. The road was proposed in the 1960s and was intended to run 5500 km along the eastern side of the Andes through Colombia, Ecuador, Peru and Bolivia to Paraguay. Rather than linking already productive areas the road was intended to stimulate the colonization of relatively uninhabited territory. It was projected that the population in the zone of influence of the road would increase from 150 000 to 1 500 000 and that the addition to the national cultivated area would range from 5% in Colombia to 12% in Bolivia. It is significant that the only major stretch to be completed is in Bolivia where two productive areas around the towns of Cochabamba and Santa Cruz have been linked. Elsewhere the direct stimulus appears to be lacking, and there is reluctance to initiate the highway through completely virgin territory. It is doubtful if the construction of the road by itself would effect much improvement. Only as part of a carefully integrated and wider development programme, including health, education and agricultural advisory centres, could the scheme hope for success. Even then it may be questioned whether the road is correctly oriented. The colonizers of tropical lands to the east of the Andes would surely derive greater benefits from trade with the highland area, with its greater population and different products, than from trade with each other.

Finally, the Trans-Amazonica is typical of a number of spectacular road schemes proposed and developed in Brazil (the Belem–Brasilia road is an early example, completed in the 1950s and leading to land colonization and rapid population growth in its vicinity). The Trans-Amazonica, proposed in 1970 and now almost complete, runs for 3500 km from Recife through Itaituba and on to the Bolivian frontier. The major reasoning behind the road was to relieve overpopulation in north east Brazil. Although large numbers of people have moved west from north east Brazil, much of tropical Amazonia has land of low fertility and the road is not accompanied by the necessary network of feeder roads to nearby settlements which would help the marketing of bulky products. Thus, agriculture remains at little more than subsistence level. As the road progressed, the plan was for blocks of land to be opened up by settlements of from 48 to 64 colonist families, each with a 100 hectare lot. Higher-order centres were to be established also, with populations of 1500–3000. In reality, the land has rarely been cleared owing to lack of suitable machinery and labour. Instead of this settled cultivation the colonists practise shifting cultivation, using only about 10 hectares. Fertilizers are not used and animals are not incorporated into the system.

More recently, small farmer colonization has received less attention and the Government has shifted the focus of economic development in the region to mining and large-scale ranching. Quite apart from the disappointed hopes of colonization, a further set of problems relate to the impact of the highway on the indigenous Indian population of the area. The creation of new communications has brought them into contact with 'civilization' for the first time, and for them it has been a largely unpleasant experience. Colonization and clearance has taken place without regard to traditional Indian economic practices, whether agriculture or hunting and gathering. Disease has spread, owing to lack of immunity, and alcohol has ruined many people. For the Amazon Indian the Trans-Amazonica and its associated schemes probably spell extinction.

4. Air transport

Air transport is extremely expensive in terms of the infrastructure it requires and is thus beyond the means of many LDCs, yet often they are well suited for it. Competitive forms of transport are often poorly developed and subject to physical or seasonal limitations. Many countries are large with population and activity scattered into clustered 'islands' of development, separated by relatively empty areas. Against this, many export commodities are bulky and not well suited to air transport. Most LDCs possess a national airline, although often for prestige rather than economic reasons, and the proportion of the national population who benefit is minimal.

Air transport plays its biggest role in countries such as Fiji and the Philippines which consist of scattered islands. Passenger and freight traffic by air is of considerable importance in maintaining national cohesion. 99% of all visitors to the Fiji group now arrive by air (see Table 7.4) and, in Melanesia, more than 90% of the passenger services to and from the islands since the Second World War have been in the form of air services. Between 1959 and 1969 the number of smaller airfields has increased considerably and these act as feeders to the main routes.

Table 7.4 Air fares and origin of visitors to Fiji Islands, 1977. (Source: Varley, 1978, p. 90)

(a) Air fares   (b) Visitors' origins

Town flown from	Total fare (US $)	US cents per kilometre		Number	Percentage of total
San Francisco	630	7.03	USA &		
Vancouver	615	6.50	Canada	39 456	23.4
Toronto	731	5.82			
New York	772	5.89	Australia	66 591	39.5
Honolulu	508	9.95			
Sydney	258	8.13	New		
Melbourne	317	8.18	Zealand	37 601	22.3
Auckland	164	7.58			
Wellington	200	7.59	Elsewhere	25 017	14.8
Singapore	690	8.11			
Hong Kong	1049	9.94			
Tokyo	862	10.43			
New York–London	387	6.96			
New York–Antigua	192	6.70	Total	168 665	100.0

Note. The population of Fiji is estimated at about 573 000 (1975)

In general, the significance of air transport tends to depend on the absence of other competitive forms of transport, the size of the country, and its geographical configuration.

5. Ports and sea transport

(a) Factors influencing port development

The provision of adequate port facilities is, like the provision of adequate transport, a major condition for economic growth. The efficiency of ports relates to several factors. Among the most obvious are the actual capacity of the port in relation to its traffic and its speed and efficiency in dealing with this traffic. However, external factors are also important.

(i) The nature of the hinterland is a major influence on the size and significance of the port. Many hinterlands have been profoundly affected by the arbitrary division of territories into political divisions; this is especially the case in Africa. Transport developed to serve the needs of these 'artificial' political units rather than the natural trading areas or hinterlands. A clear example of this is the port of Freetown in Sierra Leone. No other harbour in West Africa has such natural advantages. Instead of the normal coastal features of heavy surf and shallow muddy creeks, Freetown is a deep-water inlet, with the deepest part of the harbour close to land. Despite such unique advantages, the port remains under-utilized, partly because of the small size and relative underdevelopment of Sierra Leone but mainly because the boundaries of Sierra Leone provide an artificially small hinterland for the port of Freetown.

(ii) The capacity of a port is ultimately related to the capacity of the transport network serving it. Thus, the size and facilities of the port must be planned in relation to other aspects of the infrastructure. There is little point in building a large port with many berths and modern facilities if the transport links to the interior are inadequate.

(iii) Keeping abreast of technological development poses a major problem for Third World countries, yet there have been significant developments in the technology of shipping and cargo handling in recent decades. The size of bulk carriers has increased and this creates problems for poor countries in coping with such vessels.

It is obvious that many local factors can influence the viability and success of seaports. We shall now illustrate some of these factors in the context of East Africa.

(b) East African seaports

East Africa has four main seaports: Mombasa, Tanga, Dar es Salaam and Mtwara. These four have emerged in the twentieth century while several formerly important ones have faded into obscurity. Environmental factors have played a part in the evolution of the port pattern. From medieval times East Africa was easily incorporated into the Indian Ocean trading system because of the monsoon winds (Figure 7.7), but in the era of the sailing ships, Pangani, Bagamayo, Mikindani and Kilwa were important ports as they possessed sheltered anchorages from both monsoons and were easily defensible sites. Among the modern ports, only Mombasa and Zanzibar were important. The latter port grew to prominence in the nineteenth century. Its central location on the East African sea coast, its good supply of fresh water, and the commercial skill and strength of its merchants were its main advantages. On a global scale, however, East Africa, was a relative backwater and remained so until the opening of the Suez Canal in 1869 when several ports were brought back into major commercial activity. However, the development of the railways and the emergence of larger ships signalled the relative decline of

Figure 7.7 East African seaport hierarchies, 1500, 1850 and 1960. (Source: Hoyle & Hilling, 1970, p. 233)

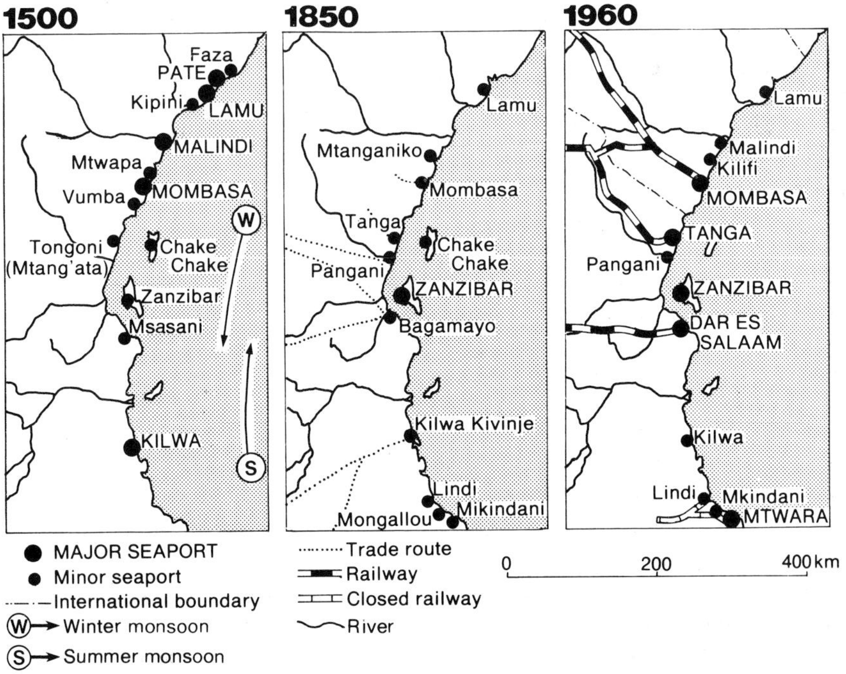

Zanzibar in favour of ports with deep water and more direct access to the interior. Dar es Salaam took the place of Bagomoyo, Tanga replaced Pangani and fifty years later, Mtwara replaced Mikindani and Lindi. The colonial era produced changes that were especially favourable to Mombasa. Although the immediate hinterland of the port was unpromising, European settlement and economic development in the Kenyan highlands greatly stimulated the growth of the port, especially after the completion of the railway. A wide variety of exports and imported goods passed through the port. More recently, Dar es Salaam has received stimulus through the links established between Tanzania and the landlocked state of Zambia (Figure 7.5). Zambian copper exports and the import of more oil have necessitated further growth in the physical capacity of the port of Dar es Salaam.

Conclusion

A fundamental objective in the LDCs should be complementarity in their transport systems. In many cases this is lacking. For example, in Colombia, the Magdalena river was the major route to the interior and to the capital, Bogotá (via Honda), for many years. Feeder railways were built to give access to the river from the mountains and in 1950 a World Bank mission recommended the building of a railway along the Magdalena Valley, linking these feeder routes and providing an outlet along the valley to the Caribbean at Santa Marta. The whole line was officially opened in 1963 but at the same time Bogotá and Medellín were linked by road to the Caribbean, not along the valley but along the mountain ranges on either side. The newly built railway has found it impossible to compete effectively with road transport and illustrates the all too frequent lack of co-ordination in the field of transport in the Third World.

Transport investment in the LDCs is frequently on a massive scale and, as we have seen, may involve spectacular projects (Plate 7.2). Institutions such as the World Bank also make major contributions to transport investment. While there are many achievements in transport planning and transport policy in the LDCs, the motives behind transport improvement are often open to question. The spectacular Brazilian road-building programme owes as much to the political desire to occupy the national territory as any realistic attempt to integrate it economically. Similarly, the Malaysian Government is attempting to give a major stimulus to Port Kelang (formerly Port Swettenham) primarily for political motives. Now that Singapore is independent they wish to challenge its supremacy and develop their own international port.

Thus, as in so many aspects of Third World development, the growth and improvement of transport facilities is not the straightforward matter that it may, at first sight, appear to be.

ASSIGNMENTS

1. Examine the patterns of railway expansion and port concentration shown in Figure 7.5. To what extent do they conform to the model shown in Figure 7.3, and to the example of Ghana?

2. (a) Describe the economic character of each of the hinterlands of the four East African ports shown in Figure 7.5.

(b) Examine the role that transport (especially railways) has played in the development of these hinterlands.

(c) Comment on the likely future prospects of the four ports.

172

C. Tourism

1. Transport and tourism

The development of tourism is a marked feature of recent change in the LDCs, and one with wide ramifications. It is a development that, more than anything else, is due to the transport innovations of the mid-twentieth century, especially air traffic growth. Furthermore, although various elements in the physical environment are important in the location of the tourist industry (e.g. climate, the sea, beaches, beautiful and spectacular scenery), it is as fundamentally affected by the transportation system and accessibility as other forms of economic activity. However, the relationship is a two-way one, for the demands of the tourist industry and the hopes of attracting increased traffic provide a major incentive for airport improvement, road building and the provision of berths for ships. For example, there is little doubt that the development of Fiji's tourist industry has been allowed through the expansion of air services. The number of visitors increased from about 15 000 in 1961 to about 200 000 in the mid 1970s, although it has subsequently dropped a little from this peak. Table 7.4 shows the main air fares and origins of tourists and it must be noted that the vast majority of tourists fly in on foreign airlines. The cost of air fares helps to explain why Australia and New Zealand supply most visitors. Although the introduction of new air services would undoubtedly help the tourist industry, it is difficult for Fiji to promote such services. In 1975 Singapore Airlines wished to open a service to Fiji and were granted traffic rights by the Fijian government. However, for the route to be fully viable, Singapore Airlines wished to continue the flight to Auckland. Unfortunately, the New Zealand government refused permission. Thus, it can be seen that small countries such as Fiji depend largely on the policies of foreign governments and airlines for the growth of their tourist industry. In addition, the Fijian government can do little to influence fares from abroad to Fiji and, on the whole, fares within the South Pacific region tend to be higher than elsewhere. Many other small and poor countries, for whom tourism offers significant potential for development, face similar external obstacles in attempting fully to realize this potential.

2. The significance and impact of tourism

In many LDCs and MDCs, tourist receipts are now the biggest single item of world trade. During the 1950s the rising incomes of the MDCs and the falling real costs of transport encouraged the growth of international tourism. Although the LDCs' share of this tourist traffic remains small, its contribution has to be seen against the rest of these nations' economies. Many governments are anxious to encourage further growth. Tourist expenditure can be widespread, including spending on internal transport, accommodation, restaurants, and general shopping. Tourism is also a labour-intensive industry, and its role in creating employment is held to be important. Such employment is not limited to work in hotels and restaurants but also includes guides (both official and unofficial), transport, street vending and various forms of entertainment. Furthermore, tourism is frequently perceived by local people as the only way of improving their incomes and quality of life.

Figure 7.8 gives a measure of the distribution and significance of tourism in the LDCs. Between 1962 and the mid 1970s the number of annual tourist arrivals in LDCs increased from 6 million to over 30 million. However, tourism is concentrated into specific areas such as the Caribbean Islands, Mexico and some parts of the Pacific. Even within such countries, the major tourist areas are extremely localized, and a distinction may be made between 'sunlust' tourism (and tourists), primarily oriented towards hot climates and

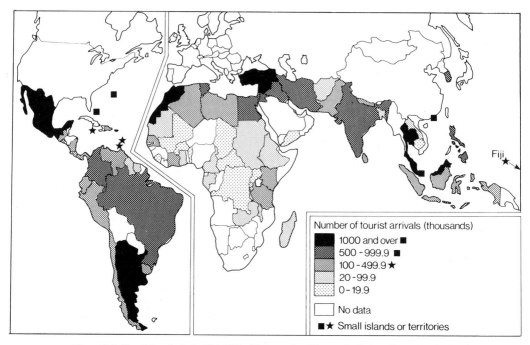

Figure 7.8 Tourist arrivals in Third World countries. (Own calculations from data in Kurian, 1979)

sandy beaches, and 'wanderlust' tourism, where the emphasis is on experiencing a 'different' culture. Most of the destinations of the former are, as one would expect, coastal but, in the latter case, interior areas of specific interest also play a tourist role. For example, the game parks of East Africa, or the archaeological sites of Central America (Plate 7.4). However, these tend to be of much less significance than the coastal areas. In Mexico, the economy has an annual contribution of $2 billion from tourism yet the vast proportion of this is generated from the 'tourist ghettos' of Tijuana, Acapulco and Cancun.

Apart from this concentration on specific locations, and the consequent limited spread of benefits for the country in general, the full economic potential of tourism may not be realized in a number of other ways. To the tourist, the relevant cost of the holiday is the total price, including travel to and from the destination, but this travel element is likely to accrue, not to the receiving country, but to the foreign carriers. In the case of most LDCs that are tourist destinations, this is likely to be a substantial proportion of the total tourist revenue because of their relative isolation from the higher-income tourist-generating MDCs. In some package tours, travel costs may amount to over 60% of the package. Furthermore, a substantial proportion of the total tourist trade in some LDCs, especially in island areas in the Pacific and Caribbean, is 'call-in' trade from cruise liners. The revenue accruing to a LDC from this kind of tourist traffic is likely to be only a fragment of the total revenue expended, the vast majority going to the cruise organizers and their affiliates.

The realization that only a fraction of the potential revenue from tourism was benefiting the LDCs has prompted some of them into more formal tourist planning, as the case of Mexico illustrates.

174

Plate 7.4 The archaeological site of Chichen Itza, Yucatan, Mexico. The Yucatan peninsula was the homeland of the Mayan Indians who achieved a sophisticated civilization long before the Spanish conquest of Mexico and who were noted for their artistic achievements. In the tenth century the Mayas were conquered by the Toltecs who founded their capital at Chichen Itza where they built magnificent monuments in a style derived partly from their own culture and partly from Mayan influences. The site is dominated by the great pyramid, dedicated to the 'plumed serpent', Quetzalcoatl. Chichen Itza is also famous for its 'cenote', a natural well about 30 metres deep in which human sacrifices were made in times of drought. The site also contains the famous Ball Court where a sacred game was played, after which the winner was put to death! Chichen Itza lies half way between Mérida and the new resort of Cancun, and is one of the most visited archaeological sites in Mexico. (*Photograph: G. P. O'Hare*)

3. Tourism planning in Mexico

Until recently, tourism was not planned in Mexico but since 1969 all new tourist developments have taken place under the control of FONATUR (Fondo Nacional de Fomento al Turismo). One of the first projects planned by FONATUR was the development of Cancun as a major tourist resort. The intention was to locate the resort next to an area of rural poverty, and to use the development as an instrument of regional growth, with new agricultural, industrial and handicraft activities in the zone. When construction began in 1971, only 200 people inhabited the site and much of the adjacent territory was thinly populated (Plate 4.1). Construction workers were soon attracted, nearly 75% originating in the Yucatan peninsula, and by 1975 over 7000 jobs had been created. Other important local developments have been in agriculture and related activities. A large modern poultry farm has been established at Ejido Bonfil, just outside Cancun. Formerly, poultry keeping was a backyard subsistence activity but Cancun's hotels and restaurants have stimulated this commercial development. Similar projects are under way in fishing and cattle raising. However, rapid inflation, a feature found in other tourist regions, has led to Cancun and the whole state of Quintana Roo being declared a duty-free zone. The site of Cancun was selected largely because of the ease of promotion as a 'typical' Caribbean beach resort and environment.

Cancun represents a deliberate attempt to channel tourists to new locations in Mexico. The airport has been planned to take international air connections and it was projected that by the 1980s the Yucatan peninsula, which attracted only about 4% of Mexico's tourists in the early 1970s, would attract over 25%. Cancun is intended to be the major destination for these people.

4. Tourism in Fiji

Tourism is now Fiji's second most important industry, after sugar. However, the industry is not dispersed (Figure 7.9). More than 90% of the tourists arrive by air and so the industry is tied by the transport network to the airport–hotel axis. Few visitors are adventurous enough to explore very far by themselves, a feature recurring in other tourist areas. The hotels and other tourist facilities are overwhelmingly concentrated near Nadi Airport, in Suva city and the 'coral coast' in south west Viti Levu. Over 90% of the tourist accommodation is in these areas, and in two of them, the 'coral coast' and the Nadi–Lautoka area, tourist accommodation grew by 25% and 40% respectively in the 1968–76 period. Hotels employ over 3000 people and it may be that in various other tourist-related services at least double that number are employed.

However, tourism does have an adverse effect on other sectors of the economy. For example, it competes with agriculture for land and labour, and it is significant that sugar output has dropped by 25% in Fiji as a whole and by 33% in the 'coral coast' area. Although the availability of jobs in tourism cannot be blamed entirely for this, many of the other sources of employment that have grown–road building and maintenance, taxi-driving, etc.–have absorbed labour from the land and are related, if in a loose way, to tourist development. A further consequence has been the rapid inflation of land values with the tourist boom, something of little benefit to local interests. An alleged 'spin-off' from tourism is supposed to be the greater demand for locally produced food and drink,

Figure 7.9 Fijian tourist industry. (Source: Varley, 1978, p. 22.)

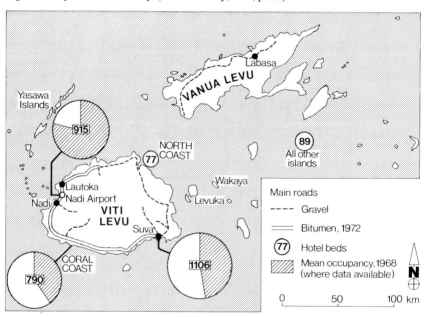

Table 7.5 Purchases of food and beverages in Fijian hotels. (Source: Varley, 1978)

Purchases	Percentage locally produced	Percentage imported
Meat/poultry	41.6	58.4
Fish/sea food	45.8	54.2
Fruit/vegetables	45.7	54.3
Bread/dairy products	85.9	14.1
Other food	18.5	81.5
Beverages	46.8	53.2
Cigarettes/tobacco	87.8	12.2
Total purchases	47.3	52.7

yet Table 7.5 indicates that this is far from being the case as over half the food and beverages are imported. Finally, a sad accompaniment to all tourist developments, and one present in Fiji, is the growth of tourist-related crime, whether prostitution, theft or even violence. Undoubtedly, this is one reason for the growth of highly localized tourist 'ghettos', often with private beaches, and for the reluctance of many tourists to be more adventurous in their explorations.

5. Some general problems

In this section we have examined some of the benefits and some of the costs of tourism. While there is little doubt that tourism can make a major contribution to many Third World economies, it is obvious that there are also many problems associated with it. If we have stressed these more negative views, it is to counter the frequently over-enthusiastic and rather naive embrace given by Third World governments to the tourist industry. For example, much of the ownership of the hotels is, in fact, foreign. Hotel receipts usually comprise 50–80% of all receipts from tourism, but if most of these go abroad then little benefit can be claimed. The smaller West Indian islands are particularly affected by this, for example, in the British Virgin Islands only 20% of the hotels are indigenously owned, and in Antigua only 11%. The involvement of local entrepreneurs tends to be confined to small guest houses. In Sri Lanka, which has attempted to expand its tourist industry in recent years, most of the 'infrastructure' has to be imported. Tourists fly in on other national airlines and, although hotels are largely owned by the Government, they are operated by foreigners. Because of these factors it is estimated that only a half of all tourist expenditure is retained in the country.

The problems of tourist expansion are not purely related to economics; some are also of a social nature. In extreme cases the number of tourists may outnumber the local population. For example, the annual visitors to the Bahamas and Bermuda outnumber the local population by 8 to 1. It is inevitable that the indigenous way of life is massively disrupted and eventually destroyed under such circumstances. Some authors have warned of what is called the 'demonstration effect' where high-spending tourists, consuming imported luxury goods, have considerable social impact on the local population who also wish to share in these artificial and luxurious consumption patterns. It is argued that these 'consumerist' desires, either imposed or learnt from wealthy transients, are a hindrance to more fundamental, locally based, self-sustaining growth, and militate against the success of longer-term development programmes. Some writers even go so far as to call this a new form of colonialism.

1. (a) Describe the patterns of tourist arrivals shown in Figure 7.8.

   (b) Give possible reasons for the patterns, with reference to: (i) location, (ii) political stability, (iii) natural environment, (iv) special interest, such as nature reserves, archaeological remains.

2. Examine the data in Tables 7.4, 7.5, and Figure 7.9, and re-read the sections on tourism in the Fiji Islands.

   (a) (i) Calculate from Table 7.4 the approximate ratio of tourists to indigenous population.

   (ii) From Figure 7.9 estimate the likely distribution of these tourists within the whole of the Fiji Islands.

   (iii) From Table 7.5 describe and account for the patterns of food and beverage consumption shown.

   (iv) With the aid of a good atlas, comment on the likely source of imports of non-locally produced food and drink.

   (v) From Table 7.4 describe and account for the pattern of tourist origins.

   (b) Using these findings discuss the implications for the impact of tourism in the Fiji Islands, under the following headings:

   (i) the spread of economic benefits through the islands, including improvements to the infrastructure,

   (ii) the impact on indigenous culture,

   (iii) the dependence of Fiji on its more developed neighbours.

Key Ideas

Introduction
1. Transport is a vital element in the process of development.
2. Transport is a fundamental factor in bringing about spatial change.

A. The Role of Transport in Economic Development
1. In any specific area transport may help in the process of economic development but it may also be a negative factor.
2. Transport provision, by itself, is rarely sufficient to lead to economic development and it is best interpreted as a factor permitting development.
3. It is possible to formulate a model of the sequence of stages in the development of transport networks in a Third World country.
4. Such networks are oriented very strongly to the coast and the principal towns and ports, and developed primarily to serve the interests of external powers rather than to maximize internal benefits within a country.

B. Characteristics of Third World Transport Systems
1. River transport is locally sufficient in Third World countries but physical obstacles limit use on a wider scale.
2. Railway lines were often initiated for one specific purpose, such as mineral extraction.
3. Early railways in East Africa induced considerable spatial change and economic development, while more recent schemes have been less successful.
4. In most LDCs, road has replaced rail as the principal transport medium.
5. Major road schemes in Latin America have been varied in their success, the main problems being the tendency to promote national interests only (in international schemes), and the lack of additional infrastructure, for example to aid colonization effectively.

6. Air and sea transport are especially important in island communities.
7. The nature of the hinterland is a major influence on the size and significance of the port.
8. The capacity of the port must be related to the capacity of the transport network which serves it.
9. The importance of ports has varied through time in response to a variety of natural, economic, and technological factors, such as the depth of harbours and the nature of their hinterlands.

C. *Tourism*
1. Tourism is a major growth industry both globally and in the Third World.
2. Many LDCs are anxious to promote tourism.
3. The development of tourism in the LDCs has been enabled largely by improvement in air transport, although distance and air fares still strongly influence tourist origin and destination patterns.
4. The impact of tourism is extremely concentrated spatially, usually at a few coastal sites and one or two interior locations.
5. Some countries have deliberately tried to plan for tourism by spreading it wider and building specific resorts.
6. Tourism brings social and economic problems, and only a proportion of the economic benefits go to the country concerned.

Additional activities

1. Study Tables 7.2 and 7.3.
   (a) Construct two maps to show the time–distance relationships between Bombay and the cities mentioned in Table 7.2. The method of construction is as follows: choose an appropriate scale (e.g. 10 hours = 1 centimetre) and plot the time–distance relationships shown in Table 7.2 for (i) railway travel time, and (ii) road travel time. Use a good atlas to help you plot the orientation of the towns from Bombay.
   (b) Compare the two maps with each other and with the straight-line distance shown in the atlas.
   (c) Plot the transport costs against distance for the four commodities shown in Table 7.3.
   (d) Describe and explain the patterns shown.
   (e) Comment on the significance of your results (with respect to time involved and costs) for the transport of materials in India.
2. With reference to specific examples, discuss the ways in which transport investment (i) may, or (ii) may not, stimulate economic development.
3. Debate the advantages and disadvantages of promoting tourism in an imaginary Caribbean island. The class may be divided into several groups, each of which can represent a particular point of view, for example, landlords (wealthy islanders), poor peasants, the island government with responsibility for all aspects of development, a trans-national development company with interests in luxury tourist hotels.

Population

Introduction

During 1980 and 1981 more than 80 countries in the world conducted a census of their populations. The preliminary results of these population counts indicated that, in many countries, the rate of population increase is slowing down and as a consequence estimates of the future world population are being revised downwards. Nevertheless, the LDCs include some of the more populous nations in the world and, more importantly, those with the fastest rates of increase (Figure 8.1), although there is now considerable diversity within the Third World in this aspect. Equally important is the fact that the distribution of world resources available for social and economic development does not match up to the distribution of these populous and rapidly growing countries (see Chapters 2 and 3). In this chapter we shall examine current trends in population growth in the LDCs, then turn attention to the question of carrying capacity and overpopulation. Finally, we shall study migration and its role as both a negative and positive agent of change in the Third World.

A. Population Growth

1. Factors of growth: applicability of the demographic transition

Despite the relatively more optimistic view emerging from recent census findings, the growth of population in LDCs remains staggeringly high and in some places has reached crisis proportions. It took all of human history until 1850 for the human population to reach 1000 million. Only eighty years later 2000 million people inhabited the earth and by 1975 the global population had reached 4000 million. By the year 2000 a further 2000 million is likely to be added. The fear of many people is that the earth's resources simply cannot sustain such numbers of people and that the periodic famines of Africa and Asia, together with persistent malnutrition in a large proportion of the Third World's population, are signs of this.

At the level of individual countries, population growth may result from large-scale migrational gain (e.g. Canada, Australia) but in most of the countries of the Third World it is the changing balance between births and deaths that contributes by far the largest quota to national population increase. Figure 8.2 shows some trends in birth rates and death rates for several Third World countries.

To relate the changing relationship between births and deaths to overall population growth, we can use the model of the demographic transition (Figure 8.3), which hypothesizes four stages:

(1) a high stationary phase where both birth rates and death rates are high and therefore there is only slow population growth or, in some cases, a fluctuating population;

(2) an early expanding phase where the birth rate remains high but where the death rate begins to decline (often through medical improvements), thus causing a rapid increase in the rate of population growth;

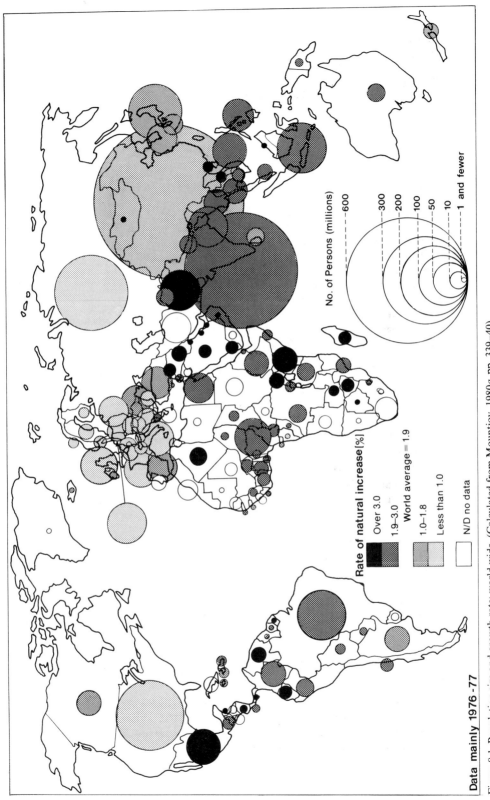

Rate of natural increase [%]

Over 3.0

1.9–3.0

World average = 1.9

1.0–1.8

Less than 1.0

N/D no data

No. of Persons (millions)

600

300

200

100

50

10

1 and fewer

Data mainly 1976-77

Figure 8.1 Population size and growth rate: world wide. (Calculated from Mountjoy, 1980a, pp. 339–40)

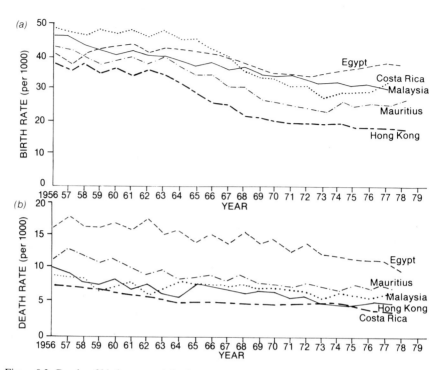

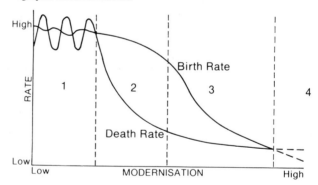

Figure 8.2 Graphs of birth rates and death rates: selected LDCs. (Sources: *United Nations Demographic Yearbooks* and own calculations)

Figure 8.3 Demographic transition model.

(3) a late expanding phase where the death rate continues to decline but where the birth rate also now begins to fall; the population continues to increase, however, as there is a large proportion of young people in the total;

(4) a low stationary phase where both birth rates and death rates are very low, causing a very slow rate of increase of total population or a fairly stationary figure.

Most of the countries of the Western world, and others such as Japan, have passed through this demographic transition. Thus, a critical issue in Third World population studies is 'At what stage in this cycle of events are these countries?' This is an important

182

Table 8.1 Birth rates, death rates and per capita GNP: selected countries, 1981
(Source: *World Bank Development Report, 1983*

	Birth rate	Death rate	Per capita GNP($)
Mali	49	21	190
Bangladesh	47	18	140
Afghanistan	47	26	160
Sierra Leone	46	18	320
Sri Lanka	27	6	300
Uganda	50	18	220
Philippines	34	7	790
Zambia	49	16	600
Liberia	50	14	520
Colombia	29	8	1380
Malaysia	31	7	1840
Algeria	45	13	2140
Mexico	36	7	2250
Yugoslavia	17	9	2790
Hong Kong	19	5	5100
Venezuela	35	6	4220
Spain	14	8	5640
Czechoslovakia	16	12	ND
France	15	10	12190
West Germany	10	12	13450
United States	16	9	12820

question because we are really asking if there is a prospect of stabilizing population growth in the future.

Table 8.1 sets out a range of data on births, deaths and level of development as measured by per capita GNP. It is clear that the wealthier countries have considerably lower birth rates than the LDCs and that the highest death rates occur in the LDCs. Thus, we might expect that countries falling into quadrant I of Figure 8.4 would be at the lowest levels of development and those falling into quadrant III at the highest, i.e. they have completed the demographic transition.

Figure 8.4 Crude birth rates and death rates for countries at different stages of the demographic transition. (I) Pre-transition stage: (II) transition stage; (III) late and post-transition stages. (Source: Heenan, 1980, p. 8)

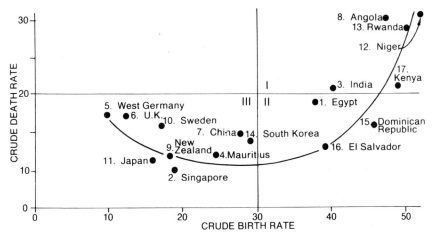

2. Global patterns of birth rates and death rates

Figure 8.2 indicates that, while the decline in birth rates is a recent phenomenon, the fall in death rates took place earlier, although the death rate in the LDCs is still typically twice that in the MDCs. Nevertheless, this does represent a major improvement since the Second World War, and medical and public health programmes are largely responsible. Over much of Asia, birth rates have fallen appreciably, if not always dramatically. The most marked declines have been in smaller countries such as Singapore, Malaysia, and Sri Lanka. Most heartening of all is that in the two most populous countries of the world, India and China, birth rates do appear to be on a downward trend. Despite this, population will continue to increase in many Asian countries because birth rates are falling from a previously very high level and the age structure of the population is very young (Plate 8.1). In other words, there are a great many potential parents of the future. In Latin America, remarkable reductions have taken place in Mexico, Colombia, Chile and some of the smaller countries, but in Brazil the birth rate is still rising. Many African countries have some of the fastest rates of population growth in the world (Figure 8.1), hardly surprisingly when they have some of the highest (and still rising) birth rates. In the northern and southern extremities of the continent, however, birth rates are appreciably lower than elsewhere.

Reasons for decline of birth rates

(i) *Health care.* Over much of the Third World, a large family is regarded as a necessity, both as a potential workforce and, in the absence of proper welfare provisions, as a means

Plate 8.1 Children at Rotifunk, Sierra Leone. Rotifunk is a town of some 5000 population located about 70 kilometres from Freetown. It is a 'head of navigation' town which, in the past at least, owed its importance to the difficulties of overland transport. Small coastal vessels still sail up the Bumpe river to Rotifunk, where commodities are collected from the surrounding area and then shipped either to Freetown or elsewhere on the coast. Like many such settlements in Africa, the age structure is very young–it is likely that over 40% of the population are aged under 15 years–and, in the absence of local employment opportunities, many of these children are destined to end up in Freetown. (*Photograph: M. Barke*)

of support in old age. Thus, in countries like India, where infant mortality is high, there is considerable incentive to produce large numbers of children to ensure that some at least will survive. The availability of health care (see Chapter 3, Section B) is clearly important in changing this trend and there is considerable evidence that greater use of health services results in a lower death rate (especially of infants) and, consequently, may assist in lowering the birth rate as people have confidence that their children will survive infancy. The spread of health facilities over an area is therefore highly significant. For example, the number of government hospitals and dispensaries in Sri Lanka, a country noted for its health service provision, rose from 357 in 1938 to 868 in 1968 and the number of beds per 100 000 population rose from 172 to 320. At the same time the death rate fell from 21 per 1000 to 7.9 per 1000 and the infant mortality rate from over 140 to 50. Countries such as Costa Rica, the Korean Republic, Barbados and Mauritius also show such trends in association with the spread and greater use of health facilities.

(ii) *Family planning* (Plate 8.2). Much has been claimed for programmes of family planning in the past and it is clear that the availability of such services is vital so that families can take the practical steps necessary to carry out family limitation. But family planning facilities by themselves are unlikely to produce significant reductions in birth rates. Equally important are changes in people's attitudes to persuade them against the necessity of having a large family; such changes may be induced by greater health care as outlined above. The improvement of both literacy and the means of communication, through more education facilities, is also important. In northern Bihar, India, a number of factors were found to be significant in explaining the 'take up' of family planning measures: people showing a greater degree of acceptance were those of higher caste who were more literate, and those with large families. The simple provision of family planning facilities is likely to be received differently by different people and, although an integral part of the reason for a decline in the birth rate, rarely stands alone as an explanation.

(iii) *Education.* Education is one of the most important and effective means of bringing about changes in attitudes towards population growth and contraception. This may happen directly or indirectly. If people can read and write then ideas such as family limitation may be communicated more readily (Plate 8.2). More indirectly, education is one of the most important factors in affecting changes in the status of women and in postponing the age of marriage. Both these trends ultimately lead to a reduction in population growth rates as women tend to become more economically independent and to find employment in the modern sectors of the economy.

3. Population structure

In the geographical study of population, it is necessary to focus not only on numbers but also on population structure, i.e. the composition of the population in terms of age, sex, marital status, family size, economic activities, language, religion and race. There are two main reasons for this. First, population structure has obvious implications for future growth and, secondly, it has implications for a country's future social and economic welfare.

(a) Population structure and future growth

The most obvious features that affect future demographic trends are age and sex structure, and the conventional way of illustrating this is by the age and sex pyramid. This is a type of bar graph with age groups (at five-year intervals) on the vertical scale and the number or percentage of males and females in each five-year age group on the horizontal scale. Males

Plate 8.2 Family planning poster in Singapore. A variety of methods have been adopted by Third World countries in their efforts to reduce their birth rates: the most usual being to offer various incentives. Singapore, however, is one of the few countries to adopt quite deliberate *disincentives* to having a large family. Despite the humorous poster and the politeness implied by using the word 'please', Singapore's policy has been quite strict. Income tax relief is limited to the first three children, paid maternity leave is restricted to the first two pregnancies, after the first two childbirths the cost of hospitalization increases, and in the allocation of public housing priority is given to small families. (*Photograph: Popperfoto*)

are conventionally placed on the left and females on the right. As the chances of dying obviously increase with age the shape should be pyramidal. However, a symmetrical pyramid rarely occurs because of the greater longevity of women, and because men tend to be more involved in migration. Also, although more boys are born than girls, the rate of infant mortality among boys is higher. Finally, previous events such as warfare and famine may have affected the structure of the population generations earlier but still have some influence on the shape of the contemporary age and sex pyramid.

Figure 8.5 shows the age and sex pyramids of England and Wales and several LDCs. A considerable variety of shapes can exist but the LDCs are characterized by an 'expansive'

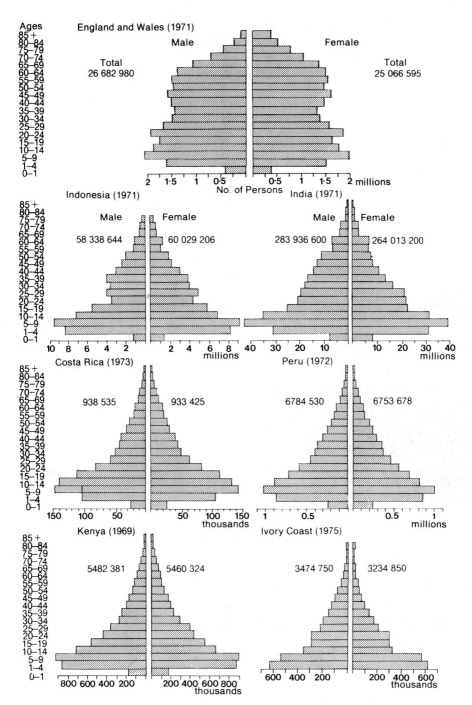

Figure 8.5 Age and sex structure pyramids. (Sources: *United Nations Demographic Yearbooks* and own calculations)

pyramid (e.g. for Kenya) which is the nearest to the true pyramid with a wide base and steep sides indicating a high birth rate, large numbers of children, and declining death rates so that population is growing rapidly.

Age structure is directly influenced by three variables: mortality, fertility and migration, but these variables often inter-relate quite closely. Thus the immigration of young men into African towns has immediate consequences on the age structure of such towns and, subsequently on overall mortality and fertility trends. The relationship between birth rates, death rates, age structure and future population growth is probably best understood as a cyclical process. Changes in fertility and mortality affect the age structure, but this then itself influences the future volume of births and deaths for decades. Thus a population with more older people will obviously have a higher death rate than a younger population and this explains the apparent anomaly of LDCs such as Costa Rica (4.9 per 1000) and Belize (6.1 per 1000) having a lower death rate than England and Wales (12.2 per 1000). The extreme juvenility and potential for future growth in most Third World countries is illustrated in Figure 8.6 where it can be seen that most LDCs have over 40% of their populations aged under 15 years (Plate 8.1).

(b) Population structure and social and economic welfare

Population structure may have a direct impact on the social and economic welfare of a country in a number of ways. One of the most obvious is in the 'dependency ratio', i.e. the proportion of non-productive people (children and the elderly) who have to be supported by the productive population. However, dependency ratios may also be interpreted in terms of the overall resources available to support the non-productive population. A

Figure 8.6 Percentage of population aged under 15. (Source: Mountjoy, 1980b, p. 37)

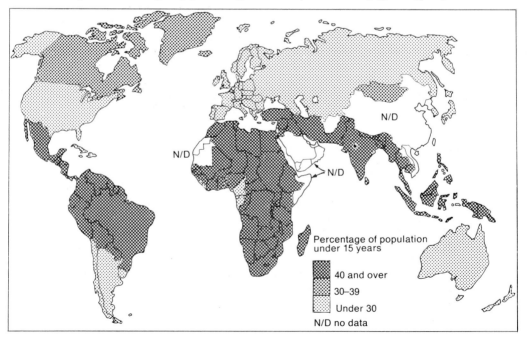

high dependency ratio may be tolerated in a wealthy country like the USA but not in a poorer one, so much so that in the latter both children and elderly may be forced into economically useful roles (Plate 6.2).

Other aspects of population structure are of equal significance for the future economic and social welfare of the Third World countries. We have already stressed (Chapter 3) the rather illogical boundaries of many such countries and noted that they frequently have little meaning for some of the indigenous peoples. Plural societies, i.e. societies with diverse ethnic composition, are characteristic of many LDCs, and their continued existence may be an impediment to development in the widest sense. We can identify four features of plurality which may impede development:

(i) *Lack of national political coherence.* The strength and morale of a nation is probably related to the existence of a sense of common purpose, which may possibly be inhibited in a plural society.

(ii) *Internal social conflict.* There are many examples of this in Africa because of the superimposition of national boundaries over tribal territories. This has led in part to conflicts like the Nigerian Civil War, where the Ibo people of the south east wished to secede from the federation. In Iran, a key reason for internal conflict is the variety of groups living there: Kurds, Turks, Azerbaijanis, Baluchis as well as Iranians.

(iii) *Inequality.* Specific groups often dominate wealth, power and resources in a country while others have only limited access to them. One of the classic examples of this is South Africa where inequality is expressed, at the crudest level, in the fact that although blacks constitute 60% of the total population, the black homelands granted for 'separate' black development occupy not only some of the poorest land but also constitute only about 14% of South Africa's total area.

(iv) *Geopolitical implications.* The external political relationships of countries can be quite fundamentally influenced by their population compositions. These geopolitical relationships are of two kinds. The first is where the existence of a plural society leads to internal conflict which can then be exploited by some external power. It is no coincidence that the strategic confrontations between the 'super powers' in recent years have been in the LDCs in South East Asia and Africa, and have been triggered off by internal conflict, for example in Korea, Vietnam, Palestine, the Congo (Zaire). Secondly, the part played by one country in relation to another may be fundamentally influenced by that country's own population structures. It could be argued, for example, that the USA's continued support for Israel is largely due to the prominent position of many Jews in public life in the USA.

ASSIGNMENTS

1. *Carefully examine Figure 8.1.*
   (a) *Describe the constrasts in population size and distribution within the Third World.*
   (b) *Examine the contrasts in population growth rates within the Third World.*
   (c) *Attempt to account for the contrasts in growth rates of population in Latin America, Africa and Asia.*
2. (a) *Describe carefully the age and sex pyramids shown in Figure 8.5 and note any significant variations between them.*
   (b) *How do the age and sex pyramids for the countries shown in Figure 8.5 relate to patterns of juvenility for the same countries (Figure 8.6)?*
   (c) *Discuss the significance of Figures 8.5 and 8.6 for future population growth in the countries concerned.*

3. *(a)* *Examine Figure 8.6 in relation to Figures 1.3, 1.4 and 1.5.*
      (i) Do those countries with large numbers of children have adequate diets (Figures 1.3, 1.4)?
      (ii) Do those countries have high or above-average PQLI values (Figure 1.5)?
      (iii) Comment on these relationships from the point of view of the likely future social welfare conditions in different LDCs.
  (b) *Examine Figure 8.6 in relation to Figure 3.4.*
      (i) Comment on the relationship between inadequate water and sewage services in the major regions of the Third World and the distribution of young children.

B. Population Distribution and Carrying Capacity

1. Population distribution

So far we have largely neglected any explanation of the factors influencing population distribution in the Third World. Many factors come into play, but it is clear that different factors may operate at different scales. Thus, those factors which explain the global distribution of population may not explain distributions within a 10-hectare segment of Tanzania.

(a) Global distribution

Figure 8.7 shows the global distribution of population. The most striking feature is the unevenness of the distribution, and the principal factor explaining it is the ability of an area to enable people to make a living there. Thus the main concentrations lie on the

Figure 8.7 Global distribution of population.

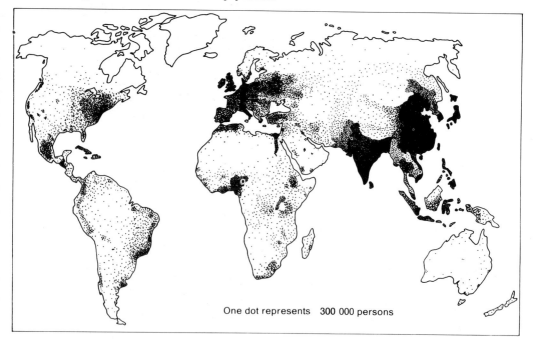

One dot represents 300 000 persons

periphery of the continents. As noted in Chapter 2, physical factors, especially climatic ones, play a major part. However, technical innovations from the Industrial Revolution onwards allowed high densities to be supported in Europe and North America. Thus the potential of the physical environment does not provide the total explanation. It must be stressed that the world population distribution is also dynamic. The distribution at any one time reflects the limits of human culture and technology, but these themselves operate within the framework of the physcial environment.

(b) National distribution

Figure 8.8 shows the distribution of population in the African country of Cameroun. The country penetrates into the continent and has physical environments ranging from the semi-arid north to the moist mangrove coast, but these cannot explain the detailed distribution patterns. Seven main zones can be identified. The economic basis of zones 1 and 2 was established at the time of European occupation and these are the main zones of in-migration at the present time, including the main zone of commercial agriculture near the coast and extending north east, and the Yaounde region in central southern Cameroun. The former has fertile volcanic soils and contains the main plantations producing bananas, coffee, rubber and tea. The second zone does not have commercial plantations but produces 80% of Cameroun's cocoa output and is centred on the capital Yaounde. Two other zones of quite dense population exist (zones 3 and 4) but these are mainly engaged in traditional agriculture and are zones of high population pressure. One expression of this is the high rate of out-migration to the commercial plantations and chief towns of Yaounde and Douala. The two zones (3 and 4) do contrast, however, since the northerly area (zone 4) has fewer natural advantages than the Ramileke district to the

Figure 8.8 Distribution of population in Cameroun. (Source: Zelinsky, Kosinski & Prothero, 1970, pp. 353, 354. Copyright 1970 by Oxford University Press, Inc. Reprinted by permission.)

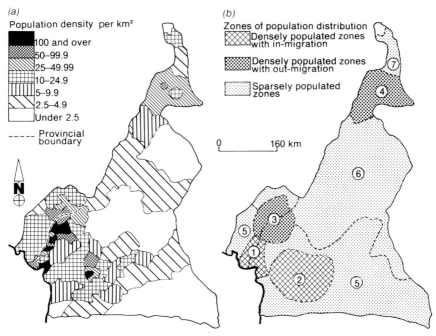

south (zone 3) which has volcanic soils and a more productive agriculture. The rest of the country is sparsely populated. Zone 5 is the forested southern area, while zone 6 is the savanna, used mainly for cattle farming. Zone 7 in the extreme north is seasonally flooded and inhabited only by a few fishermen and stock raisers. Cameroun is in many ways typical of modern Africa. 'Islands' of dense population exist, associated either with productive traditional agriculture (itself associated with favourable physical conditions such as volcanic soils) or with areas of in-migration and employment opportunities created by the impact of a modern economy, either in commercial agriculture or in the urban areas.

2. Overpopulation and carrying capacity

The concepts of overpopulation and carrying capacity, or the ability of land to support population, are difficult to define precisely because, when applied to any specific area, they are likely to be modified by a wide range of factors including technological change and extreme physical events. But the two concepts are clearly related in the sense that an area may be said to be overpopulated if the number of residents is in excess of its ability to provide them with the necessities of life. At the simplest level this would be the ability of the area to grow sufficient food to feed the population, but in more complex societies it would mean the ability of the area to produce the commodities and degree of social organization necessary to promote the import and export of the necessities of life. Features other than numbers of people could interfere with this capability but this merely serves to illustrate the difficulty of the concepts involved. An area which may not be considered overpopulated may, because of some external event, with no increase in population, suddenly find it difficult to support its residents.

In discussing the question of carrying capacity, reference must be made to the work of Ester Boserup, a Danish economist. After summarizing her theory we shall then develop a geographical critique of the ideas. It must be stressed that her ideas apply only to a predominantly agricultural population.

(a) The Boserup hypothesis

The Boserup hypothesis is concerned with the ability of a particular area, or agricultural system, to support a particular number of people. This ability clearly depends on the possibilities for increasing food production in that area. Boserup believes that population growth stimulates innovation and development in agriculture. To put this view crudely, 'necessity is the mother of invention' or the increase in population provides a major incentive for ways to be found of increasing food production, as demonstrated in Table 4.2. Boserup argues that the frequency with which a plot of land is cultivated is an important factor in agriculture in the Third World and that by modifying this and adopting appropriate techniques and innovations the challenge of population increase may be met. From Boserup's ideas we can suggest a continuum of cultivation frequencies (cropping length) and population carrying capacities (density) (Table 4.2). The figures shown should not be taken too literally and are included as being broadly representative of some of the relationships between cultivation frequencies, fallow periods and carrying capacities.

The argument is that as population and population pressure increase, changes in the agricultural system are stimulated in order to cope with this, and this possibly involves a shift from one stage of the continuum shown in Table 4.2 on to the next. The implications of this argument are of the utmost importance for it appears to suggest that a significant proportion of Third World population growth could be catered for by adaptations of indigenous agriculture, and that such growth will lead to improvements in agricultural technology and therefore to increases in carrying capacity. It is clear that the theory is a persuasive and optimistic one as far as the ability of the Third World to deal with population growth is concerned, yet it must be treated with caution and even some scepticism. The reasons for this become clear if we examine the theory in the light of geographical factors.

(b) A geographical critique

There are five major points to make in criticism of the Boserup hypothesis.

(i) The hypothesis gives no consideration to the qualitative aspects of diet and nutrition. For example, although permanent cultivation may be able to support a population density of about 250/km², there is no comment on how well fed these 250 people are. Some tribes rely on cassava for up to 90% of their calorific intake—yet although cassava is a filling food because of its high starch content, it provides very little nutrition or vitamins. Thus the qualitative aspects of diet at each stage of the continuum are vital and it would be a mistake to assume that they are always adequate.

(ii) Boserup tends to neglect the impact and role of physical factors. The physical environment and its potential or limitations is fundamental for agricultural change. Some areas that are currently supporting, say, 12 people/km² under shifting cultivation could, with improved techniques and the judicious application of manure and fertilizers, support, say, 300 people/km². However, as we saw in Chapter 2, tropical soils are fragile and need careful handling, so not all areas could increase their carrying capacity in this way. Also, climate and especially rainfall are fundamental factors. In many areas the average annual rainfall may be a meaningless statistic; the variability and incidence of the rainfall is much more important. For example, totals may vary from the average by up to 50% or more from one year to another and climatologists have established that dry spells tend to occur in groups. That is, there may be a period of four or five years where the rainfall is considerably less than average. The impact of this is likely to be cumulative where bad harvest after bad harvest leads to the consumption of available stocks of food and probably the seed for the next crop, resulting in famine. The incidence of rainfall is equally important. At Sokoto province in north west Nigeria, where there is an average annual rainfall of 680 mm, good harvests have been achieved with a well-distributed annual rainfall of 406 mm, while near famine conditions have resulted from an annual rainfall of 1016 mm most of which fell at the wrong time.

Finally, when considering physical factors, we must remember that many parts of the Third World are especially prone to natural disasters (see Figure 2.7) which have catastrophic effects on agriculture and food production. Earthquakes, floods, locusts, tsetse fly, plague and sickness epidemics may severely disrupt the production of food and therefore the number of people that an area may support.

(iii) It is clear that the necessary agricultural adaptation hypothesized by Boserup would take time. Innovations in agricultural techniques cannot be presumed to occur immediately. A period of trial and error may be necessary before more intensive systems can be adopted. However, if the rate of population increase is sufficiently rapid, then it may be the case that population growth will overwhelm the agricultural system in its process of adjustment. In other words there may simply not be the time available for the necessary agricultural adjustments to occur.

(iv) A fourth point is the rather simplistic assumption in Table 4.2 that just one area is characterized by just one agricultural system. In fact different systems can occur within the same local area (see Figure 4.5), these often being well adapted ecologically to local conditions. Although the less intensive systems could possibly receive more intensive effort this may imply breaking the already delicate ecological balance that many farmers have attained.

(v) The Boserup hypothesis is meant to apply to relatively unsophisticated subsistence economies and implies that change comes from within the community and its economy. However, this implies a degree of 'closure' of the community, and such communities are becoming increasingly difficult to find in the modern world. Most are susceptible to outside influences and most peoples are in fact being drawn into a larger economy than the purely local. So, for example, the problem of population pressure may be solved by migration (either temporary or permanent) of people to sources of wage employment. In fact, many authorities regard out-migration as a symptom of population pressure.

None of these five points can by themselves disprove the Boserup hypothesis but taken together they do represent a set of arguments which suggest that Boserup may be over-optimistic in her view of the capability of much of the Third World to support more people by subsistence agriculture.

ASSIGNMENTS

1. (a) Examine Figures 8.1 and 8.7 and describe the global distribution of population.
   (b) With reference to contrasts between the LDCs and MDCs, discuss the factors influencing the distribution of population under the following headings: (i) distribution and character of physical features (see Figure 2.2, 2.5 and an atlas), (ii) historical factors such as a major movements of people, (iii) levels of technological development.
2. (a) Examine Figures 8.1, 8.7 and Table 2.1, and note from the latter those countries claimed to be overpopulated and underpopulated.
   (b) With reference to Figures 8.1 and 8.7 suggest examples of other countries in the Third World that might be said to be overpopulated or underpopulated.
   (c) What factors other than density may be important in determining whether a country is overpopulated or not?
3. Refer to Table 4.2 and Section B.
   (a) Review the reasons for the apparent increase in population carrying capacity from shifting cultivation to permanent agriculture.
   (b) List the conditions which may prevent this increase in carrying capacity from taking place.

C. Migration and Mobility

Migration is a topic of great complexity. It is possible to classify migrants in terms of the distance they travel; the time period over which migration takes place (e.g. seasonal, annual, once in a lifetime); and in terms of the character of origins and destinations (e.g. rural to urban, rural to rural, urban to rural). A further possibility would be to attempt a classification based on the motives of the migrants; these could be economic, cultural or educational, or to do with whether migration was voluntary or forced in some way. Finally, one could classify on the basis of the characteristics of the migrants themselves:

age, sex, occupations, educational levels, etc. It is obvious that migration has many dimensions and the most appropriate method of classification depends on the purpose of the study.

1. Theories of migration

(a) Ravenstein's laws of migration

These are really generalizations about the characteristics of migrants, their motives, and origins and destinations. Devised in the context of late-nineteenth-century Britain, the most important of Ravenstein's 'laws' are the following.
(1) Most migrants move only a short distance.
(2) The volume of migration increases with the development of industry and commerce.
(3) The direction of migration is mainly from agricultural to industrial areas.
(4) Most of the long-distance migration is to the major industrial and commercial areas.
(5) Migration takes place step by step.
(6) Each migration flow has a counter flow (i.e. return migrants).
(7) Migrants are predominantly adult, and families rarely move long distances.
(8) The majority of migrants are females but males are more significant international migrants.
(9) Migrants are more likely to have rural than urban origins.
(10) The major causes of migration are economic.
It must be conceded that a number of observations made about migration in late-nineteenth-century Britain are likely, as with many other Eurocentric models, to have limited application to the contemporary Third World, the most obvious example being 'law' 8. In the LDCs, males constitute by far the largest proportion of total migrants, since most of the jobs available in cities and mining areas are for men. However, as these observations remain an important starting point for most migration studies, it will be interesting to consider at a later stage the similarities and differences between late-nineteenth-century Britain and the contemporary Third World.

(b) Economic approach to migration

In an economic approach migration is seen principally as an adjustment to economic inequalities, which can be viewed in a variety of ways, either as the threat of over-population, differences in regional employment (or unemployment rates), or differences in wage levels. Thus, we have a series of factors which may 'push' people from one area and 'pull' them towards another. However, in most LDCs, rates of rural-to-urban migration exceed rates of urban job creation (see Chapter 9), so we have the paradox of accelerated rural-to-urban migration and rising urban unemployment. Such a paradox would, at first sight, appear to invalidate the purely 'economic' approach to migration. Many people migrate more in the hope rather than in the certainty of obtaining an urban job, and they migrate also for other reasons.

(c) Behavioural approach to migration

The behavioural approach attempts to understand some of these other reasons by examining the decision processes of migrants. The argument is that most people will not behave in a totally rational way (as an economic theory presumes), but that they perceive and respond to their social, economic and physical environments with differing degrees of rationality. The movement of people is bound up with individual psychological factors, and also with the structure of society, its cultural attributes and norms of behaviour. These may predispose an individual to move or not to move. They may also influence the perception of opportunities in an alternative location. Equally important may be the range of options known to and available to the individual. In the LDCs this knowledge is likely to be at least partly a function of the friction of distance, with decreasing knowledge of the attributes of distant places. Thus, the actual act of migration depends on the information available to individuals and how their individual preferences and motivations, and those of the society in which they have been brought up, influence their perception of their opportunities.

2. A classification of mobility

One of the problems in attempting to apply these general models of migration to the LDCs stems from the use of the word 'migration' itself. At this stage it is important to stress the difference between migration and mobility. We take migration to mean a change in one's place of permanent residence, a concept readily understood in the developed world but, as we shall see, of limited meaning in many LDCs. Mobility is a much broader term and may be taken to include a whole range of population movements, varying in scale from one's journey to work, school or shop, up to long-distance international migration, and varying in time from the trips one makes each day, up to a 'once in a lifetime' movement. 'Mobility' is perhaps the most appropriate term to use in the Third World context.

Figure 8.9 is a classification of African population mobility and has general applicability to much of the rest of the Third World. The classification illustrates two of the main themes of this book: the diversity that exists within the Third World, and the

Figure 8.9 Classification of African mobility. (Source: R.M. Prothero, unpublished paper)

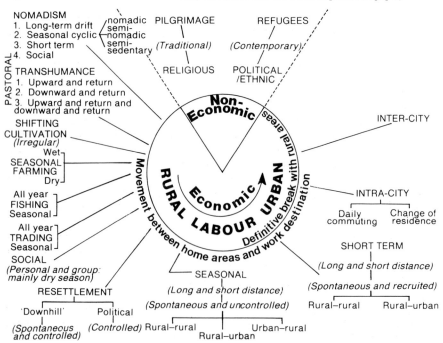

impact on such countries of being drawn into the global economic system. Initially, this classification divides mobility into two major types: that motivated by economic factors, and that which results from non-economic forces. The two most important of the latter are pilgrimage and the displacement of people (refugees) because of warfare or other disturbances. Mobility for economic reasons can be further subdivided into rural oriented and predominantly urban. The former ranges from nomadism through to the complete resettlement of villages. It also includes those moves resulting from the desire of rural people to secure wage employment, either on a seasonal basis, for two or three years, or permanently. Urban mobility takes place simply within or between cities.

Before we proceed to an empirical examination of these aspects of mobility, two further points must be made. First, we have already made a distinction between migration and mobility and Figure 8.9 makes it clear why this is necessary. Many aspects of mobility shown would be difficult to classify as migrations in the Western sense of a change of one's permanent residence. Nomadism is the most obvious example of this. True nomads simply have no permanent place of residence; they are perpetual migrants. Similar problems may be met in studying the various types of shifting cultivators. Some may settle at one point for a period of years and cultivate plots around this point, moving on when the plots are exhausted. Others may make regular seasonal moves between several locations, none of which are permanently inhabited. Thus, migration in the limited Western sense is hardly an appropriate term. A second general point is that it is obvious that many aspects of mobility represent continuity from the past while others represent more recent changes brought about by incorporation into a wider economic system.

3. Mobility patterns in the Third World

(a) Some general features

Severe regional economic imbalances exist within the LDCs and these may produce migration streams. The attractions of a weekly wage plus all the other apparent advantages offered by the town may be a magnet, but equally important may be the population pressure on the land, which may provide a significant push from rural areas.

This population pressure is unlikely to be relieved by overseas migration in the contemporary Third World. Since the 1950s, such intercontinental migration has been only on a very limited scale. Some movement of Latin Americans into the USA has taken place, and other examples are the movement of West Indians, Pakistanis and Indians to Britain, and people from North Africa and the Near East to north west Europe. However, in relation to the population problems of the LDCs, the numbers are very small and there is no prospect of overseas migration to the MDCs offering a major solution. However, as we have already seen in the context of mineral extraction in the Middle East and Africa, there is substantial transnational migration between some LDCs.

Despite the attention given to rural-to-urban migration in the literature, rural-to-rural moves are numerically more significant in most LDCs. In Ghana in 1960, 60% of all moves were rural to rural, and in India in 1961, 73.7% of all moves were between rural areas and only 14.6% were rural to urban. Admittedly, much of this rural-to-rural movement was of women on marriage but its contribution to the overall volume of migration is clear. Another reason for the significance of intra-rural moves has been the marked increase of the cultivated area up to the mid 1960s (Chapter 4), sometimes as a result of new irrigation schemes or malaria eradication programmes. Thus, movement to new frontiers of cultivation has been a viable alternative to migration to urban areas for many Third World people.

Nevertheless, rural-to-urban movement is obviously important and, as we shall see, is possibly the most important feature of mobility from the point of view of its impact on other features. Most studies demonstrate that it is only a particular segment of the population who move. Most are young adults, aged between 15 and 30 and (contrary to Ravenstein's law) predominantly male. One of the major reasons for this sex bias is that it is women who tend to perform the agricultural tasks and it is necessary for them to remain behind to retain a hold on the land. Furthermore, most of the migrants' jobs are heavy manual tasks (e.g. mining) and are more likely to recruit male labour. These migrants frequently possess better levels of education than the rest of the population and this has obvious implications for the areas they leave. Although there are some long-distance migrants, the majority are short range. For example, 20% of migrants in Djakarta had formerly lived as close as within 30 minutes travel time of the city and, in Bangkok in 1960, 50% of the migrants came from within an 80-km radius of the city.

In summary, the major general features of mobility patterns in the LDCs are: limited overseas migration, a high degree of rural-to-rural mobility, at least formerly associated with an expanding frontier of cultivation, and the movement of young males to the urban areas. With these general observations in mind, we shall now examine those features of mobility that represent continuity from the past and those due to more recent change.

(b) Continuity from the past

One of the major types of population mobility that has continued from the past is pilgrimage. It is estimated that 3 million people are involved in these moves each year. Pilgrimage is particularly associated with the Muslim religion. Some movements may be only over a short distance to worship at a local shrine while others take place over huge distances. Mecca and Medina are the main destinations for most of these pilgrims, because Muslims are supposed to make a pilgrimage to those cities at least once in their lifetime. This feature of mobility has increased in importance as Islam has spread rapidly, especially in Africa, and also as travel has become safer and easier, in the twentieth century. The movement of pilgrims from West Africa across the southern margins of the Sahara to Lake Chad and thence to the Nile basin and the Red Sea coast represents one important example of this mobility. As most routes converge on the Republic of the Sudan, it is not surprising that there should be a significant number of West Africans living there. Although other reasons may be important, many of these people are pilgrims making a long stay on their outward or homeward journey, or simply people who did not get any further. It is estimated that there are 0.75 million West Africans living in the Sudan and they are of considerable economic significance, being prepared to pioneer new areas. West Africans are particularly important in the Gezira scheme where they constitute about 90% of the workers in the cotton ginneries.

One of the most striking forms of population mobility to continue from the past is nomadism. The Fulani people of Northern Nigeria are of particular interest as they show two aspects of mobility. First, they have been involved in long-term drift over several centuries. Fulani people originated from the north of the Sahara and migrated originally in a south westerly direction to the Fouta Toro in Senegal. From there they have spread eastwards since the twelfth century, resulting in their present scatter through the northern parts of West Africa. They are now relatively stable as they are limited in their southward movement by the tsetse fly. Their second type of mobility is seasonal. In the dry season they tend to move south away from the increasing aridity of the fringes of the Sahara and in the wet season they move north to escape the advancing tsetse fly (Plate 2.2).

Another form of mobility that has continued from the past is shifting cultivation (see Chapter 4). Clearly, this is an aspect of rural-to-rural mobility where either the settlement or the cultivated land (or both) is moved in response to declining fertility. Of a similar nature are movements associated with fishing where people move in response to the rise and fall of the major rivers.

(c) Mobility of more recent origin

Development and modernization in LDCs in the twentieth century have produced new types of population movement. Many of these arose when the LDCs established, or had imposed upon them, wider economic and political relationships.

The imposition of stability associated with colonial rule reduced tribal confrontations and the slave trade. Significant population shifts resulted as the need for defence became less important. More recently, compulsory 'resettlement' schemes have resulted from nationalist movements and their struggle for independence. Such schemes forcibly removed people to new villages in Kenya (see Chapter 10) and Malaysia.

The major aspect of recent population mobility, however, is migration from rural to urban areas and centres of commercial agriculture or mining activity (Figure 6.6). It is undeniable that the employment opportunities apparently offered by the industrial, administrative, port and transport functions of the main cities have acted as a powerful magnet for people. Strong migration streams may be identified in most countries, focussing on the capital or the main city. Figure 8.10 shows such streams in Ecuador, yet they are by no means the only movements. While Quito and Guayaquil dominate the migration pattern between the provinces of Ecuador, other patterns may be discerned (Figure 8.10*b*), suggesting a movement down from the sierra to the more productive

Figure 8.10 (*a*) Net inter-provincial migration *excluding* Guayaquil (Quito's population was 800 000 in 1980). (*b*) Net inter-provincial migration to Guayaquil (population 1 116 000 in 1980). (Source: Blakemore & Smith, 1971, pp. 289, 290)

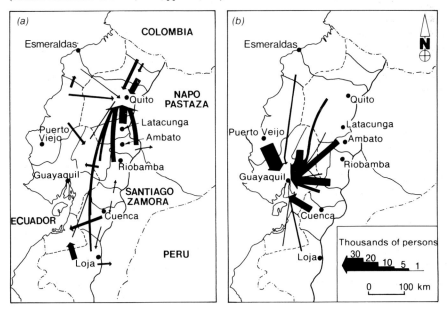

coastal regions. Finally it must be noted that each migration stream has a counter stream of return migrants.

Although movement to the city may be the largest single migration stream, it appears that it is the search for economic, rather than strictly urban, opportunities that is important. Wage labour migrants in Africa go to the mining areas and areas of cash crop production as well as the major towns. In West Africa such movement tends to be from north to south and is usually seasonal. The men leave in the dry season in late September, October, or November and return home the following April or May to cultivate their farms at the beginning of the rainy season. In many areas a third of the total male labour force may be involved each year, and of these most travel outside northern Nigeria to areas of greater economic development. In Central and East Africa, wage labour migrants tend to be away for longer periods, as they are often recruited under contract to South African, or what were formerly Rhodesian, mines on an annual basis or for a period of several years.

These examples show that the economic opportunities created in recent times have had a profound influence on mobility patterns.

A final aspect of mobility resulting from change in recent times is the enforced movement of people (Plate 2.5). Refugees have become a familiar part of twentieth century life, whether in Zimbabwe, Uganda, Chad, Somalia, Afghanistan, Kampuchea, Vietnam or El Salvador. The expulsion of 2 million 'illegal' immigrants from Nigeria in January 1983 is a similar politically based instance of population movement, although the refugees were not fleeing from warfare.

Although many types of population mobility in the Third World do represent a degree of continuity with the past, rapid change in social and economic conditions has superimposed a whole new set of patterns and causes.

4. Migration and change

Migration or, more correctly, the migrants may be viewed as significant in the processes of change. Migrants carry with them ideas, skills and labour power. These attributes are gained by the area of immigration but lost to the area they leave. Furthermore, migrants are important in the process of demographic change. A large proportion of young migrants carry with them a high reproductive capacity which has obvious implications for both areas of origin and destination. Finally, as most migrants are male, women tend to be left with the agricultural tasks and the responsibility for bringing up the children. Thus important social changes ensue from migration. This section will examine some of the more important themes in the geographical impact of migration.

(a) The impact of out-migration

The depopulation side of migration, or the impact on the areas that migrants leave, has been little studied but it is just as important as the study of the impact on the 'receiving' areas. The qualities that migrants possess are obviously lost to their areas of origin. It is frequently the better-educated and more adventurous members of village society who are the most likely to migrate, and the loss of such people may result in declining agricultural productivity and the persistence of conservative attitudes. However, some studies have shown that the break with the village is often not clear cut. For example, in a study of 14 villages in Java, 90% of the permanent migrants visited their village of origin at least once a year and only 10% felt that they would never return to live there. Such close ties with the place of origin seem to provide both economic and emotional security for the future.

Under these circumstances the impact of out-migration is likely to be minimized and, although the labour force may be reduced, the level of contact is still high. On a more economic level, the return of remittances to the home village is very important and one of the main reasons for moving in the first place is to enhance the total family income. In the Java study, 95% of all migrants who were in employment sent money back to the village, and those households with no representatives away were claimed to be noticeably poorer than those with workers in the city. The loss of the younger and more active members of the village did have a negative effect however. Leadership in the village was adversely affected and the loss of the stronger members of the workforce was felt when heavy agricultural tasks had to be undertaken. Also there is the long-term prospect that the village could cease to be a viable unit and come to rely almost entirely on its absent members.

(b) Migration and health

There is considerable evidence that disease is spread by the movement of people. For example, the movement of refugees within and from Bangladesh in the mid 1970s resulted in the spread of smallpox in the country and into adjacent areas of India. A more significant disease in the contemporary Third World is malaria and there is considerable evidence, especially from Africa, that attempts to eradicate malaria are being impeded by mobility patterns. In north east Africa, nomadic pastoralists move south to sources of water and pasture available only in the wet season. This brings them into contact with the malaria vectors (mosquitos) breeding in the water sources. The nomadic pattern of mobility alone would create major problems in dealing with the disease as their north–south movement makes it difficult to maintain contact in order to spray dwellings and distribute drugs. This is further complicated by the pattern of short-term mobility practised within this annual north–south movement, when the young men go off long distances with the camels in search of pasture while the older members of the family remain with the sheep and goats. Such mobility is a natural response to environmental conditions but makes any attempt at effective eradication extremely difficult. This is further exacerbated by the fact that the north–south movement takes place across an international boundary, which makes co-ordination necessary between two national health agencies if effective measures are to be taken. Thus, mobility can be a highly significant factor both in the diffusion of diseases and in their effective control.

(c) Migration and social change

The major generalization that has been made about migration and social change in the Third World is that it is part of the 'modernization' process. The claim is that, in the migration experience, 'traditional' values and ways of life will be transformed as the individual comes into contact with a wider range of influences, especially more Western, 'developed' or 'modern' ones. Such a generalization assumes a number of things: first, that migration is primarily from 'backward' rural areas to 'advanced' urban areas, and second, that migrants are permanent enough to absorb the new set of values, etc. that they find in the city.

From the evidence studied in this chapter it is clear that mobility patterns are far more complex than this generalization suggests. In many LDCs, temporary and seasonal circular mobility are obviously important and may even be the major forms of mobility. In addition we have seen that many traditional forms of mobility co-exist with modern ones, rather than being replaced by them. This is true of many aspects of life, but in mobility studies the example of temporary mobility between rural and urban areas is a case in point. Seasonal rural movements became common in many traditional societies as a response to environmental conditions. In more recent times seasonal or temporary urban movements have become equally common as a response to the economic necessity of having both a rural and urban means of livelihood.

In such circumstances it would be false to claim that migration in the Third World is inevitably resulting in fundamental social change. By making an individual familiar with an entirely different residential and work environment, migration may be contributing to a process of 'modernization' and social change, but the evidence suggests that it is much slower and much less spectacular than some have claimed.

ASSIGNMENTS

1. *Having re-read Chapters 6 and 8, suggest how, in the Third World, a rural dweller's attitudes to migration may be influenced by: (a) age, (b) sex, (c) education, (d) cultural background (including religion).*
2. *Attempt to provide examples of the various types of movement shown in Figure 8.9.*
3. *Refer to Figure 8.10a, b.*
   (a) Describe the patterns of interprovincial migration shown.
   (b) Attempt to explain why there is a reduction in the numbers of migrants with increasing distance from the two main cities of Guayaquil and Quito.
   (c) Examine some of the possible reasons for moving to the city.
   (d) Discuss why many may wish to return to their rural origins.
   (e) Make a list of the main effects of rural-to-urban migration in the Third World, both on the sending and receiving areas.

Conclusion

Third World population growth, although apparently slowing down in some areas is still at a dangerously high level. Great attention continues to be given to increasing food supplies and to controlling population growth through the promotion of family planning. Some commentators argue, however, that with economic growth and development in the Third World, and the development of Western patterns of living and consumption, many people will have fewer children. Furthermore, medical improvements reduce the necessity of having large families. In this view, the process of development itself is seen as the principal means of controlling population growth. It is argued that this is what happened in the developed world and that the same process will be transmitted to the Third World.

It seems possible that such a process could take place, yet is must be stated that over many parts of the Third World the prospects for even a modest improvement of economic growth and development are remote. The fact that very large numbers of children already exist in the Third World has further implications (Figure 8.6). Large numbers of children mean a high dependency ratio and although these children will ultimately provide a large labour force, a high proportion of non-workers puts stress on all other services. We have seen that Boserup regards population growth as a stimulus to development, but the key issue in her argument is that population growth must be slow. In much of the Third World, population growth is not slow, and it seems likely that very large and still growing populations with high dependency ratios are a considerable handicap to development.

In summary, it is clear that many countries of the Third World are characterized by an imbalance of population and resources and do not possess enough of the latter to maintain their populations at a reasonable standard of living. The symptoms of this situation are not only manifested in the periodic famines which afflict several countries from time to time, but are also present in the persistently low quality of the diet of many Third World inhabitants, in malnutrition, and lack of resistance to disease. This imbalance manifests itself in other ways, such as in the volume of migration either to find new lands to cultivate or to find alternative employment in the cities. One result of this rural-to-urban migration is urban unemployment which is indicative of the same imbalance. Lastly, the debts that burden the national economies of most Third World countries are due, at least in part, to this shortfall between indigenous resources and the needs of the rapidly growing population. Any general conclusion on Third World population must therefore remain pessimistic. The best that can be hoped for is that the situation can be held constant, but for a large proportion of the world's population the prospect of any significant improvement in their life chances seems remote.

Key Ideas

A. Population Growth
1. Although there are signs that the rate of population growth in the Third World has begun to fall, the rate of increase is still very high and the absolute numbers enormous.
2. A number of countries in the Third World do appear to be passing from a stage of high birth rate/death rate to low birth rate/death rate (through the demographic transition).
3. The population explosion in the Third World is essentially due to medical improvements which reduced death rates without modifying birth rates.
4. Birth rates have fallen dramatically in some countries but continue to be at a high level in others due to the overall youthfulness of the population.
5. Improved health care, family planning advice and education have made important contributions to the decline in the birth rate.
6. The structure of a country's population in terms of age and sex is of major importance for its future growth.
7. The structure of a country's population in terms of other factors such as tribal, ethnic, or religious dimensions is of major importance for its social and economic welfare.

B. Population Distribution and Carrying Capacity
1. The distribution of population at different scales–global, national, local–is a response to a complex set of physical, cultural and economic factors.
2. The distribution of population is dynamic and may change through time as people find new ways of responding to and utilizing the environment.
3. While some authorities believe that increases in food production are necessary to allow an increase in population, a second school of thought represented by Ester Boserup, argues that population increase stimulates innovation in agriculture and the use of more intensive techniques.
4. The 'Boserup hypothesis' suggests that the population carrying capacity of an agricultural area can be greatly increased by increasing the frequency of cultivation.
5. This hypothesis does not appear to take into account a number of fundamental geographical and socio-economic factors that may prevent an increase in food production from occurring.

C. Migration and Mobility
1. Migration may be studied in many different ways, the most appropriate approach depending on the purpose of the study.
2. In many Third World countries 'mobility' is a more appropriate term than migration because of the variety of movements for different purposes.

3. A classification of mobility may be devised using the motives for movement, whether economic or non-economic, and the origins and destinations, whether urban or rural.
4. Although the rural-to-urban movement is highly significant there is a great deal of movement within rural areas.
5. Most migration is age and sex selective, young males predominating.
6. Many aspects of mobility in the Third World have been continuing for many centuries.
7. Superimposed on these movements are a relatively new set produced by greater external contacts and economic development.
8. Migration is an important agent of change both in the area of reception and in the area of out-migration.
9. Mobility may be important in the spread of diseases into new areas.
10. Migration to urban areas in the Third World does not necessarily produce fundamental social change in those areas nor in the migrants.

Additional Activities

1. Using the data on birth rates, death rates and per capita GNP shown in Table 8.1, examine contrasts in the stages of the demographic transition.
   (a) Produce a graph similar to Figure 8.4 and categorize the 21 countries.
   (b) Plot the birth rates and death rates against per capita GNP for the 21 countries.
   (c) Comment on the relationships between both sets of data.
2. Using the data shown in Table 8.2 and Figure 8.11, examine migration in Malaysia.
   (a) Map the net migration rates for each district in Malaysia.

Figure 8.11 Districts in Malaysia. (Source: Pryor, 1979, p. 81)

Table 8.2 Peninsular Malaysia: Indices of internal migration (70 districts). (Source: Unpublished census data, 1970, Department of Statistics, Kuala Lumpur)

District	District net migration rate (% gain/loss)	District	District net migration rate (% gain/loss)
1 Batu Pahat (Johor)	−10.52	38 Jerantut	+17.95
2 Johor Bahru	+12.77	39 Kuantan	+16.29
3 Kluang	+11.99	40 Lipis	−1.49
4 Kota Tinggi	+14.47	41 Pekan	+6.38
5 Mersing	+3.67	42 Raub	+4.50
6 Muar	−11.41	43 Temerloh	+9.74
7 Pontian	−9.98	44 Penang Tengah (Penang)	+6.32
8 Segamat	+0.78	45 Penang Utara	+3.26
9 Baling (Kedah)	+4.65	46 Penang Selatan	−2.49
10 Bandar Bahru	−9.82	47 Penang Timor Laut	−2.04
11 Kota Setar	−5.58	48 Penang Barat Daya	−1.32
12 Kuala Muda	−2.53	49 Batang Padang (Perak)	−2.81
13 Kubang Pasu	−2.32	50 Dindings	−1.70
14 Kulim	−7.10	51 Kinta	−3.59
15 P. Langkawi	+0.63	52 Krian	−9.28
16 Padang Terap	+19.29	53 Juala Kangsar	−6.48
17 Sik	+17.97	54 Larut/Matang	−4.25
18 Yan	−13.69	55 Hilir Perak	−6.26
19 Bachok (Kelantan)	−11.87	56 Ulu Perak	+5.45
20 Kota Bharu	−10.05	57 Perlis (Perlis)	+1.00
21 Machang	−4.64	58 Klang (Selangor)	+5.18
22 Pasir Mas	−13.94	59 Kuala Langat	−8.37
23 Pasir Puteh	−11.58	60 Kuala Lumpur	+10.64
24 Tanah Merah	+19.95	61 Kuala Selangor	−1.47
25 Tumpat	−10.05	62 Sabak Bernam	−4.39
26 Ulu Kelantin	+27.94	63 Ulu Langat	−1.07
27 Melaka Utara (Melaka)	+0.66	64 Ulu Selangor	+8.14
28 Melaka Selatan	−3.25	65 Besut (Trengganu)	+5.37
29 Melaka Tengah	−4.78	66 Dungun	+21.88
30 Jelebu (Negeri Sembilan)	+0.57	67 Kemaman	+5.75
31 Kuala Pilah	−10.01	68 Kuala Trengganu	−9.53
32 Port Dickson	+10.06	69 Marang	−1.31
33 Rembau	−8.17	70 Ulu Trengganu	+11.97
34 Seremban	−7.87		
35 Tampin	+16.00		
36 Bentong (Pahang)	+11.28		
37 Cameron Highlands	+10.36		

(b) With the aid of a good atlas comment on the patterns revealed, in terms of (i) the influence of relief and other physical factors, (ii) the major urban areas, (iii) transport and accessibility, (iv) areas of commercial agriculture and mining activity.

3. Having read the chapter through, return to 'Ravenstein's laws of migration' (page 195). Discuss the extent to which they apply to the Third World.

Urban Development

Introduction

The significance of urbanization in the Third World goes far beyond the numbers of people involved, huge though these are. In the past, the growth of towns and cities was seen largely as a consequence of development: one of the products of economic expansion. More recently, urbanization has come to be regarded as, in itself, a fundamental and integral part of development since urban areas are not just a product of growth but may themselves generate social and economic change. Thus, an understanding of the processes of development in the Third World must, in part, involve the study of urbanization. The facts of urbanization, the nature of Third World urban systems and their role in the development process form the subject matter of this chapter.

A. Urban Population Trends

In this section we examine the varied patterns of urban population growth in the Third World and assess the relative significance of migration and natural increase in such growth.

1. Patterns of urban population growth: diversity and change

Table 9.1 shows that on a proportional basis the world pattern of urban population continues to be dominated by the MDCs. The degree of economic development in the

Table 9.1 Urban population trends by world regions. (Sources: Davis, 1976; *World Development Report, 1981*)

Region	Urban population, 1950s (thousands)	(%)	Urban population, 1970s (thousands)	(%)	Mean rate of change, 1970–80 (% per year)
Latin America	65 052	40.3	153 464	54.4	+3.6
Asia	213 154	15.4	511 644	25.4	+4.5
Africa	28 951	13.8	76 986	21.8	+5.9
Oceania	115	4.9	305	8.5	—
Total LDCs	307 272	18.4	742 399	29.1	
Australia/ New Zealand	7 116	70.0	12 877	84.3	+1.9
North America	105 643	63.8	171 877	75.1	+1.6
Europe	209 851	53.4	292 225	63.0	+1.7
USSR	76 500	42.5	152 000	62.3	+2.2
Total MDCs	399 110	53.3	628 979	66.1	

world regions is almost directly paralleled by the proportion of their total populations who are urban dwellers and it is clear that the majority of people living in the Third World still live in rural environments (Chapter 5, Section A). However, trends of change are important and these are also shown in Table 9.1, demonstrating that the fastest rates of growth in urban population in the 1950–70 period were in the LDCs.

Thus Figure 9.1 contrasts markedly with Figure 9.2. Many LDCs (especially in Latin America) now have considerably more than 20% of their total populations living in cities of 100 000 +. Furthermore, if we examine the changing geographical pattern of cities with over 1 million inhabitants ('million' cities), not only is the high rate of recent Third World urban population growth reinforced, but the concentration of that urban population into very large cities is revealed. In the early 1970s there were 63 'million' cities between the equator and the 35th parallels. Of these, 51 were in the LDCs. Thus, one of the most significant recent changes in the human geography of the LDCs is the growth of urban population and of very large cities.

(a) Regional variations in Third World urban population growth

The popular stereotype of the LDCs is that they are characterized by a limited number of mushrooming cities whose growth appears to be totally out of control. Yet close inspection of Figure 9.3 shows that, although the proportion of urban dwellers has increased substantially, there is still considerable diversity in the proportion of urban dwellers in the LDCs. The average for all Third World countries is about 28%, but the range is from virtually 100% in Singapore to the minimum levels found in places such as the New Hebrides and Cocos Islands. Such diversity is the result of a complex set of forces.

Figure 9.1 Percentage of population living in cities of over 100 000, 1927. (Source: Jefferson, 1931)

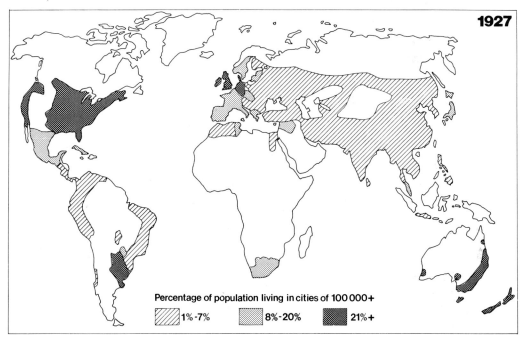

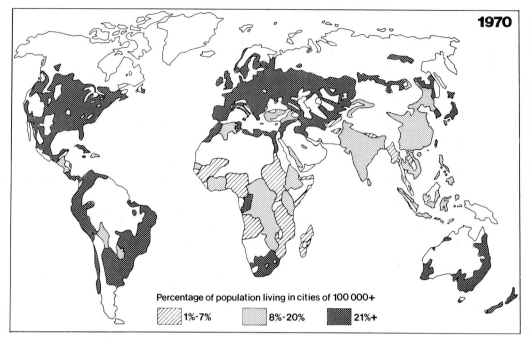

Figure 9.2 Percentage of population living in cities of over 100 000 in 1970. (Calculated from Davis, 1976)

Figure 9.3 Percentage of urban dwellers in the Third World, 1980. (Sources: *World Bank Development Report, 1981* and own calculations)

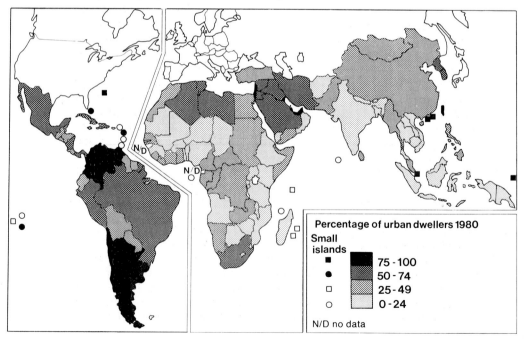

We might expect that the most powerful explanation for levels of urbanization is to be found in the level of economic development of various Third World countries. While it is true that countries with a high percentage of urban dwellers tend to be located in the more economically advanced areas of South America, or include small but relatively highly developed islands or enclaves such as Hong Kong and Singapore, it is also true that many of the least developed regions have shown large increases in urban population. Therefore, we must seek explanations beyond the current level of economic development. Some of the reasons for recent urban growth will be dealt with later in this chapter but here it is necessary to outline briefly some of the historical causes of differing degrees of urbanization.

Africa is one of the least urbanized continents of the world (Table 9.1), but such an observation hides a range of diversity. There is a contrast in Figure 9.3 between the more urbanized area of North Africa and the regions to the south of the Sahara. The North African coast has a long urban history and has been subject to successive waves of colonization from before Roman times. A long-established set of cities, supported by localized hinterlands of fertility but acting as trading gateways to and from the vast interior, are characteristic. West Africa too has, in certain regions, a long urban history. However, this was relatively localized and contemporary levels of urbanization are modest. In many regions coastal cities have been 'implanted' by colonizing powers on an almost totally rural indigenous population. Thus, the urban populations of the coastal countries of Senegal, Ivory Coast, Liberia, Ghana and Nigeria all exceed 20% while countries in the interior – Mali, Mauritania, Niger and Upper Volta – range from 2% to 9%. East Africa has very low levels of urbanization reflecting the predominantly rural interests of colonial settlers and the absence of any previous indigenous urbanization. In Central Africa, however, several countries have moderate urbanization levels owing to the presence of mineral resources and the consequent establishment of towns by mining companies. The most highly developed country, Sourth Africa, is, in every sense, a special case and its 50% urbanized population is a reflection of this.

By contrast with much of Africa, Latin America was colonized at a much earlier date and many of its countries have been incorporated into the international economic system for a longer period. As Figures 9.2 and 9.3 show, Latin America is more urbanized than most other areas of the Third World. In part this is a reflection of the origins of population, since much of Latin America was peopled by immigrants from the urban cultures of Europe, but economic factors were important too. The Spanish colonial economy was based on extracting raw materials for export, and a system of towns developed to perform and administer this function. In the post-independence period, in the later nineteenth century, investment from the USA and Western Europe has been concentrated in such localities and the high rates of European immigration to Argentina, Chile and Uruguay in particular have added to the degree of urbanization. The present distribution of large cities is largely a product of the exporting role of former colonies and the earlier economic development of the southern rather than the northern regions of the continent (with the exception of Mexico), especially Uruguay, Argentina and southern Brazil.

Urban development in Asia is masked by the overall size of the population, for although cities are a long-established phenomenon (Asia saw the origins of urbanism), the degree of urbanization is relatively low. Throughout history, the number of people living in Asian cities has probably been greater than in any other continent but the number of rural dwellers has far surpassed this. Traditional Asian cities, for example those in ancient China, owed more to cultural and political forces than to economic. It was the expanding European trading interests that introduced a new type of city, sited for the purchase of overseas trade rather than for control of the interior. Yet the majority of Asians have remained agriculturalists.

(b) Recent change in Third World urban growth

Between 1950 and 1960, the urban population of the Third World increased by about 156 million people and, between 1970 and 1980, by about 240 million people. East Asia accounted for roughly one-third of these increases, but urban population growth rates vary markedly.

(i) *Growth rates.* Table 9.2 shows the distribution of annual urban growth rates for some LDCs in the 1960s and 1970s. The 4.1% to 6.0% band is the most significant for the LDCs in both periods, but of the countries with growth rates in excess of 6.1% the majority are in Africa and few in Latin America. We have already noted that Latin America heads the Third World urbanization table (Table 9.1) so the fastest growth rates in urban population appear to be in areas like Africa, that were least urbanized in 1960. However, the rate of urbanization is a crude indicator by itself as it depends on the size of the starting figure. A growth in urban population from 10 000 to 20 000 over 10 years represents a 100% increase or 10% per annum. A growth from 1 000 000 to 1 500 000 over the same period is obviously a much greater absolute increase but is only a growth of 50% or 5% per annum.

(ii) *Urban growth by size of urban area.* A further feature of recent change concerns what form contemporary urbanization is taking. We have already noted that the popular stereotype of Third World urban development is that of the explosive growth of already overcrowded large cities. Between 1950 and 1970, 42% of the total urban population growth in the Third World was in cities of over 1 000 000 inhabitants. Despite this, well over half of the total growth was still in cities of less than a million and over one-third was in the quite small towns of 20 000 to 100 000. Such figures run counter to the extreme view that urban growth is concentrated exclusively on a few very large cities.

The theme of diversity is enhanced if we examine growth by size of place on a regional basis (Table 9.3). Once again, there is a wide range of experience, with South America and East Asia leading the way in big-city growth. Yet, in most other regions, the smaller places (20 000–100 000) accounted for over one-third of the total urban population growth and in parts of Africa these places constitute the norm for the majority of urban dwellers. Thus, while we must not underestimate the significance of very large cities in the Third World, the data analysed here suggest much more diversity in the recent urbanization trends than is often recognized.

Table 9.2 Third World urban growth rates. (Sources: *World Bank Development Reports, 1981, 1983*).

Percentage per annum	Number of countries 1960–70	1970–80	Number of countries 1970–80, by region Latin America	Africa	Asia
Less than 2.0%	4	4	4	—	1
2.1–4.0%	25	32	10	6	12
4.1–6.0%	42	37	7	15	12
6.1–8.0%	18	17	1	11	3
8.1–10.0%	2	5	—	5	2
10.1% +	3	0	—	1	1

Table 9.3 Third World regions: proportion of total urban population growth, 1950–70, by size of city. (Source: Davis, 1976)

Region	Proportion of growth in cities of		
	1000 000 +	100 000–1000 000	20 000–100 000
North Africa	33.6	28.0	38.4
West Africa	—	41.7	58.3
East Africa	—	62.3	37.7
Mid & Southern Africa	—	44.4	55.6
South Africa	47.9	17.3	34.8
Middle America	37.0	27.3	35.7
Caribbean	11.9	45.3	42.8
Tropical South America	49.9	21.2	28.9
Temperate South America	61.3	25.8	12.9
East Asia	51.8	10.1	38.1
South East Asia	46.6	19.2	34.2
South West Asia	33.5	33.7	32.8
South Central Asia	32.0	34.4	33.6
Oceania	—	—	100.0

2. Dynamics of urbanization: migration and natural increase

Urban population, like any population, grows in two main ways: by *migration*, i.e. people from non-urban areas coming to take up permanent residence in a city; and by *natural increase*, i.e. the excess of births over deaths of the residents of the cities. These two factors rarely operate in total isolation but the relative significance of one or the other is very important for the process of development. If the proportion of migrants is high, then there will be a substantial number of people for whom urban living is a relatively new and strange experience and we have already seen that migration to urban areas is indicative of other aspects of a country's social and economic geography. For example, the attractions of the city for employment or a better quality of life (note that these may be perceived attractions rather than real ones), or the lack of opportunity in the area of origin, whether for education and employment, or through shortage of land to acquire a decent standard of living. The relative balance between migration gain and natural increase also influences the rate of urban growth and therefore the capability of the authorities, both local and national, to cope with such growth.

However, it must be noted that cities which experience high rates of permanent or semi-permanent in-migration are likely to grow more as a result of subsequent natural increase than those where rates of in-migration are low or more temporary.

(a) Migration

Table 9.4 shows two types of migration data. Part (a) gives details of the proportion of the total population of specific cities born elsewhere. Thus, in Santiago, 50% of the population were born outside the city, while in Lagos the figure was 63%. This evidence suggests quite high levels of mobility, but in general is not sufficient to demonstrate that current urban growth is predominantly a function of in-migration. It must be remembered that the migrants in Table 9.4a could have moved to their respective cities at any stage in their lifetimes. This being the case, the data suggest that the majority of the population in each city was likely to have been made up of well-established migrants and those born in the city. The data in part (b) represents the proportion of urban population

Table 9.4 Migration to Third World cities.

(a) Percentage born elsewhere, 1960s		(b) Increase over set period: percentage due to migration	
Istanbul	59	Rio de Janeiro, 1920–40	75
Ankara	38	Rio de Janeiro, 1970	43
Huancayo	60[1]	Guatemala City, 1950–64	40
Lima & Callao	42	Abidjan, 1955–63	76
Lagos	63	Bogota, 1956–66	33
Santiago	50	Bombay, 1951–61	52
Kampala	52	Caracas, 1960–6	50
Bangkok	27	Djakarta, 1961–8	59
Phnom Penh	48	Istanbul, 1960–5	65
Singapore	34	Nairobi, 1961–9	50
Kuala Lumpur	50	Sao Paulo, 1960–7	68
Kuwait	50	Taipai, 1960–7	43
San Salvador	42	San Salvador, 1954–9	58

[1] Males only

growth over limited periods that was attributable to in-migration. Many of these figures are quite spectacular. For example, the city of Sao Paulo was receiving 1000 new immigrants per day between 1960 and 1967! Yet it is worth noting that the proportion of migrants declines over time in the case of Rio de Janeiro, and for many other places the proportion is around 50%. While migration is clearly important, natural increase, which tends to receive less attention, is an equally significant component of urban population growth.

(b) Natural increase

One of the most widely accepted generalizations about population in the developed world is that urban birth rates are considerably lower than those in rural areas. Easier access to contraception and abortion, the high costs of bringing up a family, and the possibility that potential parents may choose to spend more time and money on personal and social pleasures have all been suggested as reasons for this difference. A number of authorities believed that the rapid urban population growth in the Third World would soon be followed by a fall in birth rates.

However, in LDCs the urban birth rate exceeds the rural in many cases, and the urban death rate is lower than the rural death rate. For example, in India the urban death rate is 10.2 per 1000 while for rural areas it is 17.3 per 1000. Corresponding figures for Egypt are 12.4 per 1000 and 15.8 per 1000. This evidence does not support the general view that deaths, especially infant deaths, tend to be catastrophically high in the urban areas of the Third World. The difference in mortality between urban and rural areas appears to be slight, and frequently favours city dwellers.

It appears, therefore, that natural increase may well be higher in the cities than in the rural areas of the Third World. Access to clean water and better sanitation as well as public health facilities, however rudimentary, is likely to be greater in the cities and therefore mortality is likely to be lower. Also cities are likely to have a younger age structure than rural areas and this in itself will increase the birth rate and reduce the death rate. Thus, we can suggest that migration is unlikely to be as dominant a component of total urban population increase as is sometimes assumed.

Table 9.5 Estimated components of Third World urban population growth 1960–70.
(Source: Davis, 1976)

Region	Percentage of urban population increase due to	
	natural increase	migration
North Africa	57.8	42.2
West Africa	43.6	56.4
East Africa	41.3	58.7
Mid & Southern Africa	34.6	65.4
South Africa	63.3	36.7
Middle America	65.6	34.4
Caribbean	68.0	32.0
Tropical South America	57.8	42.2
Temperate South America	70.0	30.0
East Asia	22.8	77.2
South East Asia	51.9	48.1
South West Asia	51.1	48.9
South Central Asia	72.5	27.5
Oceania	41.7	58.3

(c) *The components combined*

Despite the lack of precise data on the components of urban population growth in the
Third World we can attempt to come to some conclusions using the data already discussed
and adding a simple calculation. Only a few Third World countries are significantly
affected by international migration, so at the national level most population growth is due
to natural increase. We can relate the rate of natural increase to the rate of urban
population increase over the same period and, if we assume for a moment that the rate of
natural increase for both rural and urban areas is the same, it follows that the extent to
which urban population increase exceeds national population increase must be due to
migrational gain from rural areas. The results of this calculation for major Third World
regions between 1960 and 1970 are shown in Table 9.5. The lack of equally comprehensive
data for the 1970–80 period makes it impossible to bring the situation right up to date, but
it is clear that migration is still a major factor in the growth of Third World cities; we are
also correct in stressing the equal, or greater, significance of natural increase. In 9 out
of 14 regions of the Third World, natural increase appears to be the most important
component of urban population growth. This is especially the case in Latin America but
less true of the least developed areas of Asia and Africa. While a proportion of this
natural increase may be due to immigrants themselves, the role of natural increase in
urban population growth appears to be more significant than many authorities indicate.
This fact alone has important implications for policies to contain and control urban
growth in the Third World.

ASSIGNMENTS

1. (a) *Describe the patterns of urbanization shown in Figures 9.1 and 9.2.*
    (b) *Which areas have experienced (i) the most, and (ii) the least, urban development?*
    (c) *Attempt a reasoned account of the patterns and variations shown.*
2. *Use the data in Table 9.1.*
    (a) *Calculate the total increase in urban population in the world between the 1950s and
    the 1970s.*
    (b) *Calculate the contribution of each major world region to this increase.*

(c) *Calculate the percentage that each world region contributed to the total increase in world urban population.*

(d) *Comment on the results.*

3. *Carefully examine Figure 9.3 and Table 9.3.*

   (a) *Describe the contribution to total urban population made in each region by cities of different sizes (Table 9.3).*

   (b) *Contrast the regions where large-city growth predominates with those where urban growth is due to smaller-sized settlements.*

   (c) *Give some reasons for these contrasts.*

B. Urban systems

So far in this chapter we have been discussing urban places as if they possessed common attributes of location, size and function. These attributes obviously vary and the variation leads to the need for contacts and exchanges between towns. The functional interactions between a country's urban places are important features of its economic and social life. Such interaction and interdependence suggest that the urban places in a country may form a 'system', which has a structure.

Two main types of structure have been recognized. The first is known as a 'primate' pattern where one major city (or sometimes two) dominates the whole country. The second is the 'rank-size' pattern where the size of the city is proportional to its rank in the national hierarchy of cities. The rank-size rule represents a 'balanced' system of cities and reflects the degree of national integration. Primacy, however, has been associated with the negative impact of colonialism where external forces led to growth being concentrated in one city. Although most developed countries tend to conform to the rank-size rule, evidence suggests that the structure of urban systems is not clearly related to the degree of development. It is affected by a whole range of factors. A prerequisite for understanding the present urban systems of the Third World countries is a study of their past.

1. Development and change in Third World urban systems

While a number of Third World countries possessed long-established indigenous towns, for many of them large-scale urban development was a product of colonialism. Thus the town was an instrument of political and economic control, imposed from without. The principal urban centre was frequently a port, through which trade was channelled. Subsequently, further inland 'trading post' type centres were established, particularly if the colony covered a large area. These would act as local gathering places for products before they were channelled through the major port (Figure 7.3). At this early stage the system consisted of the primary urban centre together with a network of newly established small towns. However, one may question if the term 'system' was appropriate at this stage for integration was likely to be weak and each small town would be the focal point of an isolated region with only occasional external contact. In a later phase, consolidation of the formerly independent territories occurred and certain ports became the dominant international gateways, cargoes from other coastal areas being concentrated there by coastal shipping. Inland transport (usually by rail) emphasized such concentration and aided the development of the primacy of certain favourably located ports. The pattern of port concentration in Ghana (Figure 7.4b) illustrates this process, the early wide spread of ports being replaced by concentration on Accra and Sekondi.

Similar processes operated in Latin America. In early-nineteenth-century Mexico the expansion of the export economy (often associated with the 'opening up' of new areas for

Table 9.6 A classification of urban systems development in Third World countries.

Phase	Urban systems characteristics
Pre-colonial	Few or no indigenous towns. Marketing periodic rather than based on permanent urban market places
Early colonial 1700–1840s?	Development of major port/capital. Smaller local administrative and market/service centres develop. One major city and a number of small equally-sized centres
Late colonial 1840s?–1930s?	Development of railways allows concentration on major port/capital. Primacy develops or accelerates. Foreign investment increases and exacerbates the trend. Classic primate pattern but rank size may apply to lower levels
Independence 1930s?–	Takes two forms, depending on degree of development and whether country is truly independent (Israel, Argentina) or subject to neo-colonialism. In the former, rank-size rule begins to emerge, often helped by national/regional planning strategies. In the latter, primacy continues or grows

commercial products) stimulated regional economies and the growth of smaller towns. By the early twentieth century, however, penetration by rail integrated such areas more closely to the major ports and capital, leading to the increasing primacy of such cities. As the centre of government, the primate city was also likely to attract elite groups whose purchasing power became concentrated there, thus stimulating further commercial and service activity. Furthermore, investments from abroad are likely to relate to increasing the administrative efficiency or the economic infrastructure for exports. Inevitably, such investment is concentrated on the major city through which such exports are channelled. Thus, we might expect that the historical pattern of foreign investment would relate to the degree of primacy. Contrasts between Argentina, Mexico and Cuba and other countries suggest that this was so. In 1920, Argentina had the highest degree of primacy in Latin America, closely followed by Cuba and Mexico. Argentina had 37% of total British investments in Latin America, Mexico 16% and Cuba 5%, while the latter two countries took 52% and 17% respectively of USA's investment in Latin America. On the other hand, Colombia and Venezuela had little foreign investment in the early twentieth century and neither country had a primate pattern. Overall, primacy was well established in most former colonial territories by the early twentieth century and was strongly related to past colonial experience and the pattern of foreign investment.

This historical analysis has suggested a classification of urban systems development for the majority of Third World countries (Table 9.6). As this classification indicates, the recent past has seen divergent experiences for Third World countries and the concluding section will elaborate on these using more recent data. It must be noted, however, that the urban systems of a few LDCs such as Tanzania and Mozambique may develop along different lines as these countries have adopted deliberately anti-urban policies.

2. Recent trends

Recent change will be analysed using the changing rank-size pattern of urban places in selected LDCs. The rank-size rule states that the population of a city is related directly to its rank in the national set of cities. Thus, the second largest city would be half the size of the largest city, the third largest would be one-third the size of the largest, and so on. If we

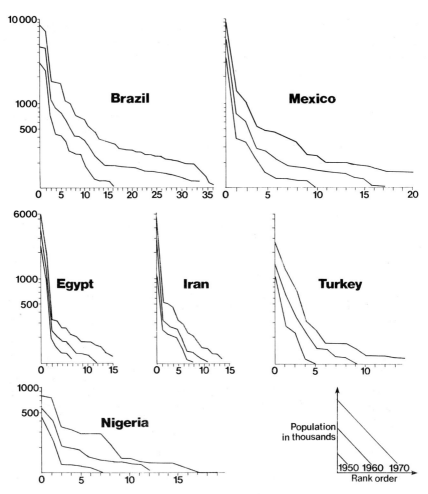

Figure 9.4 Changes in rank-size patterns, 1950, 1960 and 1970. (Source: Davis, 1976)

plot the populations of a set of cities against their ranks on logarithmic graph paper, then a perfect fit with the rank-size rule would be indicated by a straight line sloping from left to right. Figure 9.4 shows urban population plotted against rank for cities of over 100 000 in several countries. A very steep slope from left to right (Iran) indicates a primate pattern; a gentler slope (Nigeria) indicates a more balanced urban system. Figure 9.4 shows the trends of change in the rank-size pattern for 1950, 1960 and 1970.

In several cases primacy is a marked feature throughout the two decades, for example in Mexico and Iran. Other countries, such as Egypt and Brazil, show a bi-primate pattern, i.e. they possess two dominant cities. However, a marked feature of many of the graphs is the rise of a number of smaller, intermediate-sized cities, for example in Mexico, Nigeria and Turkey. The rise of such cities is a significant feature of patterns of urbanization, yet it is an aspect of urban development that is all too often ignored in favour of the much more dramatic growth of the major cities. These graphs show that primacy and conformity to some aspects of the rank-size rule are not incompatible: both elements may be present in a national urban system. In terms of development, the growth of intermediate-sized cities is of great importance. These cities are frequently regional or local centres, and their role at this local level should not be overlooked. The next section explores how the urban system functions and the impact that such centres have in their localities.

ASSIGNMENTS

1. *Study Table 9.7 and, using logarithmic graph paper, produce graphs of the rank-size distribution of cities in the four countries (as in Figure 9.4). Comment on*
   (a) the changing urban system in each country from 1950 to 1970,
   (b) the contrasts between the urban systems of the four countries over the same period.

Table 9.7 Size of major cities in four selected LDCs, 1950–70.

City	Population (thousands)			City	Population (thousands)		
	1950	1960	1970		1950	1960	1970
Pakistan				**South Africa**			
Karachi	1086	1884	3246	Johannesburg	863	1153	1400
Lahore	826	1262	1902	Cape Town	560	807	1100
Hyderabad	232	419	741	Durban	477	681	950
Lyalpur	169	402	931	Pretoria	278	423	750
				Port Elizabeth	182	291	450
Multan	182	344	636	Germiston	145	214	235
Rawalpindi	147	277	472	Bloemfontein	105	145	175
Peshawar	148	214	307	Springs	118	142	185
Gujranwala	110	186	304	Benoni	105	141	160
Sialkot	156	165	176	Pietermaritzburg	—	129	235
Sargodha	—	125	207	East London	—	116	155
Quetta	—	105	135	Vereeniging	112	—	105
Sukkur	—	101	136	Welkom	—	—	130
Jhang Maghiana	—	—	127	Roodegort-	—	—	115
Bahawalpur	—	—	161	Maraisburg			
Mardan	—	—	121	Kimberley	—	—	105
Okara	—	—	127	Krugersdorp	—	—	100
Argentina				**Colombia**			
Buenos Aires	4231	7000	9400	Bogota	607	1241	2500
Rosario	560	672	806	Medallin	341	579	1090
Cordoba	426	589	814	Cali	269	486	915
Mendoza	256	427	712	Barranquilla	287	414	645
La Plata	325	414	527	Cartagena	124	185	320
San Miguel de	224	288	370	Bucaramanga	107	177	315
Tucuman				Manizales	123	167	285
Santa Fé	217	260	312	Pereira	113	137	235
Mar del Plata	142	225	357	Cúcuta	—	129	235
San Juan	139	212	323	Ibague	—	116	200
Parana	154	175	199	Armenia	—	101	185
Bahia Blanca	128	150	176	Palmira	—	—	150
Salta	—	123	185	Bello	—	—	145
Corrientes	—	106	161	Santa Marta	—	—	145
Santiago del	—	103	129	Buenaventura	—	—	100
Estero							
Posadas	—	—	135				
Resistencia	—	—	120				
(San Fernando)							

2. *Use Table 9.7 and a good atlas.*
   (a) Plot the location and size of the cities in the four countries.
   (b) Examine the spatial patterning of large cities in these countries.
   (c) How important do you think that an even spatial distribution of cities of similar sizes is for the social and economic development of a country?

C. The System in Action

The purpose of this section is to show how the urban system functions in reality and how many facets of the social and economic life of a country are channelled through and between, and spread out from, the component parts of the urban system. Three features will be examined: the relationship of migration to the urban system, the flows of commodities and information within the urban system and, finally, the internal economic structure of Third World urban systems.

1. Migration and the urban system

Migration may take the form of a direct movement from the place of origin to the final destination or it may be accomplished in a series of stages (see Chapter 8). The migrant may begin by moving from village to nearest town, then to provincial capital, then to national capital. In other words, such migrants are 'filtered' through the urban system in a

Figure 9.5 Migration streams to (a) Istanbul and   (b) Adana. (Source: Philipponneau, 1973, pp. 416, 417)

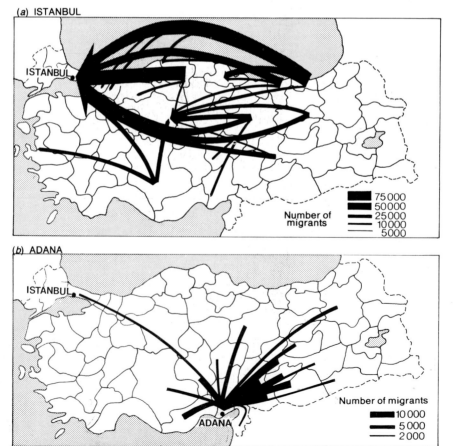

series of stages. In these cases we would expect that smaller towns would have a localized 'migration field' around them while the larger cities would attract migrants from considerable distances, eventually attracting those who initially moved from their village to the nearest town. The example of Turkey will be used to illustrate the process.

As in many other LDCs, Turkey's population has become more likely to migrate. In 1935, 6.8% of the total population left their district of birth. By 1965, the proportion was 12.6%. Although Turkey has a quite well-developed urban system (Figure 9.4), Istanbul is by far the largest city with 9.6% of the national population living there in 1970. With such primacy we would expect Istanbul to attract migrants from further afield than other large cities in Turkey. Figure 9.5 shows the main migration streams to Istanbul and Adana. Istanbul has a much more extensive migration field than the latter, reflecting its dominance within the country. However, Turkey does provide evidence of step migration (Figure 9.6) and quite well-defined migration paths existed dependent on the provinces of

Figure 9.6 Migration paths in Turkey. (Source: Philipponneau, 1973, pp. 422, 423)

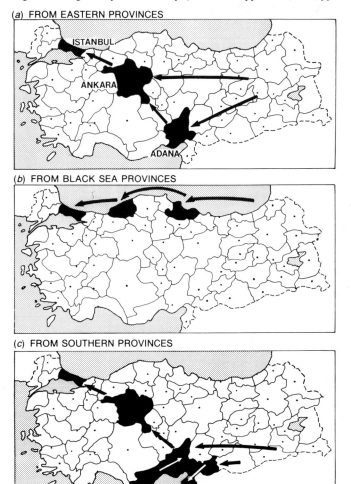

(*a*) FROM EASTERN PROVINCES

(*b*) FROM BLACK SEA PROVINCES

(*c*) FROM SOUTHERN PROVINCES

origin. Migrants from the eastern provinces tend to stop in Adana or Ankara first. Migrants from the Black Sea provinces first look for work in Samsun and Zonguldak, while those from the south and south east stop in Mersin, Adana, Tarsus or Hotay, and then go on to Ankara and to Istanbul. Migrants from western provinces follow the Izmir–Bursa–Istanbul route. This step migration is a feature of migration in Turkey but it does appear that direct (although possibly short-range) movement to Istanbul was more common.

Recent studies, especially in Latin America and East Asia, suggest that direct migration from origin to destination has grown considerably. For example, in the *barrios* of Bogota, 58% of the people moved directly to the city and in Santiago 51% of males were direct migrants. Improved transport played a significant part in this trend. The type of migration, whether direct or by stages, is important in its likely impact on social and political attitudes. Step migration may ease the cultural adjustment of the migrant from rural areas, while the sudden transition of the direct migrant may have other consequences. Chapter 10 draws attention to the survival of 'traditional' rural-based ways of life in the large city and it is possible that this is in some measure due to the problems of adjustment faced by the direct migrant with no previous urban experience.

2. Hierarchies and flows in the system

We have examined the idea of a system of cities through the medium of the rank-size rule. An alternative way of examining such systems is through their hierarchical and nodal structure. The territory of any region may be viewed as being organized around a series of 'nodes', these centres of organization being the major urban areas. Space is 'organized' around them in the sense that it is from them that commodities and new ideas are spread. We shall examine the nature and significance of this aspect of the urban system in Kenya.

Figure 9.7 shows the urban hierarchy in Kenya and indicates that it is characterized by spatial and structural imbalance. Almost two-thirds of the urban population is concentrated in the cities of Nairobi and Mombasa. Figure 9.8 shows a further aspect of the structure of Kenyan space: newspaper circulation. The circulation of English-language newspapers reflects the dominance of Nairobi and, to a lesser extent, Mombasa. The circulation of Swahili newspapers is rather different, the relative significance of Nairobi being considerably reduced. The ratio of Swahili to English-language newspaper circulation is only 0.3 in Nairobi while it is 1.2 in Nyeri and Kericho and 0.9 in Nakura and Kisumu. Therefore, it seems more appropriate to talk of two sub-systems, one indigenous and the other primarily 'European'. The evolution of Kenya's urban system supports this view. In the pre-colonial era, urban influences were felt only on the coast, mainly owing to contact with Arab traders. Colonial government introduced a system of provinces and districts, each centred on a settlement. Away from the coast this was usually an entirely new creation. Such administrative centres (many located along railway lines for convenience) provided a network of settlements in which commerce could be located. In the 'White Highlands' in the south west a cash economy was introduced by European commercial and agricultural interests and this produced a denser pattern of towns, but industry played little part in their establishment. This network of towns also attracted Asian traders, providing commodities for Europeans but also buying and selling in the rural hinterland.

Thus, African participation in an urban way of life and in the urban economy was extremely limited and has only recently grown to significance. The importance of non-Africans in the major urban centres of Nairobi and Mombasa is an illustration of this (Figure 9.7). But Africans are increasing their contact with urban culture through

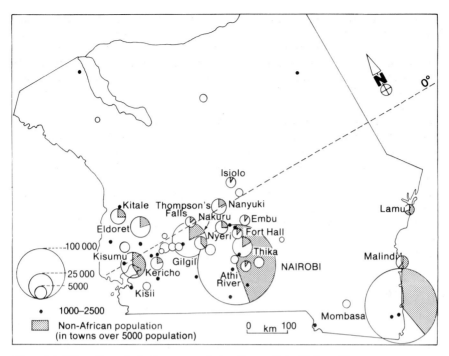

Figure 9.7 Urban hierarchy in Kenya: population (Source: Soja, 1968, p. 50)

Figure 9.8 Newspaper circulation in Kenya. (*a*) English-language newspapers,   (*b*) Swahili newspapers. (Source: Soja, 1968, p. 43)

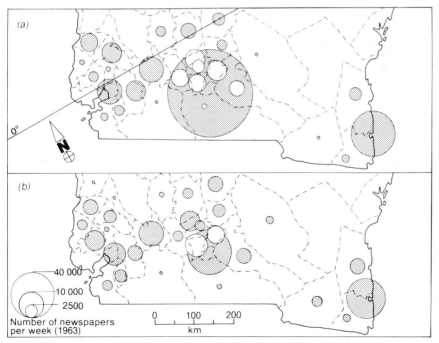

221

temporary migration to the town and 'European' farming areas for wage labour. Close contacts are kept with tribal areas but dissemination of urban culture has resulted. All this suggests that Western style measures of urban hierarchy may be increasingly inappropriate in the African context. Figure 9.8b showing the circulation of Swahili newspapers in Kenya indicates different urban hierarchy from Figure 9.8a. Possibly the best way to view the Kenyan urban system is as a 'dual' one with an African and a non-African component. In some senses these are separate, but in others they overlap.

We have seen that the network of urban places provides a basis for the spatial organization of human activity in the Third World countries as well as in the developed world. Flows of commodities and information are channelled through the system and so, too, are the forces of modernization and development. However, we have noted that participation in this urban system is not the same for all groups and Third World urban systems appear to be characterized by 'duality': one predominantly Western orientated, being partly a product of colonization and modern patterns of investment; the other being more indigenous and of a much lower economic order.

3. Economic and social dualism within the urban system

(a) The two circuits

This dual urban economy has been given many names, the 'formal' and 'informal' sectors and, more recently, the 'upper economic circuit' and the 'lower economic circuit'. The two sectors have particular characteristics (Table 9.8). The *upper circuit* consists of large-scale, usually foreign-owned, enterprises, financed by overseas or international capital and using technology developed elsewhere. Its products cater for the 'elite' market. Also involved in the upper circuit is the government. Many Third World governments invest a large proportion of their funds in economic enterprises, whether in basic industries or the provision of infrastructure. Thus the state itself becomes a significant source of employment, particularly for the 'elite' (Plate 9.1) with sufficient education or influence to compete for such jobs. Many are, of course, in the bureaucracy of government.

The *lower circuit* is predominantly small in scale, is financed by small amounts of local capital, is indigenously owned and often based on the family and kinship network.

Table 9.8 Characteristics of the two circuits of the Third World urban economy. (Source: Santos, 1979).

Variable	Upper circuit	Lower circuit
Technology	Capital intensive	Labour intensive
Organization	Bureaucratic	Primitive
Capital	Abundant	Limited
Labour	Limited	Abundant
Regular wages	Common	Exceptional
Prices	Fixed	Negotiable: bartering
Credit	Banks: institutional	Personal: non-institutional
Relations with customers	Impersonal	Direct; personalized
Fixed costs	Substantial	Negligible
Cycling of goods	None	Frequent
Government aid	Substantial	Almost none
Dependence on overseas	Great: externally oriented	Small or none

Plate 9.1 Luxury house in Mérida, Yucatan, Mexico. Mérida was an important colonial city established in 1542 by 70 Spanish colonists led by Francisco de Montejo. By 1549 some 178 communities of Mayan Indians were administered from Mérida. The development of administration and the wealth created by the henequen industry (Plate 6.3), led to the emergence of an economic and social elite. These people built the Paseo de Montejo, a Parisian-style boulevard, lined with trees and running northwards from the city centre. The house shown in the photograph is located on the modern extension of this avenue which remains the wealthiest social area in what is now a city of over 300 000 people. Most of the rest of the city consists of simple single-storey houses or squatter housing areas. It is indicative of the relatively unchanging class structures of many LDCs that many of the families living in the Paseo de Montejo and the adjacent high-class area are descendants of the earliest colonists and, despite land reform, still derive much of their wealth and status from inherited land. (*Photograph: G. P. O'Hare*)

Technology is limited and the enterprise is likely to be labour intensive. The average number of people per enterprise is small, but the number of concerns means that total urban employment is considerable.

The lower circuit of the urban economy has two major components. First, there is the traditional bazaar sector, based mainly on family enterprises. This consists of small trade and service establishments and industrial or craft workshops. It may account for between 35% and 45% of the labour force and its major feature is the production of traditional goods or services for the low-income mass market. The whole kinship group may be involved and there is intense competition between similar enterprises. This keeps prices and profits at a low level. The financial returns are near the minimum for subsistence for the family group. The second sector in the lower circuit may be termed the 'street economy' (Plate 9.2). Included in this group are the lottery ticket sellers, street hawkers, shoe shine boys, water sellers, professional beggars and petty thieves, prostitutes and pimps. According to Berry (1974), this sector accounts for between 25% and 40% of the total labour force. Earnings are on, or below, the minimum for subsistence and most people engaged in this sector lead highly marginal lives.

The upper circuit of the urban economy includes government, 'Westernized' commerce and bureaucracy, capital business and modern manufacturing activity. This sector provides between 15% and 50% of urban employment but this varies enormously

Plate 9.2 Human porterage in Istanbul, Turkey. One of the most striking visual features of LDCs is the amount of human porterage to be seen, and the heavy loads that are carried. This reflects the lack of transport and equipment for handling and transferring goods in bulk and, as in this scene, the unsuitability of the streets for motor transport. This old man had struggled up the steep slope to the right, which led down to the Bosporus. He is one of many casual labourers who daily gather on the dockside or near the markets and who are employed on an irregular, delivery by delivery, basis. Warehouse workers, merchants and retailers employ them to carry specific loads to specific destinations in the old city. Another element of the 'street economy' may be seen on the corner in the form of a stove on wheels, used for the cooking of maize-cobs for sale to passers-by. (*Photograph: M. Barke*)

from city to city, its significance being greatest, of course, in the capital or primate city (Table 6.4). In manufacturing industry, units tend to be large (Plate 6.5) and levels of technology quite high but in most Third World countries 'modern' manufacturing employs only 10-20% of the total labour force. In the commercial and bureaucratic sectors, some education is required for entry, and employment in it confers middle-class status.

This dual economic structure in the urban areas of the Third World is, as one would expect, reflected in the consumption patterns of different social classes and emphasizes the different 'social worlds' which exist in large Third World cities. Contrast, for example, Plates 9.1 and 10.5 and note the contrast in Plate 9.3.

Plate 9.3 Modern shops and Indian woman, Mexico City. The photograph gives a clear indication of what is meant by the 'dual economy'. On the one hand are the modern clothing stores, selling Western-style shirts, and suits. Seated on the pavement outside, however, is an Indian woman from the countryside, attempting to make a few pesos by selling nuts to the passing pedestrians. The street is called San Juan de Letran, one of Mexico City's main thoroughfares. The Indian woman is fortunate to have acquired such a 'pitch', for the competition for sites among the many street sellers is intense. However, it is only a matter of time before the police force her to move on. (*Photograph: M. Barke*)

(b) 'Dualism' and its significance for development

The bazaar economy represents more than just an economic system; it represents a traditional way of life where the objective is not merely profit but also the effective employment of the family. Jobs that offer little return may be regarded as useful activity if they employ an elderly relative or small child. With this in mind, it becomes easier to understand the persistence, or even the growth, of the lower circuit of urban economic activity. In its intensive use of labour the lower circuit facilitates the transfer of people from a rural to an urban way of life, enabling them to persist in a slightly modified form with their previous existence. In some cases this tendency is so strong that some authors have spoken of the 'ruralization' of Third World cities (see Chapter 10). One of the striking facts about Third World cities is the number of animals that are kept or the persistence of small agriculture to supplement income derived from other forms of employment (Plate 9.4).

Ethnic and kinship groups are extremely important in Third World cities as they perform vital functions in a situation where economic opportunities are limited. The existence of such groupings creates a small localized monopoly of jobs and clients, as well as providing help in times of illness, assistance with small loans, advice, and information. Therefore, the existence of lower-circuit activities with their apparently backward and marginal economic characteristics should not be interpreted as producing a socially disorientated urban population, for in fact this circuit performs several positive functions for the urban poor.

Plate 9.4 Housing and garden plots in Freetown, Sierra Leone. This photograph was taken about 1 kilometre from the centre of Freetown, well within the built-up area of the city. The discontinuous nature of development is clear, as is its semi-rural character. Two-storey houses of a reasonable quality are intermixed with tin shacks. Nearby garden plots help to supplement food supplies or possibly add to income. The fairly steep slopes have prevented more intensive development in the past but, as migration to Freetown continues, it seems likely that more squatters will try to occupy the available sites, despite the physical difficulties. In Freetown, such squatters are likely to face more opposition from existing residents than from the authorities. (*Photograph: M. Barke*)

ASSIGNMENTS

1. Describe the ways in which the dominance of one major city in a LDC may be considered harmful to its social and economic development.
2. Refer to Figures 9.5 and 9.6.
   (a) Describe the patterns of migration shown in Figure 9.5.
   (b) Explain the patterns in terms of (i) the relative size and opportunities offered by the two cities, and (ii) the friction of distance.
   (c) To what extent do the migration paths shown in Figure 9.6 support the idea of step migration?
   (d) With reference to these examples, discuss how people involved in step migration are likely to differ in their adjustment to an urban way of life compared with those who move straight to the city from a rural background.
3. Examine Figures 9.7 and 9.8.
   (a) Describe briefly the urban hierarchy shown in Figure 9.7.
   (b) Compare the urban pattern shown in Figure 9.7 with Figure 9.8a and b.
   (c) What other measures could be used to indicate the urban hierarchy in Kenya?

(d) Comment on the value of each measure in depicting the urban hierarchy of Kenya.

(e) Explain your findings in terms of the socio-economic dualism discussed in the chapter.

D. Third World Cities: Generative or Parasitic?

This chapter has examined recent trends of urbanization, the characteristics of urban systems and some aspects of how such systems function. We have seen that urban growth and change have been significant features but that 'traditional' elements are still characteristic of many Third World cities. In particular, urbanization has not necessarily been associated with industrialization and rapid economic development. Thus, several authorities have argued that rather than being generative of economic growth, cities in many Third World countries are parasitic, i.e. they make very few positive contributions to fundamental economic development. In this final section we shall explore this important debate and attempt to come to some conclusions about the role of cities in the development process.

1. The alleged advantages of towns and cities in the Third World

(a) Commercially, towns provide the market (Figure 10.10) and exchange centres which are necessary in the conversion of a predominantly subsistence economy to a cash economy. For example, it may be argued that the possibility of obtaining cash for agricultural produce may stimulate productivity and efficiency among farmers.

(b) Industrially, towns may provide a stimulus for development as they are large agglomerations of population and therefore of labour (Plate 6.1). From the point of view of industrial developers, the larger the town the better. They have a greater possibility of finding a work force with a wide range of skills or with the aptitude to be 'trained up' to the necessary level of skill. Also, the presence of a large pool of unskilled manual labour, something that is likely to be present in the large city, helps to keep labour costs down.

(c) Politically, towns may assist in the development of a more 'nationalist' orientation. Many Third World countries are characterized by heterogeneous populations. This diversity of tribal, religious and ethnic backgrounds has been a major problem in the attempts to achieve political unity (see Chapters 3 and 8). The city, in the very nature of its daily life, may lead to greater mixing of peoples which may assist in the breaking down of the tribal or racial tensions which are damaging to political stability.

(d) Administratively, the town provides economies of scale. This is especially so in the provision of public services such as education and health (Plate 3.2). The congregation of people into settlements of relatively high density facilitates such provision.

(e) Socially, the mixing of people in the city exposes them to a diversity of ideas and stimuli. These may be important in the change of attitudes, beliefs and values which constitute a part of the modernization process. The influence of traditional, mainly rural, beliefs and customs may be limiting. Contact with others may help to weaken such ties and lead to a greater readiness to accept new ideas and techniques.

Clearly, there are counter-arguments which could be put to each of these points. Nevertheless, they, or variants of them, have been suggested at different times as possible benefits of urbanization in the Third World. Many early strategies for development therefore incorporated the notion of encouraging urban growth as part of the development programme. (Note, however, that some LDCs have subsequently discouraged urban growth; for example Tanzania).

These alleged advantages have been presented in a rather oversimplified way but we can now examine the changing attitudes to urban development and trace the factors which have been important in shaping these changing attitudes.

2. Pessimistic views in the 1960s

As shown in Figure 3.2, Rostow identified five broad stages of economic growth. In his second stage 'the preconditions for take-off', he outlined some of the necessary dimensions of change and it is clear that he considered urban growth to be part of the precondition. Brian Berry's analysis (1962) of the relationship between urbanization and a variety of indices of economic development point to the same conclusion for he demonstrated a high positive correlation between economic development and urbanization. The most urbanized countries were the most advanced countries economically.

During the 1960s, however, this view was increasingly questioned. A major reason for this was the availability of better data. For the first time, conclusions could be based on reasonably accurate figures rather than on guesswork. These features revealed that the rate of urbanization, and especially that of migration, was very high. This had clear implications for (1) urban employment and unemployment, and (2) urban housing and social conditions.

(a) Urban employment, unemployment and underemployment

Few among the growing city populations appeared to be securing permanent and stable employment, and even fewer were working in industry. That is, few were experiencing the transition from agricultural to urban industrial employment. The role of cities in economic development therefore began to be questioned. We have already noted the existence of the dual economy in Third World cities and that few people have been able to participate in the 'modern' sectors of employment. Even when growth in manufacturing output has taken place it has usually failed to generate significant employment. The growth of manufacturing output is, typically, three or four times the growth of employment.

It seems highly unlikely that modern-sector industrial development can solve the employment problems of Third World cities. For example in Brazil in 1970, 40% of the population lived in urban areas of 20 000 or more but only 18% of this urban population was engaged in manufacturing. Inevitably, cities in the Third World are characterized by extremely high rates of unemployment.

However, we should not forget the chronic underemployment in Third World cities. As many as 30% or over 100 million people, in Third World urban areas may be considered as heavily underemployed. Many of these are, of course, the casual street employees in the lower circuit. Rapid urbanization in the Third World has outstripped expansion in manufacturing employment resulting in many people making a direct shift out of agriculture into services and casual street employment, if not unemployment. In other words, in addition to chronic unemployment and underemployment, the employment structures of Third World cities are dangerously top-heavy. In this sense, many Third World cities may be regarded as 'parasitic'. They make very little wealth-creating contributions to the economy, being centres of the non-productive bureaucracy, the inflated consumption patterns of the elite, and the teeming underemployed masses engaged in non-productive services. Furthermore, the massive influx of migrants (Table 9.4) creates the demand for more basic services, the most rudimentary of which cost money to provide. Yet, if such people are not engaged in productive work they are adding to national costs without adding to income.

Thus, in the 1960s, arguments based largely on the employment and unemployment characteristics of Third World cities led to increasingly negative attitudes being expressed about the role of the city in development.

(b) Urban housing and social conditions

Also in the 1960s, attention was drawn to the appallingly low standards of housing accommodation in Third World cities. Social problems such as lack of services and amenities (e.g. piped water and sewage disposal: Figure 10.13), illiteracy, squalor, ill health, crime and prostitution were noted. Much of the physical growth in Third World cities has taken the form of uncontrolled shanty or squatter settlement (see Table 10.3). Estimates of the numbers existing in 'minimum' standards of housing must be extremely tentative, but a recent World Bank report on six selected cities suggested that the proportion varied from 33% to 66% of the total population in each city.

Chapter 10 illustrates housing conditions but here we can note the links which have been made between these appalling conditions (or lack of housing) and manifestations of social disorganization. Perhaps the most influential theory in the 1960s was that developed by Oscar Lewis who put forward the notion of 'the culture of poverty', whereby the poor withdrew from the larger society and created their own norms of behaviour. According to Lewis, the individual growing up in this culture is likely to be fatalistic, and feel helpless and inferior. These characteristics, together with the poverty of the family or individual, increase the likelihood of social disorganization. Stealing from those who are better off may be regarded as acceptable, prostitution may be regarded as a legitimate way of 'earning a living'. Thus, the existence of appalling social conditions was linked to tendencies towards crime and delinquency and led to a totally negative view of Third World cities and their role in development.

(c) Over-urbanization and excessive primacy

Several authorities also began to cast doubt on the assumption that urban development was beneficial to economic growth and the modernization of LDCs. They argued that terms such as 'parasitic' were more appropriate descriptions and that a state of 'over-urbanization' existed, especially in those countries characterized by a primate urban system. Far from being a catalyst of change and development in a national context, the primate city may be a positive hindrance. Four major problems associated with primacy may be identified.

(i) We noted that several of the alleged benefits of urban development are based on economies of scale. That is, it is cheaper and easier to provide services to a dense urban population than to a widely scattered rural population. However, excessive growth produces numerous problems: housing shortages, traffic congestion, pollution, inadequate service provision, etc. Although these problems may not directly cost money, they certainly detract from the quality of life. The solutions to them do cost money and are often beyond the financial means of the city or even national governments in the LDCs.

(ii) Excessive primacy has a cumulative negative effect on other regions of the country. The world trading and financial system is, understandably, concentrated in the primate city. As the economic dominance of large organizations grows more significant, this tendency increases. Thus, the skyscrapers that exist in Lima are not a symbol of the progress and development of the city and the nation, but a symbol of the international power of huge companies and international banks. This concentration of international commerce on the primate city leads to demands for greater public investment there: expensive 'Western' urban planning schemes, urban motorways, airports, international hotels (Plate 10.8). Both public and private investment are therefore disproportionately concentrated in such cities while other areas are deprived of investment.

(iii) Similarly, the fact that most of the elite foreign business people and diplomats are concentrated in the primate city means that the lower classes in the indigenous population are in visual contact with the products and life style of the developed world. This helps to create a desire for the 'trappings' of Western-style culture: cars, clothes and records. Scarce resources are poured into this consumer-oriented sector rather than into more fundamental development schemes. So the primate city leads to the creation of 'artificial' and superimposed consumption patterns.

(iv) Finally, excessive primacy has an impact in a rather less obvious way. For example, in Peru the attitude of the Government, the elite, and the media is such as to perpetuate the notion that Lima is the only place to be in Peru. In the Press (controlled from Lima) the provinces are largely symbolized as holding back the progress of Lima and the nation. Government decisions frequently protect the interests of Lima first, because it is here that the Government and the elite reside (70% of the jobs in government and public services are in Lima). The majority of teachers have urban (mainly Lima) backgrounds, but on qualification they may be sent out to schools in the provinces. Frequently, their dissatisfaction with their present abode and the unfavourable comparisons they make with Lima are passed on to the children they teach. The idea that Lima is the 'best' and 'only' place to be in Peru may be passed on to the next generation whose potential for migration is considerable.

The late 1950s and 1960s saw considerable questioning of the view that urbanization was a major force in development and economic growth, and rather pessimistic views developed on the relationship between the two. A 'classical' body of theory developed about the nature of cities and their role in social and economic change. If we take the hypotheses that were formulated about migration and social change, the expectations of urban scholars ran something like this. 'People migrate to the cities of the Third World in the hope of improving their material status but, rather than experiencing this, they have to endure material deprivation and the frustration of their hopes. This is likely to lead to social disorganization and disruption and, in time, to the development of more radical political attitudes. These tendencies will be exacerbated by the continued influx of migrants and the widening gap between urban population growth and industrial employment growth, leading to increasing competition for scarce resources.' Therefore, the expectation was that rapid migration would produce alienation, disillusionment, psychological and social problems and possible political disruption. Such was the thinking which coloured attitudes to Third World cities in the 1950s and early 1960s.

3. Cautious optimism?

However, the late 1960s and 1970s have once again seen a shift in the consensus view about urbanization and development, and a more positive view of urban migration is being taken (see Chapter 10). The major view of migrants is that their life chances have frequently been improved by moving to the city. As we have also seen, rural-based customs have continued in the city and, in order to assist in coping with their new environment, the migrant population has adapted or devised means of mutual support. This is not to deny that problems exist. Unemployment, desperate poverty, criminality and deviance are relatively commonplace in many Third World cities. But the massive social disorganization and revolutionary political activity predicted by early theories has not taken place. Furthermore, many recent studies of shanty towns and squatter settlements have shown how they are capable of considerable self-improvement over time (see Chapter 10). Thus, the social consequences of urban growth may be seen in a more positive light than previously. However, much of the writing on the city and development has been concerned with economic factors. How has this come to be seen in a more positive way?

As Table 9.9 shows, it is not the case that migrants to the city experience limited employment opportunities and continuing poverty. However, much discussion has concentrated on the negative aspects of the growth of tertiary employment. It is surely an error to do so since tertiary employment also incorporates the growth of essential services such as medicine and education. Even the petty trading activity that is characteristic of Third World cities may be viewed in a more positive light. The concept of over-urbanization fails to take into account what the people employed in such services would be doing if they were not engaged in the selling of lottery tickets or matchboxes. At least in the city they have the possibility of access to some services such as medicine and elementary education for their children. In the rural areas from which they came, such facilities may be totally lacking.

Finally, many of the criticisms of urban development, if they are examined closely, appear to be criticisms of excessive primacy. Although the primate city may dominate, we have seen that in many Third World countries not all urban development is necessarily centred there. Smaller intermediate centres may still have beneficial and positive effects. They possess economies of scale for serving the needs of the population in their region. Hospitals, clinics, schools, agricultural advisory centres and marketing facilities may be located in them. Thus, such centres may grow, not on the basis of industrial expansion, but through the performance of commercial and administrative functions. Their effect, both for the populations of such centres and their hinterlands, may be nothing but beneficial. It is therefore important to distinguish between the problems of excessive primacy and the rest of the urban system. To stress the problems of primate cities is not to suggest that all Third World urban development is negative in its impact. Therefore, while urban development can again be seen in a more favourable light, much attention needs to be given to the most appropriate pattern of urban development for particular regions. It may be that the promotion of a pattern that approximates rather more to the rank-size rule, with towns that occupy nodal positions with respect to the regions they serve, may prove to be the ideal pattern for the urban system.

Table 9.9 Percentage of migrants and natives in various types of employment in three Latin American cities. (Source: Gilbert, 1974, p. 119)

	Santiago		Mexico City		Guatemala City	
	Native	Migrant	Native	Migrant	Native	Migrant
Professional & managerial	17.3	24.8	7.2	6.7	13.5	13.1
Office workers	11.4	11.6	18.1	15.9	8.3	8.6
Salespersons	12.1	9.7	15.8	15.9	7.6	7.3
Drivers & delivery workers	7.5	5.0	5.9	10.1	7.9	10.1
Farmers & miners	1.3	2.1			5.0	5.9
Skilled manual	35.1	29.5	48.8	43.4	46.2	33.2
Unskilled manual	4.6	4.8			5.5	8.4
Personal service	7.9	11.3	6.2	7.9	1.9	10.7
Seeking work	2.8	1.2	—	—	4.2	2.6

1. *Why should towns and cities play an important role in social and economic development? Make a list of their advantages.*
2. *Refer to Table 9.9.*
   (a) *Describe the nature of employment of migrants to the three cities.*
   (b) *How far do the data support the view that migrants experience limited job opportunities and continuing poverty?*
   (c) *Given that Latin American cities tend to be among the most developed in the Third World, would you expect similar patterns to be found in African cities?*

Key Ideas

A. Urban Population Trends
1. The highest proportions of urban dwellers occur in the MDCs.
2. The majority of the Third World's population are rural dwellers.
3. Nevertheless, there has been massive recent growth in Third World urban populations.
4. There is considerable diversity in the proportion of urban dwellers in Third World countries.
5. To a large extent such diversity may be explained by historical patterns of development.
6. Although very large cities account for a large proportion of the recent urban population growth, smaller urban places also account for a very significant proportion.
7. There is considerable disagreement over the relative contributions of migrational gain and natural increase to urban population growth.
8. Despite the greater attention given to spectacular increases due to migration, the available data indicate that natural increase is the more important component of urban growth in most regions.

B. Urban Systems
1. Urban areas do not exist in isolation and their inter-actions with their hinterlands and each other suggest that they form part of a system.
2. This system has a structure, the two extremes of which are a primate pattern and a pattern that conforms to the rank-size rule.
3. The nature of the urban system in any country is not easily explained by simple measures of current economic development.
4. The development of a 'balanced' urban system (rank-size rule) depends on the degree of integration and interdependence within the country and the intensity of external contacts.
5. Primacy and a rank-size distribution are not mutually exclusive properties of a national urban system.
6. Trends of change in rank-size graphs for a number of countries since 1950 show a growth in the number of intermediate-sized cities.

C. The System in Action
1. The degree of migration to urban places is related to their size in the urban system.
2. Although step migration exists in Third World countries, direct migration to the major centres is also common.
3. Step migration may help in the gradual transition from rural or small-town attitudes to those of the big city, while direct migrants are more likely to retain their rural values.
4. Flow of goods and information are related to the structure of the urban system, so that larger places dominate at the expense of smaller.

5. However, in some Third World countries the nature of the urban system may only have meaning for certain groups, i.e. those participating in the 'modern' economic sector.
6. It is therefore possible to identify a 'dual' economic structure in most Third World countries: one modern and one 'traditional'.
7. The modern sector is likely to be almost exclusively concentrated in the capital and other large cities, while the traditional sector may also be found there but predominates in small towns and rural areas.
8. The traditional sector, although frequently viewed as economically backward, performs many positive functions in a social sense and may also adapt itself to some of the needs of the modern sector of the economy.

D. *Third World Cities: Generative or Parasitic?*
1. Urban places perform a number of important functions in the process of development.
2. Studies in the 1960s found that there was little employment being created in the modern industrial sectors of Third World cities.
3. Other studies showed that many of the rural-to-urban migrants were enduring appalling housing and social conditions.
4. For these reasons it is possible to argue that many Third World countries may be considered 'over-urbanized'.
5. For these and other reasons, the role of cities in economic development in the Third World was called into question.
6. More recently, positive views have again emerged, partly due to more detailed studies of so-called 'shanty-towns'.
7. Many of the criticisms directed at Third World urbanization are really criticisms of excessive primacy.

Additional Activities

1. (a) Using the data in the most recent edition of the *World Bank Development Report* (Oxford University Press), construct a graph by plotting the figures of per capita GNP against urban population increase for a selection of MDCs and LDCs.
   (b) Is the rate of urban expansion related in any way to the degree of development as measured by GNP?
   (c) Which groups of countries experienced the greatest and the least expansion in their urban populations?
   (d) What other factors may influence the rate of urban expansion, especially in the Third World?
   (e) Attempt to explain your results for different groups of countries, namely: (i) MDCs, (ii) oil-exporting LDCs and NICs (see Chapter 1), (iii) the poorest LDCs.
2. Examine Plates 6.1, 6.2, 6.4, 6.5, 9.1, 9.2 and 9.3. For each photograph answer the following questions.
   (a) Write a brief description of the urban scene.
   (b) Comment on the extent to which the scene indicates 'dualism' in the urban economy.
   (c) Comment on the photographs as evidence of the 'generative' or 'parasitic' nature of cities in the LDCs.
3. '... urban development in the West and in the underdeveloped countries today is the same process although greatly separated in time and place.'
   (a) Read Carter (1981), Chapter 16, pp. 380–404.
   (b) Discuss the validity of the statement above.

10

Forms of Settlement

Introduction

In this chapter we look at settlement patterns and the internal structure of settlements in the Third World. We are concerned with both rural and urban settlements. In the MDCs it is not always easy to distinguish between the two, and national definitions vary widely. In the Third World the distinction is even more difficult to make but we shall adopt a functional definition in this chapter. A rural settlement is deemed to be one that is mainly concerned with primary activities, especially agriculture, while an urban settlement obviously performs a much wider range of functions.

A. Rural Settlement

In this section we shall examine the dynamic forces influencing rural settlement patterns and the internal structure of settlements. We shall consider firstly the factors influencing settlement in the past and secondly those which have, more recently, changed 'traditional' patterns.

1. Factors influencing settlement patterns

A number of physical factors influence the pattern and extent of rural settlement in any area and, although the need for defence may in the past have governed the nature of the settlement pattern, this too may be closely related to physical factors. Yet social and economic factors also are important, such as those concerned with agricultural systems, land availability and ownership, and the social organization of the group. It is only rarely that a single factor will operate in isolation and offer a total explanation of a particular settlement pattern. For example, the need for defence may be the primary consideration, and this may lead to the search for a suitable site in a specific type of environment. But, within that environment, the precise location may be governed by other factors, for example the availability of water.

(a) Physical factors

The presence or absence of water is perhaps the most fundamental influence on settlement patterns. Without water no permanent settlement can develop, yet the precise relationship between the siting of the settlement and the availability of water may vary. It is not always the case that settlements locate as near as possible to the water supply, especially where water is generally fairly readily available. As indicated in Chapter 3, Section B, many diseases are waterborne and this often provides a good reason for not wishing to be too close to the water supply. It should be noted also that the carrying of water is women's work in many LDCs, but decisions about the locations of settlements are made by men.

Villages may be located at some distance from available sources of water, resulting in long daily journeys for the women (Figure 10.1). In more marginal environments, however, water can dictate the pattern of settlement as in the case of oasis settlement. In the northern province of Sudan, linear settlements occur along the banks of the Nile, on a narrow strip of irrigated land, each land holder occupying a strip of land at right angles to the river.

Other physical factors may also be important. Many countries have patterns of movement associated with transhumance, a feature related to the need to find pasture and water in very difficult terrain. During the summer, herds are moved from the aridity and heat of the valley floors to the higher grazing pastures where the snow has melted. In the winter months, movement may take place away from the low temperatures of the interior mountain valleys to the adjacent lower-lying areas, as for example in central Turkey.

Figure 10.1 Villages and water supply in Ghana. (Abstracted from topographic map)

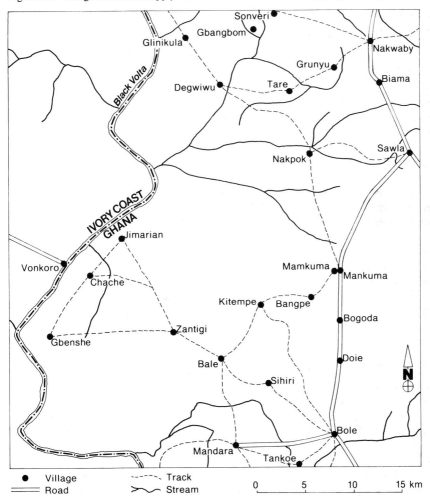

(b) Defence

Although this is a factor that has declined in importance in recent times, it remains an explanation for the distribution and siting of many long-established villages. In areas of India where disturbances were frequent, for example the north west frontier, villages may be grouped around a small fort, and the close-packed houses with blank outer walls and few entrance points give the villages a defensive appearance.

Hill settlements were a widespread feature of tropical Africa and were often associated with boundary zones, for example between the Hausa and Fulani in northern Nigeria, and, further south, between the Yoruba empire and the kingdom of Dahomey. These hill settlements were most common on the periphery of strong military states where weaker tribes sought defensive sites to survive slave raids, holy wars and the influx of stronger tribes. Figure 10.2 shows tightly nucleated villages on the extensive hill masses of the Jos plateau where the farmlands are usually to be found close to the village, within the walls. Such settlements may still be found but many have begun to disintegrate in recent times.

(c) Social organization

Although less obvious than the factors we have been considering so far, the type of social organization in an area may be a powerful influence on the settlement pattern. We can distinguish between two major types of social organization: those that are hierarchically structured and those that are more individualistic. The former would have a pyramidal structure, with the chief at the top, the elders below and the mass of the population at the base. Decision making is likely to be from above and this is expressed territorially in a highly structured and organized pattern of settlement (Figure 10.7). In the more individualistic and socially fragmented type of society, where the unit is likely to be the man and his immediate family, a more fragmented settlement pattern is likely to result, as for example among the Tiv people of northern Nigeria (see Plate 5.1).

Figure 10.2 Hill villages in the Jos plateau of Nigeria. (Source: Gleave, 1966)

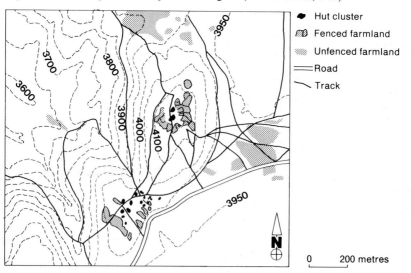

(d) Economic organization

The type of economic activity prevalent in an area is also a powerful influence on rural settlement patterns. We have already dealt indirectly with some of the influences, in Chapter 4. Here we look at some examples. Figure 10.3 shows the highly distinctive settlement type that occurs in Malaysia in association with the cultivation of paddy rice. These settlements are commonly of a loose linear nature and are built along the edges of paddy fields and on *levées* along the banks of rivers or canals. This linear pattern is a response to several factors, but the nature of the agricultural system is among the most significant. Linearity maximizes the proximity of each householder to his paddy field, and it also maximizes the amount of land that can be used for the cultivation of rice. A dispersed pattern of settlement would waste valuable land through the need for connecting paths. Individual land holdings are placed at right angles to a stream or irrigation canal, providing access for the maximum number of holdings to the available water supply. A linear pattern of houses is the result.

A more complex agricultural system is to be found in the Chimbu area of the New Guinea Highlands. The basis of the Chimbu agricultural system is the cultivation of sweet potatoes and the rearing of pigs. The former are grown in small fenced enclosures under a system of shifting cultivation. The 'farm' consists of several plots of land scattered over a wide area and has three or more focal points: the men's house, the separate houses for wives and other dependent women, and the shelters built for the family pigs. Chimbu houses rarely last for more than four years and thus mobility is a feature of Chimbu social and economic organization. Superimposed on this pattern of mobility, however, is a longer-term pattern known as the 'pig cycle', it being the practice to hold a religious ceremony every several years at which all the adult pigs are slaughtered. It is held at a permanent site upon which a temporary village grouping of huts is built. Thus, during the pig ceremony the pattern of settlement is radically transformed. Dispersed houses are vacated and people move to the temporary village, which would be begun up to two years before the ceremony and remain at least partly inhabited several years afterwards. Up to 1000 people may congregate at the ceremonial site. Thus, the interweaving of economic, social and religious practices produces a highly complex and dynamic rural settlement pattern.

Figure 10.3 Linear settlement in paddy field zone, Malaysia. (Source: Hodder, 1959, p. 66)

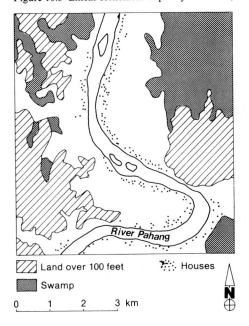

River Pahang

```
▨ Land over 100 feet     ⸭ Houses

▓ Swamp

0    1    2    3 km
```

N

Although transhumance has already been referred to under physical factors, in Turkey it results also from the economic organization of the village. Expansion of the cultivated area in Turkey has considerably reduced the amount of good-quality grazing available, and many former nomads have become settled. Nevertheless, livestock are an important part of the economic structure of the village in central and northern Turkey. It is common for livestock to be tended by full time herders who have no land of their own and, as the more favourable areas are used for cultivation, lower-quality upland pastures are used for the *yaylas* or summer grazings.

2. Change in rural settlement patterns

(a) *The transient nature of Third World rural settlement*

Many village sites in Britain have been occupied for centuries. This is much less the case in the Third World. Figure 10.4 shows the changing location of villages in the Ra province on the Fijian island of Viti Levu. In the pre-conquest period the main function of the village was the protection of its inhabitants, so hilltop sites or moated coastal sites were sought. When Fiji became a British colony in 1874, a period of rapid change began. More peaceful conditions meant the abandonment of hilltop sites (as happened in Africa) in favour of more easily cultivated sites near the sea. Such changes were often accompanied by the disintegration of the village into smaller hamlets. However, many of these new sites were found to be unhealthy and were abandoned in turn. Provincial administration played a part in finding new locations, some for medical reasons, and others near lines of communication for administrative convenience. This latter type of location has grown more significant in the recent past and most new village sites are either on or close to roads. This helps the villagers to obtain a cash income from their produce.

Similar features may be found in West Africa. The abandonment of former hill villages has sometimes had ironic consequences: the intensive and conservationist techniques forced upon the inhabitants in a restricted locality have often been abandoned in favour of rotational bush fallowing on the plains. Also, nucleated villages have broken up as people spread over the plains. Isolated compounds surrounded by their cultivated areas become more common. In many parts of Africa the abandonment of villages is also due to the development of new lines of communication, new roads 'pulling' settlement towards them and causing the abandonment of more distant sites.

(b) *Planned rural settlement*

Settlement planning was a feature of the colonial period. For example, in the Caribbean Islands the British Board of Trade drew up plans for effective colonization in the eighteenth century, regulating the distribution of plantations and smaller plots for colonizers. Recent years have seen numerous attempts at settlement planning in the Third World, although the reasons for these vary considerably. In some cases settlement planning was a device used to control and supervise the population in times of emergency, the Kenya emergency in Kikuyuland in the 1950s being the best example. Other schemes have resulted from public health programmes, for example the anti-sleeping sickness campaign in western Tanzania in the 1930s.

Another common reason for planned settlement has been the relief of population pressure. There have been many such schemes in Latin America (Chapter 5, Section C), as almost every country there has large areas that are virtually uninhabited. Planned colonization occurs where selected families are moved to areas of new settlement and where there is close supervision of agricultural practices and the marketing of produce.

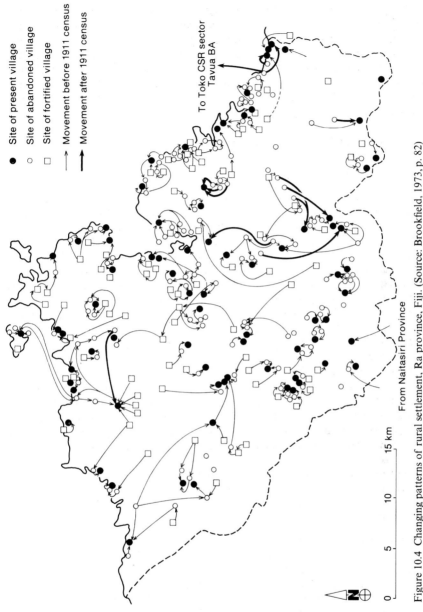

Legend (top left):
- ● Site of present village
- ○ Site of abandoned village
- □ Site of fortified village
- → Movement before 1911 census
- ⟶ Movement after 1911 census

To Toko CSR sector
Tavua BA

From Naitasiri Province

0   5   10   15 km

N

Figure 10.4 Changing patterns of rural settlement, Ra province, Fiji. (Source: Brookfield, 1973, p. 82)

239

Roads, houses and other basic services should also be provided to ensure success. Inevitably, planned colonization is expensive and time consuming. In fact, despite good intentions, the record of planned settlement in much of Latin America is not good. Indeed the record in Colombia is so negative that the state now limits itself to support for spontaneous colonizers and in most countries the latter are in fact more significant than the planned schemes.

Political and ideological factors have also been important. One of the most spectacular attempts at the planned reorganization of rural settlements has taken place in Tanzania, where rural development is now being pursued through *ujamaa* villages, or co-operative communities. The dispersed nature of the rural population and settlement pattern makes it difficult to increase agricultural production and provide services, so a policy aimed at the voluntary nucleation of people into ujamaa villages was introduced (Figure 10.5). This encourages the communal ownership of land resources, the formation of village committees with power to plan and implement local projects, and the provision of local services such as schools, dispensaries and water supply. From 1967 to 1969 a few villages served as models and by 1969 some 180 ujamaa villages with a combined population of 60 000 people had been formed. By the later 1970s, there were well over 5000 such villages with a population of over 2 million. In some regions progress has been slow: for example, in the fertile Kilimanjaro district where there was hostility to the programme. In regions with problems such as flooding, drought and famine, greater progress has been made. The Tanzanian case provides an interesting example of a political philosophy being expressed in a spatial manner. The village is to be the focus of development in Tanzania, not the city or the steel works.

3. The internal structure of settlements

Internal structure, or morphology, takes several forms. Firstly, it may relate to the spacing of buildings within a settlement. For example, the buildings may be nucleated or scattered, they may be arranged in a linear or circular fashion, they may be regular or irregular in their layout. Secondly, the internal structure of settlements may be examined through land-use variations: how the use of land and buildings is distributed throughout

Figure 10.5 The formation of ujamaa villages in Tanzania. (Source: Mabogunje, 1980, p. 146)

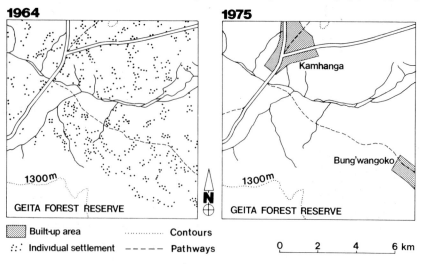

240

the settlement. Thirdly, there is an aspect of internal structure that is not immediately visible on the ground or on a topographic map. This relates to the distribution of different kinds of people within the settlement, for example different religious groups or social classes.

(a) Settlement morphology

Figure 10.6 indicates the variety of rural settlement forms that may be found in Sierra Leone. The long history of tribal wars has affected the form of many villages. For example, Betaya was built by peasant farmers as defence against Fulani cattle herders, and

Figure 10.6 Settlement types in Sierra Leone. (Source: Clarke, 1969, p. 63)

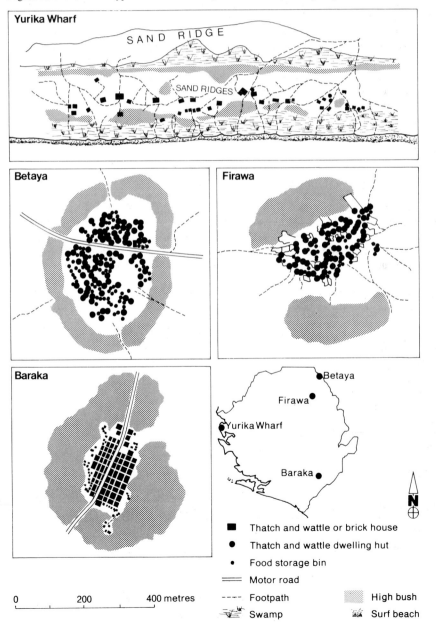

protected by ditches and a ring of cotton trees. Five 'gates' led into the village which has not yet been greatly affected by the modern motor road. Kinship may also be an important influence. At Firawa, the clustering of kinship groups into roughly circular compounds (12 in Firawa) gives spatial expression to social relationships. In complete contrast is Yurika Wharf, a Temne village on the west coast of Sierra Leone. Environmental factors have obviously been important here, and each house has its own pathways to seashore and swamp. The remaining example demonstrates more recent influences. Baraka is obviously a planned form, and many such villages are set up after the destruction of an older village by fire. The opportunity is taken to regulate the layout and it is significant that neither the defensive function nor the kinship ties appear to be a strong influence on these layouts.

(b) People within a settlement

As there are many aspects of population, each may vary considerably within any one settlement. At the village level in many Third World countries, two aspects are particularly important in internal differentiation: kinship ties and social status or caste. Figure 10.7 shows the complex pattern of settlement morphology that can result from

Figure 10.7 Kinship ties and compound morphology, Nangodi, northern Ghana. (Source: Oliver. 1971, p. 50)

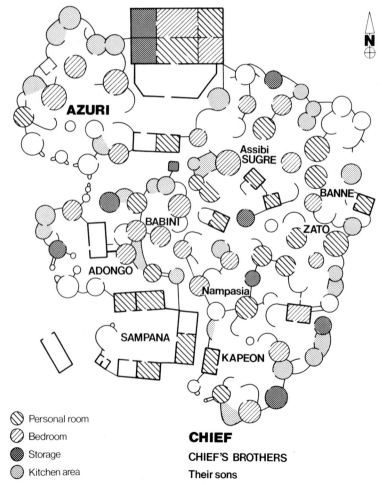

N

⊕

AZURI

Assibi
SUGRE

BANNE

BABINI

ZATO

ADONGO

Nampasia

SAMPANA

KAPEON

⊘ Personal room

⊘ Bedroom

● Storage

◍ Kitchen area

CHIEF

CHIEF'S BROTHERS

Their sons

kinship ties, in this case an extended family. Just one compound in the Nangodi district of northern Ghana is shown. The chief was Azuri and also living in the compound were his seven brothers, Adongo, Babini, Sampana, Banne, Kapeon, Sugre and Zato and their wives. Azuri's son Nampasia and Sugre's son Assibi also stayed with their wives in the compound. The land-use needs of each section of the family were met within their section of the compound. Each brother had his own hut, there were associated huts for each of their wives, other bedrooms, kitchens, grain stores and animal yards.

In some parts of the Third World the caste structure of society is an important influence on settlement structure. Figure 10.8 indicates this feature in the Indian village of Aminbhavi, where separate areas are given over to the various castes. The population structure is indicated in Table 10.1. The culturally dominant groups are the Jains and the Brahmins whose larger houses stand on the best sites in large compounds. The other castes tend to occupy blocks of contiguous houses. The Lingayats are the tenant farmers and predominantly an agricultural caste while the Talwars are domestic servants and agricultural labourers. The Harijans (the untouchables) and other low caste groups tend to live on the periphery of the village or beyond.

Figure 10.8 Aminbhavi village, India. (Source: Spate, 1960, p. 174)

☐ Harijans	▓ Lingayats	◉ Mosque
▨ Muslims	■ Jains	⊕ Temple
▤ Talwars	▦ Brahmans	★ Well
▥ Shepherds	■ Shops etc.	0 100 200 300 metres

Table 10.1 Population structure of Aminbhavi.
(Source: Spate, 1960)

Caste group	Number	Percentage
Jains	250	6
Brahmins	75	2
Lingayats	2650	65
Muslims	550	13
Talwars	300	7
Harijans	200	5
Other low caste	75	2
Total	4100	100

Caste groups arranged in approximate order of status.

ASSIGNMENTS

1. *Refer to Figure 10.1.*
   (a) *Measure the distance from each village to the nearest water supply.*
   (b) *Produce a histogram of the range of distances.*
   (c) *Calculate the average distance.*
   (d) *Discuss the implications of these findings for everyday life and work in the villages.*
2. *Refer to the text and Figures 10.1 to 10.6.*
   (a) *List the factors of importance in selecting the site of an initial rural settlement in a LDC.*
   (b) *Attempt to arrange these factors in order of priority.*
   (c) *Give reasons for your answers.*
3. *With reference to Section 2, discuss the factors that have brought about change in rural settlement patterns in the LDCs in the last 40–50 years.*
4. *Refer to Figure 10.8 and Table 10.1.*
   (a) *Describe the distribution of the different caste groups in the village.*
   (b) *Using transparent graph paper make an approximate calculation of the relative space allocation for each group.*
   (c) *Using this information and the numbers in each group, calculate the population densities of the groups within the village.*
   (d) *Attempt to explain the location and density of the groups in relation to their relative rank (see Table 10.1).*

B. Urban Morphology

This aspect of the geography of the Third World has generated much literature. Many authors talk of the 'Third World city' as if all urban areas were much the same. The use of this term masks the diversity of urban forms that exist in the Third World. Cities of the Islamic world, for example, contrast vividly with the colonial 'implants' of Latin America. Nevertheless, in this section we shall explore some of the general features of Third World cities.

1. Indigenous urban forms

It is often said that cities mirror the cultures that create them. We have already seen how aspects of Third World cultures affect the form of rural settlement, and much the same is

244

true of urban places. The Islamic city of the Middle East and North Africa is a clear example (Plate 10.1). The first impression is of disorder and haphazardness: narrow alleys wind irregularly among densely packed houses, mosques, workshops and bazaars. There are few open spaces, many cul-de-sacs, and, from the street, house walls are high and only broken by small windows. Yet internally, the layout is regular, each house having its open courtyard. The overall impression is one of privacy and introversion, the streets and alleys

Plate 10.1 Alleyway in Tangiers. The traditional Islamic city of the Middle East and North Africa is characterized by narrow alleyways, winding among densely packed buildings, and by a mixture of land-uses. House walls tend to be blank except for high windows, cul-de-sacs are common, and there are few large open spaces. This apparently haphazard urban form does have some logic, however. Narrow alleyways are partly a response to the climate as they provide shade, retain the cool night air, and prevent excessive wind movement. The urban morphology is also partly a reflection of the Islamic philosophy that stresses the separation of public and private life. The house is for the immediate family only, and behind the high walls the houses are inward looking, built around an internal courtyard. Meetings with friends would take place in public areas; for example, in coffee shops. (*Photograph: G. P. O'Hare*)

are little more than the spaces left over after the buildings have been erected. They are also well adapted to the climate, in that they provide shade and retain cool air. In the Islamic culture there is a clear separation between public and private life. The former involves religious worship, manufacture, retailing, discussion and education, and demands the close proximity of school, mosque, bazaar and workshop to the home, hence the apparently haphazard mixture of land-uses. On the other hand the home is the centre of private life and these other activities are not allowed to intrude upon it.

Over much of Africa, the town is a European introduction although one major exception is Yorubaland, Nigeria. Many towns were established in this area between the seventh and tenth centuries by invaders from the north. These traditional towns tend to be rather amorphous, the compound being the dominant element, lacking any regular street pattern or building line. Markets and the chief's compounds are centrally located, but the whole structure is foreign to the Western conception of urban form. In addition, many of the inhabitants are farmers.

2. Urban forms associated with colonial impact

Probably the clearest examples of the colonial urban impact are to be found in Latin America. The town was a deliberate instrument of colonization used by the Spaniards and was the base for mineral and agricultural ventures as well as a centre of administration. Many urban sites proved unsuitable and many others never grew, yet the Spaniards were ruthless in demonstrating their superiority. For example, Mexico City was deliberately established on the site of the former Aztec city of Tenochtitlan. The native city was destroyed and the colonial grid town laid out on top of it. Symbolically, the plaza, with cathedral, law courts and government buildings was located over the spiritual centre of the native city (Plate 10.2).

Plate 10.2 The cathedral and main square, Mexico City. Spanish colonial town planning was repeated throughout Central and South America. A rectangular street layout was used, with the central square surrounded by the main administrative buildings, but the whole scene was dominated by the cathedral or colonial church, symbolizing the spiritual dominance of the Church. Often the cathedral would be built over the demolished remains of Indian temples, as here in Mexico City. Unfortunately, the site was formerly a lake and subsidence is taking place at the rate of 250–300 mm per year, causing the 'tilting' of the cathedral towers and the constant need for restoration as evidenced by the scaffolding. Mexico has no pollution controls and the rather murky photograph is due to vehicle exhaust fumes. (*Photograph: G. P. O'Hare*)

Elsewhere in the Third World it was frequently the case that a colonial administrative town would be grafted on to an older settlement, giving such cities a dual structure. In Indian cities the planned layout of the British area contrasts vividly with the irregular layout of the adjacent indigenous Indian settlement. Figure 10.9 shows the form of Allahabad in 1904 after 100 years of British rule. The main elements are the fort, the traditional Indian city, the cantonments (areas set aside for the military), and the civil lines. The fort, originally built by an Indian prince, commands the confluence of the Ganges and the Jumna: a sacred site for Hindus. The old city of Allahabad lies to the west of the fort and in 1900 it housed some 150 000 people at very high densities. Retailing was dominated by the Chowk or principal market and scattered bazaars. To the west of the old city lay Khusru Bagh, an old formal garden with the mausoleums of the Indian princes. To these traditional elements were added the colonial elements. The railway line marked the division between the two, perhaps appropriately, as more than anything else the railway was the symbol of British rule in India. To the north lay two cantonments. The first was built to the north east of the old city and was spaciously laid out with hospital, cavalry and infantry 'lines', schools and even its own bazaar. It was almost a

Figure 10.9 Allahabad, India, in 1904. (Source: *The Imperial Guide to India*, 1904, p. 98)

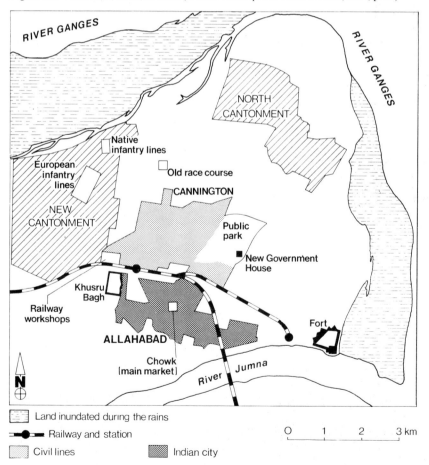

247

self-contained unit. Between the old city and this cantonment was the civilian area, with government houses, a large park and, immediately to the north of the old city, the civil lines. Nothing could present a greater contrast than the old city and the neat rectangular layout and low densities of this area with its well-spaced parks, schools, clubs and churches. Finally, to the north west of the old city lay the second or new military cantonment. Allahabad was considered to be an important strategic centre and therefore had a large garrison. Within this second cantonment there was clear segregation of the European infantry lines and the native infantry lines, even to the extent of having separate bazaars and hospitals. Thus Allahabad in 1904 gives a clear illustration of the impact of a colonial presence on the form of the city in at least one part of the Third World.

3. Recent changes in urban form

The elements of form examined so far originated mainly in the past, but the last few decades have seen significant change (Plate 6.5). In many cities, multi-storey office blocks (Plate 10.8), large department stores, international airports, blocks of flats, sports stadiums have all been built in the capital cities of the Third World (Plate 10.3). Such developments may seem to imply that there is a global convergence of urban form. Opinions are divided as to whether this is the case. Some authors see the form of the city as a product of the stage of development of a country, and argue that cities will pass through a series of stages of modernization until, presumably, they approach similarity to the most developed Western economies. Other authors argue that, although modernization does take place, the influences are modified by the specific cultural contexts within which they

Plate 10.3 Sports stadium, Freetown, Sierra Leone. The stadium was a 'gift' from communist China. Such developments in the LDCs are often the result of political motives as the major powers attempt to gain influence in the territories of other countries. However, sport is of great and increasing importance in the LDCs both for reasons of national prestige and, in many African countries where there are strong tribal divisions, because it helps to foster a spirit of nationalism and unity. (*Photograph: M. Barke*)

operate. Even though a central business district (CBD) may be recognized in both developing and Third World countries, its detailed character and role may be different in the former case and, although similarities may exist in other aspects of urban form, they are only superficial.

After we have looked at more detailed evidence on urban land-use, we shall be in a better position to reach a conclusion on the issue of the convergence or divergence of urban form.

4. Urban structure: business activities

The models of urban land-use patterns in Western cities are now well-known and provide us with generalized descriptions of the structure of the Western city. The task of providing a similar model for the Third World is fraught with difficulties for, as we have already noted, it is misleading to speak of the 'Third World city' as if they were all the same. This point will be readily understood if we examine one of the most important urban functions, business and commerce, in a variety of urban areas in the Third World.

A detailed study of Ibadan, Nigeria, shows that African cities can only be understood as an amalgam of two different urban processes: the 'traditional' and the 'Western', both of which appear to be flourishing side by side. The centre of the old city is called the Iba market (Figure 10.10), while the modern town is focused on the Gbagi business district. The Iba market used to be held in the open, filling an area of 4 hectares in the core of the old city. Earlier in the twentieth century two roads were developed across the market area, but although the open area of the market has been reduced to 1.2 hectares its activities spill out along the roads that focus upon the market. During the nineteenth century the Iba market was the centre of long-distance trade, and it still has a very large hinterland, with fleets of lorries replacing the caravans of the previous era. The market performs political and social roles as well as economic ones. News of local events are announced and discussed there, and the head of the city is installed there. It is the meeting place for

Figure 10.10 Markets in Ibadan. (Source: Mabogunje, 1968, p. 208)

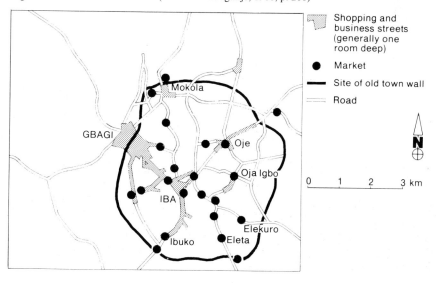

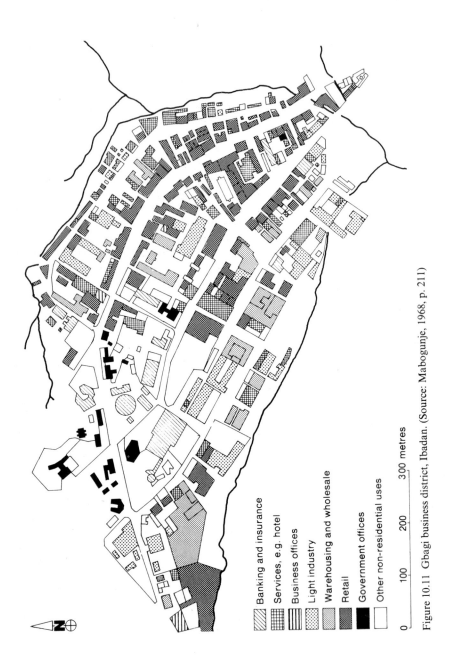

Banking and insurance

Services, e.g. hotel

Business offices

Light industry

Warehousing and wholesale

Retail

Government offices

Other non-residential uses

0   100   200   300 metres

Figure 10.11 Gbagi business district, Ibadan. (Source: Mabogunje, 1968, p. 211)

youth societies, the burial ceremonies of relatives, and the festivals held by different groups.

The Gbagi district is shown in detail in Figure 10.11 and, like many European focal points, is actually not centrally located but is placed towards the west. The reason for this is that the major stimulus to its growth came with the railway. The line was opened to Lagos in 1901 and, of necessity, was located at what was then the periphery of the city. The Gbagi centre grew up in close proximity and was set aside for European traders. Leases were granted in 1903 and shops, offices, banks and stores began to be laid out in orderly fashion, in complete contrast to the Iba area. Also, unlike the latter the greater amount of space used for permanent buildings gives scarcity value to plots and has encouraged competition for choice sites and therefore to significant spatial variation within the district. The site value of certain plots has also led to the building of high-rise blocks. These can be seen in the larger building blocks in the centre of the district (Figure 10.11), a feature absent from the 'traditional' centre. To the western fringe and nearer the railway station are the government offices, some light industries and, as one would expect, warehousing and wholesaling. Similar functions demarcate the southern edge of the Gbagi district and to the north are a number of motor sales and repair garages. On the eastern side, away from the railway station, the European firms give way to Levantine and Indian-owned shops and businesses. These tend to be considerably smaller and deal mainly in textiles, clothing and jewellery.

The two districts reflect, to some extent, the distribution of different social groups in Ibadan. The western part of the city contains the wealthier population while towards the east live most of the low-income people (Figure 10.12). It is also significant that most of the recent urban expansion has occurred in the west, while in the centre and east, although population has grown, this has been accommodated by filling in available space at high densities (Figure 10.12b). Figure 10.10 indicates that in addition to these two major nodes there are a number of smaller markets distributed through the city, and also several business streets. Many of these markets are held at periodic intervals, and their frequency is related either to the income density of the neighbourhood or to the specialized character of the market. This periodicity is common throughout the Third World (Plate 10.4) and is an important adaptation to the circumstances of low income and infrequent demand for more specialized goods. For example, Mokola market in the north of Ibadan is held every day. A wide range of goods are sold: local fruit and vegetables, china, haberdashery and imported groceries. In the lower-income east of the city, however, the peripheral Ibuko, Eleta, Elekuro and Oja Igbo markets are held only every four days and rural farm produce from the vicinity of the city is sold there. In the north east the Oje market is highly specialized; it is held every eight days and sells alternately traditional woven cloth and home-made soap. In spite of the modern developments, these traditional elements exist and flourish, and show no signs of being replaced.

In many of the medium-sized and smaller towns of Asia, business and commerce takes place in the so-called 'shophouse core': the compact intensively used central area with a very high population density. Although retailing is carried out from fixed sites on a daily basis and therefore has superficial similarities with Western urban structures, there are many differences. The shophouses are usually two storeys high, with a frontage of about 6 metres, and a depth of about 18 metres. The open-fronted outer part of the ground floor is used for business activities while the rear portion and the upper floor provide the living space, usually for several households.

Coffee and eating places are significant, because of the limited facilities for cooking and storing food in the overcrowded shophouses. The shophouse core is usually dominated by small-scale Chinese businesses. This itself is an important cultural factor

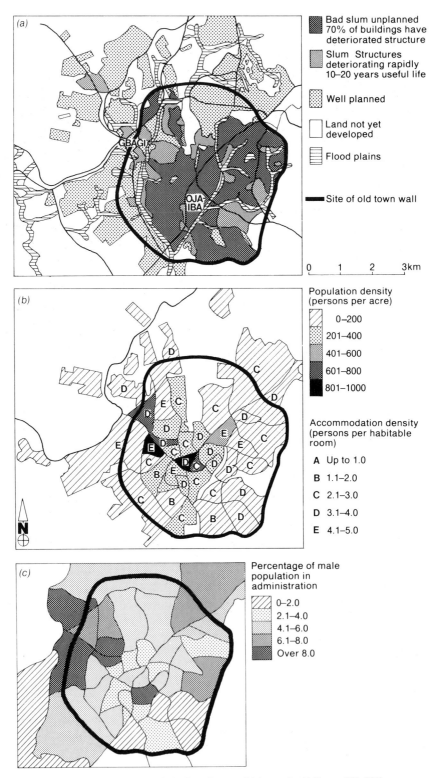

Figure 10.12 Social geography of Ibadan. (Source: Mabogunje, 1968, pp. 222, 228)

Plate 10.4 Periodic market, Sierra Leone. In many LDCs the sale and purchase of goods takes place outside urban locations, at long-established rural sites. Such markets are frequently 'periodic' in the sense that they are held at regular intervals, for example, every Tuesday or Friday, and often form part of a market 'ring' or 'cycle'. The market traders move to other long-established sites some distance away, each market being held on a specific day. The size of the 'ring' and the frequency of the markets will depend on factors such as population density and the level of purchasing power in the region. Such markets provide a lively and colourful scene and play an important role in rural social and economic life. (*Photograph: M. Barke*)

influencing urban structure, for the Chinese attach considerable status to being in business on one's own. Yet, because capital is limited and purchasing power is low, a multiplicity of small units results.

ASSIGNMENTS

1. *Discuss the major ways in which the urban structures of the cities examined in Section B depart from the models of urban structure suggested by Burgess and Hoyt. For details of the latter see Daniel & Hopkinson (1979, pp. 84–120).*
2. *Compare Figure 10.10 with the map of population density in Ibadan (Figure 10.12).*
   (a) Describe the distribution of population in the city.
   (b) Describe the distribution of markets within the city.
   (c) Attempt to relate the distribution of markets to the distribution of population.
   (d) With reference to Figure 10.12, suggest some reasons why there may not always be a direct relationship between population density and the number of markets.
3. *Carefully examine Figure 10.11.*
   (a) Describe the distribution of the main land-use categories.
   (b) Attempt to explain the distributions.

C. Urban Social Geography and Housing Problems

Much of the recent literature on the city in the Third World has been concerned with the problems of very rapid urban growth. Chapter 9 has already analysed this growth so here we concentrate on its implications for the city as a form of settlement. Two themes are particularly important: the internal social geography of the city and the problem of accommodating its expanding population.

1. Social geography

(a) General spatial patterns

It must be stressed at the outset that the social geography of cities in the LDCs is in a state of flux. It is possible to identify a development continuum for the social geography of cities (Table 10.2). Although generalized, it acts as a useful frame of reference. Only twenty years ago many authors described most Third World cities as 'pre-industrial'. Some undoubtedly were, especially those of indigenous growth, but as we have seen many had a 'foreign' or 'alien' element grafted onto them. Nevertheless, the pre-industrial city is a starting point for the development continuum. In contrast to the Western 'model' the pre-industrial city has the core and inner areas as the zones of highest status. In conditions of limited intra-urban transport, proximity to the central institutions is desirable and confers status, especially if they are the main religious, educational and administrative institutions. Therefore there is a reversal of the normal Western pattern where status rises with distance from the centre.

However, cities in the LDCs have experienced rapid change and this has influenced the distribution of different social groups within the city. In the next sections we shall examine the changes affecting such groups.

(b) Elite residential areas

As the members of the elite in any society have access to financial and other resources, they are also able to exercise greater choice in where they live. They are therefore likely to be an important element of change in the social geography of the city. In the Third World, as industrialization has developed, commerce grown and new transport facilities been introduced, many cities have moved away from the pre-industrial model. One of the main

Table 10.2 A development continuum for the social geography of cities.

Stage	Population trend	Main aspects of residential differentiation
Pre-industrial city	Slowly increasing	Elite dominate central area. Place of work and residence often the same. Occupational specialization takes place within the city. The poor and noxious trades are relegated to the periphery.
Industrializing city	Rising very rapidly	Transport improvement allows peripheral expansion; and this plus population increase at centre encourages elite to suburbanize. Workplace and residence become increasingly separated. Different socio-economic groups become clearly segregated.
Modern industrial city	Falling in centre; rising on periphery	Suburban areas dominated by nuclear families (mother, father and children). Inner locations mainly slums or development. Some inner areas favoured by single people. Different ethnic/migrant groups, socio-economic status, family status, and minority groups are all more clearly segregated.

components of this has been the decentralization of the upper-income groups (Plate 9.1). In cities such as Ankara and Mexico City, the elite have left the centre and moved to a specific part of the periphery. The processes behind such movements are relatively straightforward. As development began to gather momentum in many cities (if not in the whole of the national territory), rural-to-urban migration increased dramatically. This increased the numbers and proportions of lower-income dwellers and, inevitably, put pressure on inner city housing areas. Densities increased in areas already inadequately provided with services. This increase in population and decline in the quality of the environment provided a strong impetus for the wealthier groups to leave the centre for newer suburbs, especially if they provided direct and easy access to the centre. This trend has been assisted by the increase in car ownership among such groups in the last four decades, and their ability to ensure that they will be provided with urban highways, etc.

In Africa and parts of Asia, suburbanization, although present, may not be as marked. Here the elite often live in 'closed' areas, formerly inhabited by colonial officials. The best example is the 'civil lines' in Indian cities. Today the colonial administrators have been replaced by indigenous leaders but their spatial pattern remains much the same and relatively central. Several reasons may account for this: there are lower levels of development than in Latin America, less industrialization and, in Africa, migration to the cities has a strong seasonal component and therefore pressure on the centre is possibly less significant.

(c) Migrant clustering

It is clear from the studies examined so far that migrants in the cities of the Third World are a major component of the social geography of any city. As they tend to have particular characteristics of age, sex and occupation (or lack of it), they obviously affect the distribution of these elements within the city. Furthermore, as they are new arrivals they must either add to the existing area of the city, or increase densities in some locations, or force the re-location of other groups by the invasion of their territory.

One of the most commonly observed features of migrant behaviour is the tendency to concentrate in specific parts of the city according to their place of origin. It is not difficult to see why such clusters should emerge. Information on which the decision to migrate is based is acquired from friends or relatives who have moved to the city or themselves have contacts there. It is only natural that migrants should move first to a locality that allows them to adjust to the strange new environment. Friends and relatives from their village of origin are likely to provide support, they can provide food and shelter, introduce new migrants to others and pass on information about employment opportunities.

This clustering together of people from the same village or district has further implications. It leads to the mutual reinforcement of traditions, customs and many other aspects of behaviour which may provide a cushion against the impact of the city and its different customs. In Cairo in the late 1950s there were no fewer than 100 village associations, maintaining the links between the migrants in the city and their home villages. Other less formal features are also important. For males especially, the coffee shop (the Middle Eastern equivalent of the British pub) plays an important role. Many Egyptian and Turkish coffee shops in the big cities are run by villagers to serve the men from their particular village and function more like a select club than a profit-making business.

Evidence of the lack of a clear distinction between rural and urban ways of life may also be found in the location and physical layout of migrant communities. Those on the rural–urban fringe may incorporate garden plots (Plate 9.4), and animals are often kept well within the built-up area of a large city. For many migrants the ties of the extended family and the links between city and village still play important roles. It is significant, for example, that in Africa de-tribalization has not taken place to any great extent along with urbanization. Many associations that typify political and social life in African cities are based on tribal divisions, or a common language, and help urban residents to retain strong ties with the rural area they consider to be their home.

The evidence from studies therefore suggests that the process of urbanization in the contemporary Third World may be taking a very different course from that experienced in the West.

2. Housing problems

Introduction

The urban poor in the Third World face considerable problems in obtaining adequate shelter together with other basic services. Indeed, the lower-income housing areas in most cities are a major influence on urban form and character. Figure 10.13 gives an indication of this in the city of Calcutta. The maximum height above sea level is only 10 metres and the area is consequently very badly drained. Only half of Calcutta proper is adequately sewered (Figure 10.13*c*) while in Howrah and most of the rest of the conurbation there is no sewerage system at all. In addition the piped water supply is clearly insufficient and the basic services on which housing depends are woefully inadequate. Many of the houses are themselves appalling. There are some 3000 pockets of *bustees* in Calcutta (Figure 10.13*a*), these being collections of huts built of non-permanent materials such as cardboard. In 1966 some 1.75 million people (many of them single males) were living in bustees in the conurbation as a whole.

However, it is all too easy to assume that all the urban poor are condemned to live in such shanty towns or squatter settlements. These terms usually refer to areas of apparent chaos and squalor where people have squatted with no legal rights to the land and property they occupy. In fact there are many forms of housing provision for the poor in the Third World. The best term to encompass all such areas is 'low-cost housing', but this may be subdivided as follows:

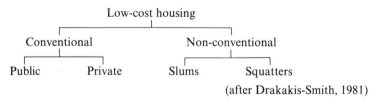

(after Drakakis-Smith, 1981)

Conventional housing is that built in accord with accepted standards, through recognized institutions. Non-conventional housing is that which does not comply with the accepted procedures and often does not conform to the legislation. Private housing for the poor is virtually non-existent. Although the private sector does build most of the conventional houses in the Third World, they are built for the wealthy. In the MDCs publicly provided housing is a major source of shelter for poor people, but in very few Third World countries is this true. Some of the richer ones such as Hong Kong, Singapore and Venezuela have undertaken such schemes, but they tend to be in the form of massive high-rise blocks with quite high rents. They are most commonly located at the periphery, which means costs of travel to work in the centre are higher, and alternative employment opportunities for

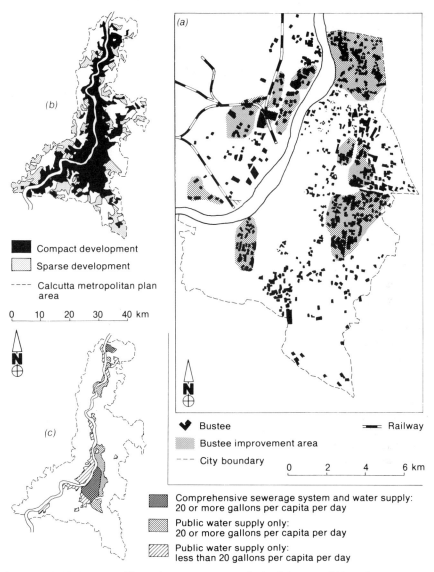

Figure 10.13 (*a*) Bustees and bustee improvement areas in the Calcutta and Howrah municipalities. (*b*) The Calcutta conurbation. (*c*) Water supply and sewerage in the Calcutta conurbation. (Source: Dwyer, 1975, pp. 216, 218)

wives and children are drastically reduced. Therefore, even when public housing schemes are provided, they are frequently inappropriate for the needs of the urban poor.

Thus it is clear that for the vast majority of poor people in Third World cities, non-conventional housing is the norm, i.e. slums and squatter settlements. Yet such areas are often the target for demolition because in the eyes of the bureaucrats and planners they disfigure and disrupt the city. Governments fear that they are centres of political and social discontent so raids, 'clear-outs' and demolition are carried out at frequent intervals.

(a) Distribution and characteristics of slums

The word 'slum' is a familiar one but is difficult to define with any precision. In this section the term is used to mean legal permanently built houses that have become sub-standard through time. The causes may be many: excessive sub-division, neglect, or simply age. Slums are characterized by overcrowding, both within dwellings and within rooms, and the sharing of facilities. In many cases a tenant will rent part of a dwelling from the owner and then sub-let parts of this rented accommodation to others. This is especially common in the 'Chinatowns' of South East Asia. In Hong Kong such accommodation is provided in three-storey or four-storey tenements (Plate 6.4), each floor of the tenement being managed as a unit and reached by a common stair. Each floor is divided up into cubicles that may be let separately to individuals or family groups who would share the use of a kitchen and lavatory. It is not surprising that under these conditions, people in Hong Kong and in other parts of South East Asia choose to spend most of their time outside the 'home', on the streets or in restaurants. Hong Kong is of course an extreme case of congestion, but in many of the larger cities of the Third World similar inner city slum housing, usually in the form of tenements, exists (Plate 10.5).

(b) Distribution and characteristics of squatter settlements

Possibly even more significant than the inner city slum areas are the squatter settlements which are often, although not always, located on the periphery. For example, the Peruvian census of 1968 revealed that 431 000 people were living in the inner city tenement areas of

Plate 10.5 Tenement housing in Mexico City. The photograph shows some quite recently built rented housing in the inner city. These four-storey tenements, mostly with two-room or three-room apartments, replaced older housing that had deteriorated into slum property. Most houses appear to have a television, but the tenements suffer from severe overcrowding, and 'roof-top' squatting takes place on the flat roofs of several of them. These houses seem certain to deteriorate into overcrowded slums. (*Photograph: M. Barke*)

Table 10.3 Estimates of squatters as a percentage of total population in selected cities. (Source: Drakakis-Smith, 1981)

Dakar	60 (1970)	Djakarta	25 (1971)
Dar es Salaam	50 (1970)	Karachi	23 (1970)
Kinshasha	60 (1970)	Kuala Lumpur	37 (1971)
Ankara	65 (1970)	Manila	35 (1972)
Baghdad	25 (1970)	Arequipa	40 (1970)
Casablanca	70 (1970)	Brasilia	41 (1970)
Istanbul	45 (1970)	Lima	40 (1970)
Calcutta	33 (1970)	Mexico City	46 (1970)
Colombo	57 (1973)	Montego Bay	40 (1971)
Hong Kong	10 (1979)	Rio de Janeiro	20 (1975)

Lima, while 649 000 were living in the *barriadas* or squatter settlements. By 1970 the latter figure had risen to 800 000. Table 10.3 gives some idea of the significance of this form of housing in a variety of Third World cities. In some cities it clearly forms the major housing sector.

It is difficult to generalize about squatter settlements. Some may occur singly (Plate 10.6) or in small groups of 12–20 dwellings; others occur in huge agglomerations of thousands of houses. They can occur through organized rapid (almost overnight) invasions of an area by large numbers of people, or by gradual accretion, family by family. It is also possible to subdivide the category of squatters into further groups. There are those who build houses intended to last for a reasonable period while there are others who wander the city like intra-urban nomads looking for somewhere to put up their shelter for

Plate 10.6 Single squatter house, Uskudar, Turkey. Uskudar (Scutari) lies across the Bosporus from Istanbul but is still part of the urbanised region. Links provided by ferries and, more recently, by the new road bridge have led to considerable expansion, much of it in the form of squatters' housing. The photograph illustrates the variety of squatter housing that exists in LDCs. The fact that this house is built mainly of breeze-blocks suggests that a degree of consolidation or improvement has probably taken place in this dwelling. The initial construction material would almost certainly have been more flimsy and impermanent. (*Photograph: M. Barke*)

Plate 10.7 Railway shanties, Port au Prince, Haiti. Haiti was colonized by the French who developed sugar plantations using African slaves. Blacks still constitute about 80% of the population. Haiti is one of the poorest countries in the world with a per capita GNP in 1979 of $260. Coffee and sisal are now the main products and Port au Prince is by far the largest city with a population of 500 000. Narrow gauge railways like the one shown in the photograph run out to the sugar cane fields and vacant land adjacent to these lines provides sites for squatters. The photograph shows the extremely high densities of such sites and the different stages of improvement of dwellings within one shanty area. Some buildings are now constructed of permanent materials. The higher-status area has developed on the hillsides to the south east of the city, leaving much of the centre to the poorer people. (*Photograph: T. D. Douglas*)

the night. Others have no shelter at all and simply sleep on the streets. It is estimated that in 1966 Calcutta had 100 000 pavement dwellers.

For semi-permanent squatter settlements the availability of land is the vital factor. Squatter settlements are found in a variety of locations, the most common being land with little value for other uses. One often finds them located on steep hillsides, along river banks on land subject to flooding, on swamp land and on spare pieces of land left unused by organizations such as the railways (Plate 10.7).

(c) Improvement and self-help in squatter settlements

Official feeling about squatter settlements in the Third World is negative. The response of officialdom has normally been to try and eradicate them. In Rio de Janeiro, local government officials have repeatedly singled out individual *favelas* for demolition and moved their residents to the urban periphery. These evictions often involve the police and, in extreme cases, the military. Other governments have gone even further in their attempts to discourage squatting and have forcibly returned residents to the distant countryside by the truckload. Some relocation policies have involved the movement of people from squatter settlements to government-provided housing. The most spectacular attempt at this was in Caracas, Venezuela. In the 1950s some 97 superblocks (Plate 10.8) of fifteen storeys were built to house 180 000 people. It was intended to rehouse people from the

Plate 10.8 The modern townscapes of Caracas, Venezuela. Caracas was an isolated colonial centre of no great importance until the 1920s. The city was built at the western end of the valley of Caracas, an enclosed valley some 25 kilometres long and 5 kilometres wide, and throughout the nineteenth century it remained compact. In the late 1920s oil was discovered in Venezuela and the wealth generated by it became focused in Caracas. In 1920 the population of the city was only 92 000 but by 1948 it was 600 000 and by 1962 over 2 million. The major focus of expansion has been to the east. The photograph was taken looking northwards across the valley and shows the high-rise developments, modern roads and car parks characteristic of much of the urban development on the valley floor. Higher-class residential areas, with their own 'out of town' shopping centres (bottom right) and supermarkets are strung out along the main east–west thoroughfares up to 16 kilometres from the old city centre. (*Photograph: T. D. Douglas*)

261

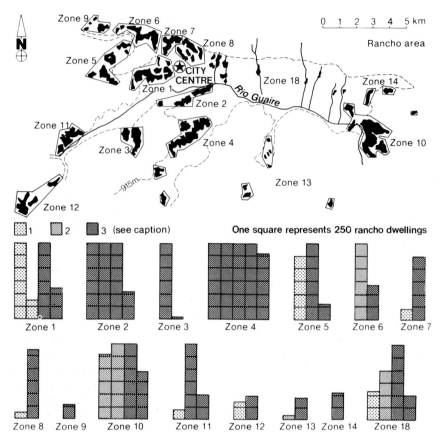

Figure 10.14 The distribution of ranchos in the Caracas metropolitan area. The possibilities for improvement indicated by shadings 1–3 on the graphs are explained as follows: 1. little danger in topographic situation: improvement possible *in situ*, 2. street and house alignments irregular: very limited improvement *in situ*, 3. complete re-location necessary: no improvement possible *in situ*. (Source: Dwyer, 1975, p. 138)

ranchos of Caracas (Figure 10.14), but the scheme misfired badly. The superblocks attracted more people into the city and many social problems resulted. Rents were not paid, and maintenance was neglected. In short, the scheme was an expensive failure which Venezuela could only afford because of its oil wealth.

Demolition is not the answer in squatter areas, and rehousing on the scale required in most countries would be prohibitively expensive. The most realistic alternative policy is to recognize the opportunities for self-improvement that exist within the squatter areas themselves. A study of three *colonias paracaidistas* (literally meaning parachutists, or people who appear from nowhere) in Mexico City reveals that these may be considerable. The oldest area, Sector Popular, was first settled in 1947. Originally on the urban fringe, it is now completely incorporated within the city. The second, Isidro Fabela, dates from 1960. The most recent area, Santo Domingo, began in 1971 with an initial invasion of several hundred families. After four days there were 4000 families there and by 1974 this had risen to 10 000, such is the speed with which the squatting process can occur. All three

Table 10.4 Comparison of three improving squatter settlements in Mexico City. (Source: Ward, 1978, p. 41)

	Santo Domingo Los Reyes (incipient)	Isidro Fabela (consolidating)	Sector Popular (consolidated)
Age in 1974	3 years	14 years	26 years
Households renting	—	8.4%	46.6%
Average households per lot	1.2	1.8	4.2
Density (persons per hectare)	211	415	753
Number of industrial, commercial & service enterprises	5	34	66

Consolidation index:			Percentage of dwellings		
	'Best'	1	—	1.9	8.7
		2	—	17.8	45.2
degree of		3	—	22.4	25.2
consolidation		4	9.1	29.0	16.5
		5	21.2	21.5	3.5
		6	43.9	7.5	0.9
	'Worst'	7	25.8	—	—

'colonies' were illegal occupations of land. Table 10.4 gives a selection of data on each of the three areas. Santo Domingo lacks all basic services, and the houses are provisional or, at best, semi-permanent. Isidro Fabela has most of the basic services although these are not installed inside the dwellings. Sector Popular is fully serviced with water and drainage reaching the interior of every lot. The streets are paved and lit and many houses are two or more storeys in height. The data therefore suggest that squatter settlements can improve considerably over time. They also increase their densities over time, two processes being important here: the sharing of lots between kinsfolk, and the subdivision of lots for rental purposes. As Table 10.4 shows there is a clear increase in renting out with age of settlement. It is also clear that settlements attract commercial and industrial activities over time. However, possibly even more interesting is the trend for self-improvement of individual houses. This is indicated by the consolidation index in Table 10.4. This index is based on three things:

(i) the structure and services of the dwellings, i.e. the permanence of the building materials and the presence or absence of water, drainage, electricity, etc.;

(ii) material possessions; household goods are included because these also represent investment in the home and at some point people are likely to spend money on such things as television, etc., rather than on better building materials;

(iii) room functions; low scores were given where a room fulfilled several functions (e.g. bedroom and living room); high scores were given where separate rooms existed for specific functions.

On each of these three aspects scores were given ranging from 1 to 7, these were then aggregated for individual houses and divided into three categories.

(1) Consolidated dwellings were brick built with several rooms, full services, and a wide range of consumer goods.

(2) Incipient dwellings were shacks built of flimsy materials, without services, and with few personal possessions.

(3) Consolidating dwellings fell into an intermediate category.

Table 10.4 indicates a clear trend for the longer-established squatter settlements to undergo considerable self-improvement, and over time to demonstrate positive features.

Therefore a policy of demolition would seem to be a gravely mistaken one. It obviously causes misery, and, as we have seen, merely shifts any problems elsewhere (as, for example, has often occurred in Rio de Janeiro). It is also a completely false economy, if in a number of years such areas will start to upgrade themselves. Policy should be aimed at creating confidence in such areas so that residents feel it worthwhile to start making modest improvements.

It is, however, necessary to add a note of caution. Most of the reports of self-improvement come from Latin America and to some extent the Middle East. The evidence is less convincing and less widespread from Africa and India. Once again the theme of diversity within the Third World is apparent. The reasons for this contrast are undoubtedly complex but one factor may be the degree of development in these regions. Latin America, the Middle East, and places like Hong Kong and Singapore are, on the whole, rather more developed than the countries of Tropical Africa or India and therefore there may be a greater amount of disposable income available to finance self-help and improvement. It is also worth noting that in Africa and India there tends to be a greater proportion of male-dominated migration to the city, and a greater incidence of temporary or seasonal migration. In other words, adherence to the city is much weaker than in other regions where the whole family is resident. In the latter case there is a clear incentive to improve; in the former such incentives are largely absent. Finally, it must be stressed that not all squatter settlements are capable of being improved *in situ* as many are located in areas that are difficult or impossible to service, and others are downright dangerous. A study of the *barrios* of Caracas (Figure 10.14) found that many squatter settlements had been forced onto such marginal land that the topographic conditions meant that any permanent improvement was not really feasible, and complete relocation was necessary.

Conclusion: Convergence or Divergence?

Earlier in this chapter we raised the question of whether there was a global convergence of urban form taking place. The townscapes of many Third World cities might appear to indicate that this is so (Plates 6.1, 6.5, 7.2, 9.1, 10.3, 10.8). In conclusion we shall assess whether or not the forms of settlement we have analysed provide evidence for such convergence.

Although the forces of international capitalism are obviously affecting Third World cities, the evidence does seem to suggest that they are not producing a total transformation along Western lines. Instead, such forces are being modified in the Third World context. Four major reasons may be cited.

(1) *The extent and variety of 'low-cost housing'.* This in itself is a major urban form without direct parallel in the Western world. Its sheer physical extent and the variety of responses to the housing problem it encompasses, suggest that convergence of urban form between the West and the Third World cannot be taking place.

(2) *The relationship between urbanization and social change.* In the West the city has been seen as a producer of change in social relationships, whereby the nuclear family and a more 'private' way of life replace the extended family and more communal way of life. As we have seen, in many Third World cities it is difficult to recognize this process, and in some cases social relationships that are more characteristic of the village appear to predominate.

(3) *The vitality of the 'lower circuit' of the urban economy.* If convergence were indeed taking place then one would expect that the 'upper circuit', the Westernized commercial

and industrial sector, would replace the more traditional workshop-based activities and petty trading. Yet we have seen that the latter continues to thrive, perhaps as much because of its social and cultural role as its economic function. The lower circuit is far from moribund and has to some extent adapted to the upper circuit, for example in the repair of items like transistor radios.

(4) *The strength of tradition and its impact upon urban form.* In our studies of the morphology of Third World cities we have noticed that many indigenous elements in the urban pattern also thrive alongside more modern additions, for example in the twin business centres of Ibadan. Elsewhere the 'tradition' may be an imported colonial one, for example in Latin America and India, but the various elements still survive and appear to be valued. Such features are major components of urban form and have not been wholly replaced by the conversion to higher-order uses which, for example, the 'Western-style' bid-rent function would demand.

Therefore we may conclude that cities in the Third World, although changing rapidly, are not being changed into imitations of the Western industrial city.

ASSIGNMENTS

1. *Re-read Section C, carefully examining the Plates and Figures. Refer also to Plates 9.1, and 6.4 and Table 10.2. Then attempt to give reasons why*
   (a) the distribution of elite residential areas changes through time,
   (b) migrants from similar areas cluster together,
   (c) some of the worst housing areas in Calcutta are centrally located.
2. *Examine Table 10.4 and the relevant part of the text. Discuss various 'indicators' that might be useful in attempting to measure the degree of improvement in a squatter area. Arrange the criteria under the following headings and indicate how you would measure improvement or otherwise:*
   (a) building materials, (b) urban services, (c) personal possessions.

Key Ideas

A. Rural Settlement
1. Rural settlement patterns in the Third World are highly dynamic, changing in response to a wide variety of factors.
2. Physical factors, the need for defence, social organization and economic organization may all play major roles in different places at different times.
3. Planned rural settlement has become more important in recent times, sometimes for strategic reasons, but more commonly as part of politically motivated regional development schemes.
4. Modern lines of communication have had an important effect on the internal structure and layout of villages.
5. The internal structure of villages may reflect the social structure of their inhabitants.

B. Urban Morphology
1. Several parts of the Third World had indigenous towns of considerable size before European contact.
2. The layout of such towns, although apparently haphazard, was often well adapted to climatic conditions and defence needs, and reflected the social structure.
3. Colonial powers superimposed a whole new set of towns in previously non-urbanized countries and added new morphological elements to existing towns.

4. The morphology of many urban areas in the Third World has dual elements which are derived from both indigenous and modern influences.
5. Recent trends in architecture and planning seem to be making the appearance of some Third World cities superficially similar to Western ones.
6. There is less segregation and specialization of land-uses in the business areas of Third World countries than in Western towns.
7. In many Third World cities, retailing and commercial activities are divided between a 'modern' and a 'traditional' business area.
8. The 'modern' business centre may be interpreted in terms of centrality and economic land-use theory but the traditional elements owe their existence to other (often non-economic) reasons.
9. Much of the business activity in the LDCs takes the form of periodic marketing at non-permanent sites in the city and rural areas and is a response to limited purchasing power.
10. Specific ethnic groups often emerge as leaders of the business community.

C. Urban Social Geography and Housing Problems
1. In contrast to Western urban areas the 'elite' residential area in the Third World is often quite central.
2. In recent years there has been a marked trend for suburbanization of the wealthy in the largest cities.
3. Migrants from the same area of origin often cluster together in the urban area.
4. Such clusters give rise to strong social cohesion and the maintenance of powerful links with the area of origin.
5. These groupings plus economic stresses are leading to a process known as 'ruralization' in parts of some Third World cities.
6. Many urban areas in the Third World are characterized by severe housing problems.
7. There are many varieties of low-cost housing, ranging from inner city slum tenements to peripheral squatter settlements.
8. Many squatter settlements, especially in Latin America, show a tendency to improve over time, and government policies should assist this trend rather than viewing such areas in a totally negative way.

Conclusion: Convergence or Divergence?
1. Although recent changes in Third World cities may suggest superficial similarities with Western urban forms, several factors suggest that global convergence of urban form and character is not taking place.

Additional Activities

1. Examine Table 10.3 and note those cities for which the data relate to 1970 or 1971.
   (a) Using a good atlas note which countries these cities are located in.
   (b) Attempt to find the total population size of each city. A good atlas will contain this information; alternatively, the relevant edition of the *United Nations Demographic Yearbook* may be used, or publications like *Whitaker's Almanack*.
   (c) Calculate the actual numbers of people inhabiting these squatter settlements.
   (d) Refer to the text, including the relevant Plates and Figures and discuss the quality of life likely to be experienced by these squatters.
2. Carefully examine Figure 10.14.
   (a) For each zone shown, i.e. zones 1–14 and 18, tabulate each category of improvement possibility.

(b) Calculate the numbers of dwellings involved in each zone and the percentage of the total dwellings in each zone.

(c) Calculate the numbers and proportions estimated to be involved in complete relocation (category 3).

(d) Describe the pattern of rancho improvement possibilities in Caracas.

(e) Given that 20% of the total urban area of Caracas is already occupied by ranchos, and given the difficult nature of the city's site, discuss the extent to which it appears likely that the city's poorer people could ever be adequately housed.

(f) Refer to one of the following books: Rodwin (1970), Dwyer (1981, pp. 141–50). Discuss the extent to which the new towns in Venezuela (Ciudad Guayana, Tuy Medio, and El Tablazo) may help to solve some of the housing problems in Caracas.

3. Having read Chapter 10, also refer back to Chapters 1, 3, 4, 6, and 9.

(a) Make a list of the ways in which 'village life' differs from 'urban life' in the Third World. Refer to specific figures and plates in your answer.

(b) Do your results suggest why there should be migration from rural areas to the city?

11 Interdependence: Trade, Aid and Technology

A. Demands of the Periphery

It may be recalled from Chapter 3 that, despite the decolonization and political independence movements of the nineteenth and twentieth centuries, the LDCs (the South) have remained economically dependent on, and disadvantaged compared with, the MDCs (the North). Accordingly, wherever possible the LDCs have pressed vigorously for improved terms in their dealings with the industrialized countries, especially in the areas of aid, trade and technological transfer.

Responsibility for reforming international trade and finance in favour of the LDCs rests primarily with the General Agreement on Tariffs and Trade (GATT) conferences founded in 1963, and with the United Nations Conference on Trade and Development (UNCTAD) established in 1964. In 1974, at the UN General Assembly, a group of Third World countries (initially 77 and now about 115), who were disillusioned with the lack of real progress made by the UNCTAD and GATT forums, and inspired by the unilateral action of OPEC which successfully raised world oil prices, called for a New International Economic Order (NIEO). This action, which later became known as the 'revolt of the periphery', called for widespread economic, political and social reforms in the relations between North and South, and stressed the importance of international co-operation in solving the problems of the LDCs.

Many of the reforms and objectives of UNCTAD and NIEO were tackled afresh by the now famous Brandt Report (Brandt & Sampson, 1980). The Brandt Emergency Plan draws attention to the need to implement four major programmes to help solve North-South problems: (i) an international energy strategy; (ii) a global food programme; and most importantly (iii) a massive transfer of financial and technical resources from North to South and (iv) major reforms in the international economic system. Table 11.1 summarizes the details of the two latter programmes. A quantitative increase as well as a qualitative improvement in the flow of aid and assistance from the MDCs to the LDCs is called for; and a plea is made for the LDCs to receive better terms of trade and freer access to the markets of the MDCs.

B. International Aid

1. Trends and types of assistance

International aid can be defined as the transfer of resources including the supply of finance, food and technical assistance (engineers, teachers) from the MDCs to the LDCs. The transfer of assistance from the rich to the poor countries is of two distinct forms.

Table 11.1 Agencies and suggestions for reform.

Agencies and forums of reform
GATT (1963)
UNCTAD (1964)
UN General Assembly 'Group of 77' (1974)
Brandt Report (1980)

Suggested reforms	
Aid	*Trade*
1. Greater volume	1. Better terms
2. Fewer strings	2. Freer access

Firstly, there is aid in the normally accepted sense. Much of this is in the form of Official Development Assistance (ODA) donated or lent by governments either directly to other governments (i.e. bi-laterally) or indirectly (i.e. multi-laterally) through international agencies of the United Nations. Most ODA, whether bi-lateral or multi-lateral, is made available to finance welfare and development projects and is usually given as outright grants or as 'soft' loans where repayment is on reduced or concessionary rates. 'True' aid also comprises important (but quantitatively less sizeable) grants and donations given by the various voluntary agencies. The latter range from *ad hoc* (spontaneous) organizations dealing with famine, earthquakes, floods and similar emergencies to long-established charities such as Oxfam, War on Want, and Christian Aid.

A second type of assistance involves private sources. This includes bank loans to be repaid at higher commercial rates, and even direct private investment such as given by trans-national corporations. It is questionable how much of this sort of assistance should be included in general 'aid' totals, however.

Since 1960, and in particular since the oil price rises of 1973–4, a fundamental change has taken place in the relative importance of the two major channels of resource flow. Private financial flows, from the early 1970s, have been the major overseas source of capital in the Third World and reached a total of about 53 billion dollars in 1980 (two-thirds of total aid). In contrast, official aid has increased much more slowly and has accounted for a progressively smaller share of total resource flow (about 35% in 1980). If inflation is allowed for, the real value of ODA stabilized during the 1960s and even declined during the 1970s.

2. Analyses of financial transfers

(a) Official aid

(i) *ODA donor groups and countries.* Figure 11.1 shows the breakdown of ODA supplied by major group and country on the basis of (*a*) total value and (*b*) as a percentage of the donor's GNP. In terms of total value, the major regional contributors were the Western industrial countries of OECD (Organisation for Economic Co-operation and Development) who supplied almost 75% of total official aid in 1981, i.e. $26.5 billion out of $35.7 billion. The USA was the major single contributor of aid in 1981 (as in 1975–9) and provided over $7 billion, about seven times the value of the tenth largest single donor,

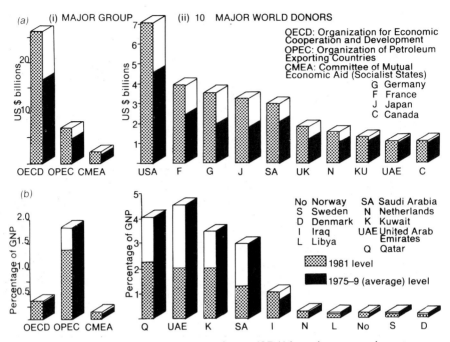

Figure 11.1 Analyses of official development assistance (ODA) by major group and country on the basis of (*a*) total value, and (*b*) as a percentage of the donors' GNP, 1975–9 and 1981. (Source: *World Bank Development Report, 1981*)

Canada. Aid measured as a percentage of the donor's GNP gives an altogether different picture. In this case the major suppliers are the OPEC countries (themselves within the Third World) which individually hold the first five and seventh positions. As a group OPEC gives almost 1.5% of its GNP in aid as opposed to only about 0.37% of GNP from OECD.

The amount of ODA given per capita in each donor country is a third way of presenting aid contributions. Figure 11.2 illustrates the spatial distribution of aid expressed in this way. Using this new measure the very high per capita donations of a few countries such as Kuwait ($1343), Qatar ($1966) and the United Arab Emirates ($4982) stand apart from those given by most of the OECD countries of NW Europe, the USA, Canada and Australia, and the remaining OPEC countries of the Middle East and Africa, which contributed between $20 and $100 per head. A third group of countries provided less than $20 per head and include the UK ($16.5), most of East Europe, the USSR ($11.3) and China (£0.3).

(ii) *Destination of ODA.* Unlike the donors, the recipients of aid are many and the volume of aid received varies widely among different countries (see Figure 11.2). The largest single flows of ODA are to several heavily populated poor countries such as India and Bangladesh. The sums are not, however, proportional to the size of populations and the largest receipts per capita are obtained by the smaller countries: for example, Martinique $512 per capita, Netherland Antilles $176 per capita, French Guiana $1087 per capita. It may be that the benefits of aid are expected to be more readily apparent among small countries and so greater amounts are given!

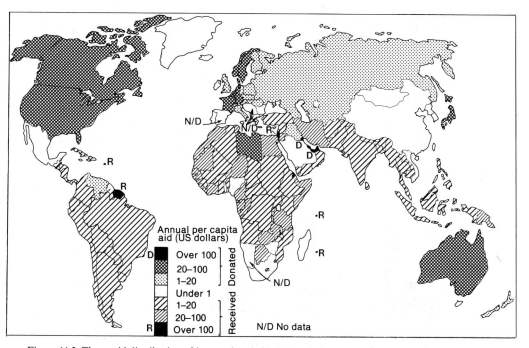

Figure 11.2 The world distribution of international aid (ODA) showing the per capita value of aid donated and received. (Copyright *Third World Quarterly*, 1981)

In general terms, aid does not go where it is most needed. The Least Developed Countries, a group of about 30 countries concentrated in the poverty belts of mid-Africa and South East Asia (see Figure 1.6) receive less than 20% of total ODA. It is therefore difficult to explain aid distribution on strictly humanitarian or economic grounds. More critical perhaps are political, strategic and historical factors. Among countries with particularly large receipts per head are those of strategic significance, and some are former or existing colonial territories which receive special treatment. Israel, Jordan and formerly South Vietnam have received large sums of ODA from OECD while countries such as Cuba, North Vietnam and Angola appear to have received similar benefits from socialist countries. Only a limited group of countries benefit from OPEC assistance which is heavily biased towards the Arab World. British and other European aid seems to be influenced by former colonial ties. Very large amounts per head are received by small (often former colonial) territories whether British (British Honduras, now Belize; West Indies); French (Martinique, Réunion) or Dutch (Netherland Antilles).

(b) Private capital flows

The recent rise in the availability of private commercial as opposed to official 'soft' loans has also had a differential impact on the LDCs which has largely worked against the poorest countries. The heaviest borrowers have been those LDCs able to afford the higher interest rates on this type of assistance. The richer LDCs (GNP > $1500), including Argentina, Mexico, Brazil, Venezuela and Algeria, account for over 70% of gross private borrowing. LDCs with a GNP between $370 and £1500 take a further 25%, leaving the poorest countries (the Least Developed Countries with a GNP of less than $370) with only

3%. However, the 1982 financial crises in several rich LDCs (e.g. Mexico and Argentina) cast serious doubts on the long-term ability of these countries to repay their private loans.

3. Effectiveness of aid

Aid can assist economic and social development in a number of ways; some of the main supporting arguments for aid are shown in Table 11.2, column 1. At the same time aid can be ineffective. Much of it can be misused and wasted, and it may even be directly harmful to the economies of the LDCs. Such counter-arguments are shown in Table 11.2, column 2, and have contributed to a recent faltering in aid policies.

It is not really possible to come to some final assessment about the overall advantages and disadvantages of aid since supporting and counter-views tend to be rather diffuse and depend ultimately on one's point of view. What is clear, however, is that firstly the MDCs must reduce the extent to which ODA is 'tied'. In other words ODA (especially bilateral) should be provided free of strings and obligations. The recipient countries should not have to purchase, for instance, an arranged amount of the donors' manufactures to receive financial assistance, thereby reducing the effective value of that aid. Secondly, private loans should be offered at lower interest rates. In 1981 over $35 billion was borrowed by the LDCs on the commercial market, but because of high interest rates they have had to pay back about twice as much ($60 billion) to the MDCs over the same period! In the case of some of the larger borrowers between one-third and one-half, and sometimes more, of their annual export earnings are used to repay interest and principal due on commercial debts. Indeed, if profits from private investment by the MDCs in the Third World are included there is probably a net outflow of capital from the LDCs to the MDCs! Thirdly,

Table 11.2 Some arguments for and against the provision of aid to the LDCs.

Supporting arguments for aid	Counter-arguments against aid
1. Moral obligation to transfer wealth from rich to poor peoples and countries	1. Aid is maldistributed and does not go to those most in need, i.e. poorest countries and peoples
2. Helps to redress the former exploitation of the LDCs by the MDCs	2. Widens income gap within the LDCs by going to the already better off
3. Strengthens global welfare and solidarity	3. Reduces self-help attitudes, i.e. may cause reduction in domestic savings and food production
4. Valuable supplement to the LDCs' domestic savings	4. Creates harmful dependence on the rich countries: often ties the LDCs to import MDC products
5. Source of scarce foreign exchange for the LDCs	5. Capital is often squandered by inefficient and corrupt governments: reduces private enterprise
6. Increases spending power in the recipient countries and thus helps exports from, and employment in, the donor countries	6. Restricts choice of techniques, by e.g. bias towards high technology, such as steel, petrochemicals
7. Method for dumping surpluses of various kinds from the MDCs, e.g. food	7. No real benefit to donors; capital is not efficiently used by inflexible LDC economies
8. Capital transferred to the LDCs can, initially at least, be very productive	8. Causes internal social disruption
	9. High interest on many private loans

the present distribution of aid needs to be re-examined because not enough aid goes to those countries in most need of assistance. Finally, any evaluation of aid policies must suggest a quantitative increase in aid flow. Present ODA contributions are only about 5% of the world expenditure on armaments and are grossly inadequate to meet essential needs. The Brandt Report has argued for a doubling of ODA from 0.37% of GNP to 0.7% GNP by the OECD countries as well as more financial help from OPEC and the socialist states.

ASSIGNMENTS

1. *(a) Examine the regional and national contribution of ODA shown in Figure 11.1a.*
   (b) Compare your results with ODA donations shown in Figures 11.1b and 11.2.
   (c) Explain the reasons for any variations found.
2. *Using Figure 11.2, summarize and explain the international pattern in the destination of ODA under the headings: economic factors; strategic and political motives; historical issues.*

C. International Trade

1. Opportunity or constraint?

A number of considerations favour trade-based rather than aid-supported economic development in the Third World. Firstly, the value of trade to the LDCs is quantitatively greater than aid. In 1981 exports from the LDCs to the MDCs were costed at $145 billion and were thus equivalent to about four to five times the value of Official Development Assistance (about $35 billion) in the same year. Secondly, the Third World is highly dependent on trade which provides, compared with the industrialized countries, a relatively large share of its GNP. Thirdly, trade has fewer economic, political and bureaucratic strings attached than aid has. Thus, when export prices are favourable, trade seems clearly beneficial to economic growth and development.

On the other hand, the LDCs are not completely convinced about the supposed benefits of trade. It appears historically to be associated with colonial domination, dualistic patterns of development, an emphasis on primary production, and low and unstable export prices (see Chapter 3). These historical patterns are preserved to the present day so that the current international trading system works to the disadvantage of the LDCs. Prices for primary products in which the Third World tends, or is forced, to specialize have remained low (except for oil) and new markets have been difficult to find. Apart from the major oil exporters, the LDCs' world share of exports has continued to fall since the 1950s. Further, although the LDCs received $145 billion in 1981 for their exports of largely primary products, these materials were processed by the MDCs and sent back to the LDCs in the form of manufacturing and capital equipment. Indeed, two-thirds of the total GNP of the Third World in 1981, equivalent to about $160 billion, was spent on the purchase of these manufactured products.

2. Patterns of international trade

In real terms there has been a nine-fold increase in the value of world trade between 1950 and 1980. Despite this rapid expansion, the overall structure of post-war trade has remained remarkably stable. The Developed Market Economies (DMEs) have throughout dominated world trade and have accounted for close to a 66% average share of world exports. Similarly the Third World has contributed consistently around 24% of world exports and the Centrally Planned Economies (CPEs) about 10%. Within the LDCs, however, certain areas and countries have experienced different trends. The major petroleum exporters (OPEC) have increased their share of world exports from 6% to 15%. The thirty or so Least Developed Countries (incomes of less than $370 per capita) have seen their contribution to global trade severely slashed from 1.5% to a mere 0.4%, and all other LDCs from 23% to about 11%. Figure 11.3 shows the breakdown in percentage terms of the origin and destination of exports by major country group. More than 70% of the DMEs exports (total value $1215 billion) were to the DMEs. Thus the most important feature of global trade is the flow of goods between the DMEs themselves. The advanced countries tend to trade with each other rather than with the LDCs (24% of total) and even less with the CPEs (5% of total).

Most importantly the LDCs tend to trade overwhelmingly with the advanced industrial countries. The non-oil-exporting LDCs channel almost two-thirds of their exports to the DMEs while about three-quarters of OPEC's export trade is similarly directed. A much smaller proportion of LDC trade is with their own group (about 27%) (see Plate 11.1) and even less flows to the CPEs (about 4%).

A more detailed impression of the world trade system can be seen from Figure 11.4 which illustrates the structure of world trade by major area and commodity group. Trade within the DMEs (no. 1) consists predominantly of the exchange of manufactured products which comprise 76% of total trade between countries of this group. While the movement of primary products (food, fuel and raw materials) within the DMEs is relatively small (about 24% of total), it still represents a large absolute exchange of materials because of the very large value of total trade between the DMEs (e.g. $617.6 billion in 1978).

In the case of the LDCs, however, trade within this group (no. 5) is characterized by the movement of primary products. When we focus on trade patterns between the LDCs and the DMEs the extreme nature of the specialization of trade becomes apparent. Essentially this consists of exports of primary products from the LDCs to the DMEs (79% of total in no. 4) and the export of manufactures from the DMEs to the LDCs (85% of total in no. 2). Thus one section of the globe, the DMEs, produces industrial manufactured products and the other, the LDCs, provides the raw materials to enable that manufacture to take place. If trade patterns in the Third World are dominated by the export of primary products, a very narrow range of such production is also characteristic. One-half of the 90 LDCs listed in the *United Nations Statistical Yearbook* (1978) depended on one export product for

Figure 11.3 Structure of world exports by regional groups, 1980; percentage distribution by value. (Source: GATT, 1981)

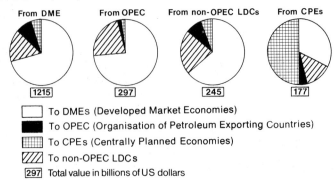

Home DME   From OPEC   From non-OPEC LDCs   From CPEs

1215   297   245   177

☐ To DMEs (Developed Market Economies)
■ To OPEC (Organisation of Petroleum Exporting Countries)
▦ To CPEs (Centrally Planned Economies)
▨ To non-OPEC LDCs
297 Total value in billions of US dollars

274

Plate 11.1 Banjul docks, the Gambia, West Africa. Trade dependency and dominant LDC–MDC trade patterns are illustrated by the sacks of groundnuts on the left. Groundnuts or peanuts are the main crop of the Gambia and account for over 90% of total exports. The groundnuts shown are destined for export to the MDCs. The bales of cotton yarn on the right, imported from the Republic of China, emphasise trading links between the LDCs themselves. (*Photograph: G. P. O'Hare*)

Figure 11.4 World trade by area and commodity group, 1978; percentage distribution by value. (Source: United Nations, 1981)

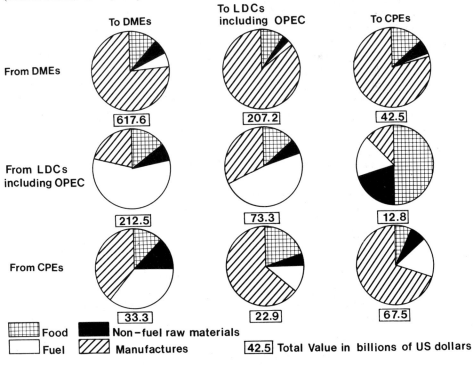

Table 11.3 Trade dependency by major commodity and trading partner for selected LDCs and MDCs (1976). (Sources: *United Nations Statistical Yearbook, 1978*; United Nations, 1981)

Country	Exports and imports as percentage of GNP	Major export	Major export as percentage of all exports	Major trading partners	
				Export partner and share of all exports (%)	Import partner and share of all imports (%)
Argentina	10	Wheat	11	Brazil 11	USA 18
Colombia	11	Coffee	56	USA 31	USA 40
Dominican				USA 70	USA 48
Republic	36	Sugar	55		
Ghana	14	Cocoa	76	UK 15	USA 16
India	6	Clothing	6	USA 12	USA 25
Liberia	64	Iron ore	75	USA 22	USA 31
Malaysia	49	Rubber	23	Japan 21	Japan 21
Mexico	5	Petroleum	16	USA 63	USA 57
Réunion	61	Sugar	80	France 69	France 61
Saudi Arabia	98	Petroleum	94	Japan 20	USA 19
Sri Lanka	21	Tea	44	China 10	S. Arabia 13
Venezuela	29	Petroleum	65	USA 39	USA 49
Zambia	46	Copper	90	Japan 16	UK 24
UK	21	France and especially the UK trade widely with			
France	16	over 100 countries			
World	15–20%				

50% or more of their export income while nearly three-quarters depended on the export of only two such products. The most dramatic example of primary export specialization is by the oil-exporting countries where petroleum accounts for over 90% and in some cases (e.g. Saudi Arabia, Libya) for over 95% of total export value (see Table 11.3). In addition, over 90% of Zambia's and 72% of Chile's exports are represented by copper; coffee dominates the export trade of Uganda and Rwanda where it accounts for 89% and 76% respectively of total export earnings; while 75% of Liberia's export income is obtained from iron (Plate 11.1). Moreover, as shown from Table 11.3 the LDCs tend to rely on a small number of major trading partners. The implications of these patterns are discussed in the next section.

3. Implications of international trade

(a) Low and fluctuating raw material prices

One of the most unfortunate aspects of Third World trade concerns the poor prices paid for their raw material exports. Most primary products, with the exception of oil, have stagnated relative to other products (e.g. manufactures) and have been subject to wide variability over time (see Figure 11.5).

There are a number of reasons for this. Firstly, both natural and synthetic substitutes may be found for these products: for example, aluminium for copper and polyester fibres, nylon and plastics for cotton, wool, rubber and some metals. Secondly, natural hazards such as drought, pest and disease often cause the yield and therefore the price of agricultural products to be unstable. Thirdly, a tendency to overproduce, caused by a relatively large number of similar suppliers, keeps prices low. In fact, many Third World

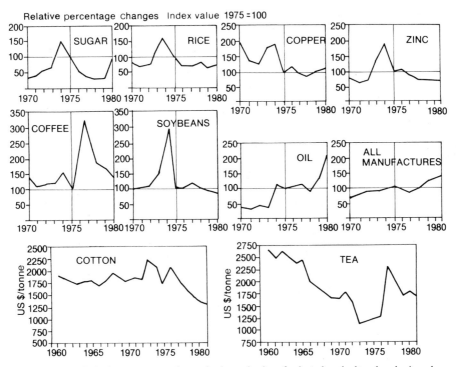

Figure 11.5 (*a*) Relative percentage change in the real price of selected agricultural and mineral commodities, oil and manufactures 1970–80. (*b*) Changes in the real price (in US dollars) of cotton and tea, 1960–80.

countries compete with each other for the same products and markets. Fourthly, primary products, compared for instance with manufactures, have what is called 'low demand elasticities'. This means that a given increase in the standard of living in the MDCs does not generate a proportional increase in imports of primary production from the LDCs.

When a country is small, depends heavily on trade for a large proportion of GNP, and over-relies on a small range of export commodities and trading partners, the consequences of low and fluctuating export prices are exacerbated. Most of the LDCs shown in Table 11.3 show some or all of these forms of trade dependency. The most extreme case perhaps is that of Réunion, a small French protectorate. This territory obtains 61% of its GNP from trade, 80% of its export revenue from one product, sugar, and depends on France for 69% and 61% of its exports and imports, respectively. Though trade in Colombia contributes only 11% of its GNP, such trade is heavily reliant on the export of coffee to the USA. Trade in India appears to be much more widely based but trade dependency on the USA is still relatively significant.

(*b*) Terms of trade

As the price of most primary exports has tended to fall relative to that of manufactures, many LDCs, except the major oil producers, have suffered a long-run deterioration of what is called their 'terms of trade'. Two examples illustrate the effects of such an international poverty trap. In 1971 in Tanzania 2 tonnes of tea could buy one Land Rover but in 1981 6 tonnes were required. In the early 1970s a bicycle could be purchased in Mali from the sale of 5 tonnes of cotton. Ten years later, it took the sale of 25 tonnes of cotton to buy the same bicycle.

Some of the wealthier LDCs have been able to compensate for a deterioration in their terms of trade. Apart from greater external borrowing many have increased their purchasing power by increasing the volume of exports. One of the dangers inherent in this process is, of course, that, as primary export supply increases, demand and usually prices sharply decline. In 1975, when there was a glut of coffee on the world market as a result of overproduction (5000 million tonnes), prices collapsed to about 60 cents/lb. But they rose to around 320 cents/lb two years later as production was slashed by about 30%. Coffee prices in 1978 fell again as a consequence of expanded production.

4. Trade reform

(a) *Better terms of trade*

The MDCs dictate to a large extent the (high) price the Third World has to pay for imports of manufactured goods and the (low) price the LDCs receive for their own exports of primary products. Accordingly, the LDCs have attempted (1) to reduce export price instability, and (2) to raise long-term commodity prices by seeking various commodity agreements among themselves. Few commodity agreements, however, other than the oil price cartel established by OPEC, have ever worked satisfactorily, except for a short time. For instance, Brazil, the leading world coffee producer, was at various times during the 1970s very keen to establish fixed levels (quotas) of coffee production, to avoid market changes in output and price. Yet attempts to control coffee production by fixing individual producer supply has failed because the Central American and some of the African countries have refused to join.

(b) *Better access and free trade*

The LDCs have also complained that the MDCs are guilty of restrictive trade practices. Many MDCs limit the import of manufactured and processed goods from the LDCs to protect their own industries. These quota restrictions (called non-tariff barriers) are particularly severe on the LDCs since they impose trade limits on manufactures that are within the technical capacities of the LDCs (e.g. textiles, leather goods and food processing). In addition to quotas the MDCs also reduce the competitiveness of Third World manufactures in international markets by increasing their effective price. This is done by imposing financial taxes and penalties on these products. These tariff and non-tariff barriers to trade discriminate against the LDCs, and force them to continue producing primary products.

(c) *'Internal' regional trading organizations*

In recent years, in order to lessen their external dependence on the MDCs, the LDCs have sought a number of 'internal' trading solutions. They have pressed for closer integration between their national economies through regional trading organizations. However, there are many obstacles to such developments.
(1) Before progress can be made, dominant colonial (MDC–LDC) links have to be broken.
(2) Intra-LDC trade is often limited by similar commodity production by member countries.

(3) Any benefits from an increase in intra-regional trade tend to accrue to the more powerful and better-off countries.

(4) Suspicion exists between states as to what should be traded and what intra-LDC developments should take place. For instance, which country receives the steel mill to serve any two or more countries and which gets the tooth-pick factory?

To date, most progress towards greater inter-regional trade has been in Latin America with groups such as LAFTA (Latin American Free Trade Area) and CACM (Central American Common Market). Other regional organizations in Africa and Asia have experienced more limited success.

5. Trade and aid: a case study

Tanzania: a low-income oil-importing socialist economy

Tanzania's current economic position is precarious. Already one of the world's poorest and Least Developed Countries (see Figure 1.6.), its GNP fell by 5% in 1980. Initial analysis would suggest that Tanzania is only moderately dependent on international trade. The contribution of exports to GNP fell from 25% to 11% during the 1970s and trade with the rest of the world is relatively evenly distributed. In 1979 59% of Tanzania's exports were to the MDCs, while 41% went to other LDCs. Yet the country is very dependent on the export of primary products. Indeed 94% of Tanzania's foreign exchange is obtained from the sale of agricultural commodities with 65% from food and beverages (coffee, cloves, cashews and tea) and a further 25% from other agricultural products such as sisal, cotton and tobacco.

As with many oil-deficient LDCs in the 1970s, the need to import fuel and capital goods to sustain economic development meant (1) a deterioration in Tanzania's terms of trade. In 1980 oil imports absorbed more than two-fifths of the country's export earnings. Such difficulties have been compounded by (2) the effects of the Sahelian drought which necessitated the import of food grains. Between 1974 and 1978 these imports were among the largest in Africa and absorbed a further 20% of export earnings. There has also been (3) a marked fall in the volume of exports. In 1980 these were 28% down on the 1966 figure and 34% less than in 1973. Such shortfalls have been assisted by socialist programmes within the country which have attempted to switch production from cash crops to local foodstuffs. The country therefore has experienced a worsening trade deficit which reached $550 million in 1979.

Less effective trade has meant more aid. Since 1973 there has been a 150% increase in the real value of such aid. However, because of Tanzania's socialist policies, private investment and capital has tended to stay clear of the country. A substantial proportion of total aid is Official Development Assistance from the industrial market economies. This reached $32 per capita (see Figure 11.2.) in 1979 and currently amounts to two-thirds of total domestic investment. As a result, Tanzania has gone into increasing debt which presently stands at around $1150 million.

ASSIGNMENTS

1. (a) Carefully analyse and describe the overall pattern of world trade shown in Figure 11.3.
   (b) How far does Figure 11.4 improve your understanding of world trade?
2. (a) Use the data shown in Table 11.3 to support the idea that the LDCs are highly dependent for their prosperity on (i) trade in general, (ii) a narrow range of crops and products, (iii) a small number of trading partners.

(b) Can you identify any LDCs which are not heavily dependent in some way on trade?
(c) Explain, with reference to the text, why countries having a greater dependency on trade for their income and prosperity are in a more vulnerable position.
3. How far does Figure 11.5 confirm
   (a) the highly variable price of most primary raw materials exported by the LDCs,
   (b) the deterioration in the 'terms of trade' of the Third World?

D. Technological Transfer

A particularly important aspect of trade and aid concerns the transfer of technology, usually of the advanced kind, from the rich to the poor countries. There are, however, a great many technologies in existence, from simple to advanced. One of the great issues facing the LDCs today concerns the optimal adoption and use of these different sorts of technology for their development effort.

1. Technological dominance and dependency

There is no doubt that the MDCs dominate the production and control of technology. Different indications of the imbalance in the generation of technology between the MDCs and LDCs are contained in Table 11.4 which illustrates the meagre attention given to research and development (R & D) by the LDCs. In fact, in the non-socialist countries some 98% of all R & D expenditure takes place in the MDCs. As a consequence Third World countries are highly dependent on Western technology. For instance, almost 90% of the LDCs' imports of machinery and transport equipment come from the DMEs, 5% from the CPEs and 5% from Third World countries themselves.

Adverse effects of dependence: inappropriate technology

A number of arguments have been directed against the 'inappropriateness' of the current wholesale import of advanced technology to the Third World: for example, iron and steel mills, petrochemical plants, the green revolution (see Chapter 5, Section D). First of all, as capital is scarce and labour generally abundant in the LDCs, the transfer of Western

Table 11.4 The technology gap between the MDCs and the LDCs. (Sources: Stewart, 1978; Open University, 1976)

	MDCs	LDCs		
	(DMEs)	Africa	Asia	Latin America
Ratio of scientists and engineers per 10 000 population	112	5.8	22.0	69
Scientists and engineers engaged in research and development (R & D) per 10 000	10.4	0.35	1.6	1.15
Expenditure on R & D as percentage of GNP	1.2	0.6	0.3	0.2
Total expenditure on R & D between DMEs and LDCs as percentage	98	2		

Plant 11.2 Advanced or inappropriate technology? These tractors, a gift from the Soviet Government, are lying idle in Bangladesh because of a lack of local technical and maintenance support. (*Photograph: R. P. Wainwright*)

technology, which is capital intensive (i.e. expensive) and labour saving, seems paradoxical. The transference of such advanced technology consumes much of the Third World's scarce and expensive capital, and offers relatively little employment in countries where underemployment and unemployment are acute problems. (It has been estimated that about 350 million were unemployed in 1981 in the LDCs as opposed to about 30 million in the DMEs.) Secondly, there seems little point in giving sophisticated equipment to the LDCs, if they are not able to use, maintain and repair such technology effectively (see Plate 11.2). It has also been contended that the adoption of advanced technology by a small well-paid or skilled elite living in cities and industrial areas tends to create a dualistic economy and to exacerbate income inequalities.

2. Appropriate technology

(a) Concept of appropriate technology

The realization in the 1960s of the failure of advanced technology to solve the development problems of the LDCs drew attention to the need for alternative technologies more appropriate to the objective requirements of the Third World. These have evolved as various 'self-help' technologies which, as shown from Table 11.5, can be afforded, are easy to use and maintain, and draw upon local skills and resources. They have come to be known as 'intermediate' technologies, since they are suitable for small-scale operations, and lie between the traditional handicraft and the fully mechanized advanced technologies. Given the capital scarcity and labour abundance in the Third World such intermediate technologies may be the optimal technology.

(b) Problems of adoption and adaptation

The effective pursuit of alternative intermediate technology and a more even distribution of benefits threatens the interests of not only the MDCs themselves, which supply the

281

Table 11.5 Types, characteristics and examples of appropriate (intermediate) technology.

Types of appropriate technology	Characteristics of appropriate technology	Examples of appropriate technology
1. Older technology from the MDCs	1. Inexpensive, i.e. capital extensive	1. Simple locally made ploughs; tools for working the land e.g. simple wind-driven pumps for irrigation
2. Traditional technology from the LDCs	2. Simple to make, operate repair and maintain	2. Equipment to grade and thresh corn and groundnuts; hand milling equipment
3. Recently developed technology designed for the LDCs	3. Labour intensive and employment providing	3. New devices for storing food and water, often using concrete and cement
	4. Uses local skills and raw materials	4. Energy-saving equipment in cooking
	5. Small-scale operations	5. Simple metal and wood industrial equipment, e.g. use of bicycle wheels for spinning
	6. Low productivity/worker-hour	6. Simple mechanical presses (vibrators) in concrete block and brick manufacture
	7. Low on prestige	
	8. Second best?	

advanced technology, but also of the powerful groups in the LDCs who currently benefit from its use. The switch from advanced to more scaled-down techniques requires scientists and decision makers to demand and use appropriate techniques, a task which may not be easy. Unfortunately, intermediate methods tend to have generally lower productivity, especially in terms of output per worker, often produce a lower-quality product, are less prestigious and have an air of being 'second best' (see Table 11.5).

Also, not all forms of intermediate technology are successful when applied, and care has to be taken in the adoption and adaptation of techniques. For instance, the supply of spades (rather than mechanical digging equipment) to the LDCs as a self-help gesture may be futile if agricultural workers are not at the same time supplied with decent footwear. Technology, no matter how simple or advanced, is a 'package' (as in the green revolution) so that if one element only of the new technique is transferred it will only be efficient if the associated parts (in this case shoes) of the technical system are also adopted (see Plate 11.2). Likewise, the provision of simple ox carts built largely to Western design specifications often do not suit the highly rutted lateritic road surfaces of the LDCs. Western cart design needs to be locally modified with special axles before they can be adopted successfully by the Third World.

(c) Appropriate technology in practice

Some significant developments in the manufacture, design and use of intermediate technology have, however, been taking place. Only a few examples can be given. In Sri Lanka, as part of a programme of industrialization, an intermediate technology which uses bicycle wheels for textile spinning has been devised. Simple labour-intensive industries making moulded concrete products which satisfy local demand and do not require high capital investment have been established in many LDCs, including the Sudan and

Kenya. In agriculture, wind-driven pumps for irrigation have been constructed using discarded motor vehicle and bicycle parts, and in Nigeria (and now elsewhere) simple mechanical cassava grinders, which take the toil out of hand grinding, have been made, again with bicycle components. Where proper bicycles themselves cannot be obtained, simple wooden adaptations may be used (see Plate 3.1).

ASSIGNMENT

1. (a) How does Table 11.4 assist in illustrating the gap in technology (i) between the MDCs and the LDCs, (ii) within the Third World itself?
   (b) What are the implications of the technology gap for the LDCs?

E. International Interdependence

The world today is ravaged by hunger and disease in the Third World and by growing economic recession in the highly industrialized countries. While millions die of hunger and disease in the LDCs, millions are being thrown out of work in the MDCs. Though there is widespread agreement about the nature and causes of poverty in the South and economic collapse in the North, there is widespread disagreement on how these problems should be tackled. In particular, there are no easy answers to the complex problems of Southern poverty.

1. Separate versus interdependent development

In recent years possible solutions to global poverty have become increasingly polarized so that today two quite distinct scenarios can be discerned. One view is that the MDCs, and (even more) the LDCs, need to 'get their own house in order' first, before further development can take place between the two groups of countries. This view is inward looking, short-term and emphasizes the division between the MDCs and the LDCs. Its message is clear: 'help yourself before you help others'.

The other viewpoint is more outward looking, longer-term and draws attention to the interdependence of North and South. It argues that the prospects of economic recovery for all nations are interlinked in an increasingly interdependent world. The South can only help itself and in turn help the North if it is first given assistance by the MDCs. The message of interdependence is clear: 'help others to save yourself'.

2. Unequal interdependence

As already outlined in the previous sections of this chapter, the present structure of world trade and finance locks the MDCs and the LDCs together as unequal partners in a closely interdependent world. The LDCs tend to trade overwhelmingly, but on unfavourable terms, with the MDCs. They rely on the MDCs, who control the basis of international trade, for about 70% of their exports and 75% of their imports. In their turn the MDCs depend more than is generally acknowledged on the Third World. The EEC exports more to the LDCs than to either the USA or Japan; 22% of Britain's and 50% of Japan's exports go to the Third World; in the USA one job in 20 depends on links with the South.

The international flow of finance and investment also draws North and South inextricably together. Though a great deal of capital and investment flows from the MDCs to the LDCs, there is evidence that the net movement of capital may be reversed, that is from South to North. True aid, or Official Development Assistance, may provide some net capital benefit to the LDCs, but this source of finance is declining relative to other flows. Private capital and investment flows to the LDCs, now quantitatively the largest form of supply, have a habit of filtering back to their place of origin through interest paid on loans and investment profits. While some LDCs do receive a net inflow of capital, there seems little doubt that the vast majority of them are losing capital to the MDCs. In other words, the real direction of financial flows is from the LDCs to the MDCs! And the MDCs 'depend' on this return flow.

3. Balanced interdependence

Balanced interdependence means changing the international economic, social and political order so that the benefits which accrue from the interaction between countries can be more equally shared. Real interdependence is also about bringing the North and South closer together in mutual assistance.

Unfortunately the present international economic system seems to be driving the MDCs and LDCs further apart. The oil price rises of the 1970s hit the non-oil-producing LDCs especially hard. They have had to borrow heavily and have gone into increasing debt ($400 billion in 1982) in order to maintain imports and the possibility of sustaining economic growth. Increasing indebtedness of the South has been especially severe because it has coincided with relatively reduced aid donations from the MDCs. Furthermore, with recession in the MDCs, the LDCs have been less able to sell their exports to the MDCs and have thus lost considerable export earnings. One consequence of these events has been for the LDCs to cut back on their own imports from the MDCs. This in turn has worsened recession in the MDCs. The MDCs simply cannot afford to lose the large market potential of the Third World.

All over the globe, examples can be found where closer interdependence between North and South would bring mutual benefit. For instance, in 1981 British Rail contributed to the unemployment problem in the UK by closing its locomotive factory in Ashford, Kent, because of declining markets. Yet Third World countries such as Tanzania and Zambia are desperate for, but cannot afford, new rolling stock for their transport systems. If more aid was made available to these countries, they could better afford the new rolling stock they need. Ashford could have supplied this capital equipment and might not then have been forced to shut down. The resultant saving in unemployment benefit could have been used as aid. Such an example demonstrates that the North will have to increase its financial assistance and liberalize its trade with the LDCs. Only in this way will the South be saved from hunger, poverty and underdevelopment. Only in this way will the South be able to help the North in turn.

ASSIGNMENT

1. (a) *Examine the evidence which suggests that the LDCs are being increasingly drawn into an interdependent but unequal partnership with the MDCs.*
    (b) *Why is 'balanced interdependence' possibly a better long-term solution for global problems than 'unequal interdependence'.*

Key Ideas

A. *Demands of the Periphery*
1. In their international and financial dealings with the MDCs the LDCs occupy a weak and inferior position.

2. The LDCs, in association with a number of international organizations, have consistently called for more aid from, and better trade with, the MDCs.

B. *International Aid*
1. Aid can be regarded as a strategy for transferring resources from the rich to the poor countries.
2. There are basically two types of international financial flows: (i) true aid which includes Official Development Assistance (ODA) together with donations from voluntary charities, and (ii) private loans.
3. Since the early 1970s private loans have become the largest form of financial flow from the MDCs to the LDCs.
4. Official aid contributions vary according to whether such aid is expressed as a total amount, as a percentage of the donor's GNP or in donor per capita terms.
5. Most ODA is directed not to the poorest countries but to those with historical, political and strategic importance.
6. Private financial flows are directed principally to those LDCs which are able to 'afford' it.
7. It has been stated that aid helps to tackle the cycle of poverty in the LDCs and improves global relationships.
8. It has also been claimed that aid is maldistributed, is wasteful and may even harm socio-economic development in the LDCs.
9. There is a clear need to change the direction, increase the quantity and improve the terms of aid.

C. *International Trade*
1. Trade can and has exercised both a positive and negative role in the economic development of the Third World.
2. Despite a massive increase in the volume of world trade since the 1950s, overall trade patterns have remained remarkably constant.
3. Though the LDCs tend to trade overwhelmingly with the DMEs, quantitatively the most significant feature of world trade is the flow of produce between the DMEs themselves.
4. The LDCs tend to export primary products to the DMEs, in exchange for manufactured goods.
5. Most LDCs are highly dependent on a narrow range of primary exports and trading partners.
6. Prices of primary raw materials have tended to remain low and are subject to wide fluctuation.
7. Because the price of manufactured products and energy (oil) has continued to increase, many LDCs have suffered a long-term deterioration in their 'terms of trade'.
8. The LDCs have attempted to improve their terms of trade by seeking various commodity agreements.
9. The Third World has also sought to remove trade barriers and restrictive practices of various kinds in order to gain better access to international markets.
10. To lessen their dependence on the MDCs, the LDCs have attempted (with only moderate success) to establish greater economic and trading links between themselves.

D. *Technological Transfer*
1. An important aspect of aid and trade concerns the transfer of advanced technology from the rich to the poor countries.
2. The MDCs dominate the generation and control of advanced technology.

3. The LDCs are highly dependent on the MDCs.
4. Advanced technology which is capital intensive and labour saving may be inappropriate to the needs of the LDCs where labour is abundant and capital scarce.
5. Intermediate technologies which can be afforded, which are easy to use and maintain, and which draw upon local skills and resources, may be more appropriate to the LDCs.
6. The switch from the use of advanced to more appropriate intermediate technology faces many political and institutional difficulties.
7. Not all forms of intermediate technology are in fact adequately adapted to the specific Third World environments within which they must operate.

E. *International Interdependence*
1. Solutions to the world's problems may be found in either the separate development of North and South, or, more realistically, the interdependent development between North and South.
2. World trade and the international flow of finance continues to lock the North and South closer together in an interdependent but unequal partnership.
3. Real or balanced interdependence will demand a radical change in the whole international economic order and involve bringing the North and South closer together in mutual assistance.

Additional Activities

1. (a) With reference to Tables 5.2 and 6.1, examine the contribution of agriculture, mining and manufacturing to national incomes (GDP) in the Third World.
   (b) Using Table 5.2 and Figure 6.7, compare the relative importance of agriculture and manufacturing as sources of employment.
   (c) Outline the role of agriculture and mining in export earnings using Tables 5.2, 6.2 and 11.3.
   (d) How may your results and the information in Figure 6.2 be used to explain the structure of world trade shown in Figures 11.3 and 11.4?
2. Read the now famous Brandt Report (Brandt & Sampson, 1980) and using the information contained in Chapter 11 examine in detail the following areas:
   (a) the logic, scope and potential benefit of greater mutual assistance between North and South,
   (b) the likelihood or otherwise of the MDCs giving to the LDCs (i) a massive transfer of resources, and (ii) better terms of trade and access to international markets.
3. 'More trade, less aid'. To what extent do you agree with this statement in relation to the Third World?

References and Further Reading

Chapter 1

Cole, J. P. (1981) *The Development Gap: A Spatial Analysis of World Poverty and Inequality*, Wiley.

Connell, J. (1971) The Geography of Development, *Area* Vol. 3(4), pp. 259–65.

Dwyer, D. J. (1977) Economic Development: Development for Whom? *Geography* Vol. 62(1), pp. 325–34.

FAO Production Yearbook, 1981, Food and Agricultural Organisation.

Mabogunje, A. L. (1980) *The Development Process: A Spatial Perspective*, Hutchinson University Library.

Morris, D. M. (1979) *Measuring the Condition of the World's Poor: The Physical Quality of Life Index*, Pergamon.

Mountjoy, A. B. (ed.) (1971) *Developing the Underdeveloped Countries*, Macmillan.

Mountjoy, A. B. (ed.) (1978) *The Third World: Problems and Perspectives*, Macmillan.

Myint, H. (1980) *The Economics of the Developing Countries*, Hutchinson University Library.

Open University Press (1977) *Values, Relevance and Ideology in Third World Geography*. D204 Sect. III Units 27/28.

Steel, R. W. (1974) The Third World: Geography in Practice. *Geography* Vol. 59, pp. 189–207.

Third World Quarterly (1980) World Food Supply: Protein Intake. *Third World Quarterly* Vol. 2(3), pp. 555–6.

Third World Quarterly (1982) Poorest of the Poor: A Glossary. *Third World Quarterly* Vol. 4(1), pp. 144–6.

Todaro, M. (1977) *Economic Development in the Third World*, Longman.

World Bank Development Reports, 1980, 1981, Oxford University Press.

Chapter 2

Auty, R. M. (1979) Worlds within the Third World. *Area* Vol. 11(3), pp. 232–5.

Biswas, A. K. (1979) Climate and Economic Development. *The Ecologist* No. 6, pp. 188–96.

Cole, J. P. (1981) *The Development Gap: A Spatial Analysis of World Poverty and Inequality*, Wiley.

Doornkamp, J. C. (1982) The Physical Basis for Planning in the Third World I, II and III. *Third World Planning Review* Vol. 4(1), pp. 11–30.

Eckholm, E. P. (1976) *Losing Ground: Environmental Stress and World Food Prospects*, Norton.

Eckholm, E. P. & Brown, L. (1977) *Spreading Deserts: The Hand of Man*, Worldwatch Institute.

Ecologist (1980) A Plan to Save the Tropical Forest. *The Ecologist* Nos. 1 and 2.

FAO (1981) *State of Food and Agriculture, 1980,* Food and Agricultural Organisation.

FAO, UNESCO and WMO (1977) *World Map of Desertification (1977) at a Scale of 1:25 000 000*. United Nations Conference on Desertification, Nairobi, Kenya. A/CONF. 74/2, 11pp. Mimeogr.

Gates, E. S. (1965) *Meteorology and Climatology for Sixth Forms*, Harrap.

Gersmehl, P. J. (1976) An Alternative Biogeography. *Annals of the Association of American Geographers*, Vol. 66(2), pp. 223–41.

Gourou, P. (1980) *The Tropical World*, Longman.

Hodder, B. W. (1980) *Economic Development in the Tropics*, Methuen.

Jackson, I. J. (1977) *Climate, Water and Agriculture in the Tropics*, Longman.

Karmarck, A. M. (1976) *The Tropics and Economic Development*. A Provocative Inquiry into the Poverty of Nations, World Bank.

Manshard, W. (1979) *Tropical Agriculture*, Longman.

Meigs, P. (1953) World Distribution of Arid and Semi Arid Homoclimates. *Reviews of Research on Arid Zone Hydrology*, pp. 203–10. UNESCO Arid Zone Programme 1, UNESCO.

Money, D. C. (1980) *The Tropical Rainforest*. Environmental Systems series, Evans Bros.

Money, D. C. (1980) *The Tropical Savannas*. Environmental Systems series, Evans Bros.

Money, D. C. (1980) *Arid Lands*. Environmental Systems series, Evans Bros.

Tivy, J. & O'Hare, G. (1981) *Human Impact on the Ecosystem*, Oliver & Boyd.

Trewartha, G. T. (1954) *An Introduction to Climate*, McGraw Hill, p. 272.

United Nations Statistical Yearbooks 1965, 1978, United Nations.

World Bank Development Report, 1981, Oxford University Press.

Chapter 3

Bauer, P. T. (1976) *Dissent on Development* (Student Edition), Weidenfeld & Nicholson.

Boeke, J. H. (1953) *Economics and Economic Policy of Dual Societies as Exemplified by Indonesia*, Institute of Pacific Relations.

Boserup, E. (1974) *Women's Role in Economic Development*, St Martin.

Buchanan, K. (1971) Profiles in the Third World, in A. B. Mountjoy (ed.) *Developing the Underdeveloped Countries*, Macmillan.

Buchanan, K. (1978) *The Geography of Empire*, Spokesman Books.

Freeberne, M. (1972) Lonely Taiwan Sows for the Future. *Geographical Magazine* Vol. 64(4).

Furtado, C. (1977) *Economic Development of Latin America*, Cambridge University Press.

Goodenough, S. (1977) *Values, Relevance and Policy in the Third World*, D204, Units 27/28, Open University Press.

Kirk, W. (1981) Cores and Peripheries: The Problems of Regional Inequality in the Development of Southern Asia. *Geography* Vol. 66(3), pp. 188–201.

Mabogunje, A. L. (1980) *The Development Process: A Spatial Perspective*, Hutchinson University Library.

Mountjoy, A. B. (1979) Taiwan Alone. *Geographical Magazine* Vol. 51(7), pp. 464–72.

Murdock, G. P. (1959) *Africa, its Peoples and their Culture History*, McGraw Hill.

New Internationalist (1981) Pure and Simple. A Review of Water, Sanitation, Irrigation and Disease in the Third World. *New Internationalist* No. 103.

New Internationalist (1979) Successful Developments in the Third World–The Facts. A Survey of the Progress made by the Third World in Education, Health and Life Expectancy. *New Internationalist* No. 88, pp. 8–9.

Nurkse, R. (1953) *Problems of Capital Formation in Underdeveloped Countries*, Basil Blackwell.

Open University Press (1976) *Inequalities Between Nations*, D302, Units 19–21, pp. 62–74, Units 22–24, pp. 139–158, Open University Press.

Rostow, W. W. (1971) *Stages of Economic Growth*, Cambridge University Press.

de Souza, A. R. & Porter, P. W. (1974) The Underdevelopment and Modernization of the Third World. AAG Resource Paper No. 28.

United Nations (1981) *Handbook of International Trade and Development Statistics*, Supplement 1980 UNCTAD, United Nations.

Weston, R. (1980) Rostow and the Real World: A Case Study of Taiwan. *Classroom Geographer*, January, pp. 3–6.

World Bank Development Reports, 1980, 1981, Oxford University Press.

Chapter 4

Barraclough, S. L. & Domike, A. L. (1966) Agrarian Structure in Seven Latin American Countries. *Land Economics*, Vol. 62(4), pp. 391–424.

Boserup, E. (1965) *The Conditions of Agricultural Growth: The Economics of Agrarian Change under Population Pressure*, Allen & Unwin.

Courtney, P. P. (1980) *Plantation Agriculture*, Bell & Hyman.

Davies, D. H. (1971) *Zambia in Maps*, Hodder & Stoughton.

Grigg, D. (1979) Ester Boserup's Theory of Agrarian Change: A Critical Review. *Progress in Human Geography*, Vol. 3(1), pp. 64–84.

Grigg, D. (1970) *The Harsh Lands: A Study in Agricultural Development*, Macmillan.

Grove, A. T. (1967) *Africa: South of the Sahara*, Oxford University Press.

Grove, A. T. & Klein, F. M. G. (1979) *Rural Africa*, Cambridge University Press.

Hodder, B. W. (1980) *Economic Development in the Tropics*, Methuen.

Manshard, W. (1979) *Tropical Agriculture*, Longman.

Morgan, W. B. (1980) *Agriculture in the Third World: A Spatial Analysis*, Bell & Hyman.

O'Connor, A. M. (1971) *An Economic Geography of East Africa*, Bell.

Ruthenberg, H. (1980) *Farming Systems in the Tropics*, Oxford University Press.

Todaro, M. (1977) *Economic Development in the Third World*, Longman, Ch. 10, pp. 204–34.

Chapter 5

Chakravarti, A. K. (1973) The Green Revolution in India. *Annals of the Association of American Geographers* Vol. 63(3), pp. 319–30.

FAO Production Yearbooks, 1979, 1980, Food and Agricultural Organisation.

FAO (1980) *State of Food and Agriculture, 1979*, Food and Agricultural Organisation.

Farmer, B. H. (1977) *The Green Revolution*, Macmillan.

Farmer, B. H. (1981) The Green Revolution in South Asia. *Geography* Vol. 66(3), pp. 202–7.

Grigg, D. (1970) *The Harsh Lands: A Study in Agricultural Development*, Macmillan.

Grove, A. T. & Klein, F. M. G. (1979) *Rural Africa*, Cambridge University Press.

Johnston, B. L. C. (1972) Recent Developments in Rice Breeding and Some Implications for Tropical Asia. *Geography* Vol. 57, pp. 307–20.

Johnston, B. L. C. (1979) *India: Resources and Development*, Heinemann.

King, R. (1973) Geographical Perspectives on the Green Revolution. *TESG* Vol. 64(4), pp. 237–44.

King, R. (1978) *Land Reform: A World Survey*, Westview.

New Internationalist (1979) Growing Inequality. A Survey of Land Ownership and the Prospects of Land Reform in the Third World. *New Internationalist* No. 81.

Todaro, M. (1977) *Economic Development in the Third World*, Longman, Ch. 10, pp. 204–34.

Whittemore, C. (1981) *Land for People: Land Tenure and the Very Poor*, Oxford University Press.

World Bank (1975) Land Reform. Sector Policy Paper, World Bank.

World Bank Development Report, 1980, Oxford University Press.

Yapa, L. S. (1979) Ecopolitical Economy of the Green Revolution. *Professional Geographer* Vol. 31(4), pp. 371–6.

Chapter 6

Bale, J. (1981) *The Location of Manufacturing Industry*, Second Edition, Oliver & Boyd.

Banks, A. S., Carlip, V., DeWitt, R. P. & Overstreet, W. (1981) *Economic Handbook of the World: 1981*, McGraw Hill.

Birks, J. S. & Sinclair, C. A. (1980) *International Migration and Development in the Arab Region*, International Labour Organisation.

Bosson, R. & Varon, B. (1977) *The Mining Industry and the Developing Countries*, Oxford University Press, pp. 12–76, 132–50.

Brown, J. A. (1969) Industrial Estate Development in India, *Pacific Viewpoint* Vol. 10, pp. 65–71.

Cheng, T. Y. (1970) Hong Kong: A Classical Growth Model, *Weltwirtschaftliches Archiv* Vol. 104, pp. 138–58.

Chiu, T. N. & So, C. L. (1983) *A Geography of Hong Kong*, Oxford University Press.

Cody, J., Hughes, H. & Wall, D. (eds.) (1980) *Policies for Industrial Progress in Developing Countries*, Oxford University Press, pp. 20–34.

Daniel, P. & Hopkinson, M. (1979) *The Geography of Settlement*, Oliver & Boyd.

Davies, D. H. (1971) *Zambia in Maps*, Hodder & Stoughton, pp. 80–95.

Dickenson, J. P. (1970) Industrial Estates in Brazil. *Geography* Vol. 55, pp. 326–9.

Eyre, S. R. (1978) *The Real Wealth of Nations*, Arnold, pp. 73–136.
Fryer, D. W. (1979) *Emerging South East Asia*, Philip, pp. 83–138.
Hodder, B. W. (1980) *Economic Development in the Tropics*, Methuen.
Leeming, F. A. (1977) *Street Studies in Hong Kong*, Oxford University Press.
Mabogunje, A. L. (1973) Manufacturing and the Geography of Development in Tropical Africa. *Economic Geography* Vol. 49, pp. 1–20.
Mabogunje, A. L. (1980) *The Development Process: A Spatial Perspective*, Hutchinson University Library.
Morris, A. (1981) *South America*, Hodder & Stoughton.
Mountjoy, A. B. (1975) *Industrialization and Developing Countries*, Hutchinson, pp. 58–194.
Mountjoy, A. B. (1980) *The Third World: Problems and Perspectives*, Macmillan, pp. 83–101.
Odell, P. R. (1974) Geography and Economic Development in Latin America. *Geography* Vol. 59, pp. 202–22.
Odell, P. R. (1979) *Oil and World Power*, Penguin, pp. 153–258.
Odell, P. R. (1981) Where there is Energy there is Industry. *Geographical Magazine* Vol. 53(9).
Odell, P. R. & Preston, D. A. (1975) *Economies and Societies in Latin America: A Geographical Interpretation*, Wiley, pp. 117–57.
Robinson, J. (1979) *Aspects of Development and Underdevelopment*, Cambridge University Press, pp. 102–20.
Warren, K. (1973) *Mineral Resources*, Penguin, pp. 75–82, 120–43, 209–25.
White, H. P. & Gleave, M. B. (1971) *An Economic Geography of West Africa*, Bell, pp. 163–93.
World Bank Development Reports, 1981, 1983, Oxford University Press.

Chapter 7
Gilbert, A. (1976) *Latin American Development*, Penguin, pp. 177–208.
Hoyle, B. S. (1973) *Transport and Development*, Macmillan.
Hoyle, B. S. & Hilling, D. (1970) *Seaports and Development in Tropical Africa*, Macmillan.
de Kadt, E. (1979) *Tourism-Passport to Development?*, Oxford University Press.
Kurian, G. T. (1979, 1980) *The Book of World Rankings*, Macmillan.
Morris, A. (1981) *South America*, Hodder & Stoughton, pp. 40–56.
Mountjoy, A. B. (1980) *The Third World: Problems and Perspectives*, Macmillan, pp. 84–92.
O'Connor, A. M. (1965) New Railway Construction and the Patterns of Economic Development in East Africa. *Transactions of the Institute of British Geographers* Vol. 36, pp. 21–30.
O'Connor, A. M. (1971) *An Economic Geography of East Africa*, Bell, pp. 176–99.
Owen, W. (1968) *Distance and Development: Transport and Communications in India*, Brookings Institution, pp. 1–74.
Stokes, C. J. (1968) *Transportation and Economic Development in Latin America*, Praeger, pp. 113–45.
Taaffe, E., Morrill, R. L. & Gould, P. R. (1963) Transport Expansion in Underdeveloped Countries: A Comparative Analysis. *Geographical Review* Vol. 53, pp. 503–29.
Varley, R. C. G. (1978) Tourism in Fiji: Some Economic and Social Problems. *Bangor Occasional Papers in Economics* No. 12.

Chapter 8
Blakemore, H. & Smith, C. T. (1971) *Latin America: Geographical Perspectives*, Methuen.
Caldwell, J. C. & Okonjo, C. (1969) *The Population of Tropical Africa*, Longman, pp. 250–332.
Clarke, J. I. (1971) *Population Geography and the Developing Countries*, Pergamon.
Clarke, J. I. (ed.) (1969) *Sierra Leone in Maps*, University of London Press, pp. 36–47.
Dickenson, J.P., Clarke, C.G., Gould, W.T.S., Prothero, R.M., Siddle, D.J., Smith, C.T., Thomas-Hope, E.M. & Hodgkiss, A.G. (1983) *A Geography of the Third World*, Methuen, pp. 46–68.
Grigg, D. (1979) Ester Boserup's Theory of Agrarian Change: A Critical Review. *Progress in Human Geography* Vol. 3, pp. 64–84.
Heenan, L. D. B. (1980) Teaching the Theory of the Demographic Transition. *New Zealand*

Journal of Geography, April 1980, pp. 4–11.

Kosinski, L. A. & Prothero, R. M. (1974) *People on the Move*, Methuen.

Mabogunje, A. L. (1980) *The Development Process: A Spatial Perspective*, Hutchinson University Library, pp. 223–49.

Mountjoy, A. B. (1980a) Population Increase. *Third World Quarterly* Vol. 2(2).

Mountjoy, A. B. (ed.) (1980b) *The Third World: Problems and Perspectives*, Macmillan, p. 37.

Prothero, R. M. (ed.) (1972) *People and Land in Africa South of the Sahara*, Oxford University Press.

Pryor, R. J. (ed.) (1979) *Migration and Development in South East Asia*, Oxford University Press, pp. 3–16, 79–97, 204–11, 305–31.

Thomas, I. (1980) *Population Growth*, Macmillan, pp. 1–18, 32–46.

Zachariah, K. C. & Condé, J. (1981) *Migration in West Africa*, Oxford University Press, pp. 57–98.

Zelinsky, W., Kosinski, L. & Prothero, R. M. (1970) *Geography and a Crowding World*, Oxford University Press, pp. 329–576.

Zelinsky, W. (1971) The Hypothesis of the Mobility Transition. *Geographical Review*, Vol. 61, pp. 219–49.

Chapter 9

Abu-Lughod, J. & Hay, R. (1979) *Third World Urbanization*, Methuen, pp. 195–241.

Berry, B. J. L. (1962) Some Relations of Urbanization and Basic Patterns of Economic Development, in F. R. Pitts (ed.) *Urban Systems and Economic Development*, University of Oregon Press.

Berry, B. J. L. (1974) *Human Consequences of Urbanization*, Macmillan, pp. 74–114.

Brookfield, H. C. & Hart, D. (1971) *Melanesia*, Methuen, pp. 384–407.

Carter, H. (1981) *The Study of Urban Geography*, 3rd edition, Arnold.

Clarke, J. I. (1975) *An Advanced Geography of Africa*, Hulton, pp. 263–303.

Davis, K. (1976) *World Urbanization 1950–1970*, Vol. 1, Greenwood Press.

Gilbert, A. (1974) *Latin American Development*, Penguin, pp. 83–127.

Jefferson, R. (1931) The Distribution of the World's City Folk. *Geographical Review*, Vol. 21.

Jones, R. (1975) *Essays on World Urbanization*, Philip, pp. 1–46.

McGhee, T. G. (1971) *The Urbanization Process in the Third World*, Bell.

Mabogunje, A. L. (1980) *The Development Process: A Spatial Perspective*, Hutchinson University Library, pp. 151–74.

Philipponneau, M. (ed.) (1973) *Geography and Long Term Prospects*, IGU. (Publications of 4th Symposium, Rennes, 15–22 July 1971).

Preston, S. H. (1979) Urban Growth in Developing Countries. *Population and Development Review*, Vol. 5, pp. 195–215.

Santos, M. (1979) *The Shared Space*, Methuen.

Soja, E. W. (1968) *The Geography of Modernization in Kenya*, Syracuse University Press.

World Bank Development Reports, 1981, 1983, Oxford University Press.

Chapter 10

Brookfield, H. (ed.) (1973) *The Pacific in Transition: Geographical Perspectives on Adaptation and Change*, Arnold, pp. 75–96, 127–62.

Carter, H. (1981) *The Study of Urban Geography*, Arnold, pp. 380–404.

Clarke, J. I. (ed.) (1969) *Sierra Leone in Maps*, University of London Press, pp. 62–4.

Clarke, J. I. et al (1975) *An Advanced Geography of Africa*, Hulton, pp. 263–338.

Daniel, P. & Hopkinson, M. (1979) *The Geography of Settlement*, Oliver & Boyd.

Davies, D. H. (1976) *Zambia in Maps*, Hodder & Stoughton, pp. 60–2.

Dickenson, J.P. *et al.* (1983) *A Geography of the Third World*, Methuen, pp. 169–207.

Drakakis-Smith, D. (1981) *Urbanisation, Housing and the Development Process*, Croom Helm, pp. 53–112.

Dwyer, D. J. (1975) *People and Housing in Third World Cities*, Longman, pp. 1–76. (Paperback edn. 1981).

Gleave, M. B. (1966) Hill Settlements and their Abandonment in Tropical Africa. *Transactions of the Institute of British Geographers* Vol. 40, pp. 39–49.

Hodder, B. W. (1959) *Man in Malaya*, University of London Press, pp. 60–83. *The Imperial Guide to India*, (1904), John Murray, p. 98.

Lloyd, P. (1979) *Slums of Hope?*, Pelican.

Mabogunje, A. B. (1980) *The Development Process: A Spatial Perspective*, Hutchinson University Library.

Mabogunje, A. B. (1968) *Urbanization in Nigeria*, University of London Press.

Oliver, P. (ed.) (1971) *Shelter in Africa*, Barrie & Jenkins, p. 50.

Rodwin, L. (1970) *Nations and Cities: a Comparison of Strategies for Urban Growth.* Houghton-Mifflin.

Scargill, D. I. (1979) *The Form of Cities*, Bell & Hyman, pp. 182–253.

Spate, O. H. K. (1960) *India and Pakistan*, Methuen, pp. 171–198.

Ward, P. M. (1978) Self-help Housing in Mexico City. *Town Planning Review* Vol. 49(1), pp. 38–50.

Chapter 11

Bird, G. & Gutman, P. (1981) Foreign Aid: The Issues. *National Westminster Bank Quarterly Review*, August, pp. 36–51.

Brandt, W. & Sampson, A. (eds.) (1980) *North-South: A Program for Survival*, MIT Press.

FAO (1978, 1981) *FAO Commodity Review and Outlook 1977–78, 1980–81*, Food and Agricultural Organisation.

GATT (1981) *International Trade 1980/81*, General Agreement on Tariffs and Trade.

New Internationalist (1978) Dancing South to South: A New Partnership in Technology, of, by and for the Third World. *New Internationalist* No. 61.

New Internationalist (1979) The Foreign Aid Link. *New Internationalist* No. 82.

Open University Press (1976) *Inequalities between Nations*. D302, Units 19–22, pp. 34–42, Units 22–24, pp. 7–48, 95–131, Open University Press.

Schiavo-Campo S. & Singer H. W. (1970) *Perspectives on Economic Development*, Houghton Mifflin.

Schumacher, E. F. (1973) *Small is Beautiful: A Study of Economics as if People Mattered*, Bond & Briggs.

Scientific American (1980) *Economic Development*. A Scientific American Book, W. H. Freeman & Co.

Stewart, F. (1978) *Technology and Underdevelopment*, Macmillan.

Tarrant, J. R. (1980) The Geography of Food Aid. *Transactions of the Institute of British Geographers* Vol. 5(2), pp. 125–40.

Third World Quarterly (1981) International Aid. Donations and Receipts. *Third World Quarterly*, Vol. 3(1), pp. 127–8.

United Nations (1981) *Handbook of International Trade and Development Statistics*, Supplement 1980 UNCTAD, United Nations.

United Nations Statistical Yearbook, 1978, United Nations.

World Bank Development Report, 1981, Oxford University Press.

Index

age/sex structure 184, 185–8
agriculture 74–99, 100–120
  commercial 68, 74, 87–90
  diversity 74–5
  efficiency 93
  employment 100–2
  importance 100–2
  improvement 67
  income from 102
  intensification 74, 79
  investment 104
  multiple cropping 26
  permanent 83, 87
  plantation 69, 94–5
  productivity 103–5
  reform 108
  rotational fallow 76, 79–83
  shifting cultivation 76–9
  subsistence 67, 87–8, 93
  technology 88–9
agricultural colonization 110
  rural settlement and 169,
    238, 240
agricultural exports 67
air transport 169–70
  tourism and 173
Asia, land ownership 92–3

Berry, B.J.L. 228
birth control 185–6
birth rate 182, 183, 184
  decline 185
  urban 212
Boserup, E. 97, 192–4
Brandt Report 268, 273

Calcutta, housing
    conditions 256–7
Cameroun, population
    distribution 191–2
capital see resources
capital flows 271–2, 283–4
Caracas, housing
    conditions 256–7
carrying capacity 192–4

Chile, copper in 132
  nitrates 131–2
China, growth of
    railways 156–7
circle of poverty 45–6, 47, 93,
    151, 229
climatic types 25, 27
  arid 27, 30, 33
  equatorial 85
  steppe 33
  tropical 27, 29, 30, 33, 84
Cole, J.P. 22
colonialism, impact of 66–71
  urban development 214–15
  urban morphology 246–8
commodity agreements 278
cores 67–8
craft industries 137–8, 149
crops 76–7
  cash 80, 88
  export 68, 83
  high-yielding varieties 113,
    114, 115, 116, 117; see also
    green revolution
  losses 36
  subsistence 80
culture
  conflicts 70
  constraints 85
  traditions 60–1

death rate 182, 183, 188
  urban 212
debt 279, 284
deforestation 40
demographic transition
    model 180–3
desertification 41
development gap 66
disease 35–6, 53–5
  cause 54
  control 67
  introduction 69
  patterns 53
  see also health, sleeping
    sickness, malaria

diversity 3–5
drought 27, 30, 33, 39, 41, 107
dual economy 139, 222–6
  urban form and 249–53
Dwyer, D.J. 14

East Africa
  railway development 166–7
  seaports 171–2
economic 'take-off' 47, 48
ecosystem 20, 24, 26–8, 31, 33,
    35, 40, 41
education 56–8, 185
elite residential areas 254–5
enclave economy 67–8
Eurocentric views 61

fertilizers, sources of 86–7, 88
Fiji
  tourist industry 176–7
  imports of food and
    drink 177
  changing rural settlement
    238–9
flooding 30, 34, 39
food production
  increase 104–7
  population and 105–6
  stagnation 105–6
  variation 106–7

General Agreement on Tariffs
    and Trade (GATT) 268
geopolitical relationships 129,
    189
Ghana
  land use 74
  industry 139
  ports 161
  transport network 159–61
green revolution 113–18
  declining impact 116
  ecological effects 116–17
  effects on employment
    117–18

293

green revolution (*cont.*)
  polarization of benefits 117
  technological inputs 116
gross national product
  (GNP) 5, 8–9

health 50–6
  economic development 55
  facilities 50–2, 66, 185, 212
  measures of 50
  migration and 201
Hong Kong
  industrialization 143–4
  land-use problems 144–6
  new towns 144–5
hunger/malnutrition 7–9, 54,
  107, 193
imports and exports 274–8
import substitution 138–9
income gap 15
income level (national) 5–7,
  11–12
India 40, 42, 59
  caste system 59, 243–4
  colonial cities 247–8
  industrial estates 141–2
  green revolution 115, 118
  village structure 243–4
inequality (within
  countries) 14, 150, 189
infant mortality 14
interdependence 17–18, 283–4
intermediate urban centres 231
international aid 268–73
  destinations 270–1
  effectiveness 272–3
  sources of 269–70
  types 269
international trade 273–9
  agricultural products 102
  patterns 273–6
  specialization 274, 276

Kenya
  land consolidation 109–10
  urban hierarchy 220–22

labour 48
  availability 85
  control 69, 85
  landless 91
  mobility 127–9, 199–200
  problems 149
  urban 227
land ownership 69, 77, 90–9,
  108

consolidation 109
fragmentation 69, 93
redistribution 108, 111–12
tenure 74, 90, 93
zonation 80, 81
land reform 91, 108–13
  agricultural production
    and 112
  political aspects 111
  social and economic
    aspects 111
  tenancy reform 109
land yields 79, 83, 105
large cities 207, 210–11,
  229–30
latifundia 91–2, 93, 94
Latin America
  road development 167–9
  urbanization 209, 214–15
latosols 37
  laterization 40–1
Least Developed Countries 12,
  274
life expectancy 14

malaria 53, 201
Malaysia
  internal migration 204–5
  rural settlement 237
marketing
  facilities 67
  domestic 67
manufacturing industry
  133–51
  decentralization 140–2
  problems in development
    149–51
  urban concentration 139–40
  wage rates 139
Mexico
  colonial cities 246
  land reform 111–13
  tourism planning 175–6
Mexico City
  improvement of squatter
    settlements 263
  slums 258
Middle East
  labour migration 127–9
  oil 126–9
  urban form 245–6
migration 194–205
  behavioural approach 195–6
  health and 201
  impact 200–2

labour 127–9, 133–5
  laws of 195
  seasonal 197, 200
  social change and 201–2
  step 218–20
minerals 121–35
  export 122–4
  external control 125
  problems in development
    124–5, 135
  transport development
    and 165
  transport problems and
    129–31
  see also resources
minifundia 91–2, 93, 94, 113
Most Seriously Affected
  Countries 12

natural disasters 18, 193, 276
neo-colonialism 70
Nepal transport problems
  157–8
New International Economic
  Order (NIEO) 268
Newly Industrializing
  Countries (NICs) 12–13,
  136–7
Nigeria
  agricultural systems 80
  industrial development
    147–9
  oil exports 147
  railways and economic
    development 165
  urban land use 249–52
  village form 242–3
nomadism 197, 198

Organization of Petroleum
  Exporting Countries
  (OPEC) 268, 271, 274, 278
oil price increases 12, 18,
  126–7, 269, 284; *see also*
  OPEC

parasitic cities 227, 228–9
peripheries 67–8
pests 36
  control 67
  pesticides 88
Philippines, agricultural
  practices 87–8
pilgrimage 198

294

plural societies 189
political changes 16
political instability 63–4
population 180–205, 206–13
  density 40, 76, 83
  distribution 190–2
  food and 105–6
  growth 104, 180
  physical environment
    and 193
  pressure 20, 69, 80, 88, 93,
    100–1, 113, 192–4
  rate of increase 180, 181
  redistribution 69, 199
  resources and 202–3
  size 181
  structure 185–9
ports, and sea transport
  139–40, 170–2
  hinterlands 166, 170
pre-industrial city 254
Puerto Rico, regional
  imbalance 140–1

quality of life 9–11

rainfall 27
  distribution 29
  intensity 28, 84
  variability 28, 30, 193
rail transport 164–7
  cost 165
  delays 164
  development of minerals
    and 165, 167
rank-size urban pattern 214,
  215–17
Ravenstein, E.G. 195
raw materials
  prices 276–7
  processing 125, 135, 138–9,
    148
refugees 200
religion 60
resources 25–43, 45–73
  capital 45–7
  development and 20
  exports 23–4
  human 20, 45–73
  inefficient utilization of 94
  natural 20–36, 37–9, 66–7
  non-renewable 24
  renewable 24
  see also labour
river transport 163–4

road transport 167–9
  agricultural colonization
    and 169
  economic impact 157–8, 169
  problems 167
Rostow, W.W. 47–8, 228
rural population 100–2, 191–2,
  207
rural settlement patterns
  234–44
  dynamic nature 237, 238
  planning 238, 240
  social organization 236,
    242–3
  terrain and 235, 236
  water supply and 234
rural-urban migrants
  distribution within cities
    255–6
  education and 198
  employment and
    unemployment 228, 230,
    231
  village links 200, 255, 256
rural-urban migration 196–8,
  199, 211–12, 220
  temporary nature of 200,
    202

salinization 42
sanitation 54–5, 257
shanty towns and squatter
  settlements 258–9
  demolition 257, 260
  improvement 257, 260,
    262–4
  numbers 259
  see also urban housing
    conditions
Sierra Leone, village forms
  241–2
sleeping sickness
  (trypanosomiasis) 35–6,
    53; see also tsetse fly
social geography of cities
  251–2, 254–6
society 58–62
  attitudes 59
  dual 58–9
  plural 62, 189
  traditional 59, 66
soil resources 37
  development and 38
  erosion 30, 34, 37, 39, 40

fertility 26, 33, 37–8, 77, 79,
  84
  irrigation 37
  leaching 29, 39–40, 76
  moisture 30, 34
South Africa 33
  inequality 189

Tanzam railway 131, 172
Tanzania 63
  game reserves 36
  health care 55–6
  rural settlement planning
    240
  trade and aid 279
technology 280–3
  agricultural 103–4
  appropriate 281–3
  gap 280
  inappropriate 280–1
  intermediate 281–2
  transfer of 280
temperature 25–7
terms of trade 277–8, 283
Third World
  general characteristics 5–11
  other terms for 2
timber production 34
  export 34, 35
tourism 173–8
  concentration 174
  'demonstration effect' 177
  distribution 173–4
  planning 175–6
  social and economic
    impact 174, 176, 177
trade 66, 68, 89; see also
  international trade
trade dependency 276
trade groupings 150, 278–9
transhumance 235, 238
trans-national firms 70, 125,
  140, 229–30
transport 154–72
  development and 89–90,
    154–8
  forms 66, 162–72
  improvement 67
  lack of complementarity 172
  mineral extraction 130–2
  networks 158–9
  physical obstacles 162, 165
  tourism and 173, 176
tsetse fly 198; see also sleeping
  sickness

Turkey
  migration paths in 218–20
  squatter housing 259
  urban system 216
  village economy 238

underdevelopment 3–5, 64–6
  spiral of 93
United Nations Conference on
  Trade and Development
  (UNCTAD) 268
urbanization 206–33
  components of 211–13
  development and 227, 230,
  231
  historical trends 209–10
  social change 264
urban employment and
  underemployment 223–4,
  228, 231

urban housing conditions 229,
  231, 256–64
urban morphology 244–53
  business activities and
  249–53
  convergence of 248–9, 264–5
  indigenous influences 244–6
  land use 244–53
urban population growth
  206–11
  growth rates 210
  size 210
urban primacy 140, 214, 215,
  216, 229–30, 231
urban systems 214–26
  development of 214–15
  duality of 220–2
  migration and 218–20
  structure 214
  urban economy and 222–6

vegetation 31, 33–5
  growth rate 33

water supply 28, 54, 88, 234–5
wet rice 76, 84–6
women
  education 58
  role in society 59–60, 185,
  200, 234–5
World Bank 11, 58

Zambia
  copper industry 129–31,
  132–5
  farming 98–9
  manufacturing industry
  133–5
  natural resources 98
  population 98
  shifting cultivation 79